TEACHING AFRICA

TEACHING AFRICA

A Guide for the 21st-Century Classroom

Edited by Brandon D. Lundy
and Solomon Negash

Indiana University Press

Bloomington and Indianapolis

This book is a publication of

Indiana University Press
601 North Morton Street
Bloomington, Indiana 47404-3797 USA

iupress.indiana.edu

Telephone orders   800-842-6796
Fax orders   812-855-7931

Library of Congress Cataloging-in-Publication Data

   Teaching Africa : a guide for the 21st-century classroom / edited
by Brandon D. Lundy and Solomon Negash.
      p. cm.
   Includes bibliographical references and index.
   ISBN 978-0-253-00815-2 (cloth : alk. paper)
   ISBN 978-0-253-00821-3 (pbk. : alk. paper)
   ISBN 978-0-253-00829-9 (ebook)
   1. Africa—Study and teaching, Higher—21st century.
2. Interdisciplinary approach in education. I. Lundy, Brandon D.,
[date] II. Negash, Solomon, [date]
DT19.8.T45   2013
960.0711—dc23
                                        2013002206

1 2 3 4 5 18 17 16 15 14 13

Contents

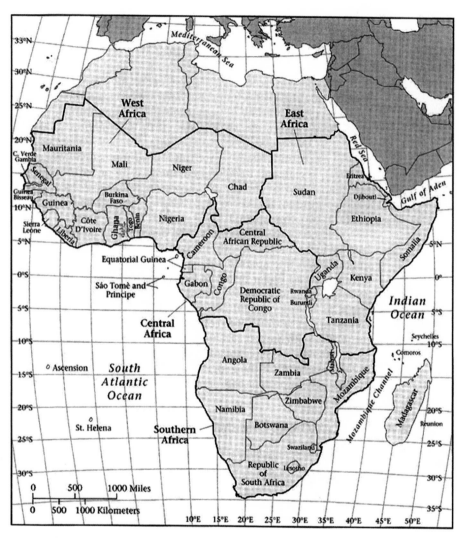

Regions of Africa (Aryeetey-Attoh 2010:2). Used with permission.

The True Size of Africa

A small contribution in the fight against rampant immappancy by Kai Krause

Graphic layout for visualization only (some countries are cut and rotated)
But the conclusions are very accurate: refer to tables below for exact data

COUNTRY	AREA x 1000 km²
China	9.597
USA	9.629
India	3.287
Mexico	1.964
Peru	1.285
France	633
Spain	506
Papua New Guinea	462
Sweden	441
Japan	378
Germany	357
Norway	324
Italy	301
New Zealand	270
United Kingdom	243
Nepal	147
Bangladesh	144
Greece	132
TOTAL	**30.102**
AFRICA	**30.221**

In addition to the well known social issues of illiteracy and innumeracy, there also should be such a concept as "immappancy", meaning insufficient geographical knowledge.

A survey with random American schoolkids let them guess the population and land area of their country. Not entirely unexpected, but still rather unsettling, the majority chose "1-2 billion" and "largest in the world", respectively.

Even with Asian and European college students, geographical estimates were often off by factors of 2-3. This is partly due to the highly distorted nature of the predominantly used mapping projections (such as Mercator).

A particularly extreme example is the worldwide misjudgment of the true size of Africa. This single image tries to embody the massive scale, which is larger than the USA, China, India, Japan and all of Europe.....combined!

© creative
commons

No Rights Reserved   This work is placed in the Public Domain

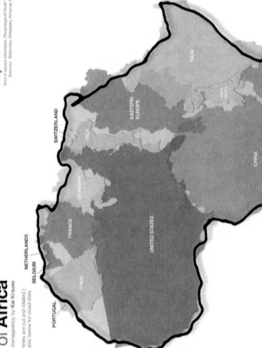

United States   Europe   India   Japan   China

Top 100 Countries

Area in square kilometers. Percentage of World Total
Sources: Britannica, Wikipedia, Pennstate 2010

Introduction

Brandon D. Lundy

THIS BOOK AIMS to transform the disparate and often ineffective ways that teachers teach Africa in American higher education and to bridge the knowledge gap between the realities and the perceptions about the continent. By focusing our attention on the tertiary level, we expect to have a direct influence on the overall education, media outlook, and societal impressions of Africa in the United States. Therefore, this book encourages a newly engaged global citizenship that recognizes the importance of transnational collaboration with the world's second-largest and second most populous continent, surpassing one billion people. We respond directly to the ongoing institutional shift from insular to multifocal education in African studies (Vengroff 2002). Each author encourages an integrated understanding of global culture without neglecting to address how these interactions play out at the regional, national, and local levels.

To challenge Western preconceptions about Africa in order to better equalize the knowledge base, increase accuracy of information, and motivate students is a slow process, but the benefit of thinking about commonalities with the peoples of Africa is a valuable and necessary undertaking in a globalizing world. Divided into 54 recognized sovereign states, the African continent covers 20.4 percent of the Earth's total surface area.[1] The histories of the West and Africa have been intertwined for more than five centuries. Africa is the birthplace of the human species, the witness to the rise and fall of some of the most powerful and far-reaching empires the world has ever known, and today the site of some of the Earth's richest natural resources. Africa's geopolitical relevance and economic and resource potential are affecting a renewed interest in the continent by the U.S. government, which in turn shapes the direction of public education in the global North. By 2040, one in every five people worldwide will be African (United Nations 2008). The U.S. government is already making strides to reinvigorate its African-based policies to take advantage of the budding labor forces, resource-rich environments, expanding markets, and prospective political allies. Students also have to better understand Africa's role in the global economy to be better prepared to fully engage with an integrated transnational world. But how do Western students understand "Africa"? How do they make sense of the various news stories, stereotypes, and myths about the continent? How can educators hope to provide relevant perspectives on such a complex and ever-changing place? The rethinking of Western teaching and learning about Africa is a necessary first step to realizing cooperative economic and political initiatives spanning the Atlantic. This book presents new ideas about Africa and Africans to demonstrate the value and necessity of teaching Africa in the 21st-century classroom. It builds on the African Studies initiatives while pushing beyond their political and disciplinary boundaries.

American students must come to understand Africa better. A proliferation of misinformation about Africa results in an incongruous student knowledge base, which leads to three serious consequences. First, nonexperts shy away from providing African content in their classrooms because it is difficult to teach to multiple experience levels, thus creating an ongoing and cyclical knowledge deficit about the continent. Second, when nonexperts do provide their students with African-based material, it is often overly vague and outdated as a direct result of the recirculation of misinformation about the continent, an overemphasis on political correctness, and a lack of appropriate pedagogical resources. As such, students are indirectly discouraged from engaging with and developing a real depth of knowledge about what is going on in Africa. Third, and in large part based upon the first two corollaries, American college and university students develop a learned helplessness in terms of a real understanding of Africa, unable to establish a strong foundation about the continent—its peoples and cultures. As a result, educators cannot be content with the status quo; business as usual when teaching about Africa disadvantages our students' employment potential in a globalized economy.

Development of Teaching and Learning about Africa

The present volume introduces game-changing strategies for teaching Africa as developed by committed and innovative college- and university-level instructors with active scholarly pursuits tied to the continent and its diaspora. Technological, regional, global, and academic developments directly related to Africa necessitate the reconsideration of teaching Africa at a consistent and academically rigorous level. The chapters of this volume give experientially-based and practical ideas adoptable by teachers within and outside traditional African Studies including nonexperts, K–12 instructors, and part-timers.

Education must advance to keep up with the shifting global landscape. New technologies have surfaced to facilitate capacity building that can lessen the divide between the global North and the global South, such as social media, online and hybrid e-learning, and online inventories (e.g., the Multimedia Educational Resource for Learning and Online Teaching [MERLOT] Africa Network, or MAN, http://man.merlot.org). These new technologies such as cell phone applications that deliver learning content via text message inspire innovation in teaching and learning about Africa. Educators and consumers no longer need to be physically proximate to share pedagogical collaboration. While Chapters 16 and 22 most readily advance this technological shift through their discussions of Francophone West African simulations and the development of an information technology (IT) Ph.D. program in Ethiopia, all of the chapter authors incorporate the latest technologies into their teaching and learning endeavors. This is just one of the many ways that the volume's contributors are innovating how they teach Africa to American college and university students. This high-tech savvy is shared with African counterparts, who, by and large, have embraced the technological age more readily than educators have in any other region in the world. To illustrate this point, the first issue of the *African Journal of Teacher Education* (2010) published five different articles related to technology in education.

Next, inter- and cross-disciplinary pedagogical pursuits are gaining traction with universities and colleges throughout the United States partly because educators are struggling to adequately prepare their students for a world beyond a narrow area- or disciplinary-based scholarship (see Chapters 2, 5, 9, and 17). While a more inclusive form of pedagogy is laudable, focused study cannot be simply discarded as somehow inadequate by the academy. In this volume, for example, Matthew Waller (Chapter 9) makes an impassioned argument for why regional geography courses on sub-Saharan Africa cannot be replaced by "area studies" or "systematic geography." In order to bring African studies into a broader range of classrooms both within and outside the traditional area studies programs, this book exemplifies a reimagining of Africa from multiple perspectives emerging out of lived experiences and encounters with the peoples and places of the African continent. This experiential approach is best suited to highlight thematic, theoretical, and methodological innovations produced by the chapter authors.

In fact, inspired by this manuscript, a colleague of the coeditors at Kennesaw State University developed the First Annual Teaching Africa Workshop for secondary school educators in northern Georgia. The proposed workshop topics included "The World in Africa" (see Chapters 17, 19, and 20); "Africa in the World" (see Chapters 4, 6, and 7); "Teaching Africa and the Diaspora: Historical and Contemporary" (see Chapters 3, 8, and the Conclusion); "Teaching Africa in Science, Technology, Engineering, and Math (STEM) Courses" (see Chapters 21 and 22); "Teaching Africa and the Visual and Performance Arts" (see Chapter 13); "Teaching Africa through Literature: Fiction and Non-fiction" (see Chapters 11, 12, and 15); "Teaching Africa through Films" (see Chapter 1); "Teaching Africa through Simulations" (see Chapter 16); "Teaching Africa across the Disciplines" (see Chapters 2 and 5); "Teaching Africa in the Internet

Age" (see Chapters 16, 17, and 22); "Teaching Africa Resources" (see Chapter 9); and "Teaching Africa and Methodology" (see Chapters 10, 12, 14, 15, and 18). As these topical selections demonstrate, this volume aids instructors in their mission to inspire, convey knowledge to, and critically engage their students on a wide range of Afrocentric themes, theories, and methodologies.

Overcoming Challenges to Teaching and Learning about Africa

Those who teach Africa at the collegiate level have three primary concerns. First, the disciplinary structure of academia penetrates the classroom, limiting and decontextualizing the content. In other words, students learn about African literatures, economics, histories, politics, music, cultures, and religions without necessarily understanding how they relate. As a multidisciplinary volume, this book provides educators a more holistic picture of Africa through specific illustrations that can then be transmitted to the students. The chapter authors provide tips and ideas for incorporating more African materials into a wide range of classes. This book contextualizes African studies from multiple and often overlapping perspectives.

Second, teachers of Africa have at their disposal limited targeted resources that can give them ideas about both classroom process and appropriate content (Alden et al. 1994; Bastian and Parpart 1999; Keim 2009). As pedagogical approaches and thematic imperatives shift with newly emergent evidence and as the need for current, up-to-date subject matter increases with each passing year, the educational resource crisis deepens. This book satisfies these needs for the educator. Contributors address controversial, newly emergent, and pressing subjects while concurrently relating their personal experiences to the bigger, more universally relevant picture by addressing inequality, oppression, marginalization, and resistance; hope, indigenous innovation, and functionalism; freedom, ethics, democracy, and civic courage; culture, power, feminism, and social justice; liberation and critical engagement; grassroots development; the effects of globalization; mediation, peacemaking, and conflict management; and the impacts of emerging information-based technologies.

Third, the chapters of this edited volume each work to push beyond the limits of Western understandings about the African continent. The authors redress African stereotypes, misconceptions, and preconceptions in unique ways. Concerns of both Afro-pessimism and Afro-optimism are covered so that the reader is left with a more accurate, nuanced, and well-rounded view of the African continent, nations, peoples, and issues. Primarily designed for undergraduate curricula of all sorts including institutions with underdeveloped African studies programs, the contributors address Afro-pessimism and Afro-optimism by providing and exploring a number of texts, oral histories, films, websites, case studies, historical documents, personal anecdotes, songs, and activities aimed at nurturing experiential, hands-on learning neatly packaged for the nonexpert or the career Africanist alike.

What Is at Stake? Why We Need Africa

On February 6, 2007, President George W. Bush and Defense Secretary Robert Gates announced the creation of U.S. Africa Command (AFRICOM) in partial recognition of the continent's strategic importance. African countries' peace and stability have a direct impact on the interests of the United States and the international community (see Chapter 3). This recognition should have a direct impact on higher education, as federal funding is increased for scholarship and research directly related to U.S. interests in Africa. Knowledgeable personnel with the appropriate training will be sought out to administer these programs. However, this shift begs the question, of what benefit for Africans is the renewed interest in Africa? While answering this question is not the book's focus, it is important as an aside to briefly mention a few benefits that could be experienced on the other side of the Atlantic. First, providing accurate information and undermining Africa-related stereotypes should help reduce culture shock for travelers from Africa to the United States and vice versa. Second, peace and stability in Africa will attract further foreign investment. Third, technological innovations paired with a renewed interest in the continent will promote collaborative enterprises and partnerships aimed at innovation and the enhancement of lifeways and livelihoods for those involved. Fourth, as globalization increases East versus West economic and political competition, Africa will find itself strategically positioned in the middle. These are just a few of the ways a renewed interest in Africa should benefit Africa and Africans.

To illustrate further, since the beginning of the 21st century, the People's Republic of China (PRC) has increasingly developed economic ties with African nations (see Chapters 9, 11, and 20). As of 2010, there are more than one million Chinese nationals working in different African countries (French and Polgreen 2007). Trade between China and Africa is expanding at a tremendous rate (Servant 2005). China is now Africa's second-largest trading partner, just behind the United States, although this gap is quickly closing. To advance China's interests on the continent further, the Forum on China-Africa Cooperation (FOCAC) was established in October 2000 as an official program to strengthen economic ties between these regions (http://www.focac.org/eng). As the geopolitical landscape changes, American students must have the relevant information to reevaluate their position and their nation's.

Social currents and educational relevancy are tightly linked. Therefore, it is necessary to address the "so what" question when it comes to teaching Africa (see Chapter 4). The histories of the United States and countries throughout Africa have been interwoven for more than five centuries, and today the United States is forging new partnerships on the continent. At the same time, since the mid-1990s, China has made an all-out effort to gain favor in Africa, with considerable success that surpasses even that of the United States in some countries (Hilsum 2005; Klare and Volman 2006; Sautman and Hairong 2007; Seddon 2006; Taylor 1998; Tull 2006). In addition, with the war on terror lasting more than a decade and eventually spreading into unstable African countries such as Somalia, and the global uncertainty caused by the Arab Spring revolutions beginning in 2010 in Tunisia and in 2011 in Egypt, clearly the continent of Africa is a major international player with global stakes worth knowing more about. And yet, for many American students, Africa remains the "Dark Continent." So how can African specialists turn the spotlight on this fascinating and varied continent?

Collaboration between Africanists, educators, students, and more than one billion Africans is our strongest option to encourage critical thinking about the continent of Africa. How can college and university students learn to recognize and incorporate the similarities, differences, and interconnections between the peoples of Africa and the United States? How can teacher-scholars foster global citizens who demonstrate respect and support for the common good of a diverse world community? And, why bring African issues into Western, specifically U.S., classrooms at all?

First, students must begin to disaggregate Africa into its highly variable, and sometimes volatile, nations, states, cultural groups, and institutions. In this way, they will begin to understand continental particularities that may or may not affect the entire global system and vice versa, such as anti-Islamic sentiments here in the United States or how certain parts of Africa are growing in strategic significance to U.S. militarism (Besteman 2008; Keenan 2008), petroleum needs (Klare and Volman 2006), and the war on drugs (Ellis 2009; Singer 2008; UNODC 2007).

Second, on the individual level, an active research agenda is a strong enhancer of teaching effectiveness. Therefore, all of the contributors to this volume continue to conduct ongoing scholarship in, on, and about Africa. Being able to speak about a research agenda from start to finish, with the kind of expertise that comes only from one's own project, is a wonderful, scholarly way to get students interested in a subject. It also lets them see the relevance of the work they are doing in class and to see why certain kinds of procedures are specified in a scientific enterprise. While it is certainly possible to teach about cultural studies and research methods without bringing up one's own research, topics come alive in classrooms when lectures and in-class activities are based on personal experience. This sometimes motivates students to read more and to consider further involvement in Africa and African issues (see Chapter 17). These classroom engagements help students understand what is occurring at the ground level in specific contexts, something they often cannot discover on their own. In other words, the overall pedagogical goal should be to develop "empathy in the context of global citizenship" (Robson 2002:337).

Third, teaching about Africa is a critical and a personal undertaking for those 35 million African Americans and more than 2.2 million foreign-born blacks in the United States today (Morris 2003:255–256). For them, U.S. and world history often fail to capture their multiple and overlapping political and historical experiences as people of African ancestry.

Fourth, Africa is a continent on the rise in industry, technology, population, and innovation. Africa also has a rich and diverse history, which must be deeply explored and understood by any global institution including colleges and universities looking to cultivate African understanding and alliances. As Curtis Keim reminds us, "Africa, because of its sheer size, population, resources, and modernization, will play an increasingly important role in the world, whether for good or ill, and will have to be taken seriously. Our long-term interest in our shrinking world is to understand Africa with as little bias as possible" (2009:12).

Fifth, and just as importantly, Africa is diverse and offers alternatives to Western philosophy in political, economic, religious, and social thinking. Keim summarizes: "Our best partners may be those who are not going in exactly the same direction as we are" (2009:62). When it comes to teaching, teacher-scholars must utilize their capacity for cross-cultural dialogue to demonstrate to their students how diverse cultures can inform our understanding of ourselves. Teaching is more than the transference of knowledge and skills. Teaching involves nurturing alternative worldviews and giving students the resources to educate themselves in a safe environment.

Changing people's attitudes about anything is not an easy task, especially long-held stereotypes that have pervaded popular culture. Many Africanists are taking on this very task because they realize the implications of not recognizing the global significance of a large and diverse continent such as Africa. Educators at all levels are beginning to innovate the teaching of cultural, regional, and interdisciplinary studies, especially in relation to so many potential cross-cultural partnerships. Educators are more acutely aware of an inherent need to "pluralize the curriculum" (Hilliard 1991) through multi- and cross-disciplinary endeavors such as those exemplified in *Teaching Africa: A Guide for the 21st-Century Classroom.* This multidisciplinary undertaking builds on the work of more traditional African Studies programs by promoting the teaching of African themes in a wider array of classrooms. In the United States, as the need increases to understand the diverse patterns and processes of African peoples in order for students to become better global citizens able to engage with a global world system, this polycentric attitude toward teaching at the college and university levels is our strongest approach. By collaborating across the disciplines and across the Atlantic, a new multi-positioned and multilayered discourse allows students to draw on different perspectives that bear upon the study of Africa, leading students to develop the "capacity to think through these issues for themselves" (Alpers 1995:9–10).

Teaching Africa: In a Globalizing World

The two most comprehensive works to date on the topic of teaching Africa to Western undergraduates are Curtis Keim's *Mistaking Africa: Curiosities and Inventions of the American Mind* (2009) and Misty L. Bastian and Jane L. Parpart's edited volume, *Great Ideas for Teaching about Africa* (1999). Keim's book is primarily dedicated to discussing what Africa is not. He suggests that "even if we want to avoid portraying Africa in stereotypical terms, we are bound to do so because we have few other models of Africa to which we can compare these images" (Keim 2009:32). Keim argues that for a majority of Americans, Africa and its people are simply a marginal part of their consciousness. This greatly worries him because, as he puts it, "if, for example, we are wrong about Africa's supposed insignificance, we will be blindsided by political, environmental, or even medical events that affect how we survive" (Keim 2009:4). Keim continues: "We also perpetuate negative myths about Africa because they help us maintain dominance over Africans. . . . It doesn't take much imagination to figure out that modern Americans who deal with Africa—bureaucrats, aid workers, businesspeople, missionaries, and others—might have an interest in describing Africa in ways that justify the importance of their own work" (2009:9). He uses Africa as a conceptual model or tool. I believe that his approach to teaching about Africa is a necessary first step for Western undergraduates. Once these students discover what Africa *is not*, however, they become ready to talk about what Africa *is* in contexts that are more thematically specific and theoretically relevant. Keim's book is primarily dedicated to refuting the many stereotypes Americans hold about Africa. He advocates for a renewed focus on diversity and dialogue when it comes to Africa-centered pedagogy. Keim concludes: "There is no one real Africa. . . . Dialogue with others implies both self-respect and respect for others, both listening and talking" (2009:186–187). Here, Keim suggests the next step in teaching about Africa, one that this volume tackles head on.

Although Bastian and Parpart's edited volume on teaching about Africa is a wonderful pedagogical resource, it is more than a decade old. Their volume demonstrates how "university-level instructors bring African issues and topics into their classrooms, breaking down stereotypical notions about the continent and engaging students with the variety, scope, and potential of societies on one of the largest continents of the world" (Bastian and Parpart 1999:1). Bastian and Parpart's book is an excellent next step from Keim's work, although an update on Africa's most recent contributions to the world is now quite necessary. So much has changed as far as relations between the West and Africa in the past 10 years including the rethinking of the neoliberal policies of the 1990s, the further advance of globalization, the rise of China, the development of AFRICOM, the Arab Spring, and much, much more. The rapidly changing political geography of Africa means that educators must be vigilant about conveying appropriate and up-to-date information in their classrooms.

Earlier works about teaching Africa in the West were routinely sponsored by the African Studies Association (ASA), although these undertakings focused primarily on issues of cultural studies and the viability of African Studies programs in the United States after World War II (Alpers and Roberts 2002; Bowman 2002; Bowman and Cohen 2002; Guyer 1996; McCann 2002; Vengroff 2002; Zeleza 1997). The ASA's mission is to bring together people with interests in Africa.

Jane I. Guyer (1996) reviewed the earliest initiatives of the ASA in the book *African Studies in the United States: A Perspective*. She defined two broad eras in Africa Studies in the United States, beginning with the independence movements of African countries and then shifting to a focus on "debt and disaster" (Guyer 1996:1). Subsequently,

James C. McCann (2002) advanced Guyer's history over the following decade. In his reflections on the specific roles of the federally funded area studies programs (i.e., Title VI) designed to strengthen national security, McCann argued for a third period in African studies. He reasoned: "Collectively, they [i.e., Title VI funds and Title VI centers] are no longer the country's sole repository for resources on the study of Africa or the production of knowledge about the continent. In this *polycentric academic landscape*, they are nonetheless institutional leaders, even if they must now share the tasks of intellectual leadership" (McCann 2002:35–36; italics mine). It is precisely this polycentric landscape that this current volume is intended to populate by engaging, promoting, and teaching African issues outside of formalized African Studies programs.

The teaching-Africa literature also contains several "how to" discussions about appropriately incorporating African-centric issues into primary and secondary U.S. public school systems (Morris 2003; Schmidt 1980).[2] In addition, it is common to find discipline-specific contributions to research and teaching in Africa, although these works usually focus on histories, scholars, and scholarship, not on the value of transmitting this scholarship to subsequent generations (in anthropology, see, for example, Bates et al. 1993; Moore 1993, 1994; and Ntarangwi et al. 2006). These disciplinary collections to the field of teaching Africa all contribute to the African studies conversation in important ways that run parallel to the intents and purposes of this book.

In the literature of teaching Africa, one also finds a few brief opinion pieces about the rewards and frustrations associated with introducing Africa-focused innovations in the classroom (Alpers 1995; Ansell 2002; Robson 2002; Thornton 2000). For example, famed historian and Africanist John K. Thornton (2000) reflects on teaching the Cultural Contacts in the Atlantic World, 1400–1800 course at Millersville University in Pennsylvania. Over a semester, Thornton challenged his students' stereotypes about the Atlantic slave trade by demonstrating how Europeans had every intention of enslaving Senegambians by force in the 16th century. However, the Africans held technological advantage in the shallow waters with their large, oceangoing canoes. This advantage led to the defeat of the early Portuguese raiders, who had to negotiate treatises with the coastal peoples to foster trade relations (Thornton 2000:125). Thornton wanted his students to realize that "African societies were ultimately complex societies, and ones that possessed differential power wielded by different social groups" (2000:126). His essay, and others like it, began to shed new light on innovative strategies in university classrooms to better "teach Africa." Their foresight led to lengthier publications about the teaching of Africa.

Potential Uses of This Volume

"Africa" is a contemporary linguistic label that is impossible to define. As a symbol, the word *Africa* comes to represent the qualities and characteristics, people and geography, and history and culture of a highly disparate, discursive, and imagined entity. This book is not about what Africa is *not*, but it is equally not about what Africa *is*. The chapters in this volume are brief and accessible and can each stand alone. The reader thus has many options for how he or she approaches this book, ranging from culling ideas from the chapters and adapting them for his or her own classrooms, to basing an entire African studies course on the book. Teachers, students, diplomats, travelers, reporters, tourists, missionaries, and businesspersons will find these personal experiential essays and the accompanying sources useful when dealing with specific African countries and themes. Therefore, although primarily intended as a teaching resource for college and university educators, *Teaching Africa: A Guide for the 21st-Century Classroom* may prove to be equally as informative to those who are not educators or students.

The book provides a good blend of analysis and practical advice, addressing many of the most important challenges faced by teachers of African studies today and offering concrete ways that those challenges can be met. The diversity of opinions, styles, and areas of expertise is the main strength of such an extensive anthology. Some of the chapters are more practical and others more analytical, some are directed more at beginning teachers and others at veterans, and some are concerned with issues specific to one discipline and others more interdisciplinary. The book offers practical advice for nonspecialists hoping to incorporate more African content into their syllabi as well as thought-provoking ideas for experienced Africanists whose teaching already focuses primarily on Africa. Although a few of its chapters might be suitable reading for undergraduate students training to be high school teachers or as part of a graduate-level course, its primary intended audience is current college instructors. The chapters in Part I would be most useful for history and social science instructors and those in Part II for language and literature instructors, while the great variety of topics covered in the chapters and the book's interdisciplinary nature provide something for just about anyone with an interest in the teaching of Africa studies.

The book is a practical guide to teaching through experiential learning in and about Africa. The authors all consider themselves Africanists, living and working in many African countries in a variety of capacities. The specialist, academic, and layperson can easily navigate the volume looking for specific chapters, ideas, references, or illustrations or read the volume from cover to cover. Headings divide the chapters into relatable themes, while all of the chapters remain true to the volume's overall scope of critically examining the teaching of Africa through the firsthand experiences of inspired and innovative Africanists.

Each of the authors throughout this volume (see the "Contributors" section) has been carefully selected for his or her background, experience, and expertise in both African study and pedagogical pursuits. In other words, all of the authors included in this volume have years of familiarity learning about, systematically researching, thinking about, engaging with, and conveying knowledge about a variety of rubrics of meaning about Africa, which they enthusiastically share with the reader. Therefore, they aptly and creatively address the central question, how teaching Africa in the

21st-century classroom is different than it was a decade ago, by highlighting the impact of an increasingly globalized economy, digital communication, greater international mobility, interdisciplinary curricula, and other recent changes on how Americans engage with and perceive Africans.

Sections and Chapters

This volume is intended as a journey for educators, students, and Africanist researchers situated in the global North. While there are many alternative approaches to reading this book, some of which are outlined above, as an expedition, it is best to consider this work holistically. In a sense, this volume typifies Bloom's Taxonomy (Bloom et al. 1956), which divides educational objectives into three progressive yet overlapping areas sometimes referred to as (1) "knowing/head," (2) "feeling/heart," and (3) "doing/hands" (Orlich et al. 2004). Within these domains, learning at the higher levels mandates contextual knowledge and skills at the lower levels. A goal of Bloom's Taxonomy, and this volume, is to motivate educators to focus on all three domains in order when teaching about Africa, creating a more holistic form of education.

Therefore, the three parts of this volume—Part I, "Situating Africa: Concurrent-Divergent Rubrics of Meaning"; Part II, "African Arts: Interpreting the African 'Text'"; and Part III, "Application of Approaches: Experiencing African Particulars"—parallel Blooms domains respectively. The volume starts by establishing a contextual understanding or knowledge base, then moves to a more dialogic and sensual approach to teaching Africa, and, finally, concludes with the application and creation of knowledge and understanding collaboratively through educationally based enterprises in and about the continent.

Part I, "Situating Africa: Concurrent-Divergent Rubrics of Meaning"

Jennifer E. Coffman in "Introducing 'Africa'" (Chapter 1) and Todd Cleveland in "Africa: Which Way Forward? An Interdisciplinary Approach" (Chapter 2) lead off Part I by presenting their personal techniques for introducing the American lay student to the continent. Coffman challenges her students on day one by administering a pretest about the continent and then goes on to provide a second set of questions that push her students to reanalyze both their responses and the questions themselves. She works hard to shore up the stability of her students' ontological and epistemological foundations before introducing Africa through film and music. Coffman, similar to Cleveland, understands that the first educational goal should be to inspire a setting in which students *want* to learn more and understand *why* this knowledge transfer is so important to them. Cleveland in "Africa: Which Way Forward?" builds on Coffman's work by challenging his students to *listen* to African voices. He provides many opportunities in this vein, even bringing diasporan Africans into the college classroom to be interviewed directly about their experiences. Cleveland also teaches about development challenges on the continent and, in the process, offers the reader a first glimpse at how the volume's contributors carefully and expertly navigate the potential pitfalls of objectification and Afro-pessimism; Cleveland opts to focus instead on concrete examples and structural implications of African development.

The next four chapters concentrate on African prehistory, history, and histories. In "Why We Need African History" (Chapter 3), Kathleen R. Smythe details the long conversation of African histories through topics such as human evolution, food domestication, and climate adaptation. She approaches these areas through historical linguistics and archaeology, demonstrating a more inclusive approach to historical analysis leading to alternative paradigms of thinking. Smythe encapsulates all four chapters' challenges to the established historical paradigm; through her detailed treatment, she is able to walk the reader through the *tragedy of the commons* in which humanity must look backward in time in order to find a viable way forward. Gary Marquardt's "Answering the 'So What' Question: Making African History Relevant in the Provincial College Classroom" (Chapter 4) advocates for the *uncovering* of historical materials through the use of primary sources in a collaborative approach to making history contemporarily relevant. Marquardt, like Coffman, invites his students to challenge not only content about Africa but also the very *coverage* of particular themes and events in the first place.

Trevor R. Getz in "From African History to African Histories: Teaching Interdisciplinary Method, Philosophy, and Ethics through the African History Survey" (Chapter 5) and Ryan Ronnenberg in "Treating the Exotic and the Familiar in the African History Classroom" (Chapter 6) both reveal historical cases, although with different intentions. Getz examines two decades of an introductory history course at the University of the Western Cape in South Africa as a potential model for U.S. colleges and universities. He adeptly shows the political nature of education generally and history more specifically by illustrating the changing faces of a single history requirement in South Africa. The fluctuating valuation of the teaching of history, from promoting racial politics to indigeneity and nationalism, is prevalent due to the contextual nature of the historical pursuit. Therefore, Getz argues that classroom debate can challenge a single historical narrative, in the process demonstrating to students the discipline's contested nature and why there is a need to understand the plethora of African histories. Ronnenberg also uses active learning in the classroom, although it is done more directly to challenge American students' worldviews. He demonstrates how precolonial East Africa was not a commodity-based economy; instead, social connections were often a truer measure of wealth. Ronnenberg gives the reader several classroom exercises that help students see the familiar and mundane in the seemingly exotic and, in the process, helps students to reflect on their own tacit cultural practices.

Carl Death and Harry Nii Koney Odamtten succeed in further establishing a relationship between politics and the teaching of Africa in the global North. In Death's "Postcolonial Perspectives on Teaching African Politics in Wales and Ireland" (Chapter 7), students are again asked to see the similarities between their own histories and those taking place throughout Africa, particularly in relation to colonial and postcolonial politics. Through a detailed comparative analysis of Wales, Ireland, and several African nations, Death reveals how positionality can lead to identification as both the colonized and colonizer at various times. This is an important lesson for students. They must begin to realize that as part of the global North, they are benefiting from structural inequality; at the same time, they may be able to empathize with the plight of powerless individuals by invoking their own multilayered identities. Odamtten (Chapter 8) returns to a specific case of sociopolitical integration by showing the relationships between Ghana and the United States. In his historical treatment, he reveals ties that bind the U.S. and Ghanaian independence movements. By reading this chapter, we are once again reminded of these countries' deep roots.

Matthew Waller also helps to situate Africa for the reader. In "The Importance of the Regional Concept: The Case for an Undergraduate Regional Geography Course of Sub-Saharan Africa" (Chapter 9), Waller uses textual analysis of popular African geography textbooks to reveal how these authors define the concept of Africa. The reader is able to glimpse what those Africanists in the global North deem important for students to take away from a geography course. Waller concludes that the region remains an important and valuable concept in spite of the turn toward more broad-based, global treatments of geography and African studies. He argues quite strongly for the advantages of particular, geographically focused courses. As a microcosm of this volume's conceptual framework, this chapter helps reveal the continued need to toggle between the local or regional particulars and the globally integrated and ever-changing world system.

The final chapter of Part I, Durene I. Wheeler and Jeanine Ntihirageza's "Teach Me about Africa: Facilitating and Training Educators toward a Socially Just Curriculum" (Chapter 10), culminates in the advocacy for an educational chain, an expansive model that has been shown to be quite effective in development work by training trainers or teaching teachers (e.g., the U.S. Peace Corps' approach). The chapter's authors argue that the years of experience, knowledge, understanding, and empathy gained at the tertiary level by experts needs to be shared with primary- and secondary-level instructors as well. Wheeler and Ntihirageza provide a model for developing a workshop to equip K–12 educators with accurate knowledge and skills to explore the topic "Teaching Africa," a commendable pursuit. Correcting misinformation at an earlier age will allow for a broader and more in-depth treatment of African study at the tertiary levels.

Part II, "African Arts: Interpreting the African 'Text'"

Part II begins with two chapters that utilize the comparative approach to African literature. Catherine Kroll's "Inversion Rituals: The African Novel in the Global North" (Chapter 11) is an excellent transition piece between the social sciences and the humanities. Her work returns to histories' multiplicity from an alternate perspective. She shows intersecting narratives in fiction to help the reader understand the salience of the concept of *sankofa*, that is, of the past providing inspiration for the present and future. By considering inversion in African literature, she helps students, and the reader, challenge power structures by enacting history for those who previously went without. By showing multiple histories, she reveals and encourages the potential for critical discourse and a challenge to the status quo. Similar to Odamtten's chapter, Renée Schatteman's "Teaching Africa through a Comparative Pedagogy: South Africa and the United States" (Chapter 12) goes on to draw a more direct comparison between, in this case, South Africa and the southern United States. By placing exemplars of these countries' literatures side by side, Schatteman reveals the struggles of the two Souths. Her comparative model to teach about Africa through literature emphasizes multiple viewpoints, highlighting the ambiguity and overlap of reality for her readers. Through the detail of daily life, room is left for alternative interpretations, changing perspectives, complex characters, and unresolved questions, which are not always as readily possible in fact-based or historical analysis of similar themes and events.

Jean Ngoya Kidula presents her personal narrative as a Kenyan musical instructor in both Kenya and the United States in "Stereotypes, Myths, and Realties regarding African Music in the African and American Academy" (Chapter 13). She shares the comparative approach with her predecessors. In addition, her insider's perspective is one of several personal accounts provided throughout the volume. Kidula's experiential story challenges the placement of African soundscapes on the fringes of the mainstream musical canon in the United States, where they are often relegated to study within disciplines such as ethnomusicology, culture studies, folklore, or anthropology.

Next, Caleb Corkery introduces the West African griot, or oral historian, in "What Paltry Learning in Dumb Books! Teaching the Power of Oral Narrative" (Chapter 14). Similar to Kidula, Corkery argues that a more Afrocentric pedagogical style may be more insightful in some Western classroom situations such as when the material being uncovered may seem counterintuitive and challenging to the worldview students have inculcated. Oral narrative, for example, may be particularly adept at revealing the contextual and socially derived nature of history.

The final two chapters of Part II provide pedagogical models useful in a variety of classroom situations. "Teaching about Africa: Violence and Conflict Management" by Linda M. Johnston and Oumar Chérif Diop (Chapter 15) focuses on several strategies and instruments for analysis of African literature and conflict management. Lucie Viakinnou-Brinson's "Contextualizing the Teaching of Africa in the 21st Century: A Student-Centered Pedagogical Approach to Demystify Africa as the 'Heart of Darkness'" (Chapter 16) gives an alternative model for teaching Africa, global simulation, which she uses to teach French from an African perspective. Viakinnou-Brinson is another author who is able to draw on her own personal inspiration as an African to reveal a unique perspective to understanding the continent. She creates a simulation environment in which students become responsible for dispelling their own myths and stereotypes about the continent. Viakinnou-Brinson not only employs active learning in her global simulation, but she has the student become the teacher, a method that has proved effective in achieving thorough comprehension.

Part III, "Application of Approaches: Experiencing African Particulars"

Similar to Cleveland in his pragmatic call to understanding and action about Africa for students of the global North, Amy C. Finnegan adroitly encourages U.S.-based activism in her classrooms and her chapter, "Shaping U.S.-Based Activism toward Africa: The Role of a Mix of Critical Pedagogies" (Chapter 17). Finnegan uses socially conscious approaches to teaching and learning such as the inclusion of African narratives, structural analysis of African problems, examination of social movements, calls for interventions based on solid analytical frameworks, and discussions of commonly held misperceptions about Africa and Africans. She strives to both inspire and empower young people to take action and emphasizes reflexivity, self-criticism, and rigorous analysis of power relations.

Babacar M'Baye also uses a homegrown approach to experiential learning about Africa, often branching outside the traditional classroom, in "The Model AU as a Pedagogical Method of Teaching American Students about Africa" (Chapter 18). The Model African Union is a Pan-African, intercollegiate organ that allows participants to consider real-time issues through simulation. Students seriously interested in learning more about Africa should be strongly encouraged to participate in such a profound experience. Not only are there regional and national competitions, but students are also granted audiences with African diplomats, who help explain their countries' social, economic, and political positions and agendas.

Also taking learning outside the classroom, the next three chapters—"The Kalamazoo / Fourah Bay College Partnership: A Context for Understanding Study Abroad with Africa" by Daniel J. Paracka, Jr. (Chapter 19); "Teaching Culture, Health, and Political Economy in the Field: Ground-Level Perspectives on Africa in the 21st Century" by James Ellison (Chapter 20); and "Beyond the Biologic Basis of Disease: Collaborative Study of the Social and Economic Causation of Disease in Africa" by Amy C. Finnegan, Julian Jane Atim, and Michael Westerhaus (Chapter 21)—all advocate for collaborative educational enterprises, ideally situated somewhere in Africa itself. What better way to learn about a topic than through immersion. Paracka's chapter starts by providing a history of the successful study abroad arrangement between Sierra Leone's Fourah Bay College and Michigan's Kalamazoo College. Although now defunct due to political instability in Sierra Leone, he advocates for this institutional model to be reinstated throughout the continent, in place of the "island" programs found today with loose or no institutional affiliations.

Ellison emphasizes the value of field-based courses in Africa, in this case a methodological field school in Tanzania, divided between Dar es Salaam and Zanzibar, which offers an incomparable way to teach students about everyday life. According to Ellison, the biggest draw to such a program is the fact that most Africanists already have the necessary skills and contacts to carry out such a field-based training opportunity. In addition, this approach allows for further integration between a scholar's academic and pedagogical pursuits. The success of Ellison's students directly evidences the potential for such programs. Similarly, Finnegan, Atim, and Westerhaus's field-based course on teaching global health in Africa builds upon reflexivity, partnerships, and empowerment by enrolling host-country counterparts. Their concurrent teaching of clinical and social medicine breaks down socioeconomic barriers to provide a balanced and collaborative understanding of global health in Uganda. This program has the potential to be emulated throughout Africa as well as establishing sister programs in the United States. Again, the collaborative focus, strongly advocated in this chapter, is the cornerstone of the entire volume.

Solomon Negash and Julian M. Bass take the reader on the final leg of this volume's journey in "Educating the Educators: Ethiopia's IT Ph.D. Program" (Chapter 22). In this final chapter, collaboration, partnership, sustainability, development, and creative pedagogy are all revealed and reinforced. This chapter demonstrates capacity building through the development of an IT Ph.D. program in Ethiopia. The success of this innovative program reveals quite conclusively that the discussion of teaching Africa cannot be couched in terms of need, or, in other words, that the United States *needs* Africa for its newly emerging markets, large potential labor force, and natural resources or that Africa *needs* the United States for political stability, technological advances, and "development." Instead, the discourse and subsequent actions should be ones of partnership and equity in which new ideas are shared and exchanged between populations that have long histories, shared interests, and long-standing amicability.

Prolific Africanist Toyin Falola reiterates these sentiments in his "Conclusion: Knowledge Circulation and Diasporic Interfacing." He concludes by advocating for extending the "frontier of knowledge" as a universal pursuit shared between Africa and the rest of the world. These educational actions still hold the most potential for advancement and development for the individual, community, nation-state, and region. Falola insists that the primary job of scholars and educators is to build bridges, acting as cultural brokers between the global North and the global South. Once these structures are in place, the free flow of information on the global superhighway may help lessen unequal positionality and allow for the further nurturing of critical consciousness and agency among vulnerable populations of the global North and South. At least this is the goal and intent of *Teaching Africa: A Guide for the 21st-Century Classroom*, empowerment of our students no matter where they may be geographically situated.

Notes

This introduction is developed from an article titled "Making Africa Accessible: Bringing Guinea-Bissau into the University Classroom," which appears in *Building Bridges in Anthropology: Understanding, Acting, Teaching, and Theorizing* (Shanafelt 2012). The impetus for the current volume emerged from a 2010 Faculty Learning Community at Kennesaw State University that met to discuss pedagogical resources available for the teaching of Africa in interdisciplinary settings. I would like to acknowledge and thank the participants of this working group for their ideas and encouragement including Samuel Abaidoo (sociology), Akanmu Adebayo (history), Nurudeen Akinyemi (political science), William Allen (history), Solomon Negash (information systems), and Jessica Stephenson (visual arts). I would also like to thank Sebastien Gregory for his editorial assistance and the team at IU Press consisting of Dee Mortensen, Senior Sponsoring Editor, Sarah Jacobi, Assistant Sponsoring Editor, Tim Roberts at Field Editorial, and the anonymous reviewer. Without their guidance and encouragement, this project would not be what it is today.

1. The Republic of South Sudan gained independence on July 9, 2011.

2. See also the Africa Access Review database, http://www.africaaccessreview.org.

PART I

SITUATING AFRICA

Concurrent-Divergent Rubrics of Meaning

IN PART I of *Teaching Africa*, "Situating Africa: Concurrent-Divergent Rubrics of Meaning," the journey begins, as all must, with preparation. Most sojourners' initial understanding of any topic is pitted with superficiality and paucity. Students of any size and type must be convinced of the value and necessity of new pursuits in order to fully engage in them. Therefore, it is the educator's primary task—as a coach, facilitator, and expert—to make a case for pushing beyond stereotypes and "convenient" familiarity. When teaching about Africa to U.S. students, there are many cases to be made about the value of the expedition.

Several of these arguments are outlined in the introduction and reinforced by the chapter authors such as (1) resource management and development (Chapters 2 and 3); (2) an historic and geographic positioning between the East and West (Chapters 4, 5, 6, and 9); (3) indigenous political models (Chapters 7 and 8); (4) historical and contemporary linkages to European and American populations and diasporas (Chapters 2, 7, and 8); (5) increasing global population mobility and information and technological integration (Chapters 2, 3, 6, and 7); (6) postcolonial perspectives (Chapter 7); and (7) a reflective representation of humanity, cultural diversity, complexity, universality, and fluidity (Chapters 1, 2, 4, 5, 6, and 10). As well, these authors also display unique avenues for conveying this material such as (1) the teaching of teachers (Chapter 10); (2) interdisciplinary engagement (Chapters 2 and 5); (3) textual analysis (Chapter 9); and (4) comparative perspectives (Chapter 7).

The first 10 chapters provide motivation and justification as to *why* learning about Africa is important and introduce the conceptual framework for the entire volume: collaboration between educators, students, Africa researchers, and a supporting staff of more than one billion Africans. How can individuals learn to recognize and incorporate the similarities, differences, and interconnections between the peoples of Africa and the global North? How can teacher-scholars foster global citizens who demonstrate respect and support for the common good of a diverse world community? It is recommended herein to engage with students through experiential learning both within and outside of the traditional classroom.

Part I, "Situating Africa," establishes context. It assists the reader in provisioning him- or herself and, additionally, his or her students with the necessities for a figurative and potentially literal trip to Africa. Once properly prepared, Part II goes on to explore avenues for managing expectations and expands the conceptual model for thinking about the continent.

1 Introducing "Africa"

Jennifer E. Coffman

How do we introduce our students to "Africa"? Learning and teaching about "Africa" may seem to be an impossible enterprise, but once we acknowledge the limitations of what is practicable in a single semester or less, we can convey useful material in engaging ways. This chapter includes examples of exercises used to introduce students to studying Africa as a concept, a locale, and a set of dynamic social and ecological systems. These exercises can be easily adapted and incorporated into introductory-level college courses specifically focusing on Africa or courses in which only a portion of the semester is dedicated to studying some aspect or aspects of the continent, and they can work in nearly any type of course, particularly within the social sciences and humanities.

Introduction

It is not an academic crime to be unaware of the details of a region or topic not yet studied—who among us is expert in everything? Most students want to learn more about "Africa," and overall they demonstrate sincere interest in and concern regarding African peoples, places, and events. Through well-contextualized assignments, they can also practice speaking deliberately and specifically about this newly acquired knowledge.

Some of the exercises below use incorrect statements and blatant generalizations with the initial goal of getting students to react—perhaps even to invoke some righteous indignation. This first-order level of investment is meant to spur students toward productive post-indignation practices (Hattam and Zembylas 2010) that lead to correction and substantiated judgment. The larger goals of these exercises are to motivate students to think more deeply about the information they are presented, to inquire further, to make connections throughout the semester to assigned materials and additional research they conduct, and to care enough to keep learning about Africa while sharing their knowledge with others.

First-Day Quiz

One good way to launch introductory Africa-specific courses is to have students complete an information sheet about the continent and its residents; this exercise could include a brief quiz. An important point before viewing the quiz: the students initially assume that there is only one part to it. The quiz section begins with a series of short-answer questions related to Africa, greatly and obviously influenced by Neil Postman and Charles Weingartner's manifesto *Teaching as a Subversive Activity* (1969:68–69).

MINI-QUIZ
Please answer the following questions:
1. How many countries are there in Africa?
2. Are the children of educated urban Africans more creative than the children of parents who did not go to school?
3. Who discovered Africa?
4. What is the longest river in Africa?
5. Is West Africa more developed than East Africa?
6. How are you feeling about being in this class?
7. Will it rain in Gabon tomorrow?
8. What is the most beautiful animal in Africa?
9. Is "text" a noun or a verb?
10. Why are some government officials in Africa corrupt?
11. Will you do well on the Africa map quiz in a couple of weeks?
12. Why is Africa called "the motherland"?

After the students complete this quiz, they receive a second set of questions to consider without altering their responses to the first set. The second set of questions, modified slightly from those put forth by Postman and Weingartner (1969:69), are key to setting the tone for the rest of the semester; these questions push students to reanalyze not just their responses to the first set of questions, but the questions themselves, as well as their ontological and epistemological premises.

SECOND QUESTION SET
1. Which of the questions can you answer with absolute certainty? How can you be certain of your answer?
2. What information would enable you to answer other questions with certainty? Where would you find that information?

3. Which questions restrict you to providing "factual information"? Which do not? Which require no facts at all?
4. Which questions may be based on false assumptions?
5. Which questions require expert testimony? What makes one an expert?
6. Which questions require the greatest amount of definition or qualification before you attempt to answer them?
7. Which questions require predictions as answers? Which kinds of information may improve the quality of a prediction?

Students reflect on the quality and precision of their original answers and discuss how they should proceed in pursuing information and analyzing arguments throughout the remainder of the course. The information sheets and quizzes should be collected while the second set of questions is held by the students as a frame of reference for additional assignments.

Readings and lectures help students with specific information (e.g., number of states, longest river) requested in some of the questions, as well as the contexts in which they should start to make sense of them (e.g., conditions of becoming states, politics of managing a river that passes through many states and human population centers). Readings, lectures, discussions, and other course materials, including films and music, help students gather information to deal with the quiz questions that include biases and false assumptions. Students get to grapple with concepts like ethnocentrism, formal schooling as a component of the broader concept of education (which also occurs outside of classrooms), and modernization theory. On the last day of the semester, the sheets are returned in order to reconsider the questions with the students' new analytical tool kit.

Encouraging Questions: Quick and Easy Introductions to Films

While other chapters in this volume describe specific films and their potential contributions to courses about Africa, this section offers a simple way to introduce films while linking back to the first-day exercise. It works by making a declarative statement, full of words or claims with which most students would be unfamiliar and that link to the film, and the request to write the statement verbatim. For example, prior to watching the film *Milking the Rhino* (Simpson 2008), students might be prompted with this statement: "As demonstrated in Il Ngwesi, group ranch members have embraced CBNRM—also known as CBC or CBWM—to protect charismatic megafauna in a non-fortress conservation setting." Students are then asked, "Any questions about that statement?" or even, "Why would I ask you to write that down?" followed by the prompt, "What questions would you ask to make sense of it?" Channeling the inquiry method as promoted by Postman and Weingartner (1969), students are then permitted to ask specific questions about the statement. These questions then frame the viewing of the film. After the film, they answer their initial questions and then build on what they learned with more questions to pursue and connect to other exercises.

In this example, the film focuses on the Il Ngwesi Group Ranch in Kenya and the Marienfluss Valley in Namibia to illustrate the complexities of designing and managing conservation and related tourism schemes. It shows how some rural people, specifically self-identifying Maasai in Kenya and Himba in Namibia, are trying to come to terms with increasing demands on land and animals (wild and domestic) and their own ideas of culture and acceptable employment. Students learn through this film how people working in conjunction with two different ecotourism camps view their duties as practical jobs that enable livelihoods, as well as how these types of work affect both cultural continuities and changes. The film also tackles the controversial topic of conservation with regard to the forms it takes, how benefits accrue, and who owns what. Further, it is a beautiful film to watch. Other multimedia tools employed in the classroom to aid in the pedagogical process include music.

Music: An Any and Every Day Introductory Exercise

Music can help introduce particular regions of Africa, as well as musical and narrative genres, diffusion and fusion, and other cultural concepts. Playing music as students filter into the classroom is a great way to establish a learning context. Well-chosen songs can set the tone for significant themes to be covered in class and can help students recall those points later. Music often accompanies a wide variety of activities worth studying in a course on Africa, such as religious ceremonies or other rituals (e.g., weddings, funerals, and healing), storytelling, political rallies, and social critique (Masquelier 1999; Zukas 1996).

Music works especially well in general survey courses such as an introductory course on sub-Saharan Africa. The box set *Africa: Never Stand Still* (Ellipsis Arts 1994) remains an excellent introduction to some of Africa's major recording stars and the richness of their music. As for pedagogical benefit, practically every song in this collection demonstrates diffusion and fusion of styles, language, and concepts (Coffman 2009).

For example, one semester a student—upon hearing the song "Heygana" by internationally renowned musician Ali Farka Toure—declared, "Wow! The blues actually started in Africa!" As it turns out, the music of bluesman Ali Farka Toure (1939–2006), born into a noble Songhai family, is a great example of global flows and borrowing. His music is a fusion of American blues and reworked, older African melodies (Ellipsis Arts 1994). Key influences in his music include Otis Redding, Albert King, and John Lee Hooker, but he attributed the roots of his sound to the music of the Tamashek, part of the larger Tuareg population. He composed many of his early songs on a Western-style guitar he received as a gift in 1957 and often sang in Tamashek and Songhai languages. Students greatly enjoy this music, as well as learning a bit more about the artist, his musical inspirations, and the subjects about which he sang. Such an introduction to topics of culture change and diffusion makes the points of the lecture stick.

From the CD *Nairobi Beat* (Rounder Select 1992), students respond to the Luo song "Jamoko Wange Tek" ("A Rich Man Is Arrogant") by Daniel Owino Misiani and

D.O. 7 Shirati, which introduces concepts like interpersonal disease theory, social *dis-ease* (à la Nancy Scheper-Hughes 2001), and interpretive drift. This song, and the story it tells of a rich man perilously ignoring "traditional ways," usually initiates an engaging conversation about belief systems and the concepts noted above. Interpersonal disease theory describes illness as a result or symptom of conflicts or tensions in social relations (dis-ease), in some cases involving witchcraft (Luhrmann 1989). By extension, and as many may have learned from E. E. Evans-Pritchard (1976[1937]), serious illness cannot easily be dismissed. Rather, it should prompt the ill person, as well as family and friends, to evaluate the larger social context to seek to amend whatever social norms may have been broken or to figure out who may have malevolently caused the illness. This course of action, in turn, sets in motion a series of rituals to find the source of conflict and heal the individual and larger community.

Interpretive drift occurs when one considers as perhaps reasonable, or begins to adopt, another's beliefs or explanations for phenomena (Luhrmann 1989). Evans-Pritchard (1976[1937]) explores how he had little to offer in terms of alternative explanations to witchcraft when one night he saw a light fly past and land on a hut, only to learn the next day that the man inside fell gravely ill during the night. With the wealthy man in "Jamoko Wange Tek," students see how he also interpretively drifted back to his ancestors' beliefs about how social relations should work. And, by the end of the semester, students should at least open up to the possibilities that worldviews different from their own may indeed have merit.

Music about Africa by non-Africans is also a great teaching tool. When teaching about South Africa, for example, the song "Biko" by Peter Gabriel (1980) never fails to have a profound, emotive impact on students. Just starting college in the late 1980s, I was moved by this song, and the movie *Cry Freedom* (Attenborough 1987), to learn more about Steve Biko. I realized that being appalled but not very knowledgeable was not good enough; the song and movie acted as a call for me to enroll in a political science course focused on South Africa; I subsequently began to work at *Africa News* in Durham, North Carolina, in large part to have access to current wire reports.

As a graduate student in the mid-1990s, I discovered the documentary *Biko: Breaking the Silence* (Kaplan, Wicksteed, and Maruma 1988), prepared in conjunction with the filming of *Cry Freedom*, which was based on the novel *Asking for Trouble* by journalist Donald Woods (1981). Gabriel's song in conjunction with excerpts from these films serves as an excellent point of entry to discussions about apartheid in South Africa. The story of Biko, his advocacy of "black consciousness" as a philosophy of self-expression and self-reliance, his controversial death in 1977, and his emergence as an internationally recognized icon of what had gone wrong in South Africa provide a focused, tangible introduction to the complicated history of South Africa. These popular culture aspects of the Biko image encourage students to consider the political and economic effects of "selling" Biko's story or making it public (internationally) via film and music.

Songs, films, and personal stories can humanize teachers, personalize historical events, and also sometimes serve as a call to action for other students, as they learn to move beyond righteous indignation. Class time then can include examples of "action," such as comparisons or moral questionings; creation and analysis of uncertainty, certainty, and critique; evocation of feelings; prompting of judgment; and, it is hoped, fomenting understanding. Of course, any musical selection incorporated into a class should be contextualized; any song, as Alex Zukas (1996) notes, comes from a specific time and place, and students must be cognizant of what those times and places mean in order to better evaluate the instrumentation and lyrics. Further, students must be made aware that no song represents all African people in all times and places, while the borrowing and fusing that has occurred within some African genres and musical styles should also be pointed out.

Music thus can be a highly effective means by which to capture students' attention, promote cultural understanding, practice analytical skills, and learn more about current and older historical events (Masquelier 1999; Zukas 1996). Every semester, a few students bring some relevant part of their own music collection to share and integrate it into the course. Therefore, this approach is collaborative, expanding my own knowledge about African music as well.

Onward

The preceding examples demonstrate ways to introduce students to different aspects of Africa. Teaching should convey certain information but also help cultivate the skills of students to question, analyze, make connections, and support their own arguments with that information, while still wanting to learn more. Educators can further emphasize these goals by modeling best practices through enthusiasm for the subject and caring for students by listening to them and making it clear why what is taught about Africa is worth knowing (Postman and Weingartner 1969). In sum, these exercises work well in a variety of courses, and they work best when educators personalize them by tying lessons to topics that invoke excitement and engagement on the part of both the teacher and the learner.

2 Africa: Which Way Forward?

An Interdisciplinary Approach

Todd Cleveland

Introduction

This chapter examines an interdisciplinary course titled Africa: Which Way Forward?, which focuses on the African continent's contemporary development challenges and successes. Explorations of current, often sensational, issues, such as Somali piracy, desertification, or the HIV/AIDS scourge, offer students familiar points of entry for further exploration, which are then historicized in order to identify their often deeply rooted origins. However, the course also examines the range of contemporary factors that hinder development in Africa. So as not to reinforce media impressions of a continent saddled with intractable problems and embroiled in endless conflict, students also examine success stories and the range of encouraging developments that the press invariably neglects. Ultimately, students increase their awareness of the Africa of today's headlines, but also develop a strong sense of how and why these newsworthy developments are occurring—as well as others that are not making the news.

In order to answer the question featured in the course title, a series of assignments require students to identify and explore contemporary development challenges (of their choosing) with which African governments, communities, and individuals are contending. Students are then responsible for considering different solutions to these problems after examining the relevant political science, history, sociology, economics, public health, legal, and development literature, as well as "listening" to African voices through film, fiction, and interviews. A central challenge for students throughout this process is to navigate the spectacular diversity of approaches to development. Indeed, the myriad prescriptions for Africa's copious challenges can be external (i.e., "Western") or organic—or both—and even within these two often dissimilar approaches, sentiments range widely as to the best practices. By familiarizing themselves with the range of development strategies, as well as with local sensibilities and cultures, students are better positioned to understand the continent's challenges, to advocate potential solutions, and to cogently argue their merits in both written and oral form.

Two sets of sources prove extremely useful to students as they fulfill the course assignments: African newspapers and interviews with African immigrants. One assignment requires that students access African-based media sources, which are increasingly available online, to follow a contemporary issue of their choosing as it unfolds in an African community, country, or region over the course of the semester. Students augment their understanding of the issue and how it is experienced on the ground by interviewing African immigrants who visit the class. Via these complementary undertakings, as well as additional research, students develop an interdisciplinary framework in order to analyze their respective topics and develop informed answers to the question: Africa, which way forward?

Genesis of the Course

This course is a collective product of my graduate course work in African history, politics, and development; direct observations and experiences living in Angola for roughly two years; and involvement in the interdisciplinary Liberal Studies (LS) program at my home institution, Augustana College. Each of these three components was essential to the formation of the class, as the absence of any of them would have rendered this a very different course or, more likely, would have precluded its creation.

From 2004 to 2006, I lived in Angola, dividing time between Luanda, the capital, and the diamond mines in the northeastern province of Lunda Norte.[1] During this time, I traveled throughout the war-torn country, sometimes as a tourist and at others as a consultant employed by various nongovernmental organizations (NGOs). In practice, Angola's protracted civil war (1975–2002), its prodigious oil reserves and, to a lesser extent, its diamond deposits, and its Marxist-cum-capitalist, acutely corrupt regime render it a superb place from which to observe the interplay between an African state, its citizenry, its natural resource endowment, and governmental practices and policies. In other words, it brought my academic training to life and daily delivered a practical example that was eventually usable in the classroom. Upon returning to the United States following this experience, I was offered a position at Augustana, where I teach African History and the LS course that is the focus of this chapter.[2]

Aware that history could inform, but not monopolize, the interdisciplinary LS course, the focus shifted to the array of African nations' more recent challenges. Purposefully rejecting an Afro-pessimistic approach, the course title reflected optimism for the future of the continent, Africa: Which Way Forward? The institutional charge was to educate students about the ways that Africans had arrived at their individual and collective challenges, but also to prompt them to attempt to *answer* the question posed in the course title by having them formulate their own informed solutions based on relevant, existing developmental approaches. As such, by the end of the term, the course objective amounted to nothing less than having the students attempt to generate prescriptions to some of the continent's most intractable challenges! The question thus became, how?

Constituent Parts: The Anatomy of the Course

Facilitating the process by which students gain an enhanced appreciation for the complexity of Africa's past and present is undoubtedly a challenging endeavor. Yet, if they are going to be able to comprehend the nature of the contemporary development challenges the continent faces and how Africa is to move forward from this point, their misperceptions and lack of knowledge need to be addressed—and quickly. It became immediately apparent that lectures that offered both foundation and context were imperative, while in-class discussions predicated on assigned readings serve to complement and deepen students' understandings of the topics covered during the lectures. Additionally, more in-depth, out-of-class assignments allow students to familiarize themselves with their chosen topics as part of the discovery-comprehension-prescription process. Finally, relevant films are sprinkled throughout the course to enhance the lectures, as well as to provide visual images of life on the continent.[3]

Classroom Learning: Lectures and Discussions

In order to begin to build the historical foundation that the students need to succeed in the course, they spend the first two class sessions going through Africa's history since roughly 1500. These chronological parameters allow them to move through different eras on the continent, to highlight Africans' increasing contact with Europeans and Asians, and, finally, to discuss the processes of colonization and independence, as well as the shifting postcolonial environment and the ways that Africans have creatively navigated these different periods. As such, the classroom represents an ideal setting in which to both raise students' awareness about the continent's past (and present) and to help them move beyond durable perceptions of African ahistoricity and hopelessness.

Just as students are beginning to develop some level of understanding concerning the continent, they read Curtis Keim's highly accessible *Mistaking Africa: Curiosities and Inventions of the American Mind* (2009) in order to highlight all the "baggage" that they bring to their study of Africa and where these (mis)perceptions originate.[4] The book is undoubtedly provocative—at times, arguably overly so—but unfailingly prompts students to reflexively consider what they *perceive* about Africa, and why they hold these perceptions. This assignment also serves to humble those students who presume to know a great deal about Africa, claiming this type of comprehension based on a friend's or relative's visit to the continent, or even, on occasion, a personal visit. More importantly, the text helps to promote the broader course objectives to move past African stereotypes and misinformation in order to identify the continent's core challenges, stripped of all the misleading—even if well-intentioned—media coverage to which they've been exposed. Indeed, while misconceptions about Africa are legion, a thorough exploration of the rich and complex histories of African peoples typically prompts students to revise any narrow (mis)understandings of the continent they may have and to begin to realize how these views became so firmly embedded in the first place.

From here, students begin to explore the root causes for the contemporary development challenges the continent faces, including: the export of slaves; colonial exploitation and underdevelopment; corruption; patronage politics; and neocolonialism. In addition to lectures, they also spend time reading and discussing pieces that examine the lingering, deleterious effects of the colonial era (e.g., Davis and Kalu-Nwiwu 2001). Students are made to understand that although the colonial era concluded roughly half a century ago in most cases, it continues to shape and, in practice, hinder in multifarious ways the current pace and nature of development on the continent. However, the students also read Pepetela's 2002 novel, *The Return of the Water Spirit*, to counterbalance notions that Africa's contemporary problems are, or have been, all externally imposed. This brilliant novel showcases corruption, privilege, and indolence in contemporary Angola, powerfully suggesting that many of Angola's (and, by extension, Africa's) problems are also organic in nature. Greed and corruption are also treated in a more discursive fashion during the associated class discussions, as the grab for wealth and power on the continent often precipitates conflict along ethnic or regional lines. In turn, this exploration leads students to discuss national and regional security and instability and the roles that these issues play in both fostering and hindering development.

Students next explore African challenges that are more recent in nature, such as the "brain drain" phenomenon and the spread of HIV/AIDS. Rather than simply dwell on these admittedly disheartening developments, however, lectures and readings also expose students to encouraging African responses to these daunting challenges. For example, governmental initiatives to mine African expatriate expertise or incentivize repatriation are tempering brain drain, while the "grassroots" organization and proliferation of HIV/AIDS-positive support groups and more visible prevention campaigns are all examples of initiatives that are largely or exclusively organic in nature. By highlighting these processes, students begin to focus on strategic responses to some of the most daunting challenges the continent faces. In addition, special attention is given to African visionaries, such as Amilcar Cabral, Thomas Sankara, and Nelson Mandela. By exploring the lives of these remarkable leaders, students learn that Africa also produces progressive, intelligent, determined leaders; they also learn that, unfortunately, many principled leaders' opportunities to pursue and implement equitable solutions can be severely circumscribed or even tragically brief.

The course's concluding units squarely address themes and controversies related to development in contemporary Africa, including the multiple forms of foreign aid, globalization, the global commercial arena, and the international trade agreements that (allegedly) regulate this exchange. Todd Moss's *African Development: Making Sense of the Issues and Actors* (2007) helps students sort out what can be a dizzying array of funding bodies, trade organizations, lending institutions, and NGOs. Collectively, these lectures and discussions squarely situate Africa in the international context, helping students understand how Africa interacts with, and is impacted by, the international community as it relates to development on the continent.

While the class in its current state is reasonably comprehensive, it is also certainly amendable. Going forward, for example, the course will be revised to add a unit that explicitly addresses gender (with a focus on women) and development. This current absence is partially addressed via considerations of women and shifting gender roles within the scope of broader discussions about, for example, the transatlantic slave trade and its social and economic repercussions on the continent. Women's experiences are also explicitly considered during discussions related to HIV/AIDS and globalization. Additionally, many students (and especially female ones) elect to focus on women as part of the array of out-of-class assignments. However, more focused examinations of the ways that women are excluded from both core development initiatives and participation in the advancement of the continent would undoubtedly enhance the class. For example, African women constitute the majority of participants in various forms of microfinance initiatives on the continent—a key social and economic development innovation. By examining the history, impetuses, and lived experiences of the beneficiaries of these initiatives, students would be afforded crucial insights into the gendered nature of development on the continent.

Out-of-Class Learning: Course Assignments

Fundamental to the success of the course are two assignments that each student is required to complete: the Media Assignment and the Inquiry (Research) Paper.[5] For these assignments, students identify a particular topic related to African development that they want to examine in greater detail. These two endeavors are intentionally designed to overlap, such that students identify a single topic and examine it using two different, assignment-specific approaches, and thus these dual endeavors are complementary in nature.

Students identify topics in a variety of ways. Often, a subject previously discussed in class stimulates many students and they want to learn more about it. Those students who have little or no familiarity with the continent prior to enrolling in the class, and thus rely on the classroom discussions and reading assignments to introduce them to various aspects of the continent's past and present, most often take this route. Occasionally, discussions with individual students are required, during which they are often encouraged to pursue topics that align with their personal interests, for example, sports or education. Other students come to the class with a previously developed interest in Africa and, in many cases, a particular topic. These students may have already conducted preliminary research as part of a previous assignment for another class and simply want to expand upon their existing knowledge.

Regardless of each student's starting point in relation to his or her chosen topic, the two-pronged approach of the assignments significantly deepens the student's knowledge of both the historical and the contemporary causes of the chosen topic. The Media Assignment draws students' attention to the coverage of an African issue that they most likely heretofore would rarely, if ever, have stopped to contemplate. Exploring the different ways that their topics are covered in African newspapers helps the students understand the complexity of many of these issues and the multitude of divergent perspectives that typically revolve around a particular issue. By requiring students to incorporate their own opinions into their written and oral work, they are prompted to familiarize themselves with the range of approaches or sentiments associated with their chosen topic so that their conclusions are well informed. Following their formal presentations, they are pressed, primarily by their classmates, on their advocations and thus have sufficient incentive to be as knowledgeable as possible about their topics, especially if tackling an issue about which many students in class will already possess some knowledge.

The Inquiry Paper ensures that students build a much deeper understanding of their chosen topic by significantly expanding their evidentiary base. Indeed, while the Media Assignment may enable students to "get up to speed" quickly by accessing foreign and domestic newspapers and online articles, the research associated with the Inquiry Paper provides students with a range of perspectives, both academic and, via the interviews with African immigrants, personal. By accessing an array of secondary sources, students familiarize themselves with scholarly approaches and debates related to their topics. Meanwhile, interviews with African immigrants enable students both to learn more about how individual Africans think about the issue in question and to incorporate elements of this testimony into their papers and presentations. These interview sessions reinforce the notion that one does not have to travel to Africa to study it and are also immensely popular, both for the students and the interviewees who visit the classes. Since many of the interviewees are in their mid- or late twenties, the sessions offer them an opportunity to learn more about American college students and perhaps dispel some stereotypes that they may hold, just as the students are busy trying to learn more about these immigrants' lives and perspectives. Even if the interviews ultimately produce little in the way of material for students' papers and presentations, this type of cross-cultural exchange and the experiential learning it offers are invaluable.

One benefit that both assignments help deliver is the generation of information literacy among the students as they learn how to access foreign newspapers, African-themed websites, and academic journals. These endeavors often represent initial forays into these digital repositories and, thus, help students not only with the assignments for this course, but also with other classes going forward.

Classroom and Assignment-Related Challenges and Solutions

Teaching this course is replete with pedagogical challenges. Perhaps most obvious is students' varying degrees of interest in and knowledge about the African continent. In the early stages of the class, however, Curtis Keim's text goes a long way toward drawing any potentially disinterested students into the fold. Keim's book is pitched at "average Americans" who are, he contends, for the most part unwitting Afro-pessimists. For Keim, nothing is sacred: both Disney's *The Lion King* and African safaris are equally, and creatively, vilified. Indeed, students feel compelled to react, at times for no other reason than to defend themselves against his relentless accusations, while at others to ashamedly agree with the author, struggling with feelings of previously undiscovered guilt.

Once students are sufficiently engaged, choosing a topic for the Media Assignment and Inquiry Paper constitutes a daunting task for many of them. Since most students enter the class knowing little about the continent, identifying a viable topic can be challenging. As with any prospective research topic, viability remains a key factor, and therefore students should be coached through this process. Students are typically directed to Anglophone countries (or regions, such as Southern Africa), since few students have the language skills necessary to adequately examine media output associated with, for example, Francophone or Lusophone nations.[6] A determination must then be made about whether there will be sufficient sources available for both the Media Assignment *and* the Inquiry Paper. This decision depends on a number of factors, including the topic itself and the geographic delineation.

Once topics have been identified, the next challenge the students face is the research itself. Navigating search engines to locate African-based newspapers for the Media Assignment presents an immediate challenge. In fact, most students are often only vaguely familiar with how to search American-based newspapers. While library sessions early in the semester provide students with a solid foundation, via both opportunities to practice using actual research topics and the provisioning of handouts that walk them through the search process, students inevitably struggle to master these investigatory techniques. Upon eventually securing access to pertinent source material, many students subsequently struggle with quantity, unable to locate a sufficient number of relevant articles.[7] The Media Assignment's instructions are purposefully vague concerning the number of sources, simply indicating that "quality is better than quantity," but also that "more is certainly better than less," and that a numerical balance of articles that offer differing or competing perspectives or approaches related to their topics is ideal.

Finally, for all of the wonderful insights that the interviews yield, they also generate a number of challenges. For example, from an ethical (and legal) perspective, Augustana's Institutional Review Board (IRB) first had to approve the interviews as a curricular endeavor. Many of the immigrants fled situations at home that were, at a minimum, disagreeable, but were just as often violent and potentially lethal, and thus interviewing them requires a conscious consideration of the risks that they have already undertaken, as well as the current challenges that they face. These realities render members of this population vulnerable, and many wish to remain "under the radar," doing nothing to jeopardize their deliberate social invisibility. Therefore, each potential interviewee must be made sufficiently aware of his or her rights regarding both participation and control over any testimony provided.

Notwithstanding the excitement associated with the first interview session (and similar levels regarding subsequent ones), a number of challenges associated with the interviews themselves have also materialized. The first, and perhaps most predictable, is that the vast majority of the students have little or no experience conducting interviews. Consequently, prior to the interviews a class period is spent in preparation, which typically features complementary readings, discussions about approaches to interviewing, and what candid dialogue they might expect once the interviews are under way.[8] Students are generally instructed to try to gather a life history from interviewees, allowing them to elaborate where and when they desire to speak about their experiences. Since there are typically three to five students per interviewee, they are instructed to inquire only briefly about their particular topic, mindful that others in the group have similar tasks. Students are also urged, to the extent it is possible, to incorporate their questions into the natural flow of the conversation.

Despite their preparation, many challenges remain.[9] In some cases, informants' English skills are simply not sufficient. In fact, many of the African immigrants living in the area come from Francophone countries, namely, Togo. To address this challenge, a professor of French has been enlisted to translate the dialogue. However, interviews of this nature tend to be less fruitful, given that they proceed at a much slower pace and therefore generate less testimony. Other times, interviews bring to the surface more serious problems, especially when informants have endured significant trauma in Africa and are therefore hesitant to discuss a wide range of issues related to their experiences. In these instances, the discussion must be moderated in order to ensure that the inexperienced students cease making inquiries about uncomfortable subjects and keep their questions focused on "safe" topics, even if this approach limits the overall effectiveness of the interview. These instances should, however, be subsequently utilized as teaching opportunities, while acknowledging that this strategy does nothing to generate testimony for students' papers even though the scenario itself can offer significant insights and lessons.

What to do with the testimony gathered presents a final challenge associated with the interviews. As part of the original IRB approval process, consent forms were produced that grant the signee complete control over the testimony offered during the course of the interview. The options available to informants are (1) to refuse to allow any of the discussion to be recorded; (2) to allow the conversations to be recorded but only used internally, by students in the class; or (3) to allow open access to the testimony, placing it digitally in the public domain. Most interviewees choose the second option, permitting the session to be recorded, and the conversations are then uploaded to the course website, which features two layers of password protection. Upon completion of the course, the audio files are removed and destroyed. By allowing the conversations to be recorded and accessible to members of the course, students may return to interviews for any pieces they may have missed, while classmates who were not part of their interviews can access them to try to glean additional insight and material for their own assignments. When an interviewee is unwilling to have the conversation recorded, participating students are asked to take very close notes and to confer with others who sat in on the interview to ensure that they thoroughly and accurately captured the testimony provided during the session. While this scenario is the least desirable from a data collection perspective, this group approach appears to have enabled students to overcome this challenge. Further, interviewees tend to be more forthcoming during sessions that are not being recorded. As such, upon closer review, this challenge may be better understood as an *opportunity* rather than as an obstacle.

Transcendent Benefits of the Course

An excellent feature of this course is that it has far-reaching impact. Well after the classroom sessions end, the course materials and experiences continue to generate broad interest about the continent on campus, which, in turn, benefits a number of other African-themed initiatives at the college. For example, a number of students who have completed the course have subsequently opted to pursue a major or minor in the recently formed Africana Studies Program. Moreover, many of these same students have participated in study abroad terms in West Africa (Ghana and Senegal). In fact, many students who participated on the most recent African trip have since declared an Africana Studies major or minor. As such, these various African initiatives appear to be synergistic in nature, or at least mutually reinforcing.

Conclusion

Although the course outlined in this chapter is a product of a unique confluence of institutional circumstances, professional training, and personal experience, there are certainly elements of the class pedagogy that can be applied in other settings, to other courses. In regard to the course topic itself, African Development has largely remained outside of mainstream academia, perhaps because scholars can be hesitant to engage in prescriptive exercises, preferring to analyze rather than to recommend. Even rarer are interdisciplinary courses that explore development on the continent; this hesitancy may well be attributable to well-established approaches, methods, and theories residing within particular disciplinary boundaries. Regardless, this course suggests that students can—and do—learn a great deal when exploring this topic, even when compelled to engage in a process that emphasizes prescription following an intense process of edification. And, beyond learning about the continent and its myriad development challenges and successes, the course also helps students hone their critical thinking, analytical, research, and presentation skills.

Characteristic of teachers everywhere, pedagogical satisfaction is felt most acutely when students have had effective and positive learning experiences. Evidence of this outcome is most apparent during students' final presentations when they showcase their knowledge and reflections about the course. Students' ability to both broaden and deepen their knowledge of Africa's myriad development challenges—from Somalia's "failed state" to racially-based economic inequity in South Africa—in such a short amount of time is duly impressive, while their classmates' engaging questions suggest that they also learn a great deal during this process. Perhaps most remarkable, though, is the optimism they display. Rather than emerge from their research discouraged, they appear to hold genuine hope for the continent and its peoples, often advocating less Western intervention and more "homegrown" solutions. Of course, it is tempting to attribute the students' sanguinity to their still reasonably limited knowledge of Africa, but their demonstrated acknowledgment of the complexities of the issues belies this explanation. Moreover, while their solutions may, at times, lack the type of comprehensiveness that a prescriptive road map produced by a government ministry or consulting agency might feature, they have consistently, boldly, and intelligently answered the central question that the course poses: which way forward?

Notes

I would like to acknowledge my students for their patience during, and contributions to, my ongoing journey of pedagogical discovery and reflection. I can only hope that I've inspired them as much as they've inspired me.

1. During this period, I was gathering archival and oral evidence in order to construct a social history of African laborers and their families on Angola's colonial-era diamond mines, all of which were located in Lunda.

2. Augustana describes its LS program as follows:

The first-year liberal studies (LSFY) program is designed for students to develop as active, critical learners. During the first year, each student's class schedule will include a sequence of three . . . courses from the liberal studies program. Each first year course is unique, yet they all have common features. To help students begin to engage in academic inquiry, each of the three courses in the sequence are framed around an overarching question. . . . In LSFY 103 students ask, "How do we embrace the challenges of our diverse and changing world?" (Augustana College, "Liberal Studies Courses," http://www.augustana.edu/x23478.xml, accessed October 5, 2012)

3. Films used in conjunction with the class include *Afro@Digital* (Bakupa-Kanyinda 2003), *Black Gold* (Francis and Francis 2006), and *Thomas Sankara: The Upright Man* (Shuffield 2006).

4. I also assign this text to an adult education class that I teach, to a mixture of defensiveness and ready acknowledgment.

5. The assignments appear on the syllabus as follows:

Media Assignment: By Class 6, students will identify a challenge that a specific African country or community faces (within the topical parameters of the class) and will follow this topic over the course of the term, compiling articles from both African *and* international newspapers, as well as other media sources. Students will then construct a 5–6-page, double-spaced paper based on the coverage of the topic and will be asked to incorporate their own opinions on the subject in the paper. At the end of the term, students will be asked to briefly (5–10 minutes) educate the class about the topic they've been following and present their conclusions for class discussion. They will then submit both the articles collected/employed and the final paper.

Inquiry Paper: This assignment requires that students craft a 5–6 page paper based on the topic they've chosen for the Media Assignment. Students are required to trace the historical trajectory of the issue, access relevant primary and secondary materials, and posit a solution to it based on the knowledge they've acquired via the Media Assignment and course materials, as well as outside research—including interviews with local African immigrants (to be arranged by the instructor) and cogently argue for this course of action. Students are required to submit a rough draft of this paper, at which point instructor-generated feedback will be provided so that students have an opportunity to revise the papers prior to the deadline.

6. Even this approach can be problematic at times, as some African countries, such as Tanzania, feature more media sources in languages other than English (in this case, Swahili).

7. This challenge can be legitimate if a student's selected topic simply does not generate sufficient media coverage.

8. Given the violence that many informants had to endure prior to their arrival in the United States, Helena Pohlandt-McCormick's superb article "I Saw a Nightmare" (2000), is often utilized in the lead-up to the interviews.

9. One interesting, though ultimately disappointing, scenario occurred when an African student in the class participated in an interview with a recently arrived immigrant. Rather than enhance the interview for everyone participating, their divergent life experiences generated an awkwardness that undermined the interview.

3 Why We Need African History

Kathleen R. Smythe

Wʜɪʟᴇ ᴛʜᴇʀᴇ ᴀʀᴇ a whole host of politically correct and culturally sensitive reasons why most college history departments in the United States should offer African history, there are also very important reasons why African history is vital during this most recent age of ecological destruction and "supercapitalism" (Reich 2007).[1] African history is essential to developing a new view of the United States' place in the world, as Chris Knight (1991:1) and Robin Fox (1975:348) call for. The *longue durée* (literally "long duration") of African history offers American students the distance and perspective that they need to understand the uniqueness of their particular moment in history and to interrogate their views on their place in the world.[2] If history is a means to teach about other times and places, then there is no area of history as well suited to taking students out of the confines of their modern, consumer-oriented culture than African history. The reason is not because Africans have lived pristine lives free of technology, markets, outside influences, or ecological collapse. Instead, it is that the discipline has had to forge a new path that has allowed it the freedom to construct narratives that are different from those of Western histories.

African histories provide lenses not only to understand defining historical ideas, such as human evolution, food domestication, and climate adaptation, but also to rethink the assumptions and narratives that have undergirded them. African histories are grounded in a very different set of methodologies, such as historical linguistics and anthropology. Such methodologies lead to different ways of thinking about and understanding history. Historical linguistics, for example, identifies points of culture contact and diffusion through shared words and ideas. Indeed, if students' responses to African history classes are any indication, African history can be an entirely unexpected journey through a set of suppositions and heretofore unexamined questions that is exhilarating, infectious, and inspiring. There are three aspects to a survey of African history that this chapter explores. First, Africa as the birthplace of humanity offers an important view of history that allows students to see the tremendously difficult environments and challenges that humans overcame on their journey to the contemporary world. On the way, early humans created some cultural responses, such as matriliny, that endure millennia later.[3] Second, students come to grapple with the realities of possibly cataclysmic climate change; Africans' multiple adaptations to not only changing climate but different climate zones with differing resource possibilities present lessons in adaptability and flexibility. They also offer an understanding of the very real limitations some environmental conditions impose. And third, African history allows students to take a different view of what is often termed the "globalization era" and to see the ways that the common assumptions behind the term mask a continuous historical trajectory of inequality.

The *Longue Durée*—Early Human Evolution

The beginning of African history is the beginning of humanity. And by turning students' gaze back to such a distant past, they can see that the most recent hominids were not always inherently superior. For example, as Ian Tattersall (2000) argues, the proper explanatory model for human evolution is a "bush" rather than a tree. *Homo sapiens* are not the endpoint of a single trajectory, but the lucky descendants of one of many possible evolutionary lines. They are the top of one branch of many different branches, most of which faced extinction at some point in time. Earlier hominids formed multiple lines of evolution, some of which were dead ends. For example, a little less than two million years ago, there was a world in which multiple hominid species, such as *Homo habilis* and *Paranthropus boisei*, coexisted and made use of the same landscape in eastern Africa. The latter species had large jaws with huge grinding teeth that enabled it to chew on vegetation rather than meat. The former is named for its ability to make tools and was likely a meat-eater (Tattersall 2000). We don't know as much as we would like about these species or about their possible interactions, but, certainly, recent evidence about interbreeding between *Homo neanderthalensis* and *Homo sapiens* makes it more likely that there was some interaction among one or more of these species (Wade 2010). Thus, while *Paranthropus boisei* seems to have been a dead end, our ancestors might have interacted enough with them to carry their skills, if not DNA, with them. For some time now, approximately 30,000 years, *Homo sapiens* have been the only surviving *Homo* species, possibly due to our possession of symbolic thought, according to Tattersall (2000). Yet even other species might have had the necessary physical infrastructure for such a development, even though they had not yet come to make use of it. Through a study of early human evolution, students realize that sovereignty is not fully understood or necessarily as unique as they thought (Tattersall 2000:56–62).

Studying early human history also challenges one of the common ways students differentiate people, and that is by race. Many assume that race is a biological reality; yet this is not what recent anthropological work demonstrates. Current understanding is that modern humans, or *Homo sapiens*, originated in Africa about 200,000 years ago; thus, all humans are African (Stringer and McKie 1996:179–193). All modern humans are very close genetically; previous notions of biological racial difference evolving over a millennium or more are false (Gilbert and Reynolds 2008:4–14). Instead, the physical characteristics so long associated with race, such as skin color, are the result of more recent adaptations to various climates but do not connote innate differences in intellectual or social capabilities (Jablonski 2004:16). Physical differences are just that, they explain adaptations to climate, not cultural or intellectual capabilities.

Students can also learn about cultural capabilities by looking at social adaptations to such challenging environments. One of the ways human forebears survived was through practices associated with matriliny. Authority is more diffuse in a matrilineal society, with the mother, maternal uncle, and father all having a role in ensuring the survival and welfare of a child. Such diffuse authority likely comes out of a strategy to try to maximize the successful raising of children in very difficult circumstances. Scholars such as Christine Saidi (2010) and Rhonda M. Gonzales (2009) are finding that matriliny or practices associated with it have been as much the norm in early societies as patriliny, if not more so. In early societies that were smaller in population and that valued people rather than access to land, the more social networks one had, the more likely the society was to withstand economic and environmental challenges (Ehret 2002).

The earliest African women more often lived with their mothers than with their husbands' families, at least while raising young children. While living with the mother's family after marriage, or matrilocality, is not always equated with matriliny, it is often associated with it. And some, like Chris Knight (2008), think that for these societies, as well as even earlier hominid societies, such a residence choice made it more likely that a mother's children would survive. Matrilocality meant that a mother had access both to the work and care of the children's father and her female relatives, while if she lived with her husband, she would lose the benefit of her female relatives' care. Though she might have been helped by her husband's family, they would likely be focused on their own offspring's children rather than an in-law's. According to Knight, there is some evidence that the *Homo sapiens* population was at one point very small. In order to recover from this small number and go on to populate the globe, they had to have had exceptional child care. And the optimal solution to ensuring such care would have included mothers cooperatively resisting male sexual control, relying on their male kin for support, encouraging multiple suitors to work hard to provide for them, and taking advantage of every available child-care resource (Knight 2008:79–82).

In the environments discussed above, early humans scavenged and gathered to make a living. Early on, *Homo sapiens* were the hunted more than the hunters until they developed the necessary cooperation and physiological capabilities (Bramble and Lieberman 2004; Hart and Sussman 2005; Rincon 2006). Prior to these social and physical developments, earlier hominids would have faced death from a variety of predators and would not have been as readily able to compete for scavenged meat. Students learn from these insights into early human history about the necessity for cooperation and maintaining tight social networks based on a mother and her kin. The male-headed household that has been the norm in the United States has a particular historical trajectory and has not always been typical in human existence. Thus, students can see that nuclear patrilineal families where resources are tightly controlled are a response to more recent historical circumstances. We evolved in very different situations where the eyes, hands, and skills of many adults were necessary for the successful reproduction of society.[4]

A second way humans obtained food and tried to ensure their survival was through deliberate manipulation of previously gathered plants and hunted animals, otherwise known as the practices of agriculture and animal domestication. A sense of the multiple challenges involved in domesticating plants and animals gives students a much deeper appreciation of the depth and richness of human history. In every ecosystem ancestors struggled to figure out how to control plants (and animals) for their own use. As Jared Diamond (1997) argues, in Africa and Latin America, people had to figure it out multiple times due to a series of climatic zone changes that run north to south on the continents. Of the thousands of available plants, early humans determined through trial and error, and sometimes by accident, those with the most favorable sets of characteristics, and these now make up the modern human diet (Diamond 1997:114–130, 157–175).

As Christopher Ehret (2002) shows, between 9000 and 5500 BCE during a wet climatic period in Africa, there were multiple independent agricultural developments in response to the different climate zones and changing climate. In the Sudan and Sahel regions (including, for example, the modern-day countries of Sudan and Chad), Africans domesticated sorghum. While in West Africa, Africans experimented with yams, a root crop. Moreover, in the Ethiopian Highlands, Africans discovered the value of the ensete plant, of which they ate the stalk (Ehret 2002:66–67, 80–83). Each environment required learning about the value of different plants, which plant was worthy of eating and which part of it, and how to grow more of it. Prior to this development, *Homo sapiens* spent most of their history as scavengers and gatherers with much less control over the environment (Gilbert and Reynolds 2008:24).

Humans are inheritors of a lineage of people who have physically, economically, and socially adapted to environments with many challenges. Through the study of history and the use of historical imagination, scholars, teachers, and students can appreciate the awesome legacy that has made our current lives possible. In the African history survey classes, most of this material in any given year is taught in the first month or so of class. Students, after learning about some of these early human dynamics, find history to be much broader than they had conceived of it previously. They see that it relates to multiple disciplines as well as their own understanding of who they are in relation to others in the classroom and the world around them.

The *Longue Durée*—Adaptation to Climate Change

A second aspect of studying early African history is that students can learn about how peoples of the past responded to drastic climate changes. Climate change discussions in the United States tend to focus on temperature variations because temperature is the principal factor that differentiates the seasons. Yet in Africa, it is the presence or absence of rain that determines climates. For primarily farmers and livestock keepers, rainfall is the most relevant climatic variable of food production and the growth of pasture (McCann 1999:262–263).

While climate change has affected many regions in Africa, there is evidence that the Sahel (including countries such as Mali, Sudan, and Uganda) might be a unique region on the continent, prone to more dramatic shifts than other regions, both over the short and long term. With droughts occurring in two out of five years in the Sahel, "normal" rainfall might not be a relevant term (Kandji et al. 2006:4). Evidence suggests that the Sahel is prone to either a desert state or a green state, as existed prior to 5500 BP. In the late Pleistocene and early Holocene (14,500 BP to 5500 BP), an ancient sea or lake, Mega-Chad, covered over 150,000 square miles. At the time, Lake Mega-Chad sat at 1,100 feet above sea level, draining into the Atlantic Ocean through the Benue River, to which it is no longer connected (see Fig. 3.1). For the sake of comparison, a lake covering over 150,000 square miles is slightly smaller than the area of the state of California. During this green state, when the lake was very big, it was the largest of many lakes in the present-day Sahara. Sedimentary deposits such as coastal sand ridges hold aquatic animal remains, including the bones of fish and crocodiles, and human artifacts such as fishing tools provide evidence of this previous wetter era when people made a living from the lake's resources (Schuster et al. 2009:603–611).

Beginning about 5500 BP, at the end of the Holocene climatic optimum, there was a sudden transition (within centuries or even a few decades) from a wet climate to a desert climate in northern Africa (Foley et al. 2003:524). This transition was possibly due to a changing orbit as well as changes in "incoming solar radiation, sea-surface temperatures, or the degree of land degradation" (Foley et al. 2003:524). Increases in sea-surface temperatures have altered monsoon patterns and thus seasonal rainfall patterns. Similarly, as the climate dries, drier plants replace moisture-loving plants and then promote the conditions for drier plants, reinforcing the cycle. Large lakes can create their own precipitation patterns due to water evaporation. Small lakes, like the current Lake Chad, cannot. As the lake shrinks, the temperature of the remaining water rises and evaporates faster as well. Thus, both 5,500 years ago and in the past century, one interpretation suggests, what might have begun as a small change in the monsoon rains, sea-surface temperature, or vegetation has

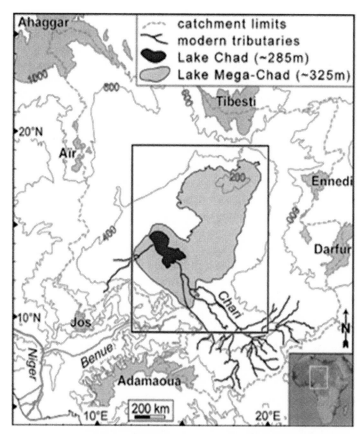

Figure 3.1. Image of Lake Chad. Present-day Lake Chad is black. Former Lake Mega-Chad is shown in gray. Note that the Benue River no longer drains Lake Chad as it did in the past (Schuster et al. 2009:605). Permission granted for reprinting by Elsevier Masson SAS on behalf of *Académie des Sciences*.

accelerated a drying phase set in motion by small shifts in the planet's orbit (Foley et al. 2003:524).

This sudden transition fits with more recent interpretations that climate changes have occurred and can occur rather rapidly, on the timescale of a few centuries, at times a few decades, and perhaps even within a few years (Adams et al. 1999). While it appears that changes in Lake Chad's size have been slow in coming, over the past 5,000 years the evidence is mounting that the climate of the Sahel (and likely the Earth more generally) "does not change in such gentle rhythms" (Adams and Foote 2010). Instead of a model of the slow effects of climate change, Jonathan Adams and Randy

Foote (2010) argue that it should be one of plate tectonics, where stress surfaces result in earthquakes rather than a gradual shifting of plates (Pearce 2007:238). Certainly, tectonic shifts suggest more radical action than global warming does.

Though the surface area (and thus volume) of the lake has varied and continues to vary significantly from season to season and year to year, there has been a general trend over the past 5,000 years of the lake shrinking, with some evidence that it nearly dried out altogether in 1908 and again in 1984. From 2,500 years ago until the early 1960s, the lake was on average 200 feet lower in depth and covered only 5 percent of its original surface area (about 9,000 square miles) (Coe and Foley 2001:3349). This change, like all climate changes, required human adaptation. Three thousand years ago, Chadic peoples, who lived in the area and whose ancestors had come from northeastern Africa, left fishing and turned to cultivating sorghum and other crops on land that had previously been under water. Some moved beyond the old lake bed, also growing sorghum and millet and keeping livestock on landscapes that were becoming more like savannas, alongside resident Sudanic peoples (Ehret 2002:59–106).

A more recent regime shift began in the late 1960s, after a wetter era. It was one of the "longest and most severe [regime shifts] in recent history. Between 1968 and 1997, precipitation over the Sahel was 25%–40% lower than the standard climatological period of 1931–1960" (Foley et al. 2003:529). In the 1970s alone, almost half the domestic livestock in the region died and nearly one million people starved to death (Foley et al. 2003:529, 532–533). Today Lake Chad covers between 115 and 200 square miles (1,000 times smaller than 5,000 years ago), and the fish yield is six times less than 50 years ago, or about 50,000 tons a day (Murray 2007).

The land that is exposed is subject to the powerful jet stream that blows over the area, creating several hundred million tons of atmospheric dust. According to oceanographer Robert Stewart (2005), the Bodele Depression in the Sahel (where Lake Chad is located) is the dustiest place on Earth. The jet stream deposits minerals needed by phytoplankton, such as calcium and potassium, in the Atlantic Ocean and the Amazon Basin (Stewart 2005). It is likely causing a decline in coral reefs as well, due to the bacteria carried in the dust masses. Peak dust production years coincide with peak coral decline years (Shinn et al. 2000). The drier and colder the climate becomes, the more desert forms and the more dust there is in the atmosphere, reinforcing the dry regime (Adams and Foote 2010).

These more recent changes are affecting the lives of those around the lake in significant ways. The water and fish resources are no longer enough for the 30 million people in the region (in Chad, Cameroon, Niger, and Nigeria) who depend on the lake. Another four countries (the Central African Republic, Algeria, Sudan, and Libya) share the lake's hydrological basin and are affected by the lake's changes. Thus, some fishermen are choosing to migrate to different regions within their own and neighboring countries in an attempt to find a way to make a living. They are environmental refugees (N. Myers 2001:609), many of whom move into already labor-poor urban

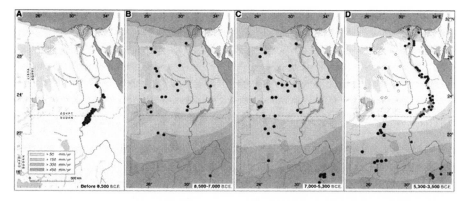

Figure 3.2. Eastern Sahara Occupation. This set of maps demonstrates the major human occupation areas (dots) of the eastern Sahara between 20,000 BCE and 3500 BCE. (A) During the last glacial maximum and the terminal Pleistocene (20,000–8500 BCE), the Saharan desert was void of any settlement outside of the Nile valley and extended about 250 miles farther south than it does today. (B) With the abrupt arrival of monsoon rains at about 8500 BCE, the hyperarid desert was replaced by savanna-like environments and swiftly inhabited by prehistoric settlers. During the early Holocene humid optimum, the southern Sahara and the Nile valley apparently were too moist and hazardous for appreciable human occupation. (C) After 7000 BCE, human settlement became well established all over the eastern Sahara, fostering the development of cattle pastoralism. (D) Retreating monsoon rains caused the onset of desiccation of the Egyptian Sahara at about 5300 BCE. Prehistoric populations were forced to the Nile valley or ecological refuges and forced into exodus in the Sudanese Sahara, where rainfall and surface water were still sufficient. The return of full desert conditions all over Egypt at about 3500 BCE coincided with the initial stages of pharaonic civilization in the Nile valley (Kuper and Kropelin 2006:806). Permission for reprinting granted by the American Association for the Advancement of Science.

areas where the likelihood of finding work beyond petty trading is limited. Others living around a much smaller Lake Chad have turned to farming the soil exposed by the drying of the lake in recent years, much as ancient Chadians did years ago. Many of those farming the areas from which the lake has recently receded are able to take advantage of good soil fertility, but others complain of desert sands encroaching on their fields. Conflicts between livestock owners and farmers are increasing as access to water becomes more limited (Muhammad 2010; Murray 2007). As rainfall decreases, communities upstream from the lake build irrigation dams to maintain their crops in a drying climate, further decreasing the water reaching Lake Chad.

If the drying trend continues, it is possible that the lacustrine (lake-dwelling) way of life in the Sahel region that dates back 9,000 or 10,000 years will disappear in the area of Lake Chad. The peoples who lived near Lake Chad thousands of years ago contributed to a distinct Nilo-Saharan civilization, from which a number of contemporary African societies descend. They developed a sedentary village lifestyle without agriculture, relying on the steady and abundant supply of fish for supporting denser populations (Ehret 2002:68–74). Unfortunately, links to that heritage are eroding as the lake dries. From this example of drastic climate change around Lake Chad, students learn that history demonstrates that climate has changed drastically in the past and that such changes have brought with them equally severe economic and social adjustments for those affected.

Dramatic changes in the climate of North Africa led to other dramatic developments in ancient Africa as well. For example, the existence of ancient Egyptian civilization is due largely to a drying climate at the end of the Holocene climatic optimum that drove the peoples living in the grasslands that once covered the area of the Sahara Desert toward the narrow strip of the fertile Nile River valley (see Fig. 3.2). The subsequent dense populations that grew there led to the developments of economic and political stratification with which most students are familiar: a royal class with access to enough labor to build monumental stone pyramids and the longest-lasting kingdom in history (Ehret 2002:107–158).

Just as Africans began to live along the Nile River to produce food, many others discovered new ways of obtaining food in a changing climate and learned to more directly control their foodstuffs in an effort to ensure a steadier food supply. Others began to rely more heavily on pastoralism, a very different means of existence requiring humans to move with their livestock as they followed pasture and water (Ehret 2002:138–141, 143–144). Ecologist Jonathan A. Foley and his colleagues note that "archaeological evidence also shows that highly mobile pastoralist cultures started to dominate the region at this time, replacing the more sedentary lacustrine traditions" (2003:527). Certainly, such an understanding of the climatic past informs researchers about the current phase of climate change.

In fact, Africans have adjusted to a tremendous variety of climates. This adaptation is one of their gifts to human civilization, just as it is a marker of the human species more generally. Anthropologist Richard Potts claims that humans are more adaptable than almost any other creature because they have had to adjust to abrupt changes in climate over a long period of time (1996; see also, Joyce 2010). One obvious and appropriate adaptation to water fluctuations is pastoralism.

Livestock pastoralism is a food production system in which a human community relies on domestic livestock for their basic subsistence (Fratkin 1991). We can learn a lot about the pastoral option from studies such as Elliot Fratkin's (1991, 1998) on the Ariaal livestock keepers of northern Kenya. There, pastoralism is one of the few viable ways of making a living. The Ariaal, who number about 7,000 (as of the mid-1990s) and live in Kenya's largest and most arid region, are masters at this livelihood strategy and have been able to withstand a variety of challenges over the past 50 years (see Fig. 3.3).

In fact, they are refugees from Samburu and Rendille societies, having fled drought, famine, and war in the 19th century. The refugees combined practices from both societies to maximize their flexibility. Over time, the refugees created a hybrid society, now known as Ariaal. The Ariaal keep camels, cattle, and small livestock in order to take advantage of the benefits each kind offers and to diversify, as necessary, to survive the

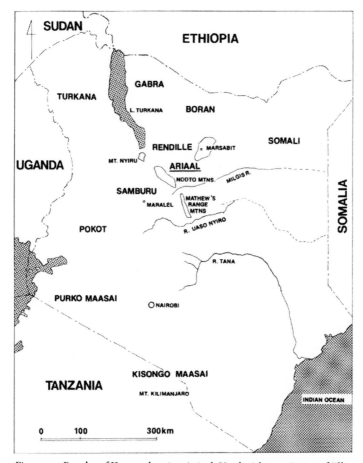

Figure 3.3. Peoples of Kenya, showing Ariaal. Used with permission of Elliot Fratkin.

too common droughts and violent raids that are part of pastoral life in northern Kenya. Camels produce more milk than cattle but do not fetch as much in the marketplace; the former graze in hot deserts, while cattle prefer wet highlands. Sheep and goats can graze in dry lands but need access to water every two to three days and so must be near springs and wells. Thus, Ariaal families must deploy members to different parts of their homeland to manage their livestock. In addition to multiple kinds of livestock, they rely on interhousehold cooperation and ties with other societies for grazing and other functions. Cooperative herding groups are necessary when a household has insufficient stock to feed its members or insufficient labor to manage its livestock (Fratkin 1991).

Keeping different kinds of livestock is one response to a challenging environment. Mobility is a second, and the maintenance of extensive social ties to people in distant areas is a third. In these ways, the Ariaal have much in common with those living around Lake Chad who over generations, and annually, have had to adjust to changing lake levels. Like the Ariaal, they deal with similar variability through mobility and a diversity of food resources and economic activities, such as fishing, soda mining, pastoralism (including cattle, camel, sheep, and goats), and farming in recessional lands. In addition, migration is another strategy for coping with sudden environmental changes. As anthropologist Jeremy Swift (1977:462–463) notes, some pastoralists leave their original economy for different work during droughts, returning to pastoralism when rains return.

Much of this material is covered midway through the first semester as students look at the various ways Africans adapted to their environments and how such modes of living were challenged in the past and still are today. This adaptation is another reason a long view of history is so important for students. Africans' adjustment to unexpected and dramatic climate changes is remarkable and is part of the larger story of human adaptation generally. The difference is that Africans have been adapting to the environment longer than any other humans have. As Potts says, that such a harsh, indifferent world "has happened to preserve us as part of its rich living fabric is extraordinary" (1996:255). Altogether, an understanding of *Homo sapiens* as a species with a history of important and long-term adaptations makes students more appreciative of their past and a bit less likely to assume that it is easy to predict the future. A primary course objective is to get students to realize that the future requires adaptation and ingenuity similar to that demonstrated by these forebears. As the climate warms, all forms of adaptation to various climates must be available as livelihood strategies. Students appreciate such an expansion of the realm of economic activity and livelihood possibilities, particularly as they face an increasingly uncertain economic and ecological future.

The *Longue Durée*—Globalization

The third example regarding the utility of African history for putting the current world in perspective is the theme of globalization. This material comes at the end of the two-semester survey course. Once one has studied in some depth the start of mercantilism and European trade along the West African coast beginning in the late 1400s, one can no longer accept the novelty of increased interconnection, as many of those, like Thomas L. Friedman (2005), writing about globalization would like everyone to believe. In fact, Africa was a part of many of the earlier phases of globalization, including the expansion of the Roman world, the Arab world, the Indian Ocean exploration, and the Atlantic Ocean commercial world. Jeremy Prestholdt (2008) argues about how cosmopolitan, for example, East Africans and Seychelleans were in the 19th century, buying, wearing, and eating the various goods that drove British expansion. In addition, he states, they sought to use their knowledge and appreciation of British objects and culture to seek British aid. Moreover, he shows how East African demands for cloth fueled growth and industrialization in Salem, Massachusetts, and Bombay, India.

Why does it matter whether or not globalization existed in earlier times? For students, realizing the centuries-long trajectory of the current global economy makes the long-term inequalities on which it is based much clearer. It is less likely that they will view current inequality as an aberration. Instead, they will see that it has been embedded in the actions and thinking of the global capitalist class for centuries. Moreover, this way of thinking about it is a significant departure from the white, neoliberal economic perspective that dominates international financial institutions and postindustrial economies and thus students' experiences and understanding. This new post-1980 era of globalization, however, marks something new—faster-paced integration, deeper interconnections, and a level of interdependency without precedent. A common current assumption is that inequality and poverty are on their way out, as both Robert McNamara, former president of the World Bank, and Renato Ruggiero, the first director-general of the World Trade Organization (WTO), have argued (Chang 2002; Peters 2008; Reinert 2007).[5] Therefore, whether globalization is new seems to hinge on whether or not it is improving Africans' lives in a way that their lives did not improve in previous eras.

This claim that the most recent era is something new and potentially better than what came before can only be embraced if there is evidence of economic equalizing. A trip today through Mississippi, Tanzania, or Haiti would suggest, instead, that the world is spiky rather than flat, as Richard Florida (2005) and James Ferguson (2006:25–49) suggest, with urban or industrial centers of hypercapitalism and the latest communication, industrial, transportation, and medical technologies surrounded by vast areas that possess little of these advances. As Swiss development specialist Gilbert Rist (2002) argues in his book *The History of Development*: "The talk about the 'world community' or 'global village' and the benefits of economic 'globalization' never ceases, but two-thirds of the planet is being increasingly separated off as the North patiently erects a wall to keep out the 'new barbarians.' Apartheid has been abolished in South Africa, only to be reborn on a world scale" (210). Globalization, he argues, asserts the opposite of the truth. It is not leveling the playing field but continuing to ensure that only some players have access. Thus, it is possible to interpret globalization as promoting the continued well-being of former imperial powers at the expense of formerly colonized nations (Rodney 1972).

From the perspective of African history, globalization masks history. It allows individuals to dump the histories of imperialism, neo-imperialism, and oppression for a potentially more benign explanatory framework devoid of any historical foundation. It is also a term that is far more widely used in the United States than in Tanzania. A search for "globalization" in the *New York Times* on LexisNexis in early March 2009 turned up 15 articles over a one-week period. A search for the same term in the *East African*, a weekly publication, turned up two articles since 2006, and AllAfrica.com, a comprehensive website of hundreds of African newspapers, did not even have "global-ization" as a search term. The closest term was "capital flows."

Not only does globalization privilege the North over the South, as newspaper cover-age attests, but it also privileges change over "repetition and restructuring," ignoring the enduring nature of some forms of social and economic relationships, according to Ali Behdad (2005:69). Two examples are useful in class to demonstrate how this continuity is evident in events that otherwise might look like "globalization." One is the United States' Project for a New American Century, developed in the early 1990s by politicians and intellectuals who sought to make the United States a more active player on the inter-national field. They called for increasing military spending, strengthening ties to demo-cratic allies, promoting the cause of political and economic freedom at home and abroad, and accepting responsibility for the unique role of the United States, and its allies, in preserving and extending the international order to achieve security and prosperity.[6]

One manifestation of the Project for a New American Century on the African continent is the installation of a combined joint task force in Djibouti, on the Gulf of Aden (Pham 2007). The goal of this base and a yet-to-be permanent African command base (AFRICOM) is to be proactive in preventing radical Islamization and to protect United States' interests. While it is a military command, the post has a humanitarian aspect focused on helping to eradicate poverty and build infrastructure.[7] From the United States' perspective, this is a new endeavor. However, the U.S. base in Djibouti is located on the abandoned French Foreign Legion outpost, Camp Lemonier (Pham 2007). Thus, in terms of the landscape memory of residents of Djibouti, the United States' presence is an extension of French colonialism. And, how, in the end, can a mission designed to meet the ends of U.S. foreign policy serve the needs of those in Djibouti and result in greater equality than rule under a colonial government did?

Another example of continuity is foreign direct investment in Africa. Such invest-ment is being lauded as part of the solution to Africa's economic woes. Foreign invest-ment in Africa is on the increase again. Much of it is in the primary sector, in oil and diamonds; the financial sector; and agriculture (Dupasquier and Osakwe 2005).[8] As such, it is primarily extractive investment, whether Chinese, American, or European. Such investment has done little to boost sustainable economic development on the continent in the past.

Africans have a nuanced vocabulary of trade liberalization, global apartheid, and neocolonialism to describe what is often glossed as globalization. African history offers students a way to interrogate the popularity of *globalization* as an explanatory term and to appreciate the fact that it is a new term coined in the North for actions and experiences that are not new to those in the South. Such realizations are impera-tive for students since they generally are exposed to only one way of thinking about globalization, and that is in terms of the economic benefits it has brought them, par-ticularly as residents of the United States. They might hear about job losses in their communities because of globalization and assume that others elsewhere are living in better conditions as a result of these jobs. Only a look at this process from the other side reveals that globalization, in fact, creates difficulties for many outside the ruling and economic elite no matter where they live. With this knowledge, students are able to question a variety of global processes, both current and past, with a more critical stance.

Conclusion

Most North American students do not know as much about their own history as educators might like, let alone that of other places. African history is a perfect antidote to such ignorance. Altogether, students' understanding of humans as a species with a long and not necessarily linear past, full of important and long-term adaptations, forces them to see recent developments and humankind as a small part of a much larger and lengthier earthly drama. Africans' participation in multiple epochs of cultural evolution and abrupt climate change enjoins the world's population to be more flexible, or versatile, and humble in any contemplation of what the future might hold. African adaptations in the Sahel suggest a need to question the linear progression of the market economy and urbanization. Finally, Africans' critique of globalization is an example of the narrowness of Western ideologies and cultural stories. All such narrowness in thinking, understanding, and visioning is dangerous to human society as it seeks revolutionary ways to think about the past and the future. Our students, particularly, must see the accomplishments and challenges of the species over the spans of thousands of years, and millennia, in order to have the humility, tools, and ideas to achieve the revolutionary thinking required to take them into the next era.

Notes

This chapter is part of a larger work, "Why We Need African History: A Continent's Past and Our Future." Some of the material in the third section on globalization appeared earlier, in Smythe (2009). This chapter and the larger work owe much to my African history survey students over the past 14 years and to my colleagues with whom I team taught a globalization course for a number of years, James Buchanan, Jamal Abu-Rashed, Gillian Ahlgren, and Anas Malik.

1. "Supercapitalism" is Robert Reich's term (2007). Other terms to describe the current capitalist system include "sociopathic capitalism," from Ian I. Mitroff and Abraham Silvers (2008:28), and "disaster capitalism," from Naomi Klein (2007).

2. The *longue durée* is an expression used by the French Annales School of historical writing to emphasize the study of long-term historical structures.

3. Matriliny is a set of ideas and ideals about kinship that tend to include placing emphasis on one's membership in the mother's family. Often this means that individuals live, work, and share resources with those related to their mother more often than with those related to their father.

4. There is evidence in early human history for aggressive behavior as well. William Burger (2003), curator emeritus at the Field Museum of Natural History in Chicago, argues that the only reasonable explanation for our significant brain expansion is intergroup competition and warfare.

5. On McNamara's philosophy, see Peters (2008). Ruggerio said in 1998 that "the potential for eradicating global poverty in the early part of the next century—a utopian notion even a few decades

ago, but a real possibility today," is thanks to the new world order (quoted in Chang 2002:15). He also noted that the "borderless economy" had the potential to "equalize relations between countries and regions" (quoted in Reinert 2007:xviii).

6. Project for the New American Century, http://www.newamericancentury.org, accessed October 19, 2011.

7. Combined Joint Task Force–Horn of Africa, http://www.hoa.africom.mil/AboutCJTF-HOA.asp, accessed October 12, 2012.

8. For a discussion of the structural biases created by foreign direct investment in Africa, primarily in oil and minerals, see the United Nations Conference on Trade and Development, http://unctad.org.

4 Answering the "So What" Question

Making African History Relevant in the Provincial College Classroom

Gary Marquardt

So what? Why is this important? The majority of scholars teaching in academia have spent the better part of their careers pursuing and justifying these questions. As teachers of African History, too few spend time in class answering or even justifying the "so what" question for students. From a personal standpoint, this is forgivable. Scholars have studied the continent and understand how its history and cultures fit into a global context. Most are even enthusiastic and passionate about teaching the continent's history. Unfortunately, knowledge and enthusiasm rarely translate into understanding the "so what" question for the average undergraduate student. As a result, the relevance of Africa seldom leaves those four classroom walls.

For today's student, connecting history to the present day is perhaps the key to getting them to understand and appreciate African history in a global context. A major part of this approach is to explore the very topics covered by Western media: contemporary social, economic, and health issues. Exploring genocide, health and disease, and trade provides fruitful avenues to understand Africa and its history.

Placing Africa at the center of international and regional topics is one way to grab the attention of students. Whether referring to the precolonial, colonial, or postindependence era, Africans have always been active participants in advocating for, rejecting, or attempting to alter events and situations on the continent. Shifting focus from passivity to activity makes Africa and Africans central to understanding African history and challenging student assumptions.

To harness this effect, teachers need to be tech savvy and original to their approach of the material, and to connect ideas about African history to major, current issues on a national and global scale. One of the main compromises in teaching African history this way is dropping any pretense of covering the material in its entirety. Lendol Calder, a U.S. historian at Augustana College, has been a major force in pushing history pedagogy away from coverage and toward, what he calls, "uncoverage." On a website titled Uncoverage: Toward a Signature Pedagogy for the History Survey, Calder argues that students need to consult and analyze primary sources in order to guide their understanding of a country's history (uncover), not read, digest, and regurgitate secondary accounts of history (cover).[1]

Packages and Threads

"Packages" and "threads" provide chronologically useful and provocative ways of allowing students to uncover comparable events and experiences in Africa's colonial and postindependence eras. The three cases examined in this chapter include (1) identity and genocide, (2) the shifting economy, and (3) changing ideas about health, disease, and power. Each case is a direct response to uncritical media portrayals of Africa that show the continent as wracked by civil war and senseless killings, and overrun by grinding poverty and AIDS. Students directly address the "so what" question by reading Western newspaper or magazine articles that address these respective issues. The students dissect the articles, identifying biases or generalizations; they then discuss what information would give the article a clearer meaning. In midterm and final take-home exams, students consistently address the media's shortcomings on these issues by writing informed and historically grounded essays on the above themes.

Identity and Genocide

The presentation of Namibia's early 20th-century genocide changes markedly every time the unit is taught. The use of photographs, oral interview notes, and observations from my research in Namibia informs and adds complexity to the comments on and methods of teaching this material. Personal experiences become vehicles to discuss the hurdles encountered in conducting oral history and how interviewees contradict some of the information stated in the readings and film clips viewed in class about this event. Students often link this event to the origins of the Holocaust, thus effectively demonstrating why and how primary and oral research conducted in Namibia matters to the greater world.

The Namibian genocide was born out of the "Scramble for Africa" when German forces eliminated approximately 85 percent of Herero and 50 percent of Nama populations between 1904 and 1908. In studying this event, students are given a brief PowerPoint overview of Germany's divide-and-rule tactics in Namibia. They also read another version of this history, covered in the essay "Colonization, Genocide, and Resurgence: The Herero of Namibia, 1890–1923" (Gewald 2003) and an account of the atrocities contained in the reprinted primary source, *1918 Blue Book* (Silvester and

Gewald 2003). Students appreciate Jan-Bart Gewald's account of this period, often stating that this essay is very accessible to readers unfamiliar with this period in Namibia's history. These chapters describe Germany's brutal treatment of the Herero during the 1904–1908 war. Witnesses speaking under oath relate extremely graphic stories of what happened to Herero women and children and also add another layer to the understanding of oral history in print form.

Combined with excerpts from the documentaries *Le Malentendu colonial* (*The Colonial Misunderstanding*; Téno 2004), which looks, in part, at the role of European missionaries in this genocide, and *100 Years of Silence* (Muurholm and Erichsen 2006), which gives another overview of the events leading to genocide, this unit introduces several salient ideas. First and foremost is the issue of identity. German identity, for example, is contrasted with that of their counterparts, the Herero. Both the Germans and the Herero had developed strong, independent nations by the mid-19th century. This fact accounts for the difficulties Germany had in subduing the Herero for over 20 years and for Germany's extreme embarrassment resulting from the early part of the 1904 war, which saw it lose many battles to the Herero resistance. It is only near the war's genocidal conclusion that one bears witness to German actions. German forces perpetrated widespread human rights abuses on the battlefield against civilians (including women and children), who were indiscriminately slaughtered. Most students find the establishment of concentration camps, developed nearly 40 years before the Holocaust, to be the most interesting phase of this event. Here they see actions that are perpetrated on the ideas of racial identity. Due to the high death rate among concentration camp inmates, colonial authorities removed many Herero skulls and shipped them to German museums and schools to advance the study of racial science. This scientific method attempted to identify superior and inferior races on the basis of body measurements and theories regarding humans from around the world, invariably favoring Europeans.

In the final part of this unit, students discuss the reconciliation of these events in modern-day Namibia. They read a brief BBC article on the events' legacy as seen by Herero today and then discuss what it means to process these historical events by discussing and understanding the differences between the terms *cope* and *reconciliation*. *Reconcile* usually refers to the final result of repairing a relationship, "to bring into consistent accord" or "harmony." *Cope* refers to the continuous act of processing what happened and how it relates to one person (or many people) later on in life.[2] *Cope* is often discussed to help students more effectively understand the term *coping mechanisms*, or the multitude of ways that humans process difficult situations in their aftermath.

Students then view *100 Years of Silence*, which tells the story of Namibia's genocide but also discusses the complexities of how the Herero cope with this event today. The film focuses on dress, symbolic and physical historical spaces, and the Otjiserandu (one of the many Herero remembrance days). All three issues usually lead to a good discussion of how one effectively reconciles or copes with an event that happened three or four generations ago. Why do women and men don German-inspired outfits during the Otjiserandu ceremony? Is it ethical to turn former concentration camp spaces into recreational parks or build a high school on top of such grounds? Both questions challenge students and also raise serious issues about how to view the past in the present day. The latter question often boils down to how historical spaces are treated in the United States. Students may be able to identify local historical spaces that have been repurposed without acknowledging the historical significance. The similarities existing between the United States and Namibia, "developed" and "underdeveloped" countries, frame the mutual experiences that each country struggles with today and again validates why Namibia remains important in understanding and debating global history.

Here, students get to respond to the "so what" question. How does the international community respond to these Namibian events as opposed to Europe's World War II atrocities (especially the Holocaust)? Does it make a difference that this genocide took place in Africa? How? Why? Is this the same thing that happened in Rwanda or Sudan more recently? Being able to thread these African genocides together, while acknowledging their differences and comparing them to events like the Holocaust, affirms their complexity and leads students to question how genocides are portrayed by the Western media.

The Shifting Economy

Another thread followed in the upper-level course, History of Africa: 1500–Present, is that of the colonial- and independent-era economies. In what Sara Berry (1992) calls "hegemony on a shoestring," the colonization tactics in Africa were predicated on making money through the extraction of natural resources with little investment.

In this vein, concessionary companies were indispensable. They procured contracts with the colonizing country, allowing them total control and virtually free rein over territorial resources and African populations. By looking at excerpts of these contracts, students are better able to understand and appreciate the clearance afforded to such companies and the widespread abuses of Africans that followed (Newbury 1971:254–255). Kevin Shillington's chapter on concessionary companies in his book *History of Africa* (1985) adds geographic balance to this discussion by focusing on southern Africa, while Basil Davidson et al.'s film classic *This Magnificent African Cake* (1984) and Berry's essay "Hegemony on a Shoestring: Indirect Rule and Access to Agricultural Land" (1992) afford excellent overviews of the extractive nature of European colonial rule in Africa.

This focus on the extractive economy primes students for the economic colonialism (or neocolonialism) that continues in the era of African independence. Some good visual starters are the short films *The Luckiest Nut in the World* (James 2002) and *The Trade Trap* (Bradshaw et al. 2002). The former is as much entertainment as it is education; done in a cartoon musical style with a documentary overlay, a singing pea-nut lays out the principles of international free trade policies, liberalized economies, and subsidies and tells how his brethren nuts from other countries (namely, Senegal) have had a "bumpy ride" on their way to consumers. *The Trade Trap* examines how international free trade policies manifest themselves in Ghana. The film demonstrates the parallels of colonial and postindependence economic policies effectively.

The short films are connected with readings on today's African economies and provide plenty of material for classroom debate about debt forgiveness and the morals of the international trade economy. Students read a chapter from Kwame Nkrumah's *Neo-colonialism: The Last Stage of Imperialism* (1965), a scathing critique of the eco-nomic, political, and social influences that Western countries use to control Africa and other formerly colonized continents. Though Nkrumah's chapter is informed by the Cold War era, many students find similar parallels in today's global trade environment.

The *Taking Sides* series on "African issues" also offers numerous possibilities for debate. For example, the respective views of Dorothy Logie, Michael Rowson, and Robert Snyder (2007) on debt forgiveness afford students the opportunity to engage in a debate over whether or not to forgive the debt of African nations. Neither argu-ment presented in their essay is entirely convincing; both sides broach issues that are discussed in class or familiar to students. The heart of the in-class debate often centers on the role former colonizers have in debt forgiveness.[3] Students assess the differences and similarities of Africa and the West over economic policies during the colonial and postindependence eras and then move on to questions. Should the West involve itself in a problem it originally created, or does Africa need to solve this problem without outside intervention? Why are so many African nations corrupt, and does this cor-ruption have anything to do with colonial governance? Should scholars be seeking answers to emerging problems only a few decades old, or will these issues sort them-selves out in the long run? These are just a few of the questions broached and debated in class.

Changing Ideas about Health, Disease, and Power

A final topic is the colonial and postindependence divide demonstrated through health and disease. A course on southern African history approaches this subject from a socioeconomic perspective that gives students another view into how colonial admin-istrations dealt with public health issues and how Africans responded. Students return to this subject later in the semester to examine how postindependence governments compare with their colonial predecessors. There is no one straightforward approach to understanding health and disease. Moreover, the overwhelming attention that HIV/AIDS receives in the postindependence era makes this topic all the more uneven and difficult to compare effectively. Students (most of whom are coming from non-health-related backgrounds) consistently identify this unit as one of the most challenging, yet gratifying, of the course.

Examining the logic behind colonial health policy and African responses to it effectively frames the unit and gives students another view of the colonial period. Four different studies are showcased over the week. The first is a lecture related to my dissertation research on the 1890s rinderpest outbreak in the border region of South Africa and Botswana (Marquardt 2007).

Competing ideas of disease management and the use of disease to access power are also discussed. Marion Wallace (1998) in an essay on South-West Africa (Namibia) considers how colonial officials responded to the threat of sexually transmitted diseases (STDs) in order to control the movements of single Herero women moving into urban spaces from other areas. Bryan Callahan (1997) concludes that results were different between British officials and Ila peoples in Northern Rhodesia (Zambia). Callahan notes that, in spite of a misdiagnosis informing the British to treat Ila for syphilis, much of the targeted population enthusiastically received drugs and medical attention that was known to improve fertility rates and thus increase their population, a major form of wealth among Ila populations. Additionally, students are tasked with reading and then explaining how JoAnn McGregor and Terence Ranger (2000), in an article on disease epidemics, tackle the politics of malaria in colonial Zimbabwe. In this piece, the basic template of colonial rulers and the African underclass is unpacked to demonstrate the complexity of the issue. McGregor and Ranger not only demonstrate the colonial state's use (or excuse) of malaria to evict Zimbabweans from prime agricultural land, but they also show how the African evictees clashed with other indigenous populations after resettlement. The article's richest contribution, however, is the discussion of how various Zimbabwean populations and the colonial government accounted for the spread of malaria. In this case, McGregor and Ranger provide a very accessible account of how Zimbabweans controlled the spread of malaria by placing restrictions on harvesting the first fruits of the year. As a result, many avoided contracting malaria, a disease known to be common in the early period of the fruit harvest, when malaria-carrying mosquitoes are most numerous and most likely to spread the disease.

Unpacking and analyzing postindependence-era health-care policies are perhaps the most difficult exercises in the course. Students are naturally interested in the HIV/AIDS epidemic but have traditionally been resistant to connecting this epidemic to its colonial-era roots. One of the few inroads to understanding the historical background of AIDS is John Iliffe's book *The African AIDS Epidemic: A History* (2006). In the fifth chapter, he provides a strong argument for the geographic spread of the disease, especially as it applies to southern Africa. Here students can readily identify how the long-established trend of labor migration in this region has led to high numbers of AIDS cases in South Africa and neighboring countries. To complement Iliffe's chapter, students view the short film *Africa: The AIDS Highway* (ABC Australia 1999) to underscore how geography, infrastructure, and urban economic opportunity have figured in the spread of AIDS. Another useful film is *Yesterday* (Roodt et al. 2006), which highlights the ineffectiveness of Western and indigenous health-care and community education in the rural communities of KwaZulu Natal, South Africa.

Alternative Approaches in Class and on the Fly

Resource selection is always a challenge when presenting varied materials on African issues. A good resource on the continent's history is the BBC's *The Story of Africa*, a set of audio programs discussing various aspects of Africa's history through time.[4] Students were mixed on the use of this series, but had some generally positive things to say about it, especially how it complemented course readings. The one improvement for students listening to an audio history today would be to convert this into a podcast format. Programs such as *Africa Past and Present* are beginning to do this for upper-level history majors; however, this medium needs to be broadened to accommodate general history learners who study in different environments and through diverse mediums.[5]

Another more traditional method is to incorporate scholarly articles into the course readings and vary how they are discussed in the classroom setting. Students often enjoy a version of the TV reality show *Survivor*, where contestants are voted off the show every week, until one emerges victorious. This format allows upper-level students to vote off readings they found particularly cumbersome. Two or three academic journal essays explore a similar theme such as health and disease in colonial Africa. Students are assigned the task of creating a case against one of the assigned readings; they judge the piece on the merits of its argument (or, in this case, lack thereof), which includes an identifiable thesis and supported evidence for the argument, organization, and prose.

This exercise achieves a number of things. First, it gives students a stake in the class reading assignments. While they do not see the direct benefits of voting out a reading from the course, they know that the weakest reading will not return the following semester. Second, it forces students to use their critical thinking skills to formulate arguments around the essay under consideration. Third, it affords the instructor the opportunity to continually research, read, and revise material in the course syllabus.

Most students who take an African history course will not become African historians. However, they will likely work at a job, meet someone in a personal situation, or be in a position where African affairs are broached. Whether this is economic, social, or political, Africa and the idea of Africa will surface. Most often this incident will be subtle; a trade or purchase of a product that contains natural minerals mined in Africa, social policies that influence international travel and migration, or even mundane, everyday decisions such as buying bananas or coffee will influence or be influenced by the continent. The chances are increasing, however, that students will have a more interpersonal connection with Africa as the number of international adoptions, refugee populations, and international students are on the rise in the United States. According to the U.S. Department of State's Office of Children's Issues, the number of children adopted from Africa rose from approximately 690 in 2005 to 2,555 in 2009, nearly a 400 percent increase.[6] Between 2000 and 2009, 29.2 percent of refugees entering the United States were from African countries; Africans obtaining legal residence in the United States during this period numbered 803,626 (Lee 2010:12, 45). In a world that is becoming ever more interconnected, students need to understand that their professional and personal decisions and relationships can have an impact on places such as Africa and vice versa.

Using a variety of pedagogical approaches and personal stories to access Africa's history and affairs can prompt students to think more critically about why the continent is relevant in the present day and, perhaps more importantly, how history has influenced its present condition. Lendol Calder's idea of "uncoverage" may be a route to free some teaching scholars from the exhaustive and uninspired chronological coverage that African history has traditionally been bound to. This chapter is influenced by what Calder calls "signature pedagogy," by tapping into topics having agency among student populations on today's college campuses. It has also brought into view the need to rethink classroom approaches to learning about African history. Group work, film critique, and "workshops" are a few ways to break the lecture cycle and give students the opportunity to think collectively and competitively in the classroom. If those in the business of teaching Africa's history cannot make a compelling case for why the continent's history is relevant today, a generation of students who cannot (or do not care to) answer the "so what" question will be alienated.

Notes

I wish to thank the students of Virginia Commonwealth University and Westminster College who have given me feedback on my African and world history courses over the years. Thanks also to the editors of this book, Brandon D. Lundy and Solomon Negash, and the Works in Progress (WiP) group at Westminster College for their critical analysis of this chapter. Credit is also due to Tom Spear and Amy E. Brandt, who provided comments on this chapter during its editing phases. A final note of gratitude is due to Lendol Calder, who, perhaps inadvertently, challenged me to rethink how to teach history in the classroom.

1. Uncoverage: Toward a Signature Pedagogy for the History Survey, http://www.journalofamericanhistory.org/textbooks/2006/calder/index.html, accessed October 19, 2011.

2. WordNet, http://wordnetweb.princeton.edu/perl/webwn, accessed October 19, 2011.

3. Logie et al. (2007:120–133) argue that loans to financially strapped African nations should be forgiven. Debt forgiveness is justified because of the alleged inequities in the global trade system, overly restrictive loan policies implemented by the World Bank and the International Monetary Fund (IMF), and the prospect that debt forgiveness could encourage (and realize) a better human rights records in the targeted countries. Snyder's anti-debt relief argument is set against the background of political corruption. He argues that "quick fixes" such as debt relief programs ignore the bigger problems, like political and economic corruption, in many African countries (see Logie et al. 2007:283–286).

4. BBC World Service, *The Story of Africa*, http://www.bbc.co.uk/worldservice/specials/1624_story_of_africa/page97.shtml, accessed October 19, 2011.

5. African Online Digital Library, *Africa Past and Present*, http://afripod.aodl.org, accessed October 19, 2011.

6. U.S. Department of State, Bureau of Consular Affairs, Office of Children's Issues, http://adoption.state.gov/about_us/statistics.php, accessed October 16, 2012.

5 From African History to African Histories

Teaching Interdisciplinary Method, Philosophy, and Ethics through the African History Survey

Trevor R. Getz

Introduction

This chapter demonstrates that in the context of the end of apartheid, South African educators were pressed to critically examine how they taught history. In this historical moment, some South African educators adopted a methodology meant to move students away from the kinds of universal narratives about the past promoted by apartheid reasoning and into critical analyses that acknowledged multiple, coexisting perspectives of and from the past. They did so partly by bundling a toolbox of skills and ideas for students together with the content they expected them to learn and partly by featuring debates and participation as the means to explore these themes and skills. In particular, this chapter focuses on the introductory history course developed over the past two decades at the University of the Western Cape (UWC) in Cape Town, South Africa. This course, and the process through which it was developed, can serve as a model that U.S. colleges and universities would do well to consider adopting on a more systematic level as part of the pedagogical repertoire.

The emergence of the formal discipline and pedagogy of history in South Africa parallels the overlapping development of British colonialism and Afrikaner political supremacy in the 19th and 20th centuries, represented in turn by English-language British imperial histories and Afrikaans-language *volksgeskiedenis* (people's history). Outwardly antagonistic, but in many ways in agreement about the framing of both history as a discipline and the main narratives of the South African past, these two histories intellectually propped up decades of white rule

(Fuchs and Stuchtey 2002; Grundlingh 1990; Saunders 1988). From the mid-20th century on, however, their consensus was challenged first by a liberal school of South African scholars and later by radical, Marxist scholars as well. Through their work—which attacked the historical arguments and narratives mobilized in support of white supremacy—these generations of historians played a valuable role in undermining apartheid's founding myths. Yet despite the agitation of many antiapartheid historians, almost all South African students continued up until the 1990s to be exposed to blatantly Eurocentric and white supremacist versions of the pasts in their primary and secondary school history classes. For black youths, specifically, these narratives were embedded in the schoolbooks of the hated Bantu education system. South African students remembered their teachers fighting back by having them cross out sections of their textbook and write replacement narratives in the margins and spaces between the lines.

Following the transition to multiparty democracy in the early 1990s, the newly elected African National Congress (ANC) administration and its supporters were frequently and deeply suspicious of the discipline of history and, consequently, professional historians (B. Magubane 2007). They also often perceived the liberal arts as less essential for the uplifting of the South African working class than "useful" disciplines such as engineering and commerce. When a committee to propose a transitional high school history curriculum was eventually constituted in 1994, it had no members who were either history teachers or professional historians (Lowry 1995). The interim curriculum they developed thus ironically continued a number of themes and approaches from the apartheid era. Consequently, a new curriculum was proposed in 1996 that attempted to make a clean break from these themes. Yet once again, professional historians were underrepresented on its formulating committee, and as a result the new system abandoned the discipline of history entirely.

Instead, the past was to be understood largely through both "folk" and "national" heritage. The folk heritage strand was intended to promote indigenous African systems of understanding the past, especially those deemed "authentic" and those that focused on the antiapartheid struggle and its heroes. The national strand of heritage, meanwhile, was largely embodied in an official narrative of the "Rainbow Nation," which emphasized the "miracle" of a new South Africa by which Nelson Mandela's "special magic" fused together a society of "many cultures" (Rassool 2000). At the same time, the broader national curriculum committee determined that South Africa was to be depicted as a country reaching for the future rather than wallowing in the past. Both of these processes were aimed at steering away from critical confrontation with the country's history rather than engaging it. This direction was only partly reversed by the minister of Education, Kader Asmal, who restored history as a high school elective in 2000 (South Africa Department of Education 2000). In the interim, the numbers of students studying history at both secondary institutions and universities dropped precipitously (Bundy 2007).

At the tertiary level, these processes of transformation, conflict, and historical avoidance left a great deal of room for the renegotiation of curricula and course offerings. They also promoted deep soul-searching among South African historians about their public roles. A great deal of their attention became focused on the processes by which history was "produced" in public and professional places. Through a vast body of papers, articles, and books, South African historians identified multiple sites of "history"—the cinema, public monuments, museums, speeches, and especially the Truth and Reconciliation Commission—and engaged one another and nonprofessionals in questions dealing with the relationships between power, knowledge, and representation (Nuttall and Coetzee 1998; Stolten 2007). One place that was not left out of their analyses was the classroom.

The Department of History at the UWC was one location where these issues were confronted. Started by the apartheid state in the 1970s as a "bush" university, the creation of the UWC was one of a series of maneuvers meant to pull the Cape's coloured lower-middle class away from the antiapartheid movement. Yet for much of the period leading up to the transfer of power, UWC academics and students had instead associated themselves with the resistance forces and especially with the banned ANC and its allies: the United Democratic Front, the South African Communist Party, and the Congress of South African Trade Unions. While intense state surveillance somewhat constrained the curricula and course content the history department faculty could offer, they nevertheless made important contributions to both liberal and radical interpretations of the South African past.

Teaching Undergraduate History at the UWC

In 2008 when I encountered the UWC history department, its members were diverse in their approaches to studying the past. To be sure, their experiences both inside the classroom and in South African society tended to have given them a certain shared awareness of social issues. Nevertheless, neither their scholarship nor their course offerings fell neatly within a school of thought. Unlike in many history departments in North American universities, members of the department jointly formulated the topics and themes of most of their undergraduate course offerings. In many cases, courses were taught collaboratively, and those members not directly involved in each course heard a report about each at monthly department meetings. This collaborative structure thrived not on a consensus among members, but on their willingness to engage one another on intellectual, philosophical, and structural issues.

The course offerings I witnessed in 2008 emerged partly from the maelstrom of new needs and new possibilities from the transformations of the early 1990s. Several principal challenges in this period are worth discussing here. First, the department had to cope with the national educational environment. Its members generally had great hopes for the new South Africa and their place within it. As a group of scholars who were publicly engaged with popular conceptions of the past, several of them sympathized with the critiques leveled by the ANC ministers that history as a profession was still an exclusive and rather bourgeois undertaking. Yet they were critical of the new regime's construction of alternate historical narratives.

Meanwhile, the department faced at least equally pressing problems in adjusting to the needs of the massive influx of Xhosa-speaking African students into the university. Many of these students came from severely disadvantaged schools in the rural Eastern Cape, and some had almost no previous history education. More worrying was that most of these students came from "schools where transmission teaching, rote-learning, and reliance on the authority of the textbook and teacher are the norm" (Cornell and Witz 1994b:50).

Another problem was that despite this influx of new students to the university, history courses continued to be undersubscribed since students saw little opportunity for economic advance through its study. Compounding the concerns of some members of the department was their growing awareness that one result of the Rainbow Nation nation-building exercise was a growing nationalist xenophobia against other Africans. In spite of this development, the department was determined to focus on what these students brought with them, rather than what they were lacking, and therefore sought to carefully identify the unique skills and possibilities of their new student body.

This combination of institutional, student-oriented, and national issues prompted a great deal of discussion within the department over several years, especially about how to design the first-year and second-year history courses. Through this debate, the faculty dealt with a number of issues. Some of these are familiar to many of us who teach history, but others were heightened by the specific situation in South Africa in the early and mid-1990s. Among the points of debate were whether to promote interdisciplinarity within a humanities or social science framework or to focus on history as a "craft." They also debated issues of scope—whether to offer at the first-year level a national history or a "world history." These were tied together with discussions of the location of Eurocentrism and discursive assumptions about Africa in history as a discipline. They debated the purpose of teaching history to both first-year majors and nonmajors and to what degree critical thinking skills, historical philosophy, and methods should be discussed or whether they should instead preference constructing a narrative for students to work with.

One of the key decisions reached through this discussion was the agreement to redevelop the first-year course from a narrative-driven national and "Western" history to a focus on "history as debate." In making this change, the department hoped to deal with contentious issues including perceptions that history was not "relevant" because it did not deliver skills, as well as incoming students' obvious inabilities to critically assess narratives placed before them. Yet perhaps most troubling for them was the realization that the long legacy of apartheid had caused students, especially those from this new influx, to view their professors as keepers of "truths" who could transmit "true facts" to be learned by rote (Lalu and Cornell 1996:197). It was through this internal conversation that members of the department came to feel that their primary task in the classroom was not just to relay to students new narratives of the past in which Africans featured positively, or even to convince them to see multiple perspectives of national and global narratives, but also to help them question the authority of all narratives—even those expounded by their professors (Lalu and Cornell 1996). In response, they developed a new curriculum whose central feature was a style of teaching in which debates among members of the faculty were featured alongside exercises that taught basic skills in research and critical reading (Cornell and Witz 1994b:53–57).

The first-year history course (History 1) is a good example of this new curriculum. The course was first developed in 1991 as The Making of the Modern World. In this incarnation, it was based on a model derived from many North American world history surveys of the time, which focused on the Atlantic world. Yet within this otherwise ordinary syllabus, the department located key debates meant to force students to think critically about messages they had internalized about Africa and Africans. In the first semester, this task was done partly by discussing African societies directly—whether Africans had precolonial states and societies and how Africans responded to the Atlantic slave trade. These debates were not just about the *content* but also about the *sources*. Through associated assignments and class discussions, students were led to question how historians worked, the nature of "evidence," and the settings in which historical research is carried out. This questioning in turn helped them develop both evidence-related skill sets and a healthy critical skepticism of historical narratives (Cornell and Witz 1994b:53–59).

In 1991, the first semester of History 1 at the UWC debated (1) whether precapitalist African societies were egalitarian, (2) whether Aztec human sacrifices were exceptional for the Atlantic world, (3) whether African rulers participated in the Atlantic slave trade, and (4) why the Aztec Empire declined. Through these debates, students acquired respective skill sets (in tutorials): (1) how to write an argument, (2) using evidence and sources, (3) avoiding plagiarism, and (4) how to structure essays.

By 1993, the department chose to modify the course further. Radically, it stepped away from world history and back into a framework of local histories. It did so both because the political meanings of the contemporary contestation of South African history had become increasingly obvious and because faculty felt that students needed to be able both to critically interpret the various narratives and to participate in them. It therefore shifted the course content to revolve around four debates in South African history. Two of these—the debate over the history and meaning of the execution of the Xhosa king Hintsa and the debate surrounding the events and interpretations of the millennialist Xhosa "cattle killing" movements of the 1850s—specifically related to incidents about which the majority of students had knowledge of the past from outside the profession and thus actively involved them in bringing the academy and the outside world together (Lalu and Cornell 1996:197).

Yet the course did not aim to reify students' own position as insiders but rather asked them to critically examine their culturally constructed conceptions of these events. A striking example of this approach was when students were asked to evaluate Helen Bradford's (2001) feminist take on the Xhosa cattle killing, which definitely met with resistance, especially from the Xhosa-speaking men in the class, although it also gained supporters over the length of the unit. Here, as elsewhere in the course, students were mentored in reading the difficult texts through not only tutorials, but also live debates enacted by two members of the department. The two other units in the course covered important topics dealing with both history and "heritage"—the archaeological and historical interpretations of the site of Mapungubwe and the destruction of the Zulu Kingdom—and also featured debates over both interpretation and commemoration.

By 2008, the units of the History 1 course at the UWC had been modified to incorporate particular primary source materials for each issue: (1) Mapungubwe (archaeological artifacts and reports, commemorations, heritage); (2) the death of Hintsa (images, written accounts, oral tradition); (3) the cattle killing (police reports, newspapers and media, images, oral tradition, intellectual histories); and (4) the destruction of the Zulu Kingdom (official documents, letters, commemorations).

These four units together involved both the UWC Department of History faculty and their students in the national discussion over what it meant to be a South African citizen in both a historical and a commemorative setting. Yet members of the department also wanted to deal with increasingly negative depictions of Africans outside of South Africa, both as a result of the internalization of apartheid-era racism and as a by-product of nationalist discourse. Thus, they developed a second-year course (History 2), Africa, Race, and Empire, to deal specifically with these issues. This course, while focusing on relationships between Africa and Europe in the 19th century, was also meant to situate the South African experience within the context of shared African experiences of the Atlantic slave trade and colonialism. Its main approach was to examine categories of analysis that emerged from the colonial era and continue to affect discourses of ethnicity, nationality, gender, and race today in South Africa (Witz and Cornell 2000:225). As in History 1, the course is taught partly as an investigation of content, but also as an exploration of historical methodology and philosophy. Almost without students' realization, they receive healthy doses of ontology and epistemological examinations. These lessons from lectures and readings are once again reinforced through debates in which one member of the department is pitted against another in representing major theories, approaches to the past, and sometimes ethical issues surrounding research.

Together these two courses aim to achieve something besides the transmission of historical fact. Rather, members of the department set out to destroy historical fact, to decenter universal narratives, and even to question the authority of the historian as interpreter of the past. They elevated Africans' perspectives, but without reifying them, and introduced to students the complexities of the relationships between history and heritage, between popular knowledge and academic knowledge, and between historical consciousness and historical knowledge.

Perhaps most importantly, the faculty of the Department of History specifically aims to deflate their own power as "knowers." They publicly dispute evidence and interpretation in debates, create classroom settings in which they elicit students' informed opinions, and admit that in many cases there are sometimes no good or no complete answers. There was, and remains, a great deal of skepticism about this approach. Yet it remains a pathway to helping minimally prepared students critically engage the specific social situations and problems of their society through the history classroom. It also helps their students to question the authoritarianism at the heart of apartheid-era society and still existing in the education system.

The United States today does not have quite the same problems (or quite the same crisis) as South Africa had in the early 1990s. Yet in view of the attacks on the value of liberal education and the humanities in recent years, this chapter proposes that African history surveys could be used for similar purposes of considering the wider value of teaching history to students as a set of skills, a method of acquiring and critically interpreting content, and a set of insights into ethical living and scholarship.

University instructors' training and experience allows them to put before students certain exceptional skill sets and issues. These can be further expanded in the context of African history since the subject has great interdisciplinary potential (Philips 2006). As a means of reconstructing the past, there is a longer history of professionally converging evidence like oral tradition, linguistics, archaeology, and archaeobotany than in most other fields of the discipline. Moreover, because Africa has been depicted through a relatively few, but very dominant key discursive formations, there is the ability to help students deconstruct narratives of the past by exposing them to evidence. Finally, issues of ethics may be discussed more openly than in other disciplines.

Can all of these things be done together? Can methodological skills be taught alongside historical philosophy, ethics, and critical thinking in a single survey-level course? Exactly such an approach has been promoted in Rwanda, where researchers from the Human Rights Center at the University of California, Berkeley, have teamed up with Rwandan teachers to develop a curriculum aimed at assisting students in questioning all narratives of the past while helping them construct their own sense of their place in a historicized world (Freedman et al. 2006). They created this program partly by adopting participatory pedagogical systems that have their origins in older ("traditional") learning systems within Rwandan society. Similarly, the most recent iterations of the South African history curriculum for 11th and 12th graders focus on ethical, methodological, and theoretical learning outcomes embedded within selected content rather than on a narrative history of the country's past or a global past; this curriculum promotes the same participatory pedagogical practices as a way to further engage the students (South Africa Department of Education 2000).

I have tried to base my own approach on this system and on my experience with the History 1 course at the UWC. One example from my African history survey is my revised approach to the topic of the Atlantic slave trade. Obviously, this episode and its human experiences cannot be omitted from any history of Africa. Nevertheless, how should it be taught? In the past three years, I have come to teach this topic principally through oral histories, oral traditions, and memoirs. Yet I do not ask students to merely uncritically consume these sources. Rather, I fold examples of songs, proverbs, and autobiographies in with the works of scholars who have interpreted them. I explain a series of debates about the value of memory for historical interpretation and how best to interpret them. At the same time, I challenge students to think about the issues of "authenticity" and "ownership" that surround these kinds of sources. I use similar approaches to topics like human relationships with the environment (archaeobotany), colonial power (archaeology and photography), and gendering the historical record (ethnography).

At the core of each unit of my survey, like the South African and Rwandan curricula on which I base them, is not an assertion of fact, but rather a series of debates. Whether epistemological, philosophical, or methodological, these debates inform one another. How can students understand historical continuity and change without a grip on data? But how can they understand the data if there is no comprehension of the cultural and institutional context in which historians and other scholars have interpreted the data? How can historians be trusted, if not confronted, with the issues of ethics and philosophy that implicitly shape their work? Finally, how can the value of history and the role of historians in society be understood if the popular narratives of the past as well as those produced by academics are not considered key to understanding contemporary issues?

The evidence that students *can* be trusted with these complex bundles comes from courses like the one at the UWC, where the department has continually sought feedback from students and used it to adjust its course offerings (Cornell and Witz 1994a). But student-learning *outputs* are only one part of the consideration of courses like the UWC's. A second aspect is student-learning *outcomes*. These outcomes can be expressed in the students' abilities to better handle their upper-division history courses, or even courses outside their major, because they leave their classes with more than just another narrative. Yet, even more, these outcomes can be evaluated in the ways that students interact in and with society.

This chapter argues that a course that bundles ethics, philosophy, methods, and content can help students strengthen each of those areas in ways that affect their lives today. Students can be expected to transfer these lessons to their daily lives to think about (1) the relationship between classroom learning and narratives of the past that they encounter at home and in civic situations; (2) the political and social purposes of stories about the past that are projected by politicians, the media, and others; (3) how to evaluate evidence by blending multiple types of data or by taking apart an argument to critically assess the data within it; (4) the way that knowledge and power are related to each other and how that affects them; and (5) multiple perspectives of the past and how people other than themselves know or are aware of that past. Imagine students applying these skills to issues of the day that are relevant to American students: immigration, the conflict in Afghanistan, political decisions, health care. Something similar was the goal of the UWC Department of History. Teaching in this manner requires abandoning the notion of a single, easily consumed African history and instead embraces the multiplicities of many histories of Africa. It requires that the instructor abandon his or her position as the only "knower" of the past and embrace the role of a facilitator of student exploration. This lesson is at the center of the approach of the historians at the UWC. It is one that teachers of African histories can offer to students, colleagues, and departments around the world.

6 Treating the Exotic and the Familiar in the African History Classroom

Ryan Ronnenberg

In 1978, THE first edition of Philip Curtin et al.'s *African History: From Earliest Times to Independence* (1995[1978]:xiii) was published in acknowledgment of African history's new place within the Western academy and with the aim of presenting this scholarly maturity to undergraduates. Implicit in the authors' stated purpose for the text was a realization that knowledge of Africa's past has grown more swiftly than U.S. college and university instructors' ability to convey this knowledge to undergraduate students. Decades later, this imbalance remains as American university students learn relatively little about Africa and its past before they matriculate into African history classrooms. This chapter represents the efforts to think through the critical problem of conveying a substantial body of historical knowledge in an African history class. This approach to teaching has been developed through experiences accumulated while living, working, and researching in Tanzania.

The students at Kennesaw State University, just north of Atlanta, Georgia, like those in other institutions of higher education throughout the United States, are frequent consumers of information about Africa, often disseminated through various American popular cultural outlets. Journalists reporting the news in Africa do so under significant constraints. American journalists are relatively few, strewn across a vast continent, concentrated in just a few major cities like Nairobi or Johannesburg. Such journalists travel to other parts of the continent primarily during times of crisis. For this reason, perhaps more so than in other parts of the world, news reports about most parts of the African continent are largely negative and superficial, concerning political upheaval or economic decline (Hunter-Gault 2007). This means not only that journalism in times of catastrophe lacks depth, but also that positive reports, for example about the successful planting of nitrogen-fixing trees in maize fields, rarely reach an American audience.

Under such circumstances, it is common to discover that the information students have absorbed about Africa is quite varied. Several students may be aware of the outbreak of violence against albinos in western Tanzania resulting from witchcraft accusations, yet those same students are unaware that Tanzania was a model of peaceful governance for East and Central Africa. Similarly, students recall Rwanda only in the context of the 1994 genocide and are surprised to learn of its subsequent commendable efforts at reconciliation and governmental transparency.

Several strategies are used to advance the level of knowledge about the African continent in the classroom. To address the perceived problem of a paucity of written archival evidence for much of precolonial African history, for example, alternative source materials (archaeology, historical linguistics, and oral tradition) can be used to construct precolonial history, each resource offering an important aspect of the historical record. For students, however, they may interpret these approaches as meaning that African history exists, but is somehow speculative or less concrete than its European or American counterparts. Overturning this myth requires more than engendering singular pedagogical breakthroughs; rather, they topple only through sustained instructional emphasis upon both general intellectual disposition and smaller details such as those presented below.

Weddings

Family size and plentiful social connections largely determined well-being in most parts of the continent prior to the 19th century. As a corollary, then, societies tended to be inclusive and assimilative with regard to strangers, and social categories, like ethnicity, were necessarily permeable, as opposed to exclusionary categories that define contemporary American society. As fundamental as these points are to understanding much of African history, they are particularly difficult to convey to students unfamiliar with this worldview. As such, they may dutifully take notes as the argument is presented in lectures, but struggle to put the ideas to work in framing events in African history. Faced with trying to bring these themes to life in a more productive way, a class exercise aimed at engaging students through an event that holds universal human interest is constructed. In the midst of a discussion about kinship and social structure, in lieu of a half hour of circle-and-triangle kinship diagrams drawn on the dry-erase board, the students participate in wedding ceremonies.

The activity begins with the selection of student volunteers to populate two nuclear families from "East Africa." A mother and father for the groom's family are picked out from those feeling maternal and paternal in the class, and three individuals are selected to serve as sons of varying ages. The process is repeated for the bride's family, making up a smaller group consisting of parents and a daughter. Each of these roles may be (and have been) filled by a person of any age or gender. Seeing their peers arrayed before them in a variety of different roles generally obtains the class's full attention. The key to walking the line between unintended classroom comedy and enlightening classroom exercise is to keep asking questions throughout. Even more importantly, students should feel comfortable asking their own.

The activity is put into motion by describing the position of the first family's eldest son. It is explained that he is of an age at which he is inclined to wed. He asks his father for bridewealth so that he may marry the young woman in the second family.[1] The exchange is simplified somewhat by stipulating that bridewealth in this instance is to be paid in cattle. Further, the teacher assumes the role of paternal uncle and negotiator and brings the offer of marriage to the second family as the patrilineal custom dictates.[2]

With the agreement and exchange of bridewealth, the daughter from the second family moves to join her husband in the first family, and the student in question walks over to the other group. This engenders a brief discussion regarding patrilocality and its significance in precolonial East Africa.[3] Students ask about in-law relationships between the bride and the groom's parents, and the teacher describes the extent to which the bride assumes the role of daughter. The teacher then asks the class, if the cattle are traded from one household to the other and the young bride is exchanged from one household to the other in the opposite direction, then does this activity amount to the purchase of a woman? Is this custom tantamount to the commodification and enslavement of an entire gender? How the class approaches these questions reveals several things about what the students have learned in the class already.

At this point, the students are reminded that in previous lectures, they learned that as land in precolonial East Africa was usually readily available and not, therefore, the foundation of a commodity-based economy, social connections were often a truer measure of wealth. As such, buying a person would amount to taking something inherently valuable (humanity) and rendering it far less valuable (a commodity). It would make little economic sense. The teacher urges the students to consider the bridewealth exchange as a means of cementing a bond between two families, representing, like the bride herself, a living symbol of that intimate connection.

This bond was historically (and is to this day) tested by life circumstances of all sorts. In some years, if the rains fail, and the harvest is insufficient, one family may come to rely upon their in-laws. The bridewealth bond, in such circumstances, is relevant to subsistence and survival. It also plays a vital role in the dissolution of a marriage. If, for instance, the new husband is abusive, the wife may remove herself to her parent's home. Her father must then return the bridewealth and the marital agreement is dissolved. The discussion then moves to how bridewealth, patrilineality, and patrilocality are deterrents of divorce. The class analyzes the difficult choice a mother would be forced to make if she were to leave her husband, given that her children would likely remain with their father. The student volunteers are asked to reposition themselves to emphasize this point and, in so doing, address, through action, the previous issue of "tradition" somehow calcifying social interactions. In transforming, in the minds of students, "traditional" marriage from a rigid institution to one that is inherently discursive and facilitates agency, they are presented with an experience that puts previously abstract principles into richer rational and adaptive context.

Students learn that social capital was more important than land, cash, or mineral wealth in precolonial Africa. They grasp the concept of land being more or less freely acquired, with people being the limiting economic factor. They understand that making social connections and sustaining large webs of kinship relationships were an essential part of precolonial East African life.

In these same history courses, the extent to which students have mastered these historical concepts is assessed by asking them to explain in a short essay the significance of cattle in precolonial eastern and southern Africa. To answer, they often reference the course discussion topics, which include the historical development of the Maasai, the Xhosa "cattle killing," and the use of bridewealth in the wedding exercise. Some students, on the one hand, fail to distinguish between cattle and currency and see them primarily as a store of material wealth. Successful students, on the other hand, understand cattle in 19th-century Xhosa society, for example, as symbols of social connections, with large herds indicating moral and socioeconomic well-being.

Students with this level of historical knowledge of Africa, however, continue to view this history as foreign to their own. The chief gain may be that students now comprehend cultural differences in a more appropriate and balanced way. They possess the right "facts" and therefore possess a more truthful comprehension of key historical concepts used to understand Africa's past. Yet their own way of life remains the norm, while Africa and its peoples reside in the cognitive terrain of the "Other" (Kolchin 2003:3–5).

So how, having worked so hard to explore and develop a notion of East African societies adhering to different values, with different social, economic, or political motivations, can students find something familiar? How are familiarity and difference kept in productive tension? One way is for the teacher to invite East African community and diasporic leaders to come and speak to the class. In addition, one of the most efficient means of maintaining the valuable tension between the foreign and the familiar is through experiential learning. For East Africa, best results can be achieved with a lesson taught not with a dry-erase pen but with a large, flat wooden spoon.

The *Ugali* Lesson

The teacher explains to the students before the "*Ugali* Lesson" that *ugali* is simply the Kiswahili term used in Tanzania and Kenya for a kind of food eaten throughout much of sub-Saharan Africa where starchy agricultural produce is available. It can be made from cassava, millet, sorghum, yam, or corn flour, and its bland flavor makes it ideal for dipping in flavorful meat and vegetable sauces. The teacher concludes the introduction by informing the class that *ugali*, although novel to the student, is as mundane a food as one is likely to encounter in Kenya and Tanzania. Above all else, the *ugali* lesson, in which the teacher cooks the omnipresent East African stiff porridge for the students, requires patience. As students enter the selected locale for this lesson, the teacher begins by serving a variety of East African foods and tea. The *ugali* lesson, then, is something like dinner theater.

The teacher lays out mats from southern Tanzania for the students to sit on in concentric arcs. This arrangement might seem a bit theatrical, but it helps on several fronts. For the students, it is immediately engaging in its novelty. At the same time, it represents a jumping-off point for a discussion, as East Africans spend some of the most important moments of their lives in precisely that posture, sitting together on the ground or floor, with woven mats defining social space.

The teacher passes around the raw ingredients (in this case, a very fine cornmeal) and gives a brief lecture about its cultivation and processing in a southern Tanzanian village. Slides are used to depict the elaborate threshing, grinding, sifting, soaking, and drying process yielding the ostensibly simple white flour. The class gains some appreciation for the sheer amount of physical labor that goes into what they are eating, something that is fundamental to an adequate comprehension of East African life, but seldom internalized as a dry fact in a classroom lecture.

Cooking in Tanzania and Kenya is still an overwhelmingly feminine activity, and it is a time for gossip and storytelling. The teacher uses the time it takes to boil water and to measure out the *ugali* flour in the same way. The talk begins by explaining that young girls, as early as their fifth year, learn to cook *ugali* under the watchful eyes of their mothers and grandmothers. They learn that its preparation is a reflection of the feminine character. Sand in the flour, making the stiff porridge gritty, or allowing caked *ugali* to adhere to and dry upon the *mwiko* (a wooden stirring implement), implies an unclean kitchen and a disorderly household. For corn-growing regions of southern Tanzania, a young woman, as part of her wedding ceremony, proves to her elders that she can cook a large batch of *ugali* in a pot that is balanced on three stones. It is useful to ask students to compare this activity to their own festivities prior to their wedding day.

Well-made *ugali* is a source of pride. In many instances, *ugali* preparation varies from one ethnic group to another, each group believing its version to be the best. This point resonates with the students. In fact, the students often mention similarities between *ugali* and hominy grits, noting that the latter, while tasting the same, is made with courser flour and is eaten with a spoon. The vigorous stirring motions required of properly cooked *ugali* amount to a skilled craft. When the *ugali* assumes a thick, smooth consistency, the students are invited to try some. They are shown how to scoop up a mouthful in their right hand and are warned that doing so may hurt. The *ugali* is scalding, and young Tanzanians and Kenyans become accustomed to the discomfort occasioned by handling hot porridge with bare hands at a very early age. Some students always try anyway, and the exercise does occasion a few yelps with singed fingers, but this experience leaves a meaningful impression as well. Those who taste the *ugali* are generally underwhelmed, remarking that the substance tastes too bland. They are asked to try again, this time dipping it in either a meat or stewed greens sauce. The students begin to understand the culinary logic. The sauces, eaten in any other fashion, would be too salty or strongly flavored, the *ugali* too bland.

There is perhaps nothing more prosaic in the life of a Tanzanian or Kenyan than cooking and eating *ugali*. Doing so in the context of a Western classroom is novel. The students are left to ponder their cooking and eating experience, to reflect upon what they find strange or familiar about it. As the students depart, they are asked to consider whether they can imagine themselves eating the thick porridge daily, the *ugali* becoming, eventually, mundane. Moments like the *ugali* lesson help students start to see the previously strange as somehow familiar.

The intent of the marriage, *ugali*, and similar lessons is that the students learn more than a mere acceptable assemblage of facts about African history. Having gained a new view from which to look about the world around them, students comprehend that who they are and how they live can be reexamined consciously instead of just being taken for granted. Such insight is what undergraduate education aimed at engaged global citizenship is intended to realize (Golmohamad 2009).

Notes

1. "Bridewealth" refers to livestock, crops, or other goods and/or services presented from a groom's family to the bride's family as part of the wedding ceremony. Bridewealth thereafter represents a part of the living contract cementing the relationship between two families, and it is returned upon the dissolution of the marriage.

2. Patrilineal societies trace their heritage primarily through the father's line, as opposed to the mother's kinship group.

3. Patrilocal societies are those in which young men, when they marry, remain in close physical proximity to their father's household while young women, upon marrying, are expected to move to live in close proximity to their in-laws' residence.

7 Postcolonial Perspectives on Teaching African Politics in Wales and Ireland

Carl Death

> You taught me language, and my profit on't
> Is, I know how to curse.
>
> —Caliban, *The Tempest* (Shakespeare 1968[1611]:I.ii.363–364)

CALIBAN'S REBELLION AGAINST Prospero in Shakespeare's final play raises questions of language, race, colonialism, power, and resistance, which have a direct relevance for the teaching of African politics. While the postcolonial context of the United Kingdom and Ireland is very different from that of North America, central themes of race, language, and political responsibility have an inescapable importance wherever African politics is taught. *The Tempest* has acquired iconic status for postcolonial analysts; Ngugi wa Thiong'o calls it "the classic text of the colonial process" (2005:157). When first written and performed in the early 17th century, the concept of "the British Empire" was first beginning to enter popular discourse, consisting of the kingdoms of England, Scotland, and Ireland and the principality of Wales (Howe 2000:13); by the 19th and 20th centuries, the text was itself a staple of English literature educational syllabi across the British Empire (Johnson 1998). Taking *The Tempest* as a starting point for discussing the teaching of African politics is perhaps counterintuitive, as one of the potential readings of the play regards the limits of education: whether with respect to the naivety and innocence of Miranda or the recalcitrant Caliban, "on whose nature / Nurture can never stick" (Shakespeare 1968[1611]:IV.i.188–189).

Prospero's impatient didacticism is not how we like to envisage the teacher-student relationship. Rather, the university lecturer tends to be seen, as in John Lonsdale's passionate call for ethically and politically engaged African studies, as tasked "to educate imaginations" in the continuing struggle for more just forms of politics (2005:393). Such a role is laudable; it is, however, as Lonsdale would doubtlessly agree, neither easy nor free from dangers. From my perspective, as a white, English, male, middle-class lecturer teaching African politics in Wales and Ireland, issues of language, race, gender, colonialism, power, and resistance have a direct and immediate resonance in the classroom. This chapter is an exploration of some of these issues, as well as a necessarily partial and incomplete account of some of the rewards and complexities of trying to adopt a postcolonial perspective on teaching and learning about African politics and development in the School of Law and Government at Dublin City University (2008–2009) and the Department of International Politics at Aberystwyth University (2009–2011). The conclusion of the chapter reflects upon some of the differences in teaching African politics on the Celtic edge of the Atlantic Ocean in comparison to North America, but the broader implications of the argument here is that issues of language, race, colonialism, power, and resistance are at stake in the teaching of African politics wherever it takes place.

A Postcolonial Approach to Teaching and Learning

For the purposes of this chapter, taking a postcolonial perspective on teaching and learning about African politics means an approach that is cognizant of some of the concerns and insights of the, broadly delineated, postcolonial politics literature (Abrahamsen 2003; Ahluwalia 2001; Appiah 1991; Hitchcock 1997; Loomba 1998; Mbembe 1992; Said 1994, 2003[1978]; Spivak 1988; Williams 1997; Young 2001). Such an approach means not "post" as in "after," in the sense of "post–Cold War," but rather "post" in the sense of a critical attitude toward the meta-narratives of modernization, progress, Enlightenment, and civilization that animated and legitimated the colonial enterprise.[1] Specifically, a postcolonial approach regards the experience of colonialism as constitutive of both metropole and colony, in which the continued existence of characteristically colonial power relations can be observed in respect to issues of language, race, gender, class, education, and religion and in which questions of identity, hybridity, and subjectivity are preeminently *political* topics that go to the heart of the educational endeavor (Wyn Jones 2005:23).

Postcolonialism, as an approach and a field of study, has had some impact on pedagogical theory, most often in conjunction with other radical, feminist, or subaltern theorists (Newstead 2009:81; Spivak 1988; Thomas 2009; Tremonte and Racioppi 2007). It is impossible, however, to identify a coherent postcolonial teaching methodology, because of both the diversity of approaches and the fundamentally ambivalent role of education itself. The university can be seen both as an institution "where people are inculcated into hegemonic systems of reasoning and as a site where it is possible to resist dominant discursive practices" (Madge et al. 2009:37). Education can be at least as much a technique of state and imperial power as it can be of subaltern resistance (ap Gareth 2009:41; Loomba and Orkin 1998:2–3). Irish priests in Nigeria, for example, were seen as "apostles of the British educational system" and hence of British imperialism (Hastings 1996:562; Johnson 1998:221). For Ngugi wa Thiong'o, "Learning—or shall we say education—is tied in with capture and enslavement" (2005:159). While the barriers to pursuing a transformative and progressive postcolonial pedagogy are not insurmountable (Mama 2007:3; Thomas 2009:254), it is important that teachers remain aware of the power relationships implicated in the classroom.

As a result, taking a postcolonial perspective to teaching African politics implies that the particular context of the classroom, and various subject positions within that classroom, will have an important effect on the forms of learning and teaching achieved. A class on the postcolonial state in Wales or Ireland will carry inflections different from those of a class on the same topic in England or the United States; a class on political ethnicity, gender, or South African music led by a white, English, male lecturer will have inflections different from those of one led by a black, Kenyan, female professor (see, e.g., Kidula, in this volume).

An active and participatory approach to teaching uses student presentations and group discussions in both lectures and seminars and aims to give all students the opportunity to engage in higher-level learning processes (Biggs 2003:100–111; Christie et al. 2008:567; Thomas 2009:254–255). In addition to a range of techniques for facilitating participation in lectures, my teaching has drawn upon e-mail surveys, questions on handouts, and short-answer forms to elicit student responses and opinions. In Dublin, the student body was predominantly white and Irish, but included a wide age range across the undergraduate and postgraduate body, largely because of a sizable part-time contingent including armed forces personnel, journalists, aid-sector professionals, and civil servants. There were a small number of African students, or students who had lived in Africa, from countries such as Cameroon, Nigeria, Kenya, Zimbabwe, and South Africa. In Aberystwyth, the student body was predominantly under age 25 and white, but included a sizable minority of first-language Welsh students, a mixture of Welsh and English nationalities, together with large numbers of European students and some African students, or students who had lived in Africa, from countries including Ghana, Zimbabwe, and South Africa.

Neither Wales nor Ireland is an immediately obvious choice for a "postcolonial" approach, and debates rage in the literature over whether they were "really" colonized and whether they are "really" postcolonial (ap Gareth 2009:31–33; Howe 2009; Williams 2005; Young 2001:302). Wales is often regarded as having the dubious distinction of being England's first colony, whereas Northern Ireland is sometimes considered one of the last. It is certainly not true to claim that Wales and Ireland were colonial, or are "postcolonial," in the same way as countries like Nigeria and Kenya. What is particularly interesting about teaching in Wales and Ireland is their Janus-faced postcolonial status. When viewed from Lagos or Nairobi, both seem more colonizer than colonized. As Terence Hawkes puts it so evocatively, "Halfway down the cat's throat, any self-respecting mouse ought at least to consider beginning to talk about 'us cats'" (1998:117).

The Welsh and Irish Postcolonies

The aim of taking a postcolonial perspective to teaching African politics is not to view the entire subject through the prism of colonial relationships, nor is it to establish colonialism as an overarching framework for interpreting Irish and Welsh perspectives on Africa. Rather, it is to foreground issues of power-knowledge, identity, and subjectivity, which arise in the postcolonial studies literature more broadly.

Despite the many obvious differences between colonialism in Wales and Ireland and colonialism across the African continent, there are also some interesting commonalities (Howe 2000:146; Kiberd 1996:197). The historical discrimination against the Welsh under British law, the monopolization of administrative positions by the English, the assumption of Welsh cultural inferiority in texts like the infamous "Blue Books," and systematic English settlement in Wales, are all pointed to as evidence of a colonial relationship (Davies 1974; ap Gareth 2009:37; Wyn Jones 2005).[2] The "barbaric Welsh" reappear throughout Shakespeare's English history plays, as a constitutive "Other" during this period of English state building. As Hawkes notes, "The very word 'Welsh' derives from the Old English *wæslisc*, meaning, brutally and dismissively, 'foreign'" (1998:118). In the Irish case, Declan Kiberd charts how over "many centuries, Ireland was pressed into service as a foil to set off English virtues, as a laboratory in which to conduct experiments, and as a fantasy-land in which to meet fairies and monsters" (1996:1). The overt Irish anticolonial resistance of the 20th century, the 1916 Uprising, the Civil War, and the Irish Republican Army (IRA) campaigns later in the century, all prefigured, directly inspired, or contained elements familiar from anticolonial struggles in Algeria, Kenya, Zimbabwe, South Africa, Angola, and Mozambique, as did the brutal policing and repression they provoked (Young 2001:293–307).

Most importantly, however, a postcolonial perspective can work to complicate the apparently straightforward binary between colonizers and colonized, ruler and ruled. The authors of *The Empire Writes Back* observe that the complicity of Wales and Scotland "in the British imperial enterprise makes it difficult for colonized peoples outside Britain to accept their identity as post-colonial" (Ashcroft et al. 2002:31–32). For Albert Memmi, "In the eyes of the colonized, all Europeans in the colonies are *de facto* colonizers, and whether they want to be or not, they are colonizers in some ways. . . . They are supporters or at least unconscious accomplices of that great collective aggression of Europe" (1990[1957]:196). The distinctions between an English vicar, Irish priest, or Welsh minister in a Church school in Lagos in the early 20th century is thus blurred— for Memmi and many others they are all de facto colonizers (Hastings 1996:418, 560; Kennedy 1992:115; Kiberd 1996:465).

The Welsh, for example, participated militarily in the expansion of the empire, and benefited economically from it, leading some to conclude that "the Welsh have been the active agents as well as the passive subjects of imperial expansion" (Williams 2005:7). In the Irish case, Liam Kennedy argues that in the later 19th century, "members of the Irish gentry and middle classes participated willingly in the administration of the imperial system world-wide. Thousands of Irish officers and soldiers manned its defences" (1992:115). Taking a rather more balanced perspective, Kiberd argues that "it is precisely the 'mixed' nature of the experience of Irish people, as both exponents and victims of British imperialism, which makes them so representative of the underlying process" (1996:5). This underlying process—and the attention to questions of power, language, and resistance that a postcolonial approach entails—has particular resonance when looking at the links between language, education, and colonialism.

Cymraeg and Gaeilge: Language, Education, and Colonialism

"The red plague rid you / For learning me your language!" (Shakespeare 1968[1611]:I. ii.364–365), Caliban curses in *The Tempest*. A central pillar of British imperialism was the imposition of the metropolitan language as the lingua franca of government, education, and culture, whether it was in Wales or Ireland or later in colonies such as Nigeria, Ghana, and Uganda (Hawkes 1998:125; Said 1994:130–132). The psychological and cultural effects of being taught that one's own culture and language were inferior have been powerfully documented by, among others, Gandhi, Wa Thiong'o, Frantz Fanon, and Memmi (Ahluwalia 2001:20; Fanon 1986[1952]:17–40; Kiberd 1996:555–557; Memmi 1990[1957]:200; Wa Thiong'o 2005). Language has also been a tool of resistance. Aimé Césaire's Caliban introduces Yoruba and Swahili words in a "creolization" of the French language that unsettles Prospero to the point of madness (Sarnecki 2000:277–281). The question of the language of education is therefore inescapably political and resonates strongly in a Welsh and Irish context.

While the speaking of Welsh (*Cymraeg*) was persecuted by the English, directly and indirectly, for many centuries, the language is still spoken and understood by over 20 percent of the adult Welsh population (Williams 2005:14). The degree of proficiency in the language varies greatly, from first-language mother-tongue speakers to those able to understand signs and a few words, and regional variations are considerable too. Aberystwyth has always been a traditional heartland of both the language and Welsh nationalism, and Aberystwyth University is officially bilingual. This does not mean that all classes have to be offered in Welsh, although many are. All students have the right to submit assessments and complete examinations in Welsh.[3] The first-year course Introduction to the Third World, for example, provides bilingual lecture handouts and Welsh-language seminar groups, although the lectures themselves are delivered in English. The module Power, Conflict, and Development in Africa is taught solely in English. In both courses, lectures and seminars contain a mixture of language proficiencies, heavily dominated by first- (and only) language English speakers, with a number who understand Welsh and a sizable minority of first-language Welsh speakers. There are therefore potential tensions and frustrations for these students studying for a degree at a Welsh university, in Aberystwyth in the heart of mid-Wales, where not all courses are offered in their first language.

This context provides an obvious opening for raising issues related to colonial education policies in Africa, the marginalization and direct persecution of indigenous languages, and the global hegemony of English as a language of research and academia. Classes therefore include discussions on the divisions between Francophone Rwanda and Anglophone Uganda (which became extremely politically significant in the context of the 1994 genocide) and the challenge of nation building in places like Tanzania, with 120-plus indigenous languages, and South Africa with 11 official languages.

The context is slightly different in Ireland, where first-language Gaelic speakers constitute a much smaller percentage of the population than Welsh speakers do in Wales. Language thus appears to be less of a political issue than it can be in Aberystwyth. However, Irish students have all learned Gaelic at school and often have strong (and divergent) views on the status and role of the language. Some students see it as an inconvenient anachronism that means little to their sense of Irish identity; others see it as an important cultural marker, whose decline is a prime example of centuries of colonial rule and British suppression.

Extirpation of the Gaelic language and the shaming of those who spoke it were central elements of English colonial policy in Ireland, and illustrious and "enlightened" writers such as Edmund Spenser (Kiberd 1996:143–144) supported these policies. In turn, this produced postcolonial resistance and a defense of Celtic culture from luminaries such as Seathrún Céitinn and W. B. Yeats (Said 1994:17). In James Joyce's *A Portrait of the Artist as a Young Man*, Stephen Dedalus realizes, when confronted with his English lecturer, that "the language in which we are speaking is his before it is mine. . . . My soul frets in the shadow of his language" (2005[1916]:219). As such, language politics in Ireland, as in Wales, provides a fascinating, complex, and sometimes dangerous context in which to discuss colonial and nationalist language policies in Africa: from the imposition of Afrikaans as a teaching medium in South Africa in 1974 (which led to the 1976 Soweto Uprising) to the call by writers such as Ngugi wa Thiong'o (2005) for their compatriots to write in African languages like Gikuyu.

This critical and reflective awareness of the links between language, education, knowledge, and power is at the heart of a postcolonial approach. "More education" is often rather simplistically proposed as a panacea for African development. Yet the questions of what should be the appropriate medium, language, subjects, and purposes of education are less frequently raised (Johnson 1998; Loomba and Orkin 1998:17). As postcolonial theorists can remind us, education can be both a source of emancipation and a disciplinary site of indoctrination (Madge et al. 2009:37). Irish and Welsh perspectives on the language of education, and the contours of power-knowledge, can illuminate important aspects of contemporary African politics.

Active and Participatory Learning in African Politics

As the sections above have shown, a postcolonial perspective can illuminate much about the contemporary politics of Wales and Ireland and their varied relationships with both England and the African colonies. This section develops some of these aspects in a more focused discussion of how a postcolonial perspective can facilitate an active and participatory approach to teaching African politics and development. In particular, there are five specific areas in which this approach has been most

rewarding: personal testimonies and family histories, tourism, global political economies of resource consumption and corruption, race and racism, and debates over
political responsibility.

Personal Testimonies and Family Histories

A useful place to begin is to have students introduce themselves, their backgrounds,
and their various motivations for taking the course. These personal testimonies and
family histories provide great starting points, but they can also be returned to in order
to illustrate examples throughout the course as new topics arise. My classes have had
students whose grandparents worked as colonial administrators in Nigeria; people
who left Zimbabwe due to threats of state violence; individuals who have run small
businesses in Nairobi and married locals; members of the Nigerian diaspora in Ireland, even some who have stood for local election there; ex–United Nations peacekeepers in Chad; white South Africans whose families left in 1994; second-generation
immigrants who have found trips back to Ghana unsettling and dislocating; and a
history teacher from Cameroon who moved to Ireland to find herself on the other
side of the classroom. There are plenty of ways to integrate these personal testimonies
and family histories into classes of various sizes—from large lecture halls to small
seminar groups. Letting the students know that they will have an opportunity to relate
their stories, in short testimonies mid-lecture, can help validate their contribution and
make classes less didactic.

There are, of course, problems and dangers with such an approach as well. Care
must be taken to ensure that classes do not become a long succession of unreflective
or rambling personal accounts, although often the class will "self-police" to ensure
momentum is maintained. Some students do also become frustrated with what they
see as overly subjective, self-involved, or insufficiently academic accounts. There is also
the danger of putting students under pressure or into situations in which they are
not comfortable. Sometimes students volunteer to speak, only to regret it when the
moment comes or when they underestimate the potential distress that recounting a
traumatic experience may cause. This appeared to be the case in an early lecture, when
a mature student offered to speak about experiences growing up in Zimbabwe, but
then froze when standing in the midst of a class of 50 people. In such a situation, the
lecturer has a responsibility to manage the situation to minimize the embarrassment
and distress of the student. In the absence of a personal testimony, there is always
another topic, or activity, that can be turned to instead.

Another danger of the "testimony" approach is the risk of privileging and valor-
izing the immediacy or exoticism of firsthand or "authentic" experiences (Madge et al.
2009:42). Students can often become uncritically in awe of particularly vocal, confident,
passionate, and authoritative individuals. The vigorous assertions of a Nigerian émigré
standing in front of them can easily appear more immediate and persuasive than a set
text by Basil Davidson, Claude Aké, or Christopher Clapham. There is a risk that such

individuals, in the context of a classroom, can adopt something akin to what Kwame Anthony Appiah describes as the role of the postcolonial intellectual: "They are known through the Africa they offer; their compatriots know them both through the West they present to Africa and through an Africa they have invented for the world, for each other, and for Africa" (1991:348; see also Newstead 2009:87). Maintaining an atmosphere of "continual criticism" (Krishna 2009:172) in this situation can be difficult, as well as politically and culturally sensitive when it comes from a young, white, English lecturer.

Tourism

Moreover, many students do not come to class with closely felt and intense personal experiences of "Africa" on which their self-identity rests; appearing to value only "African voices" can risk alienating young, white, British and European (and, in my experience, especially male) students (Newstead 2009:87). Finding ways to draw on the perspectives of these students is also important. One potential way is through discussion of tourism or portrayals of "Africa" in the mainstream media.

Asking which students have been to Africa on vacation usually provokes a few responses; asking which students have seen a television program on African wildlife usually raises a forest of hands. The politics of conservation is a useful example to highlight important broader issues related to the courses. This topic is rarely covered in African politics overview courses but links closely with many other key themes such as violence, corruption, development, and Western intervention (Dunn 2009; Van Amerom and Büscher 2005). The growth of transboundary conservation areas, or so-called peace parks such as the Greater Limpopo Park straddling South Africa, Mozambique, and Zimbabwe, raises interesting questions about the conditional, performative, and relational character of sovereignty in Africa and the growing involvement of a global industry of nongovernmental organizations, scientific institutes, foundations, private philanthropists, and concerned wildlife lovers in the management of African environments (Mbembe 2002b:76).

My own research on environmental and conservation movements in South Africa, and their mobilizations around the 2002 Johannesburg World Summit on Sustainable Development (Death 2010:51–53), has also been a useful resource in teaching, as research-led teaching is a good way to bring topics to life and introduce students to the research dimension of academia. Furthermore, by tackling topics like tourism and conservation that are often presumed by students to be at best peripheral to political analysis, and certainly not core topics of international relations, it is possible to challenge and expand students' disciplinary horizons (Tremonte and Racioppi 2007:51).

Global Political Economies

Whether students have themselves traveled or lived in Africa, or whether they have relatively little direct experience with the themes covered in the course, an important aim of the postcolonial approach is to explore the ways that we are all implicated in African politics and already have an explicit or implicit ethical relation with distant others. This can be achieved through a discussion of the legacies of the Atlantic slave trade, not just for West Africa, but also for the United Kingdom, Wales, and Ireland (Young 2001:4). The profits of the slave trade can be seen in the architecture of cities like Cardiff, Dublin, and Liverpool.[4] Stephen Howe observes how although "there was rather little direct involvement of Irish ports or Irish-owned ships in actually transporting enslaved Africans across the Atlantic," numerous Irish "prospered as slave owners and dealers" (2009:142). A more immediate and personal context for these economic linkages can be accessed through discussions of some of the contemporary global trade routes that surround and facilitate African conflicts.

Films are a powerful and accessible way to engage students with these issues. One particularly useful film is *Blood Diamond* (Zwick 2006), which, because of its treatment of the civil war in Sierra Leone and the international diamond trade, vividly shows how individual consumers, inserted within global political economies of resource consumption, can have an impact upon African societies, economies, and politics. The importance of the transnational diamond trade in the conflict in Sierra Leone, and the roles of major multinationals like De Beers, international peacekeepers, and mercenary outfits like Executive Outcomes, can help problematize the international-domestic binary (Ferguson 2006:41, 200). Whether it is the use of columbite-tantalite (coltan) from the Democratic Republic of the Congo (DRC) in mobile phones, the role of rubber from Liberia in the manufacture of Firestone tires, or oil from Nigeria that supplies 8 percent of U.S. imports, many of Africa's conflicts can be brought very close to home, even in a classroom in Aberystwyth or Dublin (Molele 2009). By raising these issues of responsibility and ethical intervention, the discussion can move from a narrowly statistical and "scientific" discussion of greed and grievances toward a more contextualized and relational understanding of political violence in Africa (Ballentine and Sherman 2003).

Global political economies, and the networks of African commodity trade routes, can also be used to discuss issues of poverty, development, and corruption. The export of coffee from Kenya or Ethiopia to the cup on the seminar table, for example, can form a mini–case study or student presentation within a session discussing the economic and mono-crop legacies of colonialism; contemporary practices of fair trade, free trade, and aid; or the effects of European agricultural subsidies. The almost unimaginable greed of Jean-Bédel Bokassa, Idi Amin, and Mobutu Sese Seko was facilitated by private banks in New York, Geneva, and London. The important point that corruption is not a uniquely African problem was made even more evident in 2008–2010 with the very public airing of the global financial system's dirty laundry. Irish students were particularly receptive to comparisons between the conduct of scandal-dogged ex-heads of state such as Charles Haughey or Bertie Ahern (the "Teflon Taoiseach") and kleptocrats such as Kenya's Daniel Arap Moi or Zambia's Frederick Chiluba. The

U.K. Westminster expenses scandal of 2008–2009 provided even more fruitful material for comparison and contextualization.

Often it seems to be these topics, and the links to everyday patterns of consumption and local economies, that resonate most strongly with students. Seminars have involved heated debates on the ethics of buying imported fruit from South Africa or jewelry made with Zimbabwean diamonds. An e-mail survey of a large (200-plus) cohort of first-year undergraduate students in Aberystwyth asked them in what ways they thought that their lives had an effect on people in developing countries, and, interestingly, most assessed their impact in terms of an imagined "shopping basket" of food, clothes, oil, and other consumables. That most students who responded tended to conceptualize themselves as consumers, rather than citizens, activists, voters, or indeed students, was quite revealing in terms of the commodification and commercialization of contemporary political identities.

It is through such explicit reflections on questions of personal responsibility, ethical conduct, and dilemmas of structure and agency that dichotomies such as public-private and domestic-international can be problematized. For Sankaran Krishna (2009:2), a postcolonial perspective can be a tactic of destabilization and resistance to the globalized hegemony of free market capitalism, and its attendant ideology of individualist consumerism, both of which have produced such attenuated conceptions of political life.

Race and Racism

The previous three topics have all sought, in some ways, to explore issues of connectedness and interrelatedness in the classroom, drawing upon students' personal experiences as a means to open up broader themes in African politics. The topic of race, however, is one of the hardest to deal with in the classroom, as it raises questions of difference quite explicitly. Although classes begin by clarifying that race is socially constructed, rather than biological (Loomba 1998:121), students in Wales and Ireland often have little experience of racially divided societies, and the dominance of "whiteness" in the classroom presents challenges of its own (Newstead 2009:82). The very small numbers of black students can mean that some individuals feel overly pressured to "speak for" a particular group or that they are being typecast as an "otherness machine" (Appiah 1991:356). Moreover, despite being in the overwhelming majority, some white students become quite defensive as soon as the topic is broached and eagerly seek to provide examples of "inverse racism" or "positive discrimination."

The topic of race and racism, because of its sensitivity, is best approached, at least initially, in a textual manner through analysis of a set text from Frantz Fanon (1986[1952]) or Steve Biko (1979). Further discussion, especially in more advanced and mature classes, covers racial tropes and stereotypes in classic literary texts such as *The Tempest* (Shakespeare 1968[1611]), Joseph Conrad's *Heart of Darkness* (1999[1902]), or Alan Paton's *Cry, the Beloved Country* (1948). Yet the question of race cannot be wholly tamed or pacified by removing it from a personal context, and the strongly felt and sometimes uncomfortable views of students must be given space. It is on the topic of race and racism that the postcolonial studies literature can offer some of its most penetrating insights (Ahluwalia 2001:20–33; Loomba 1998:121; Said 2003[1978]:206–207), and it is impossible to discuss African politics, and Africa's place in the world, without broaching the subject. Most importantly, the topic of race and racism foregrounds issues of identity and subjectivity more starkly than almost any other topic, as well as problematizing claims about the "postcolonial" status of Wales and Ireland.

The colonial nature of the historical relationship between England and Wales, or the United Kingdom and Ireland, is most often asserted in terms of land, language, the economy, the military, religion, and culture (Howe 2000:13–16; Williams 2005). When the question of race arises, however, the apparently "black-and-white" relationship between colonizer and colonized becomes considerably muddied. Notwithstanding the infamous Roddy Doyle line that "the Irish are the blacks of Europe" (Kiberd 1996:611), as well as the ubiquitous "No blacks or Irish" signs in post–World War II Britain, neither Ireland nor Wales is itself a society free from racism. Irish and Welsh attitudes toward immigrant communities, whether Nigerians in Dublin or Somalis in South Wales, have often displayed more of an imperial mentality than they have a solidarity with the subaltern (Howe 2000:156). These complex, multilayered relationships raise, quite directly, fundamental issues of ethical responsibility toward the "Other," which cut across many of the issues discussed so far.

Debates over Political Responsibility

The perpetuation of historical structures of racism and cultural imperialism raises the question of responsibility in international politics. The possibility of developing an ethical relationship between individuals and communities is an idea that lies at the heart of discussions of postcolonialism (Ahluwalia 2001:10, 135). This question is usually raised directly at the start of the courses, because it problematizes the international-domestic binary so directly and because it recurs in later topics such as the postcolonial state, corruption, violence, development, democracy, the African Renaissance, and the rise of new powers like China and India. The students are asked to read extracts from a speech delivered by French president Nicolas Sarkozy in July 2007 in Dakar, in which he declared, "The tragedy of Africa is that the African man has never really entered history," and he urged Africans that despite the violence of colonialism, "this European part of you is not unworthy."[5] This reading is accompanied by Achille Mbembe's (2007) critical response to Sarkozy and a discussion of British pronouncements on Africa, such as ex–prime minister Tony Blair's declaration that "Africa is a scar upon the conscience of the world" and the ex-chancellor of the exchequer Gordon Brown's assertion that "the days of Britain having to apologise for its colonial history are over" (Milne 2005). These three texts, in the context of the broader readings, lecture discussions, and preparation for a country report, are usually enough to ensure a heated and lively debate on the question of colonial responsibility and reparations.

In Wales, someone usually brings up the "benign imperialism" argument—associated with Niall Ferguson's (2003) claim that the British Empire ushered in modernity and global capitalism or with the famous Monty Python scene where Judean rebels ask themselves, "What have the Romans ever done for us?" (Jones 1979).[6] Although the debate has certainly never divided clearly along English-Welsh lines, students, unprompted, have often made the parallel with English colonialism in Wales, and there has always been enough of a divide in opinion within the class to have a vigorous debate over the nature and extent of colonial responsibility. A similar dynamic was observed in Dublin, perhaps somewhat surprisingly given the more prominent republican and anticolonial public culture in Ireland.

While classes in both countries were orientated toward the anti-imperial perspective, the Irish-English analogy was less readily invoked in Dublin than the Welsh-English analogy had been in Aberystwyth. It was also clear that students regarded the question of responsibility in Africa in a very different light from the Irish and Welsh experiences of colonialism. If English colonialism was seen as illegitimate in Wales and Ireland, and its effects continued to be felt quite intensely by some students, the starting assumption often seemed to be that in Africa (which was frequently homogenized), some form of colonialism or protectorate had been, if not justified or legitimate, at least "a mixed bag" and partially defensible in some respects. This position was most clearly seen when the discussion moved onto contemporary questions of power and responsibility, where many students have defended principles of international intervention or aid conditionality, while remaining skeptical about the principles of state sovereignty or formal reparations for colonialism.

What is so productive about this topic is the way its themes resurface throughout the course and how students self-consciously moderate or reinforce their earlier positions as new contexts and perspectives come to light. The discussion is also very helpful in allowing students to explain and explore their own positions and opinions, before introducing them to arguments such as Mark Duffield's (2007) critique of the liberal peace and humanitarian intervention, Pal Ahluwalia's (2001:54) view of the aid industry as the new "colonial administrators" of pathologized African states, Rita Abrahamsen's (2000; 2003:202) analysis of the democratization discourse and good governance agenda, or Graham Harrison's (2001) critique of Poverty Reduction Strategy Papers. It is in these fields that some of the insights of the postcolonial literature become most concrete and visible in everyday African politics.

Conclusion

These five examples of active and participatory approaches to teaching African politics and development, informed by postcolonial perspectives, are indicative rather than comprehensive. They should not be regarded as a template for a Postcolonial

Perspectives on African Politics course, for example, nor will they all be applicable in all courses on African politics and development. The relationship between the themes will change according to the course and the class. For example, a postgraduate masters course I teach titled Protest, Power, and Resistance in Africa draws more heavily on material on anticolonial resistance (Kenya), civil disobedience (South Africa), pro-democracy movements (Zambia), and rural-urban power relations (Tanzania), as well as on global political economies (the Niger Delta) and race and racism (South Africa).

Different aspects of this teaching program will have varying relevance in different contexts. Teaching and learning about African politics and development in the Welsh and Irish context, for example, has some similarities, but also important differences in comparison to the North American context. The topics of race, race relations, and the legacy of the African slave trade might be foregrounded far more prominently in the United States, while issues relating to the cultural marginalization of indigenous languages might carry less resonance than with students in Wales and Ireland. Most significantly, the proud anticolonial traditions of the United States, as a country that fought and won a war of independence against the old European powers, must be balanced against a prevailing view in many African countries of a post–Cold War U.S. imperium stretching out across the globe (Ahluwalia 2001; Krishna 2009). In the past half century, the United States has supported dictators like Mobutu, undermined democratic regimes in Angola and Mozambique, ignored atrocities in Rwanda and the DRC, and driven a program of financial austerity through structural adjustment programs (SAPs) that has set human development in many African countries back by a decade or more. Such issues are at the heart of a postcolonial perspective on teaching African politics and development and will vary according to the context of the classroom.

The aim of taking a postcolonial approach to teaching and learning African politics has been to encourage students in Wales and Ireland, whatever their backgrounds and histories, to think about their own personal and social relationships to the issues explored in the course. It has particular strengths in terms of understanding how events and processes in a "foreign" part of the world relate closely to our own personal and cultural contexts in the United Kingdom and Ireland. In this, it seeks to "refute tendencies to locate postcoloniality 'elsewhere' but rather recognise the interdependence and mutuality that shapes the postcolonial present" (Madge et al. 2009:44). It is important to acknowledge that we all have a connection to, and are implicated in, the themes discussed in this chapter. "This thing of darkness I / Acknowledge mine," Prospero reflects soberly at the end of *The Tempest* (Shakespeare 1968[1611]:V.i.275–276), and one of the most profound insights of much of the postcolonial literature is the mutual constitution of both colonizer and colonized and the hybrid character of identity and subjectivity in contemporary politics (Abrahamsen 2003:196; Ahluwalia 2001:128). The figures of Caliban, Ariel, and Prospero in *The Tempest* are an intriguing illustration of hybrid identities; they are mutually interdependent and yet in conflict, each embodies different aspects of the human condition, and they are fluid signifiers, which can be infused with contradictory meanings in different contexts (Loomba and Orkin 1998:7–8; Said 1994:257). Prospero himself has been variously interpreted as an imperialist in the Cecil Rhodes (English) or Henry Stanley (Welsh) mold, a Jacobean philosopher perhaps inspired by the Elizabethan John Dee, as well the more usual stand-in for Shakespeare himself, the aging writer reluctantly relinquishing his staff and books (Brotton 1998:26–30).[7] Such a co-constitution of multilayered relationships is especially relevant when teaching in Wales and Ireland, where the postcolonial relationship with England is both mirrored and inverted in many African contexts.

Notes

This chapter is indebted to contributions from the reviewers and editors of this volume, as well as from colleagues and students in Aberystwyth and Dublin. For my relationship with African politics, my attitudes to teaching, and the initial formulation of the module Power, Conflict and Development in Africa, I owe most to Rita Abrahamsen.

1. As in the use of the prefix "post-" in the concepts of post-structuralism and postmodernism. For the lengthy and sometimes circular disputes about the meaning of "post," and the relative coherence (or not) of the field of postcolonial studies, see Ahluwalia (2001:1–6) or Loomba (1998).

2. The racist and condescending 1847 *Report into the State of Education in Wales* became known as the "Brad y Llyfrau Gleision," or the "Treachery of the Blue Books" (ap Gareth 2009; Bohata 2004:9–10).

3. Aberystwyth University, http://www.aber.ac.uk/en/undergrad/general/welsh-medium.

4. International Slavery Museum, http://www.liverpoolmuseums.org.uk/ism.

5. Royal African Society, http://royalafricansociety.org/home/416.html. For the Hegelian source of this perspective, see Bayart (1993:3).

6. An ever-increasing list of answers is supplied to this rhetorical question, to the frustration of the leaders of the fractious Peoples Front of Judea, and includes aqueducts, sanitation, roads, irrigation, medicine, education, health, wine, baths, and public order.

7. John Dee, a prominent Welshman at Elizabeth I's court, is widely cited as having coined the phrase "British Empire" (Hawkes 1998:125–126).

8 Pan-Africanism

The Ties That Bind Ghana and the United States

Harry Nii Koney Odamtten

Introduction

This chapter explores intellectual, political, and sociocultural exchanges between Ghanaian nationalists and African Americans. Focusing on the similarities and interconnections between the peoples of Ghana and the diaspora, the chapter offers a historical analysis of events leading to Ghanaian and American independence and links such events to other world historical processes. I look at similarities in the martyrdom of American Crispus Attucks (1723–1770) and Ghanaian sergeant Cornelius Frederick Adjetey (1894–1948). An examination then follows of the life and times of Ghana's first president, Kwame Nkrumah (1909–1972), particularly his student days in the United States and his subsequent relationship with Pan-Africanism's cofounder W. E. B. Du Bois and American civil rights leader Dr. Martin Luther King Jr. This discussion, while focused on Ghana and the United States, embraces current trends in the field of African Studies and its interdisciplinary shift toward global African history.

Background

Teaching African history has suggested that when students are presented with images or real-life situations that reinforce what they have learned in the classroom, they are more likely to reevaluate previously held pessimisms about Africa and Africans.[1] This chapter examines the Pan-African ties between Africans and African Americans by combining historical narrative and comparative analysis: a brief narrative of the lives of individuals from both groups, on the one hand, and a comparative look at the relationships these individuals established with one another, on the other. Many students, for example, are aware of Martin Luther King Jr.'s important contributions to the evolution of the United States' political culture, but are unaware that he ever visited Ghana or had some inspirational impetus for his civil rights struggle from an African leader, Kwame Nkrumah.

Theoretical Groundings

This chapter is grounded in the contextualization of African history in a global past. This global African context is derived from sociologist Ruth Simms Hamilton's definition of global Africa as "the geographically and socio-culturally diverse peoples of Africa and its diaspora [and] is linked through complex networks of social relationships and processes" (2007:1). Building on this definition, the idea of Pan-Africanism is examined as one of the avenues by which Ghanaian scholars and politicians were linked to their African American counterparts. Pan-Africanism is defined here as the idea that people of African descent, no matter their geographic location, share historical, cultural, sociological, and kinship ties given their collective origins on the African continent. In addition, African descendants, because they face similar conditions of socioeconomic inequity based on an international hierarchy, see themselves as part of a global, African community. In light of recent trends in African studies that tend to privilege connections between Africa and its diaspora, this approach is noteworthy because it "globalizes Africa, repositioning the continent in world history" (Zeleza 2010:3). Africa thus becomes more relevant to students as an active participant in worldwide affairs rather than a static and distant continent.

Hamilton (2007) identifies four characteristics of global Africa. The first, *geosocial mobility and displacement*, captures the forced and voluntary continuous movement of African-descended peoples following initial displacements to locations in Europe, Asia, and the Americas. The later movements tend to include return migrations to the African continent. The second category, *power, domination, and inequality*, refers to the systemic institutionalization of dominance over African peoples on the basis of race, class, gender, religion, and nationality. *Agents of resistance*, the third characteristic, is the intellectual, cultural, and social resistance put up by African-descended peoples against systems of oppression and inequality. The fourth domain of global Africa, *African diaspora connections*, is the real and mythical construction of Africa as a homeland and the host of networks that are created between continental Africans and the African diaspora. This chapter shows how these four characteristics shape the individual and collective lives of Ghanaians and African Americans. In this way, the chapter shows ways that Africa may be incorporated into the limited but increasing treatment of Africa in American, Western, and world history textbooks and courses.

Crispus Attucks and Sergeant Frederick Adjetey:
Martyrs of American and Ghanaian Independence

By Hamilton's definition, Crispus Attucks of the United States and Sergeant Adjetey of Ghana not only were *geosocially displaced*, but also became *agents of resistance*. Attucks, a descendant of enslaved Africans who had been displaced by the transatlantic slave trade, faced further displacement while resisting plantation slavery. It was a racial *system of dominance* that had been instituted by white American slave owners over blacks in the United States. Sergeant Adjetey, moreover, attempted to resist colonialism, a form of authoritarian regime used by Britain to maintain control of African territories it had forcibly annexed. In their acts of resistance against racial and colonial supremacy, Attucks and Adjetey became martyrs of the struggles for independence in the United States and Ghana, respectively.

Crispus Attucks

Darlene C. Hine et al. (2002) reveal that before the American Revolution in 1776, Attucks was geosocially displaced; at the age of 27, he escaped from slavery in Framingham, Massachusetts, and became a fugitive, working as a sailor, with Boston as his homeport. Following this initial act of resistance to his slavery in Massachusetts, on March 5, 1770, together with fellow black and Irish sailors, Attucks, wielding a cordwood stick, confronted a British detachment of troops in Boston. The British soldiers shot down Attucks and four others, creating the impetus for the American War of Independence against Great Britain. Boston patriots declared Attucks, "the first martyr to British oppression" (Hine et al. 2002:76). Attucks's action as an agent of resistance to British colonialism in the United States and his subsequent martyrdom bears close resemblance to the martyrdom of Sergeant Adjetey and his colleagues on February 28, 1948, in Ghana, also against British colonialism.

Sergeant Fredrerick Adjetey

By the close of the 19th century, Ghana, then comprising three territories—the Gold Coast, Ashanti, and the Northern Territories—had come under British colonial domination similar to that in the United States before 1776. When World War II began, able Ghanaian men including Sergeant Adjetey were compulsorily recruited by the British to serve as soldiers. Adjetey served the British in Burma (1939–1945) before returning home. The Ghanaian soldiers were promised job opportunities and good remuneration on their return; however, when the ex-servicemen made their way back to Ghana, there were no prospects of sustainable livelihood. The ex-servicemen also found that talk of democratic ideals and imperialist rhetoric of the British against Germany and its allies had not been applied to them. The Atlantic Charter, which recognized all peoples' right to self-determination, was inconsequential in Ghana, where the British were on top and natives at the bottom of the colonial social structure.

Sergeant Adjetey and his colleagues therefore marched in protest to demand their rights from the British colonial administration. During the march to the Osu Castle, the seat of the colonial administration, Sergeant Adjetey and two of his colleagues, Corporal Attipoe and Private Odartey, were shot dead by Captain Imray of the British army. This incident led to riots in Accra, giving impetus for a shift in the political struggle's ideology from "independence in the shortest possible time" to "independence now," which eventually came in 1957 under the political leadership of Kwame Nkrumah.

These martyrs, Attucks and Sergeant Adjetey, even though separated by geographic location and historical time, were linked by their common status as blacks and their displacement by racism, colonial domination, and war, as previously argued by Hamilton (2007). Their resistance to the unequal social conditions they found in their respective societies ties them together both as *agents of resistance* and as members of a global Africa who were successful in leading opposition against *power, domination, and inequality.* Their individual actions thus link the independence movements in the United States and Ghana against British colonialism. More significantly in the context of teaching African history within a global context, African nationalism can be thematically linked to the ideals of the American Revolution, the Haitian and French revolutions, and colonial struggles throughout the 20th and 21st centuries. These links become even more relevant for students when contemporary examples of ties between the United States and Africa are explored.

The American Background of Kwame Nkrumah and the Great Depression

Kwame Nkrumah (1909–1972), was educated in the United States at Lincoln University in Pennsylvania, where in 1939 he received a bachelor of arts degree in sociology and economics. He later earned a master of science in education in 1942, and a master's in philosophy at the University of Pennsylvania in 1943. Nkrumah also submitted a dissertation for the award of a doctorate in philosophy in 1944, but he did not stay to defend it, leaving instead for Britain to pursue a career in law. He went on to become the first president of the newly independent African country of Ghana in 1957. Nkrumah's experience in America during his student days was no different from that of many Americans, who faced hard times during the Great Depression and World War II. In his autobiography, Nkrumah (1957) describes how he struggled to pay his rent, fend for himself, and endure racial abuse.

During the period 1929–1935, the American stock market crashed, the agricultural system was in shambles, and the economy collapsed, leading to high unemployment, which adversely affected the black population. The Depression highlighted and heightened already existing racism, urbanization, industrialization, and labor and class issues faced by black migrants to the United States.

Labor historian Lizabeth Cohen (1990), for example, has documented the rise of ethnic-based associations in Chicago during this period. Ethnic mutual aid organizations helped mitigate the effects of industry and urbanization such as unemployment and homelessness. This scenario was echoed in Detroit, as Olivier Zunz (1982) explains, with the rise of ghettoes and the eruption of racial violence against black workers and migrants as they competed with whites for industrial jobs and urban spaces. George Lipsitz (1994) buttresses the positions of Cohen and Zunz, arguing that the dire conditions faced by blacks forced them to question inequality not only abroad but at home in America, just as ex-servicemen like Sergeant Adjetey in Ghana did under British colonialism. Lipsitz notes that blacks used mass demonstrations and strikes to press their demands for equality in all spheres of American life. This public show of force was epitomized in 1941 by the March on Washington Movement led by A. Philip Randolph, who had also founded and led the Brotherhood of Sleeping Car Porters.

Nkrumah was a student in America during these events of the Depression, and his own experiences as a black migrant reinforced his Pan-African beliefs; he shared a racial, cultural, and social heritage with U.S. blacks. One of the other key figures during this period was Father Divine (1877–1965), an African American who formed the racially neutral Peace Movement. The movement sought to spiritually empower people during the Depression and also offered food relief.

Father Divine organized free banquets for his followers in Long Island and later Harlem, where Nkrumah first encountered him (Rahman 2007:66). Nkrumah, like many blacks during the Depression, faced dire economic circumstances and food shortages. A hungry student, Nkrumah found himself at Father Divine's banquets, where he was fed on a "good chicken meal for half a dollar" (Nkrumah 1957:41). Nkrumah noted that during the Depression, Father Divine was able to instill belief and hope in the future for a great number of Harlem's masses.

When Nkrumah completed his education in the United States, he left for Britain to pursue a law career and then later joined the independence struggle in Ghana. Nkrumah's actions after he became president of the young Ghana were sometimes shaped by his experiences of American racism. Nkrumah remembered his first encounter with racism on the Mason-Dixon Line in Baltimore on his way from Philadelphia to Washington, D.C. He recalled that he had asked for water from a white waiter who told him, "The place for you man, is the spittoon outside" (Nkrumah 1957:43). Nkrumah could not believe that "any man could refuse a man a drink of water because his skin happened to be of a different color" (1957:43). Nkrumah's experience of racism in the United States was a general reflection of the unequal conditions at the time. This racial incident and the sociological conditions of blacks during the Great Depression shaped Nkrumah's Pan-African beliefs. Nkrumah believed that his status as a colonial subject of Britain bonded him with African Americans, who were treated differently on account of their racial status.

This account of Nkrumah's experiences in the United States during this period of economic depression and the emergence of various social movements is also a good building block for introducing students of African history to Africa and the role of Africans in the gradual development of socialist theories and the politicization of working-class and labor movements around the world following the Second World War.

Nkrumah and King: Meeting of the Independence Struggle and the Civil Rights Struggle

Very few Americans know that some African leaders, like the first president of Nigeria, Nnamdi Azikiwe, and Ghana's president Kwame Nkrumah, were educated and lived in the United States for a significant part of their lives. Even less known is the fact that Nkrumah influenced Martin Luther King Jr., America's most celebrated civil rights leader.

When Nkrumah led Ghana to independence from Great Britain in 1957, he invited Reverend King to Ghana, which was King's first international experience. In Ghana, King witnessed the independence celebrations, and his memory of the event was the subject of his 1957 sermon "The Birth of a New Nation." In his speech, King recollected that when the Ghanaian flag was hoisted, he "started weeping. [He] was crying for joy . . . and [he] could hear that old Negro spiritual once more crying out, 'Free at last, free at last. Great God Almighty, I'm free at last!'" (Lischer 1997:84). In his sermon, King also drew parallels between the change that occurred in Ghana through struggle and the potential for change in American society.

While in Ghana, King had also been introduced to Vice President Richard Nixon, a meeting that would have been impossible in the United States. Kevin K. Gaines (2006:5, 81) recounts that Nixon was attending the independence ceremony on behalf of the United States and could not ignore King in Accra, eventually inviting him for a meeting in Washington, D.C. Nkrumah also offered King insights into how Gandhian nonviolence had been effective in the then Gold Coast struggle (Gaines 2006:79–86).

Nkrumah called his particular version of nonviolent means of social reform "positive action." So when King, who had been in Ghana with A. Philip Randolph, returned to the United States, the two leaders, together with Roy Wilkins, executed their plan to march on Washington, D.C., under the theme "Prayer Pilgrimage for Freedom" (Gaines 2006:82).

In addition to meeting with Nkrumah, King also met with Julius Nyerere of Tanzania, Trinidadian scholar C. L. R. James, and Barbadian poet George Lamming. King at this point had been drawn into a global network of black leaders fighting for social and civil reform on various fronts in the United States, in Africa, and throughout the Caribbean. These meetings also allowed King to fully appreciate the global nature of black peoples struggle for liberty (Gaines 2006:83). As such, nationalism became intertwined with the civil rights struggle in the United States. Nkrumah's relationship with King and other black leaders epitomizes the Pan-African *network* that exists between Africans and the African diaspora and those who continue to see Africa as their original *homeland*.

Nkrumah and King's relationship also goes a long way in challenging long-held views that Africa and Africans were tabula rasa and simply imbued the rhetoric of revolution, liberty, and social justice from external actors, particularly American blacks. Both Pieter Boele van Hensbroek's (1999) recent study and my own (Odamtten 2010) on African nationalism and Pan-Africanism certainly suggest otherwise, pointing instead to active African participation in the modern era through the contestation of ideas in global affairs as early as the 16th and 17th centuries.

Nkrumah and W. E. B. Du Bois (1868–1963) in the Pursuit of Freedom

Another outcome of Nkrumah's stay in America was his recognition of the intellectual and professional skills of African Americans. Following independence in Ghana, Nkrumah invited African American and West Indian nurses, engineers, doctors, and other skilled people to join in building the nascent Ghana. Many Afro-diasporans heeded Nkrumah's call. One such returnee to Ghana was W. E. B. Du Bois, arguably the most celebrated African American intellectual in present memory. Nkrumah invited Du Bois to edit the never completed *Encyclopedia Africana*, which catalogued black intellectual and social achievements.[2] Du Bois was the first black to acquire a degree in history from Harvard University and is also acknowledged as a founder of modern sociology as a discipline in the American academy.

Nkrumah first made Du Bois's acquaintance when they both helped in organizing the 1945 Pan-African Congress in London. Du Bois had been investigated by the Federal Bureau of Investigations (FBI) in 1949 on the suspicion of being a communist and was later refused a passport for travel outside the United States. So in 1961, while socially displaced as a U.S. citizen, Nkrumah offered Du Bois Ghanaian citizenship, which he accepted. When he died on August 27, 1963, he was given a state burial in Ghana. Du Bois's return migration to Ghana and his current heroic status in Ghana and among U.S. intellectuals further demonstrate the links between Ghana and the United States.

Conclusion

The late 19th and 20th centuries were times of great social upheaval as well as reform in the world. Americans and Africans all played important roles in the various movements for social justice. Americans, white and black, faced hard times during the Great Depression. Black Americans and Africans had fought and died in various theaters of war in Europe and Asia during World War II. Their participation in the war served as a prelude to the decolonization movement in Africa and Asia, as well as civil and social reform in the United States and elsewhere.

Various leaders in America and Africa saw themselves as part of a global community of African-descended peoples who were linked by their sociocultural heritage to Africa and by the unequal social conditions they faced in their respective societies. They therefore managed to establish various networks of support and resistance, particularly through the Pan-African movement to engage the conscience of the world about their humanity and right of existence in the world community of peoples. Attucks, Sergeant Adjetey, Nkrumah, King, Father Divine, and Du Bois came from different locations of the globe, yet as Africans and Americans in a global African world, they shared similar experiences of colonial domination and a common pursuit of justice and freedom for people of African descent globally. Collectively, they are an important bridge between Africa and the United States. A critical examination of their interconnections is an important step in fostering knowledge about these relationships.

As the field of African Studies reorients its "intellectual traditions" toward a more global understanding of Africa, "interdisciplinarity, and commitment to social and racial justice" (Ambler 2011:1), it is significant that it chose the career of Edward Wilmot Blyden as its classic paradigm. As a person of diasporan birth and heritage, Blyden's work often focused on the relationship between a diverse Africa and its vast diaspora. This concern for Africa and its diaspora is seen in his publications and the various addresses he gave throughout the African continent, the United States, and the Caribbean. A longtime resident in Liberia, Nigeria, and Sierra Leone, Blyden was careful not to project African diaspora and Western identities on to Africa even as he promoted emigration to Africa by the African diasporans.

Blyden did not project these external identities, because in addition to being a founder of the field of African Studies, he is also the intellectual progenitor of Pan-Africanism and one of the 19th century's most prolific African public intellectuals.[3] Blyden attained this status through his writings about the idea of an African personality. He sought a centering of an indigenous African way of life that was untainted but influenced by the amenable aspects of Western modernity. In other words, Blyden believed that global, external influence on the study and development of the African continent should be harnessed with African-derived ideas and lifeways to nurture the African personality. The field of African studies has therefore come full circle in choosing Blyden as a model for its globalizing project, which will go a long way in fostering the dynamism, complexity, and careful consideration needed in the study and teaching of Africa.

Notes

1. The gloomy characterization of Africa and people of African descent in the United States is particularly worrisome given the staggering evidence of African Americans' contributions to American culture. Systematic investigations of the African past conducted in the multidisciplinary arena of African and African American studies led to the famous debates between Melville J. Herskovits and E. Franklin Frazier and continued in the work of Sydney W. Mintz and Richard Price (1992). More recently, these debates about the agency of Africans as historical actors in a dynamic African past, as well as their role in the making of the African diaspora in the United States, has been reexamined by John K. Thornton (1998). Thornton cogently argues for Africa's significant role in the creation of Atlantic commerce and culture.

2. Inspired by W.E.B. DuBois, Kwame Anthony Appiah and Henry Louis Gates, Jr. (1999) have created the first encyclopedia encompassing the history of Africa and its diaspora.

3. As I argue in my dissertation (Odamtten 2010), Blyden is arguably the foremost intellectual who began a systematic academic articulation of the hitherto sentimental or cultural evocations of Pan-Africanism.

9 The Importance of the Regional Concept

The Case for an Undergraduate Regional Geography Course of Sub-Saharan Africa

Matthew Waller

THE REGIONAL CONCEPT in geography and outside the discipline has been promoted, criticized, or completely abandoned over the past century. Its importance within geography should appear evident, but certain geographic scholars see it as outdated and others see it as simply flawed (Eliot-Hurst 1985; Gilbert 1988; Kimble 1951; Pudup 1988; Schaefer 1953). Outside the discipline of geography, proponents of globalization make similar claims (Friedman 2005; O'Brien 1992; Ohmae 1990). However, when looking at specific world regions such as Africa, these critiques lose their merit. Regional geography has withstood the test of time as evidenced by the popularity of regional courses in higher education (Unwin and Potter 1992; Wei 2006). Geographic training in a course such as the Geography of Sub-Saharan Africa demonstrates that the "region" is not only alive and well but a critical concept for transmitting many crucial geographic concepts and skills (Murphy 2006; Murphy and O'Loughlin 2009; Wade 2006; Wei 2006).

The "Region" in Turmoil

Within the discipline of geography, an epistemological debate has been taking place between regional geographic study and systematic geographic study for the past 100 years (Bradshaw 1990; Gilbert 1988; Hart 1982; Hartshorne 1939; Holmen 1995; Kimble 1951; Paasi 2002; Pudup 1988; Schaefer 1953; Stern 1992). "Regional geography" studies most or all aspects of a particular place, while "systematic geography" studies aspects common to all places (Steinberg et al. 2002; Wade 2006). Critics of the regional approach contend that regionalists are too place-specific; critics of the systematic approach argue that systematic geographers do not put enough emphasis on "place." In higher education, the divide can be linked to course offerings such as the Geography of Sub-Saharan Africa versus a Population Geography course.

Coinciding with the previous division, a second epistemological debate has arisen between regional geography and positivist research within the discipline. Focusing on regional study's supposed lack of theory and its overabundance of description (Guelke 1977; Hart 1982; Pudup 1988; Schaefer 1953), this debate centers on the essential nature and scope of geographic study and research (Gilbert 1988; Kimble 1951; Pudup 1988). Critics of the regional approach contend that this type of geographic study is a passing trend that lacks academic veracity (Stern 1992); critics of positivism contend that positivists "[ignore] the historical roots" (Farmer 1973:365) of geography and argue that the advantages and disadvantages of regional geography concerning methods and goals were present within the discipline well before the quantitative revolution of the 1950s (Wade 2006).

Geography is a basic and indispensable part of human awareness (Murphy 2007) and is relevant to contemporary issues. Without putting America into the world context, students will be unable to adequately make informed decisions about America's future (Merryfield 2005). What better place than the regional geography classroom is there to learn about these aspects of our world and the geographic perspective: "relationships between people and the environment; the importance of spatial variability (the place-dependence of processes); processes operating at multiple and interlocking scales; and the integration of spatial and temporal analysis" (Murphy 2006:10)?

There are reasons why certain regions are different from others politically and economically, and a regional geography that incorporates systematic approaches should be at the forefront of erasing spatial inequalities between regions. Alexander B. Murphy and John O'Loughlin (2009) state that few geographers are filling the voids appearing in foreign-policy making. Despite the rise of area studies in the past half century, justification for the study of the "region" within the discipline of geography remains. First, who better suited than the regional geographer to speak to the public (e.g., policy makers and news media) on a place like China and its emergence as a world economic power (Wei 2006)? Second, if area specialists within the discipline are not being replaced (Chapman 2007; Murphy and O'Loughlin 2009), geography runs the risk of having area specialists being produced who have little geographic training. The only real difference between area studies and regional geography today is approach; the area studies approach is more cultural, linguistic, and political, while the regional geography approach is more spatial, environmental, and scientific (Chapman 2007).

There is justification for the study of the "region" within the discipline of geography even in light of the rise of globalization and global studies. First, geographic phenomena are not equally spread across the globe. Everything happens somewhere, and the "somewhere" matters (Holmen 1995). Second, regions are continually being formed, reformed, and dismantled; the world is a very fragmented place that is still characterized by regional differences (Murphy and O'Loughlin 2009). Anne Gilbert's (1988) three regional concepts still apply: (1) the region as local response to capitalist processes, (2) the region as a focus of identification, and (3) the region as a medium for social interaction. The major fault characterized by proponents of global studies has been their preoccupation with how globalization and the movement of global capital affect the West (Trouillot 2005). To claim that the world is getting smaller and that the world is more interconnected is easy when the person making the claim possesses the resources—and lives in a place that possesses the resources—to take advantage of the interconnectedness. Furthermore, globalization has done little to dethrone the nation-state as the primary seat of governmental power, and the world's economy is not so interlinked that regionalization is not noticed (Wei 2006), despite Thomas L. Friedman's (2005) proclamation that "the world is flat."

Africa as a Region

Regions are social constructions (Dittmer 2006), and *Africa* is no different in this regard. Geographers must address the discursive nature of the region of Africa. This discussion should begin with how Africa has been, and continues to be, defined. For example, regional geography textbooks have a tendency to exclude the North African nations of Morocco, Algeria, Tunisia, Libya, and Egypt (see Map of Regions of Africa) from any discussion of sub-Saharan Africa (Johnson et al. 2010; Marston et al. 2008). This ontological break has cultural and geopolitical implications. Going further into this discussion, educators must address the importance of who controls the definition of *Africa*. It is important that Africans be allowed to define Africa, because taking a region at face value ignores the fact that regions overlap one another and that they are not discrete pieces of data. It also negates dissenting voices and places convenience over the necessity for detailed examination of definitional choices. Doing this also shuts off discussion to the deeper meanings of how these places are defined.

Students and educators should study Africa to clear up misconceptions of the continent (African News Service 1990; Gordon and Wolpe 1998; Martin 1995; G. Myers 2001; Ogundimu 1994) and to dispute the claims made by globalization proponents that all regions are now becoming uniform, an assertion that oversimplifies Africa's political and economic realities. Studying the continent can reveal Africa's complexity and highlight differences from other world regions. They should study Africa in order to reduce the presence of Afro-pessimism (Gordon and Wolpe 1998; G. Myers 2001) in the United States. Studying Africa can expose students to a myriad of African successes. Students and educators should study Africa in order to put it back into history (Wilson 1995).

Students and educators should study Africa to discuss its construction as a region (Dittmer 2006). Within this area of consideration, however, a few concerns need to be addressed. The first concern deals with region building from within Africa. From this vantage point, assessment should be directed at how African societies and individuals act together in the region-development process to determine whether there is any evidence beyond tradition or the uniting circumstances of colonialism and neocolonialism that unifies the continental boundaries as an appropriate or ideal spatial area (Gilbert 1988). People associate themselves with a particular region, and they also differentiate themselves with people from other regions (MacLeod and Jones 2001). It is safe to assume that there is a possibility that Africans do not see "their region" as Western society has perceived it. The second concern deals with region building from outside Africa. From this vantage point, students and educators need to assess how Africa is constructed, who has and has not been able to decide these constructions, and the ramifications of these constructions. The third concern deals with the construction of subregions and regional organizations. Included in this process is the shaping of subregional and organizational consciousness, boundaries, scale, institutionalization, devolution of state powers, and political representation. Because subregions and regional organizations are in a constant state of formation and disintegration, their construction is an "unpredictable, contested, and contingent" (MacLeod and Jones 2001:689) process. Studying Africa as an example of a "region" addresses these questions and allows students to see Africa as more than its bounded space on the map.

Finally, educators and students should study Africa to explore geographic themes. For example, they can probe the analogous characteristics of the southeastern United States and parts of Africa, particularly South Africa, to address land tenure, redistribution, and restitution (Moseley 2005). They can also compare and contrast the effectiveness of dependency theory and modernization theory recommendations for Africa (Robinson 2004; Wilson 1995). They can analyze the effects that African socialism had on national identity and economic development in Tanzania and Senegal. In a course dedicated to the geography of sub-Saharan Africa, students gain a more complete understanding of geographic concepts.

A Course in the Geography of Sub-Saharan Africa

Choosing the most appropriate text for a course in the geography of sub-Saharan Africa is essential. Because geographers have employed textbooks for more than 50 years in their courses, their importance as sources for undergraduate geography is evident (Muller 1995; G. Myers 2001). However, "geography textbooks . . . often represent naturalized narratives of a homology between bounded spaces and national/cultural groups" (Paasi 2002:804). Consequently, the ways in which the course text defines Africa and sub-Saharan Africa are particularly important in class discussions about the construction of regions and stereotypes (Cole 2008). To make a better-informed decision concerning choices of texts, a textual study of several textbooks was conducted with the purpose of examining how Africa and sub-Saharan Africa are defined, based on a similar study by Roy Cole (2008).

Method

The main goal of the textual analysis was to examine how textbook authors define Africa and sub-Saharan Africa and to assess the degree to which they integrate regional and systematic approaches. Following Cole (2008), texts were examined to determine how authors further subdivided their study areas. For each of these endeavors, the authors' rationales for their definitions and subdivisions were sought. Currently, there are only three textbooks available in the United States that are about the geography of sub-Saharan Africa and that have been published since 2000: *Survey of Subsaharan Africa*, by Roy Cole and H. J. de Blij (2007); *Geography of Sub-Saharan Africa*, third edition, edited by Samuel Aryeetey-Attoh (2010); and *Africa South of the Sahara*, second edition, by Robert Stock (2004). Analysis of the Stock text is not included here. Instead, *Global Studies: Africa*, 12th edition, by Thomas Krabacher et al. (2009) was chosen. I was unable to obtain a copy of the Stock text, and Krabacher et al. is geared toward undergraduates in global studies. Of the three texts reviewed, Aryeetey-Attoh presents material in a systematic manner. Krabacher et al. treat their material using a regional approach, and Cole and de Blij offer a mixture of regional and systematic approaches.

The method for analyzing the texts mirrors Cole's (2008). As such, they were assessed based on the following questions: (1) What constitutes "Africa," and what is the rationale for that definition? (2) What unit is used to make the larger region of "Africa," and what is the rationale for using that unit? (3) If the larger region of Africa is subdivided, how is it subdivided, and what is the rationale behind it? (4) What unit is used for the subdivisions, and what is the rationale for using that unit?

Results

Cole and de Blij and Krabacher et al. treat continental and insular Africa as *Africa*, while Aryeetey-Attoh uses the terms *Africa* and *sub-Saharan Africa* synonymously. Krabacher et al. include North Africa in the regions treated and do not mention the term *sub-Saharan Africa* at all. Both sub-Saharan geography texts include the same countries in their definitions of sub-Saharan Africa, excluding only the five countries of North Africa (see Map of Regions of Africa). Cole and de Blij describe sub-Saharan Africa as a "geographic realm" (2007:xvii) with close ties to North Africa, and they connect topics to this subregion where appropriate in the thematic sections of the text. Conversely, Aryeetey-Attoh gives no rationale for defining *Africa* as sub-Saharan Africa and only mentions North Africa once in the entire book. Aryeetey-Attoh and Cole and de Blij use countries as the units for defining the greater region of sub-Saharan Africa. However, only Cole and de Blij give any justification for this choice, describing sub-Saharan Africa as a "conceptual region" (2007:xvii).

All three texts divide the continent into subregions (see Map of Regions of Africa). The names given to these subsections (North Africa, West Africa, Central Africa, East

Africa, and Southern Africa) are consistent among the three as well. For the most part, these subdivisions mirror one another across the texts. Southern Africa is the subregion with the greatest degree of similarity. All three books define it as Angola, Namibia, Zambia, Botswana, South Africa, Lesotho, Swaziland, Zimbabwe, Malawi, and Mozambique—only Cole and de Blij include Madagascar. East Africa has the greatest dissimilarity in terms of how it is defined. Only Uganda, Rwanda, Burundi, Tanzania, and Kenya are common to all three books, although Cole and de Blij include the Horn (Eritrea, Ethiopia, Djibouti, and Somalia) and Sudan as subregions of East Africa. Aryeetey-Attoh fails to include the island nations of São Tomé and Príncipe, Mauritius, the Comoros, and the Seychelles in any subregion. While none of the texts provide a rationale for using countries as the basis for devising subsections, Krabacher et al. and Cole and de Blij give sound justifications for their choices in deciding which countries are included in or excluded from particular groupings. For example, Krabacher et al. point out West Africa's "shared elements of a common history" (2009:203), and Cole and de Blij comment that Central Africa "is dominated physiographically by Africa's greatest river, the Congo" (2007:403). Aryeetey-Attoh (2010) provides no rationale for how his subregions were constructed, and he provides no rationale for using countries as a means of constructing them.

Of the textbooks available, the most impressive was *Survey of Subsaharan Africa*, by Cole and de Blij (2007). Although the book's focus is on places below the Sahara, the authors still link North Africa and sub-Saharan Africa quite well. Additionally, the authors provide considerable information and resources about North Africa, even though it is not a part of their study area. Most importantly, Cole and de Blij provide sound rationale for subdividing the continent and sufficient treatment of overlaps between subregions. For example, in the introduction to the section on East Africa the authors admit, "The countries of the region are internally diverse and straddle cultural as well as environmental transition zones" (Cole and de Blij 2007:449). This text does the best job of representing Africa and of integrating systematic and regional approaches in a regional geography course of sub-Saharan Africa.

Conclusion

Geographic training in a course such as the Geography of Sub-Saharan Africa can prove that the "region" is not only alive and well, but also a critical concept for transmitting many crucial geographic concepts and skills (Murphy 2006; Murphy and O'Loughlin 2009; Wade 2006; Wei 2006). Although the regional approach in geography is not complete without systematic research and although the "region" may be a contested concept, they are both appropriate for geographic pedagogy. As a world region, sub-Saharan Africa is a unique and exciting place. Through a textual analysis, this chapter provides a model of how to approach the study of and conceptualize this region.

10 Teach Me about Africa

Facilitating and Training Educators toward a Socially Just Curriculum

Durene I. Wheeler and Jeanine Ntihirageza

The 2009 CNN awards were held in Ghana, and I welcomed the guests to my place for a dinner. They moved around the city (Accra) and saw beautiful places of Ghana, but the CNN journalists decided to do a story on Ghana's slums, which was saddening because it was as if there were no attractive places or positive developments in the country.

—Chairman Krobo Edusei Jr., Safebond Africa Ltd., executive statement during a seminar on the business climate in Africa (2009)

Introduction

Chairman Edusei (2009) echoes the comments and experiences of the Northeastern Illinois University (NEIU) scholars who began developing the African Summer Institute for Teachers (AFSI) during the fall of 2003. The African and African American faculty at NEIU sought to create an opportunity that would equip educators in K–12 environments with accurate knowledge and skills to explore the topic "Teaching Africa." The scholars who started AFSI were concerned with the misrepresentations and misunderstanding of facts regarding Africa. For instance, some of the in-service and preservice teachers discussed Africa in monolithic terms, or the teachers' frame of reference was only from the colonial-rule perspective, thus presenting incorrect or skewed content to students. Some of these teachers were uncomfortable with teaching about Africa simply because they did not know how. Therefore, a vehicle, AFSI, was created to address this problem.

This chapter discusses the relevancy and practical model of the institute from the perspective of two facilitators and guest lecturers in AFSI. This institute seeks to continue the charge of its founders, taking an active role in developing solutions to the miseducation that continues to be perpetuated about the African continent in the

U.S. school system. Debunking and dispelling misconceptions regarding African history, peoples, religions, languages, and culture has taken priority in these educational endeavors. As instructors at the postsecondary level, fostering critical thinking and critical literacy through a participatory model is a double obligation to instruct both preservice teachers entering into the K–12 field and in-service teachers and administrators currently in the schools. The majority of the student-teachers teach in the Chicago Public Schools (CPS) system, while others work in the surrounding suburbs. Therefore, the task to convey a deeper awareness of diversity, cultural understanding, and global studies is woven into the curriculum approaches and instructional strategies.

Teaching Africa provides a connection to the growing global focus of the U.S. economy and future opportunities for connecting to the growing number of immigrants and refugees from Africa. For example, Alie Kabba et al. (2009) report that the state of Illinois has integrated approximately 180,000 African refugees to date. This chapter, therefore, frames a participatory model that can be utilized to teach about Africa and provides a case example illustrating the model in action so that participants can better understand their global neighbors, both figuratively and literally. The facilitators offer a discussion of how the participatory model can be an effective means for education agents to take advantage of outside resources while maintaining their core values and voice. The goal of this chapter is twofold. First, it presents a model that efficiently prepares teachers to teach about Africa using an informed socially just curriculum. An explicit and thoughtful process of engaging educators is critical when teaching for social justice and participation in the emerging global society. Second, it offers a prescription, the participatory model of educating in teaching about Africa, for engaging teachers to train true agents of change. Ultimately, this chapter offers a concise and practical model to apply in the classroom. The model is informed from the well-developed literature on teacher training, with a focus on critical learning, citizenship, and civil society, all of which have an impact on social justice (Johnston 1999; Mezirow 1996; Welton 1997). It is couched in the context of critical learning theory as an efficient framework for a teacher participatory model.

The African Summer Institute for Teachers (AFSI)

Educators in general, particularly K–12 teachers, have a very important role in changing misconceptions and misinformation about Africa. In 2002, a group of NEIU professors began discussing the limited and inaccurate curriculum on Africa offered in the elementary and secondary schools. Through personal and professional experiences, a select group of African and African American faculty decided to address the limited knowledge base concerning Africa. The first steps were to compare the educational curricula of their own children and informally assess the content of K–12 teachers' graduate classes taught by AFSI faculty. The result of this informal investigation prompted a small group of AFSI faculty from various disciplines—sociology, linguistics, education, political science, and social work—to develop a proposal utilizing the anecdotal conversations and informal assessments of in-service teachers and graduate students concerning the need and feasibility of holding summer institutes on teaching about Africa. The scholars involved in creating the institute queried their students in eight classes, with 20–25 K–12 teachers in each, in an effort to establish interest in the concept of a class or program focusing on the "teaching of Africa." Graduate students (i.e., in-service teachers) were asked the following questions: (1) Do you feel equipped to teach about Africa or any other continent in your subject area? (2) How has your current curriculum prepared you for teaching issues of diversity, multiculturalism, or cross-cultural topics? (3) If NEIU offered a course or workshop with the topic of Africa for inclusion in your subject matter, would you be interested? (4) Would you take this course or workshop? (5) Why or why not? From the 160 responses, it was resoundingly evident that many teachers were enthusiastic to have the opportunity to learn more specifics about the African continent to incorporate into their classrooms.

The results of the queries revealed an urgent need for a program to improve content knowledge and instructional strategies for teaching about Africa. The founding and core faculty of AFSI responded to this need by piloting a regional summer institute for K–12 teachers in the summer of 2003. The basis of the curriculum involved teaching content about Africa and how to use various methodologies toward teaching about Africa. Invited scholars presented on their respective areas of expertise, such as history, geography, education, languages, cultural traditions, religion, and family-kinship relations. Facilitators and guest instructors were given guidelines to create workshops that would give participants what to teach about Africa and how to teach Africa in the classroom setting. Multitudes of talents were involved in the success of the program. Facilitators came from varying backgrounds, as professors, community activists, and outreach coordinators, reflecting the richness of the continent. AFSI faculty (typically the founding cohort and select additional professors and instructors) served as the core in teaching and administration-coordination capacities.

AFSI is exhaustive in its approach to curriculum content regarding Africa. Initially, participants are offered an opportunity to declare expectations and outcomes for attending the institute. The first week's curriculum provides foundational readings and class topical presentations on prehistoric Africa, the geography of Africa, precolonial and colonial Africa, education in Africa, and exchange initiatives in Africa. The remaining two weeks consist of a variety of more specific topics addressing African traditions and cultures. The participants leave the three-week intensive institute with a breadth and depth of knowledge concerning Africa that one cannot find using a single textbook. The effectiveness of the institute is primarily due to the pedagogical approach used to impart content to the teachers: a participatory model.

The participatory model builds on the assumption that teachers already have a wealth of strategies and techniques for information gathering once given the resources. The model is couched in the framework of critical learning theory (Brookfield 2005; Mezirow 1996). In the development of critical learning theory, adult educators have long recognized issues of power and control in civic engagement as well as the promise of positive outcomes when community members are actively involved in decision-making through a process of critical reflection. Through this process, learners develop a dynamic conversation on various issues and solutions while applying them to subject matter.

The teacher participatory model allows for the application of critical learning theory. It works powerfully on two fronts throughout AFSI. On the first day, the teachers are asked to start keeping "their eyes and ears open to African content and pedagogy." Institute participants are instructed to bring related material gathered from their communities and libraries. In a relaxed, open, and inclusive environment, each individual discusses and critiques information set forth by peers. By the second day of the institute, participants start bringing to class material (e.g., books, maps, and games) related to the teaching of Africa, for content or pedagogy awareness. They are encouraged to think, from the beginning, about a topic of interest for a final project. They are, in addition, encouraged to talk about those topics to their peers during the "Guided Discussion—Classroom Techniques/Activities" session. Many end up working in groups on their final project, a model promoted by the institute faculty and staff. In conjunction with the participatory model, at the end of each day, teachers fill out a form on which they reflect on what they have learned, areas of difficulty, and recommendations. This pedagogical model requires constant feedback from staff and faculty. The following day, designated faculty facilitators respond to the participant reflections before starting new topics of the day. Each day, therefore, concurrently involves discussion and decision making about what material can go into the K–12 classroom and the strategies one may employ to teach, integrate, and infuse the acquired content of the day.

Impact of the Institute

AFSI's inaugural class was implemented in the summer of 2004 as a result of a need determined by NEIU faculty. Over seven summers, from 2004 to 2011, excluding the summer of 2008, AFSI has offered an extensive program designed to equip K–12 teachers with a wealth of information about Africa. In-service teachers meet in an intensive four-day, three-week session totaling 45 contact hours. Approximately 20 presenters are invited to share their expertise with participants at the institute, each one presenting for about an hour and a half. Sessions are interspersed with teacher discussions on the content and applicability in their classrooms.

During the three-week AFSI, participants are provided with content on at least two topics daily. For example, on the first day of class, participants play "African Bingo" or "Country Scrabble."[1] Either of these activities may be based on the geography, country names, or natural resources of the continent, allowing participants to begin exploring a working knowledge of Africa in a nonthreatening manner. Additionally, participants may employ the exercise as an icebreaker activity in their own classrooms.

AFSI cohorts are provided with multiple opportunities to develop a toolbox of activities and knowledge to adapt to their subject areas. One language arts teacher utilized her love for children's literature, incorporating what she learned from three different topics and instructors. One participant took the units on education in Africa, the African family structure, and teaching about Africa through literature and developed a final project she titled "African Breakfast." A third-grade teacher of a suburban school adapted what she learned from a number of units to create a four-week language arts unit. The unit created at the institute as her final project drew upon a comprehensive literature to teach about culture, African literature, and African children's experiences, comparing them to American children's experiences. Through developing a working vocabulary for her students and writing prompts, this teacher shared knowledge and dispelled myths. The participant felt that, without her involvement with the rich curriculum and varied instructional methodologies learned from AFSI, she would never have embarked on such an initially intimidating, yet rewarding, task.

This third-grade language arts teacher provides one example of how AFSI equips the teachers to go back to their classrooms with a way to synthesize the materials covered at the institute. Participants are provided with handout materials such as a list of books for varied grade levels that explore the topic of Africa. Through the day's agenda, participants in the institute critically reflect and share differing views and opinions in order to achieve an informed and objective consensus. Topical areas are chosen specifically for the practicality and universal fit in varied grade levels. The unit on language versus dialect allows participants to understand and discuss the differences between languages and dialects. Factual data are presented to help them in their ongoing discussions and in the creation of a unit of their own. For example, participants learn that the continent has more than 2,000 languages and more than 8,000 dialects. The instructors then ask each participant to adopt a language for a week. This unit can be adapted so that students may be assigned a particular country to research or, in the case of younger students, are given a language and words equal to their current vocabulary and developmental stage. For one week, students speak their new language and use their knowledge in the classroom. The benefit to students is learning the power of language and how the development of multiple languages can constitute an asset rather than a hindrance. Students find out that multilingualism is the norm in some places outside the United States. This lesson allows participants to have an appreciation for a more global approach and perspective to knowledge construction and production.

As one can imagine, these types of lessons and the opportunities to dialogue about the implications of the material learned prior to classroom implementation is invaluable. The participatory model allows for feedback and discussion sessions, which lead to the almost instantaneous dissipation of stereotypes and myths. This form of dialogue contributes to potential ideas for the three-week unit's project on a specific topic or subject about Africa that participants are required to produce by the completion of the institute. As mentioned earlier, participants in AFSI produce a culminating experience of topical units that are presented to a wider university audience on the last day. The units serve as models to cohorts for future incorporation of ideas and strategies for curriculum infusion within and beyond an individual's area of expertise, leading to reciprocal feedback at NEIU for both the participants and AFSI faculty.

To explore the impact of the institute, a preliminary evaluation of the program is under way in which past participants are queried in an effort to understand their experiences after completing AFSI. The purpose of this initial exploration involves describing how participation and awareness gained through attending AFSI has influenced the participants personally and professionally as educators. This process is ongoing, and we have not collected substantial data to share the findings. Our goal is to use the data not only to improve the current program, but also to conduct a purposeful investigation on how AFSI content and methodologies complement multicultural education and social justice pedagogy.

Utilizing a Multicultural Education and Social Justice Perspective

Many public school teachers model American society's values and legitimate knowledge. Schools acculturate youth to societal values, norms, and culture. Through standards in curriculum and instruction, what is provided to students is often "the linguistic codes, behavioral expectations, and value systems of the mainstream middle and upper middle classes" (Pai et al. 2006:32). Schools serve society as the conduit for the dominant perspective of what is valued and transmitted in terms of culture and appropriate knowledge to produce good citizens. The dominant perspective narrows the focus in disseminating a singular viewpoint as the only legitimate knowledge or way of knowing. This mind-set has prompted many minorities such as African Americans, Latinos and Latinas, Asian Americans, and Native Americans to seek representation and voice in curriculum and instruction practices regarding what and how subjects are taught. Reclaiming the voice of the "Other," therefore, has become the goal of multicultural education, culturally relevant pedagogy, and social justice education.

Historically, the idea of cultural diversity and multicultural education was first introduced in the early 1970s during a turning point in teacher education programs (King et al. 1997). "The belief that teachers, rather than students, needed 'fixing' also gained currency within the academic community" (King et al. 1997:9). Just as in the early movement for multicultural education, the late 1980s and 1990s brought forth an additional tool for addressing the needs of diverse learners' culturally relevant pedagogy (Delpit 1988, 1995; hooks 1994; King et al. 1997; Ladson-Billings 1994, 1995a, 1995b). Preservice teacher education programs as well as in-service professional development sessions began to include select courses and training opportunities dealing with diversity, multiculturalism, and limited social justice. These concepts emerge as the new buzzwords and practices for today's teaching force. In an effort to hold accountable current and future teachers, educators, and administrators, the National Council for Accreditation of Teacher Education (NCATE) is now including "diversity" as one of the six standards for teacher preparation programs. According to NCATE, the rationale for the diversity standard is as follows:

America's classrooms are becoming increasingly diverse; over 40 percent of the students in P–12 classrooms are students of color. Twenty percent of the students have at least one foreign-born parent, many with native languages other than English and from diverse religious and cultural backgrounds. Growing numbers of students are classified as having disabilities. At the same time, teachers of color are less than 20 percent of the teaching force. As a result, most students do not have the opportunity to benefit from a diverse teaching force. Therefore, all teacher candidates must develop proficiencies for working effectively with students and families from diverse populations and with exceptionalities to ensure that all students learn. Regardless of whether they live in areas with great diversity, candidates must develop knowledge of diversity in the United States and the world, professional dispositions that respect and value differences, and skills for working with diverse populations. (2008:36)

Educators and school staff have an obligation to meet the varied learning and cultural needs of today's students and parents. The NCATE rationale sets up a formal venue to ensure the development of multicultural and social justice issues in educational training.

All too often, however, colleges of education use the additive approach to diversity rather than an infusion approach. James Banks (2008) defines the "additive approach" as teaching about gender, race, culture, language, and religion as a single phenomenon: for example, celebrating women only in March because it is designated as Women's History Month. In contrast, the "infusion approach" views teaching about the "Other" as a conscious effort to include these dynamic alternative perspectives in every lesson as opposed to isolating them or adding them in. Multicultural education addresses five pertinent issues: (1) content integration, (2) knowledge production, (3) prejudice reduction, (4) equity pedagogy, and (5) empowering school culture and social structure (Banks 2006, 2008). At the institute, we concentrate our approach in the areas of knowledge production and prejudice reduction. Africa has been discussed in terms of myths and miseducation. AFSI provides in-service teachers with the tools and facts to confidently address the topic of Africa from varied curricula approaches. Not only does AFSI curriculum dispel myths and miseducation regarding African people, geography, traditions, languages, and societal roles, but it also provides participants with opportunities to explore many more topics that allow them to view the rich and wide-ranging facts of the continent. The institute provides a model for debunking issues of oppression, power, ignorance, and equity.

Through the in-depth curriculum of AFSI, in-service teachers gain the tools to aid in helping their students decrease prejudice and ignorance about Africa. Banks (2008) describes knowledge production in terms of how each individual understands and investigates knowing. Knowledge production reveals how the characteristics of the knower influence his or her frame of reference for gender, race, class, or culture and how these affect the consumption and production of knowledge. The lens of social justice education enables an understanding of how difference, oppression, and social power dynamics and social inequality affect society (Adams et al. 2007). Utilizing aspects of multicultural education and components of social justice education, AFSI explains and equips in-service teachers with an enlightened and accurate perspective on Africa.

Implications and Future Course of Action

Colleges of education are obligated to prepare educators to work in any environment. In fall 2008, NCATE revised standards, requiring that special attention be paid to the changing classrooms across the nation. In this regard, AFSI was designed to accomplish two main objectives: (1) to provide teachers with the interdisciplinary content required to teach about Africa in an accurate and objective manner and (2) to assist teachers in developing primary and supplementary resources for classroom use. Additionally, this institute introduces teachers and other participants to the rich heritage of African culture, music, and arts while providing participants the opportunity to discuss the continent's geography, precolonial and colonial history, oral and written history, languages and ethnicity, family systems, and political and democratic systems. Participants in AFSI delimit their scope of study through a final project for the sake of depth and analysis. Attempting to cover too much would jeopardize the impact to both participants and instructors. While cohorts are exposed to a wealth of information, it is best to make the knowledge fit their area of expertise through careful planning and dialogue. Participants in the institute can approach the subject of Africa with an understanding and passion that they would not have without attending AFSI. A socially just approach to teaching about Africa challenges in-service teachers to look beyond the media stories of poverty, civil war, and helplessness and see the wealth, justice, and happiness found throughout the continent. An explicit and thoughtful process of training and engagement is critical. Teaching about Africa allows teachers to engage in change. AFSI is a model that equips teachers to approach the subject of Africa no matter their discipline or training. The success of the African Summer Institute for Teachers is achieved through the delivery of meaningful and relevant content through a pedagogically sound approach, the participatory model in teacher training for social justice.

Notes

We would like to express our gratitude to the founding and core faculty, Dr. Wamucii Njogu, Dr. Job Ngwe, Dr. Barbara Scott, and Dr. Selina Mushi, for their contributions to the structure and content of the 2003–2010 African Summer Institute at Northeastern Illinois University. We are also indebted to Dr. Jeremy Liebowitz (2002–2003) for his early contribution to the institute.

1. The Teacher's Corner, http://www.theteacherscorner.net/printable-worksheets/make-your-own/word-scramble/word-scramble.php.

PART II

AFRICAN ARTS

Interpreting the African "Text"

As advocated throughout the first part of *Teaching Africa*, establishing a context for learning about Africa builds a necessary base, without which, the subsequent knowledge structure would crumble. The second leg of the pedagogical journey, "feeling/heart," is about pushing beyond acquiring knowledge. In terms of scientific inquiry, observations and descriptions should now start to give way to more interpretive initiatives. In Part II, "African Arts: Interpreting the African 'Text,'" the reader is encouraged to think critically about what he or she has learned thus far, challenging the "facts" when necessary, encouraged by the provisioning of both an emic or insider's worldview and, at other times, an etic or outsider's expert testimony about what is going on in particular circumstances throughout the next six chapters.

With luggage and ticket in hand, the students board their long flight to the continent. Throughout, they are free to consider what is to come. Maybe they have been there before and daydream about remembered tastes and smells. Maybe they have contacted and interviewed a diasporan, read a novel, or taken an Afrocentric course. The learning on this second leg of the journey is more personal, although it still benefits from facilitation by learned experts.

In this section, the reader is invited both to explore the authors' experiences and approaches and to bring these into his or her own classrooms and pedagogical endeavors. These dialogic and sensual techniques are focused more on specific African cases and contexts to further develop a depth of understanding about a variety of topics and teaching styles, including (1) oral narratives (Chapter 14); (2) violence and conflict management (Chapter 15); (3) African music and literature (Chapters 11, 12, and 13); (3) simulations (Chapter 16); and (4) inversions and comparisons (Chapters 11 and 12).

Parts I and II expose the reader to the disciplines of African studies, anthropology, conflict management, education, English, foreign languages, geography, history, literature, music, and political ecology. This interdisciplinary and geographic breadth in conjunction with experiential learning allows for a more comprehensive and relevant treatment of Africa in any classroom.

11 Inversion Rituals

The African Novel in the Global North

Catherine Kroll

> If narratives can bloom again, if languages, words, and stories can circulate again, if
> people can learn to identify with characters from beyond their borders, it will assur-
> edly be a first step toward peace. . . . Instead of the "we" so proudly trumpeted, the
> "we" flexing its muscles, puffing up its pectorals, it is another "we," diffracted, inter-
> active, translated, a waiting, listening "we"—in short a dialoguing "we" will be born.

—Abdourahman A. Waberi, *In the United States of Africa* (2009)

Introduction

I draw the chapter title from the Zulu inversion rituals of the 1930s, in which women
during times of seasonal dearth assumed male roles: seizing the power to suppress men,
to dress like them, and to take over their herding responsibilities (Gluckmann 1935).
The modern African novel itself functions as a kind of inversion ritual: it provokes a
radical, mind-shifting experience for Western readers. African novelists counter the
West's centuries-old depiction of their societies as "archaic," "timeless," riven by ethnic strife, and cursed by an inhospitable environment. Scholars and teachers working
in African studies have an obligation to contest the cultural and political positioning
of African peoples within such a framework of alterity and to open up an equitable,
transcultural dialogue that reveals African thinking about African identities.[1]

African literature courses such as the one discussed below challenge students to
develop their severely limited background knowledge about African peoples by entering into this transcultural dialogue. Students learn to engage with a moment in literary
studies where many African-born scholars are focusing on rewriting the history of the
roughly 80-year colonial encounter in order to reveal a more nuanced understanding of the contributions of Africans themselves to an earlier nationalist enterprise. As
Kwaku Larbi Korang argues, one central concern of African literary studies must be
with "how Africa answers to the constraints of modernity, and how African writers
carve out a place in the house that was not commodious to African literature" (2010). It

is this upending of the Euro-American claim to an exclusive ownership of modernity that awaits our students, the opportunity to experience an inversion ritual as African novelists and scholars themselves lead the way toward new historical accounts that reshape the West's familiar narrative of colonizers and abject victims. Such a project discloses an African modernity that was already under development before the colonial powers imposed their administrative structures, their educational institutions, and their resource expropriation programs (Attwell 2005; Korang 2004; Táíwò 2009). In the spirit of these inversion rituals, the present chapter sets forth some practical pedagogical strategies to make this reframing of African histories vividly real.

The benefits to students who study African literature are many: an awakening of curiosity about formerly ignored or suppressed histories, an expanded global knowledge base, and a widening of their subjectivity. In reading the work of contemporary Nigerian novelists, for example, students come to revise their assumptions about African women being subordinated within patriarchal societies and to replace these images with stories of African women working as entrepreneurs, politicians, playwrights, novelists, and academics. Likewise, instead of conceiving of history as a seamless, linear unfolding, students learn to think of the past in terms of "multihistories": intersecting narratives inflected by the ideological perspectives of an entire range of storytellers. Students learn about Africans' efforts to work toward self-governance within the frameworks inherited from the former colonial powers. And they come to understand the salience of the Akan concept of *sankofa*, the past providing inspiration for the present and future.

The central pedagogical challenge in teaching university students in the global North about Africa is to represent its literature, culture, and history as processual, fluid, and changing. This chapter demonstrates how to facilitate this shift—or intellectual migration—for students by using selected paradigms, questioning protocols, and experiential strategies from ancillary disciplines. Rather than relying solely upon the methodologies of literary and cultural studies in general education literature courses, this approach enhances the impact of teaching by drawing from critical thinking tools and principles embedded in fields such as history, economics, political science, and visual studies. Certainly, literary works offer expressive experiences that capture ambiguity and complexity in ways that only the arts can, but, in general education courses, a pedagogy that draws from a variety of disciplinary perspectives will reach more students than one that focuses exclusively on textual analysis. A multidisciplinary approach enables students from a wide range of academic majors to engage with the literature.

Pedagogical Position

Within the past 30 years, there has been a revolution both in the methods of academic inquiry and in the content knowledge about African societies. As is well known, the discipline of anthropology has subjected itself to a thoroughgoing self-critique, and thus its earlier positivist methods of cataloguing the cultural norms of "other" societies have been replaced by more dynamic analyses that investigate autochthonous epistemologies and cultural practices, as well as the role of the viewer's own situated understanding in producing knowledge (Geertz 1977). Social scientists, historians, and cultural studies theorists have all become much more circumspect and self-interrogating as they conceptualize their subjects of study. Their methodological assumptions have evolved from single-hypothesis theories to an awareness of individuals and societies as not just being acted upon, but acting with initiative, appropriation, and often subversion. As a result of Michel Foucault's works on the dynamics of power within social and intellectual discursive systems, it is now commonplace to theorize historical change and political phenomena as multidirectional and mutually informing.[2] In addition, recent works also reveal a wide range of interpretive methodologies: from attending to prophecy as a form of knowledge structuring the social and political imaginary to uncovering literacy practices embedded in the popular culture of everyday life.[3]

With these scholarly directions in mind, this chapter's pedagogical aim is to represent Nigeria, South Africa, and Cameroon as amalgamations of ethnic groups and as countries distinguished by long histories of creative, hybridic modes of cultural expression. The initial classroom discussions thus include, for example, the topic of African Christianity as syncretic, broadly informed by traditional African spiritual practices, as well as a close-up view of contemporary African life in both rural and urban settings. Short videos I made on an extended stay in South Africa in 2004, as well as photographs and music acquired from a trip to Ghana in 2006, provide visual and acoustic realia to make these introductory discussions multimodal and relevant to readings such as Chimamanda Ngozi Adichie's *Half of a Yellow Sun* (2006), Zakes Mda's *Ways of Dying* (1995), and Patrice Nganang's *Dog Days* (2006).

Chimamanda Ngozi Adichie's *Half of a Yellow Sun*

A basic knowledge of African history is essential to understanding the region today, but too often what knowledge students do possess stops with the transatlantic slave trade. In order to help them appreciate Africa's contemporary relevance to the United States and the world, I briefly examine new relationships and alliances born of globalization. China's sizable investment in Nigeria has already shifted the geopolitical balance, with China becoming a major importer of the country's oil. Nigeria, however, remains the United States' fifth-largest supplier of crude oil. I bring up these facts not to make a specific political statement in the classroom, but to illustrate the ways in which African nations and the United States remain inextricably connected and to demonstrate the continent's new global positioning between East and West.

In past semesters, I have concluded this introductory discussion with a range of activities, including screening clips from *Back to Africa* (Taylor 1993). I also show students Chimamanda Ngozi Adichie's speech "The Danger of a Single Story" (2009) in order to introduce Adichie's multivocal novel on the Nigeria-Biafra war, *Half of a Yellow Sun* (2006). Adichie's central point—that all of us need to hear multiple stories to be able to formulate accurate perspectives about one another—in fact becomes something that students reference repeatedly in discussions and in their own writing on *Half of a Yellow Sun*. Students often point out how a single character's assessment of a situation is insufficient, especially when that perspective is uttered as definitive. Coming to think in terms of competing perspectives—rather than a single plotline or linear history—helps students not only read the novel, but also conceptualize how to write about it. For students unskilled in literary analysis, the idea of a multiform framework allows them to feel more at ease with Adichie's story-within-a-story structure and her alternating narrative points of view.

Adichie performs her own inversion ritual by leveraging autochthonous perspectives against dominant versions of Nigerian history that suppress the entanglements of human relationships. Beginning the course with Adichie's novel proves to be the best possible choice precisely because of her recasting of the "official" account of the Nigeria-Biafra war. With a little assistance, students then link the inversion ritual of her novel to the course introduction on myths and realities of Africa and to the larger reshaping of intellectual and material history in African studies as a whole.

As a way of helping students make connections between the course literature and their own lives, I ask them during the discussion of *Half of a Yellow Sun* to think about the ways that "Africa" is positioned in our media and advertising. I explain a bit further: as we see from numerous "Red" campaigns launched by Starbucks, Apple, and other corporations, Africa as a whole is depicted as being in need of American charity. For example, when a consumer purchases a "Red" iPod, Apple makes a donation to an African charity on the buyer's behalf.

I suggest to the class that our assumptions about spending and global flows of wealth need to be reevaluated. Oil is extracted from West and East Africa, yet much of the profit that should filter back to local Africans themselves either ends up in federal governments controlled by African elites or travels abroad in the form of corporate profits, dividends, wages, and salaries. What we're talking about here is an inequitable flow of global capital and wealth. The problem of poverty is much more complicated to address than we are made to believe.

Subsequently, the discussion returns to *Half of a Yellow Sun* in order to examine further linkages between the United States and Nigeria. We discuss why Olanna's friend Edna, an American living in Igboland, would have been inspired by the American civil rights movement (and perhaps by Marcus Garvey's earlier "Back to Africa" campaign) to come to Africa in the 1960s. The friendship between Olanna and Edna—women from two different worlds who nonetheless find common ground—is refracted in numerous other chance relationships in the novel. Adichie shows individuals from different classes, ethnicities, and religions forging durable friendships throughout the novel, and, indeed, this fusion of varying perspectives defines the novel's formal structure and shifting centers of authority. Richard, a British writer who has come to Nigeria to study Igbo-Ukwu art and who falls in love with Olanna's twin sister, Kainene, relinquishes his "automatic" sense of entitlement to write about Nigeria. By the end of the novel, one of the most socially powerless characters, the young houseboy Ogwu, has taken over the authority and responsibility to write the history of the war, effecting, through his gain in self-confidence and understanding of his destiny, an inversion ritual of his own.

Half of a Yellow Sun, while a lengthy novel, keeps students riveted. Adichie skillfully interweaves stories of intimate relationships between the characters with stories of the Nigeria-Biafra war and its historical causes. The circumstances that unfold on both narrative levels show challenges to the human limits of endurance and our capacity for forgiveness. Because many of Adichie's main characters are drawn from the Nigerian upper class, the novel inverts common preconceptions about the socioeconomic profile of the country. Students ask sharp questions about the text. For example, one student perceptively observed: "Out of all the possible books, why did Adichie choose the *Narrative of the Life of Frederick Douglass* [1995(1845)] for Ogwu to read in his downtime as a soldier? Adichie seemed to want to show that Ogwu was searching for inspiration in Douglass's autobiography and that, for both men, writing was central to their identity." Such a subtle insight speaks to the evocative power and immediate relevance of Adichie's novel.

From start to finish, our work with *Half of a Yellow Sun* is strongly informed by discussions of pivotal historical eras that Adichie herself references throughout the novel. Adichie's story of the years of the war, while drawing on existing scholarly histories, challenges more traditional accounts of the conflict by presenting a narrative with all of the psychological ambivalence and competing personal affiliations that more macro-level histories tend to avoid.[4]

To bring Nigerian history closer to students, I vividly illustrate some of the ways this conflict was reported in the West, particularly by *Life* magazine, which used a portrait of two starving children from the Nigeria-Biafra war as the cover image for its July 12, 1968 edition. If students were to see these historical cover images on magazines at their local store today, what kinds of questions would arise in their minds? Students' reactions to the *Life* cover photographs center primarily on their own sympathy for the children. Students do not readily make connections between the textual medium they are studying and the visual images projected before them. As long as the media industry publishes images with scant context, our reactions will likely continue to be canalized along only certain preselected pathways—a result that impedes the formulation of critical questions.

At various junctures throughout the term, I make a point of reminding students of the skills they are acquiring in their analysis of each novel. Since they are responsible for producing two thesis-driven essays (as well as two midterm essays) for the course, I model how to generate analytical thesis statements. I create quite explicit lists on the board as reminders of the analytical tools students possess for engaging with the literature. By the time we finish reading *Half of a Yellow Sun*, this list includes the following skill bank and resources: (1) historical background to modern Nigeria; (2) close reading skills to examine narrative time, tropes, image patterns, tone, and counterpoints in the work; (3) Adichie's framework of political critique; (4) Adichie's speeches; (5) biographical information on the author; (6) a simplified hermeneutics: moving from part to whole, whole to part, and then repeating the circle as students read; and (7) a heuristic for thesis generation—"Adichie uses (or does) X in order to show Y"—which helps students from majors outside the humanities understand one of the basic goals of literary interpretation, as well as how to formulate rhetorically strong thesis statements.

Another course design element is a brief presentation project in which students draw from their disciplinary expertise in order to illuminate an aspect of the day's reading and then to launch the discussion for the day. While this project is actually a relatively minor assignment, students devote themselves to creating polished multimedia presentations. This work strengthens their familiarity with key issues raised in the novelists' work and provokes a greater sense of ownership of the texts, since students are able to connect them to their own disciplinary interests.

Zakes Mda's *Ways of Dying*

Next, I choose to explore Zakes Mda's *Ways of Dying* (1995) because of the ways that Mda's ethical and aesthetic vision grows out of the tumult of South Africa's new multiracial democracy coming to birth. Mda does not modulate the violence of the 1990 to 1994 transition period when the African National Congress (ANC) was unbanned, Nelson Mandela was released from prison, and the Inkatha Freedom Party (IFP) and the ANC battled for political ascendancy. Mda's vision in this novel makes possible an interrogation of issues of personal ethics, individual resolve, and the deepest existential inquiry. The novel opens up discussion of the chaos that erupts when African societies (like all societies) pass through the crucible of violence in the formation of new states.

In addition to teaching students about the shaping events and shifting political forces in 19th- and 20th-century South African history, I present pathways into Mda's novel from an economic perspective. Apartheid both invites comparison with the United States' own violent history of segregation and bears a number of salient differences, including the forced removal of nonwhite South Africans from the period of the 1950s through the early 1980s. Outlining the historical development of capitalism in South Africa, I explain the country's contested land politics, its history of labor segregation in mining and agriculture, the growth of trade unions, and the country's present-day economic challenges. Because stark economic stratification has defined the daily realities of life in South Africa, and because much of the plot of *Ways of Dying* unfolds in an informal settlement, I introduce students to the concept of the Gini coefficient, which measures economic inequality within and across societies.[5] For example, European citizens' income (sometimes represented as economic well-being) tends to be clustered in the middle, with the majority of individuals possessing wealth at about the same rate as that of their neighbors. The greater the wealth disparity in a country, the closer the Gini coefficient is to one. As of this writing, the United States' Gini coefficient is 0.41 and rising; South Africa's is 0.58, one of the highest in the world (African Studies Center 2009).

I explain to my students that the Gini coefficient is a good indicator of economic justice and social progress by stating, "By learning about the Gini coefficient, we're learning one new conceptual tool that we can use alongside of other tools of analysis. This is not the sole metric by which a country and its people are judged, but it is one piece of information to consider in your understanding of a work's context and to use in making sense of the flow of capital and economic opportunity within a country and globally." This day's discussion provides another moment where students examine the usefulness of multiple points of view or "multihistories," a framework embraced by theorists from Jean-François Bayart (2009) to Achille Mbembe (2002a:258). The more variety of analytical tools and entry points for a given text, the better students will ultimately be able to engage with the reading on their terms.

To expand the discussion on *Ways of Dying*, I also equip students with a basic understanding of the African oral tradition that informs Mda's novel. The narrator is a "we" who speaks for the entire community: "No individual owns any story. The community is the owner of the story, and it can tell it the way it deems it fit" (Mda 1995:12). Oral storytelling is defined by a number of characteristics that mark it as decidedly different from textual narratives. For example, characters are revealed through action, rather than through lengthy narrative descriptions of them. A fast-paced narrative, formulaic sayings, proverbs, stories within stories, culturally instructive digressions, repeated motifs, and statements calculated to arouse audience reaction are also prominent elements of the African oral tradition (Chinweizu and Madubuike 1983:35–38; Okpewho 1992:70–104).

Ways of Dying recounts the story of Toloki, a professional mourner, and Noria, a mother who has lost her young son to the political violence. Mda's narrative of community and personal loss, newfound love, and revitalized wisdom challenges Western readers with new epistemologies. In this novel, readers experience the "we" of collective storytelling, the "we" of collective vision, and its antithesis: the bourgeois individualism of Nefolovhodwe, a businessman who profits off of death through the sale of his coffins. At the same time, the text challenges students to understand the long- and short-term historical dimensions of the violence during the transition period: the IFP's roots in Zulu nationalism and the South African police force's alleged clandestine alliance with the IFP, which further fueled the violence during the transition to black majority rule (Giliomee and Mbenga 2007:397–399). It requires skill on the part of the instructor to keep all of the novel's perspectives actively present so that students do not retreat into explanations that ascribe the era's violence to essentialized attributes of South Africans themselves.

Like Adichie's *Half of a Yellow Sun*, Mda's novel thematizes the necessity of hearing multiple stories on an event or period, for the chaos and killings of the violent transition period of 1990 to 1994 are by no means the only issues Mda is concerned with in the text. Far more to the point is Mda's demonstration of the moral courage necessary to rebuild individual lives as well as a country that had come to the brink of civil war. A number of students compare Mda's narration to that of Adichie's multi-perspective storytelling in the discussion; they realize that this novel is as much about ways of living as it is about ways of dying. Mda's emphasis on the power of artistic expression to temper poverty and loss motivates a number of students to write on this novel. From Toloki's self-styled persona—with quirky costume and eccentric diet—to the magical realism in the text, students celebrate Toloki and Noria's drive to rebuild their lives from the ground up while also devoting themselves to their community's needs. The students point out that it is these characters' community consciousness that makes possible healing, a reoriented purpose, and a reclaimed personal dignity.

Many of the essays students produce on Mda's *Ways of Dying* center on the undaunted, joyous act of artistic expression in the midst of the terrors of the transition period, during which major political groups struggled for control. In addition to their arguments exalting the force of (South) African character exemplified in Toloki, the students try to think their way through Mda's perspective on the stunning ambiguities of death-in-life (killing "justified" by political exigencies) and life-in-death (Toloki's occupation as a professional mourner). In this sense, students reveal the ways that the novel works on them as an inversion ritual: asking them, for at least the time being, to reposition their normative Western value system of material progress, personal achievement, and social status and to consider alternative measures of meaning: community well-being, social responsibility, and a decidedly modest contentment with one's given life circumstances.

Patrice Nganang's *Dog Days*

If students eagerly embrace the existential inquiry generated by Mda's novel, they generally have trouble with the more complex formal structure of Patrice Nganang's *Dog Days* (2006). This text, like *Ways of Dying*, narrates a struggle during a political transition period: in this case, Cameroon's unsuccessful effort to unseat the government of Paul Biya and to build a democracy in the early 1990s.

Nganang's *Dog Days* is a postmodern, cross-genre work that draws its compelling force from Günter Grass's *Hundejahre* (*Dog Years*) (1963), political allegory, serious social commentary, and the inventive power of *radio trottoir* ("pavement radio," or gossip). Nganang has said that one of his aims in *Dog Days* was to capture the subversive power of speech circulating in the streets and public spaces of Cameroon (Tervonen 2001). The novel articulates competing multinarratives of political liberation and personal scamming in the face of European master narratives of "progress" and "civilization" (Kroll 2010). As postindependence Cameroon continues to labor under the sphere of French political influence, and even the Marxist revolutionary narrative has not delivered the promised liberation, Cameroon's citizens continue nonetheless to demand a democratic government. Nganang's tale, told through the eyes of the dog Mboudjak, recounts the lives of the undaunted activists, dedicated mothers, and industrious market vendors who

struggle to make their voices heard in a society that, as a whole, is beleaguered by political hopelessness and foreshortened aspirations. In Nganang's work, stories of resignation
and courage unfold simultaneously, yielding a playfully hybridic novel that allows for
a variety of tonal effects that capture the ambiguity of a moment of political potential.

Nganang's transnational perspective, borne of his graduate education in Germany
and his teaching career in the United States, positions him to read Cameroon's politics not
just through Cameroonian eyes but also through German and American eyes. His ability
to expose the hypocrisy of French "interest" in its former West African colony, as well as
the irony of violent, authoritarian governance based on the colonial example, points to
political realities that unsettle students' commonly received notions about West Africa.
Nganang's perspective reflects both a comprehensive authority and an authenticity that are
unlike anything most students have ever encountered. In a narrative voice at once urbane
and mischievously satirical, Nganang thus inverts the long-standing portraits of Africans
as powerless victims locked in the rhythms of a timeless, "traditional" lifestyle.

To gain an introduction to contemporary Cameroon, the class experiments
with a web search project on Cameroonian politics and sports. The class views web
pages devoted to countering rumors of Biya's excessive personal spending, explaining
teacher demonstrations in Cameroon, predicting Cameroon's national soccer team's
prospects for the *Fédération Internationale de Football Association* (FIFA) World Cup
in 2010, critiquing the Biya cult of personality, and demanding freedom of the press.
The students are asked to work in groups to glean as much background information on
the country as possible from these web pages. Since students' first research direction is
usually the web, this schema is a natural fit. This activity calls upon students to work
with up-to-the-minute sources, and it functions well as an experiential, spontaneous
introduction to everyday life in Cameroon.

During the same class meeting, I screen approximately half of Jean-Marie Téno's
Afrique, je te plumerai (*Africa, I Will Fleece You*; 1992). This film is an essential resource
for teaching Nganang's novel because it shows vividly Cameroonian citizens' attempts to
throw off the oligarchy headed by Paul Biya, as well as the government's repression of all
opposition groups. Viewing the film prior to studying the novel provides students with an
historical context for Cameroonians' struggle for autonomy. I summarize Frantz Fanon's
well-known prediction in *The Wretched of the Earth* (1963) that African independence will
yield nothing more than a duplication of colonial rule unless its leaders can be drawn from
"the upward thrust of the people" (164). Drawing information from a variety of sources
allows us to link the prescience of Fanon's predictions about postindependence Africa, the
reality of African power systems (armed forces and former colonial powers such as France
keeping leaders in power), and the nepotistic pathways to political leadership.

Dog Days is most productively taught alongside Nganang's literary manifesto *Le
Principe dissident* (*The Principle of Dissidence*; 2005). Nganang contextualizes his literary
goals as well as his intellectual debt to 20th-century novelists from Germany, France, and
the African continent. Nganang (2005:15, 44) identifies with the German authors who, after

the Nazi death camps were discovered in 1944 near the end of World War II, summoned the courage to write, and he asserts his solidarity with market vendors and other workers who keep Cameroon together, even under a demoralizing regime. *Le Principe dissident* describes the power of the act of reading to join author and reader: "Through his texts, the writer finds in his readers, as the readers in the writer, a soul sister, and so participates, from book to reader, from reader to neighbor, from neighbor to stranger, from stranger to stranger, in a space of possibilities, in the multiplication of invisible intimacies, in a greater fraternity that could only be that of people like him who are writing" (Nganang 2005:47; translation mine). Certainly, this irrepressible circulation of texts among our students and the building of a community of readers is what we hope for. This introductory class on *Dog Days* continues with my reading aloud of excerpts from *Le Principe dissident* and briefly translating from the French. Lastly, I hand around copies of cartoons lampooning Paul Biya, which had appeared in the Cameroonian weekly *Le Messager*.⁶

Challenges do arise in our discussion of *Dog Days*. Many students note that they have difficulty with the novel's tonal variations and rollicking shifts of scene. A number are reluctant to see the street life, male bravado, and meandering, incessant *kongossa* (gossip) as anything but self-incriminating for the men of Yaoundé. Some students either cannot or will not conceptualize the self-invention and cultural performance that is Cameroonian street life, charging, instead, that the men are "wasting time when they could have been working or doing something productive." This sentiment aligns with distinctively American meritocratic arguments and, needless to say, leaves little room for other explanations, such as Cameroon's systemic unemployment and underemployment, due in part to the president's extraction of the country's domestic resources into his personal Swiss bank accounts.

Despite this less than receptive reaction to the male characters in the novel, students do seem to grasp Nganang's neocolonial critique, in which he lambastes France's continued intrusion in Cameroon's affairs and parodies Cameroonians who fashion themselves according to French cultural norms. He also takes aim at doctrinaire Marxists in the novel: ideologues spouting effete narratives of supposed liberation. Students are attuned to the ways the novel presents the brutality of power and the fragility of life in the scenes where Mboudjak, the canine narrator, is hung in a tree and left for dead and where Nganang pays tribute to Eric Takou, the young teen who was killed during a political demonstration in Yaoundé. Students recognize the determination of "activists" such as Mboudjak and the Crow (Nganang's avatar in the novel) to stand up to power. They laugh at Mboudjak's piercingly ironic comments throughout the novel, in which he demonstrates a relentless subaltern courage to invert the power structure in which he lives. When Mboudjak reveals that his "master," Massa Yo, refers to him as "the outstretched hand," Mboudjak wittily suggests, "But doesn't it suggest that I have a hand of my own?" (Nganang 2006:8).

Although the men in the novel struggle with the quotidian realities of finding work, female companionship, and entertainment to pass the time, the narrative's more compelling concern is its resolute demand for change from the Biya regime. Nganang stands shoulder to shoulder with the courageous market hawkers, mothers, and all those who are trying to work against dispiriting odds to construct a new political narrative of defiance. In locating the "magic" potency of the Crow's poetic words, in seeing "The neighborhoods [as] the forge of mankind's creativity" (2006:82), and in the truth-telling, admonitory barks of the lowliest "dog," Nganang creates a text that serves as a ritual object capable of providing courage and sustenance to the one who wields it. He insists that if the country had come so close to democracy at the beginning of the 1990s, this goal must still be within reach.

Discussion of Outcomes

Contemporary African novelists engage in ideological inversion rituals in defense of their political and cultural perspectives, which are often profoundly anticolonial, anti-imperialist, and antimaterialist. Their works denounce domestic corruption in their own countries just as much as they counter the West's arrogant gesture of having situated their societies in "the past" or in "an earlier stage of development." As we read and teach African literary works, we find that traditional African value systems and personal identities—centered on social relationships and networks—often come into collision with American ideologies of personal success (although this generalization itself is deceptive, as one can certainly point to the influence of Western cultural values upon African societies, as well as autochthonous cultural practices intended to ensure an individual's professional success). Students are decidedly relieved to find that there are factual and literary multinarratives that offer them ways of reconceptualizing their received notions about African societies. Reading works by contemporary African novelists puts them in the position of learners listening receptively to these cultural authorities: a position of radical openness to the affective dimensions of learning.

How do I know that the teaching, discussions, and activities are successful? Occasionally, I receive some glimpses of the impact of the course on students. At the end of our discussion of *Half of a Yellow Sun* in February 2010, news agencies reported that a Christian group had set upon members of a Muslim neighborhood in Jos, in Plateau State, Nigeria. A student e-mailed me a link to CNN's reports on the story, and I devoted time in class to a discussion of the event and the differences in coverage and angles between CNN, the *New York Times*, and videos made by nongovernmental organizations in Nigeria. I directed students to the videos I had posted on the course website. It is in such spontaneous exchanges of texts, materials, and ideas that teachers can come to know their students and in which students, themselves engaged in the transfer of knowledge, can be proud of their intellectual independence and development.

With so much multimedia and realia available for circulation, our pedagogy can continue to become much more dynamic, our classrooms more "flat," and learning thoroughly ubiquitous. Whether we bring in Ghanaian highlife tunes, video excerpts of Johannesburg street dancers and mimes, websites on Cameroonian news, or kola nuts, all of these tangible media form appealing entry points into African fiction, for they connect on-the-ground, contemporary African realities to students' immediate worlds.

Using a multidisciplinary pedagogy to teach African novels contextualizes the works and energizes class discussions. It affords us the opportunity to teach critical awareness of Western media by exposing the link between commercial and political imperatives and the creation and dissemination of information about cultures. In our classroom discussions, students question who stands to gain from retaining a fixed cultural, political, and economic hierarchy in a globalized world. As students themselves come to see in reading African texts, such existing power hierarchies and assumptions about Western superiority need to be seen for what they are: assumptions.

In the field of African cultural studies itself, African novels—apart from African aesthetic, epistemological, and rhetorical qualities—are themselves evidentiary artifacts that are deployed in the service of larger arguments about the distribution of political, economic, and cultural power. One central goal of instructors' work, then, is to make students aware of how a text can itself become an inversion ritual: a kind of "argument" that shifts the grounds of fixed cultural and political viewpoints. Teaching the African novel is one means of rendering the struggle to live in the historical continuum of the colonial and "post"-colonial eras.

This is not to reduce African authors' political critique to mere ideological polemic. Tejumola Olaniyan (2009:84), for example, points to the reductive nature of textual interpretations that do little more than mirror a novel's critical stance, thereby obscuring the text's many aesthetic and conceptual strands. Close reading of the literary features of the text needs to be balanced by multidisciplinary tools of analysis. Ultimately, an African literature course ought to help students learn to scrutinize what they read and hear: both within the pages of the novel and outside of it.

But the issue here is not only one of binary exchange, of subjecting the West's master narrative of technological progress and ahistorical exceptionalism to intense ethical scrutiny and then replacing it with African multihistories. The issue is really one of seeing our territories and our histories of North and South as intertwined. Part of our pedagogical and research agenda must be to explore the ways in which the European consciousness that came to Africa was embodied in technologies of colonial control on the continent and to understand likewise that what we often celebrate as the innovative cultural verve of American life continues to draw its spirit from African diasporic culture.[7]

Conclusion

Teaching African literature necessarily involves an honest examination of the ways in which historical forces have produced not so much a "post"-colonial phase along the path to African independence as an entrapment in a "post"-colonial continuum. And yet, in their novels, African writers effect the very inversion rituals that they seek to inaugurate in their home societies. Chimamanda Ngozi Adichie wrote *Half of a Yellow Sun* to explore a mediation of the ethnic solidarities and nationalist borders that precipitated the Nigeria-Biafra war, inducing her readers to trust anew in the palpable power of human affection. Zakes Mda wrote *Ways of Dying* in the extremity of South Africa's transition to a multiracial democracy, recalling the country's citizens to their original strength. And Patrice Nganang wrote *Dog Days* out of an ebullient spirit that celebrates the role of the imagination in constructing democracy, even if this goal appears to have temporarily receded.

In terms of global cultural flows, we continue to witness a panoply of inversion rituals and other critiques of the prevailing balance of power, particularly in regions formerly designated as the "Third World." What first motivated Chinua Achebe to begin writing was the urgency of telling an Igbo story from an Igbo point of view; this sentiment continues to inform African literature today.

Notes

I am grateful to Ada Uzoamaka Azodo, Kwaku Larbi Korang, Joseph C. Miller, Mutombo M'Panya, and Hassan Sisay for their generous mentoring and support as I learned how to teach African multi-histories through the continent's literature.

1. Abdourahman A. Waberi's *In the United States of Africa* (2009) constitutes one recent African inversion ritual; his novel parodies Western exceptionalism and reverses assumptions about which countries are "wealthy" and which are "poor."

2. Jean-François Bayart in *The State in Africa: The Politics of the Belly* (2009) credits Foucault with providing the theoretical framework for his analysis. Bayart's *Global Subjects: A Political Critique of Globalization* (2008) employs a similar methodological framework to analyze the mutually informing flows of power and initiative from the developing world outward and back again.

3. Jennifer Wenzel's *Bulletproof: Afterlives of Anti-colonial Prophecy in South Africa and Beyond* (2009) probes the South African social imaginary by tracing the resonance of the traumatic Xhosa cattle killing directed by Nongqawuse's prophecies in 1856–1857. For three innovative works on wide-ranging literacy practices in West African societies, see *Readings in African Popular Culture*, edited by Karin Barber (1997); Stephanie Newell's *Ghanaian Popular Fiction: "Thrilling Discoveries in Conjugal Life" and Other Tales* (2000); and *Africa's Hidden Histories: Everyday Literacy and Making the Self*, also edited by Karin Barber (2006).

4. Eleni Coundouriotis in "Why History Matters in the African Novel" (2009) provides an overview of scholarship on the intersection of the African novel and history.

5. Developed by the Italian statistician Corrado Gini in 1912, the Gini coefficient is a complex formula. Gini conceptualized income distribution as spanning a range from zero to one, with perfect income equality within a country being represented as zero and with the greatest degree of income inequality represented at the end of the range, or one. An accessible overview of the Gini coefficient can be found at the World Bank's "Measuring Inequality" (2010). Sampie Terreblanche in *A History of Inequality in South Africa, 1652–2002* (2002) offers a meticulous study of the inequitable distribution of wealth in South Africa.

6. For a brilliant analysis of the visual rhetoric of *Le Messager*'s cartoons, see Achille Mbembe's *On the Postcolony* (2001:149–168).

7. Among the many works that explore the ways European consciousness migrated to Africa in the precolonial and colonial eras, see Ronald Robinson and John Gallagher, *Africa and the Victorians: The Official Mind of Imperialism* (1961) and George Steinmetz, *The Devil's Handwriting: Precoloniality and the German Colonial State in Qingdao, Samoa, and Southwest Africa* (2007). On the richly variegated artistic production of African diasporic culture, see Paul Gilroy's *The Black Atlantic: Modernity and Double Consciousness* (1993).

12 Teaching Africa through a Comparative Pedagogy

South Africa and the United States

Renée Schatteman

W HAT SOUTH AFRICAN poet Andries Walter Oliphant articulates in "The Struggle of the Two Souths" (1992) is the potential for comparative understanding that can be gained when placing South Africa and the United States side by side. Reading his own nation's experiences of racial persecution from the perspective of civil rights, Oliphant reaches the conclusion that change in South Africa is inevitable since "the earth belongs to the just ones" (1992:70). The poem posits that these two countries, simultaneously unknown and familiar to each other, are also closely linked in terms of influence, as seen in the way that Martin Luther King Jr.'s words helped fuel the antiapartheid movement. "The Struggle of the Two Souths" rightly suggests that numerous ideas about nonviolence, resistance campaigns, black consciousness, and black power were exchanged with impassioned interest across the Atlantic as protesters in both countries saw their own fight as part of a larger global struggle for freedom.

Scholars interested in teaching American students about the realities of life on the African continent understand the importance of getting them to relate the knowledge they learn to themselves and their own worlds. This chapter takes that pedagogical principle one step further by advocating comparative study, in this particular case between South Africa and the United States. Since the beginning of the 20th century, there has been scholarly interest in the striking historical similarities between these two countries: the early settlement in each country by northwestern European Protestants; the eradication, displacement, or domestication of the indigenous populations they encountered, the Khoikhoi and the Native Americans, respectively; the ideologies of white supremacy that took hold in both contexts, especially through the practice of slavery; the civil wars fought between factions of whites with opposing views; the racial divisions imposed by Jim Crow and apartheid legislation; the resistance struggles that emerged from these repressive environments; and the advancement of biracialism-multiracialism rather than separatism that ultimately served as each nation's most prominent liberation goal. In these ways, the political history of South Africa over the past few centuries can be said to have more in common with the United States than with most other African countries.

The study of these parallels was elevated to a new level with the publication of George Fredrickson's landmark works *White Supremacy: A Comparative Study in American and South African History* in 1981 and *Black Liberation: A Comparative History of Black Ideologies in the United States and South Africa* in 1995. These works inspired other notable studies as well as the 1999 creation of an academic journal named *Safundi: The Journal of South African and American Studies*, which publishes articles that analyze the United States and South Africa from an international, transnational, and comparative perspective. As indicated on *Safundi*'s website, the journal's title "derives from the 'S' for 'South Africa,' 'a' for 'America,' and 'fundi,' which comes from the Xhosa verb, '-*funda*,' which translates as 'to read,' or 'to learn.'"[1] *Safundi* operates from the assumption that comparative study helps define a subject by relating it to another; as Andrew Offenburger, the journal's founder, et al. state, "Looking through the mirror of one country, [we] gain perspective on another" (2003:x).

The scholarly rationale for this type of research can also be applied to teaching, since the benefits of bringing materials from parallel contexts into the classroom are multiple. Students engaged in comparative study come to better understand their own historical and cultural grounding. The contrasts between South Africa and the United States allow students to appreciate the uniqueness of their own circumstances, while the similarities encourage them to reinterpret those circumstances in a new light. American students at certain moments are struck by the extremes of racial conflicts in South Africa and conclude that their own country's history involving race is of a different nature and of a lesser degree. When they discover meaningful points of connections between the two contexts, they reexamine their culture's dynamics with a new seriousness and a greater appreciation for what those dynamics reveal about power, difference, and human relations. Students learn to look at American culture through a more objective lens and can read beyond commonplace interpretations of the past.

Comparative work also fuels a hunger in students for knowledge of the world outside of themselves. By identifying with particular realities of life in South Africa, students experience an investment in South Africa as a whole, and this naturally prompts them to expand their worldview. A heightened interest in South Africa is especially important today when students are generally far removed from the history of apartheid, often possessing only a superficial understanding of this country's unique past. Moreover, because contemporary comparative studies also consider exchanges between nations and the influences nations have on one another, students come to understand that their own national history is connected to other global narratives. In general, this analytical work teaches students to use the essential critical thinking skills of questioning, comparing, and evaluating as they seek out likenesses and dissimilarities; examine relationships across race, culture, and continents; and trace the movement of ideas and ideologies over time.

My experiences with using a comparative model to teach about Africa began when my colleague Pearl McHaney and I proposed and were granted the opportunity to codirect a 2002 National Endowment for the Humanities (NEH) Summer Institute titled "Literary Perspectives on Race and Rights in the American South and in South Africa: Eudora Welty, Nadine Gordimer, Alice Walker, and Sindiwe Magona." The institute's comparative examination of four specific authors, two from each context, enabled the participating middle- and secondary-school teachers to explore broad issues of race and rights in exciting ways. We subsequently developed a special topics course that we titled Race, Rights, and Resistance: Literature from the American South and South Africa and offered it to undergraduates in 2004 and to graduates in 2006. The courses featured short fiction and novels by the same four authors, but we added two additional works: Anne Moody's memoir *Coming of Age in Mississippi* (2004[1968]), about the life events that led to her involvement in the civil rights demonstrations, and Lauretta Ngcobo's novel *And They Didn't Die* (1990), about the women's resistance movement in South Africa from the 1950s through the 1980s.

As this description suggests, our approach in these endeavors was literature based, and the majority of our class time was devoted to discussing works of fiction. A literary approach is admittedly different from the historical analyses mentioned above, since history attempts to provide a stable accounting of the past, while literature, with its emphasis on multiple viewpoints, highlights the ambiguity of reality instead. The experience of reading literature is essentially one of exploration, "where uncertainty, and hence openness, is a normal part of the response and newfound possibilities provoke other possibilities" (Langer 1995:26). Judith Langer contrasts literature with the discursive experience of exploring language for gaining information and argues that while discursive reading moves toward closure and thesis building, the literary experience is constantly in flux, leaving room for alternative interpretations, changing perspectives, complex characters, and unresolved questions. Another contrast between the two disciplines is that history highlights crucial events, whereas literature details the daily lives of people in the spaces between those transformational moments. Literature, in this sense, translates social movements and conflicts into the everyday; this is particularly the case in women's writings, which often encompass the domestic sphere and are located on the margins of history.

Eudora Welty contemplates another insight into the uniqueness of literature when she states: "Mutual understanding in the world being nearly always, as now, at low ebb, it is comforting to remember that it is through art that one country can nearly always speak reliably to another. . . . Art, though, is never the voice of a country; it is an even more precious thing, the voice of the individual, doing its best to speak, not comfort of any sort, indeed, but truth" (1957:117). More attention is being given in recent years to the truths unveiled through the rich literary interconnections between South Africa and the United States. For example, when *Safundi* was founded, it primarily published studies based in the social sciences, but most of the issues over the past four years have each also included at least two articles related to literary studies.

While our summer institute privileged a literary perspective in the teaching, we did incorporate historical knowledge about race, rights, and resistance in both sessions by bringing in guest lecturers from the history department, showing various documentaries about the civil rights movement and the antiapartheid struggle, and assigning articles from *Safundi* that complemented or supplemented our literary study. By interweaving the discursive with the literary as well as the transformational with the translational in this manner, students examined and questioned the interplay between literature and history. Students found the historical information useful in confirming the key events depicted in the literature and grounding the specific people, legislation, and occurrences out of which the narratives arose. The literature struck students as particularly true and poignant because it could be tied to real world occurrences and settings, and they consequently approached it with a seriousness that would not as readily be granted to less historically based texts. In this manner, the historical information undoubtedly enhanced the literary study, while the fiction, with its open-ended questions and multiple interpretations, expanded historical understanding.

In our selection of literary texts to feature in our study, we chose works by women writers of different generations, races, and educational backgrounds. We also selected writers whose works brought a complexity and honesty to matters of race, rights, and resistance. Gordimer and Welty were chosen in part because of what Toni Morrison says of them in a 1977 interview: "They are fearless. Nadine Gordimer and Eudora Welty write about black people in a way that few white men have ever been able to write. It's not patronizing, not romanticizing—it's the way they should be written about" (Watkins 1994:47). Both are also viewed as masters of the short story in their ability to capture profound insights into human nature within the limited confines of the genre. Gordimer in the introduction to her *Selected Stories* (1976b) highlights the potency of this genre when she explains what, for her, distinguishes a short story from a novel: "A short story *occurs*, in the imaginative sense. To write one is to express from a situation in the exterior or interior world the life-giving drop—sweat, tear, semen, saliva—that will spread an intensity on the page; burn a hole in it" (15). While all of the short fiction by Gordimer and Welty in some manner addresses race, rights, and resistance, we chose the following specific stories because of their individual emphases and the interplay between them: Gordimer's "Happy Event" (1976a), "Is There Nowhere Else Where We Can Meet?" (1976c), "A Chip of Glass Ruby" (1986a), "City Lovers" (1986b), "Country Lovers" (1986c), "Six Feet of the Country" (1986d), and "Once Upon a Time" (1991), and Welty's, "The Demonstrators" (1980a), "Livvie" (1980b), "Powerhouse" (1980c), "Where Is the Voice Coming From?" (1980d), "Why I Live at the P.O." (1980e), and "A Worn Path" (1980f).

We paired Alice Walker with Welty as significant writers from the American South because Walker treats her subjects with an insistent determination to tell truths that have consistently evoked contradictory feelings in her readers. In addition to Walker's short fiction (in particular, "Everyday Use" [1967a], "Roselily" [1967b], and "Nineteen Fifty-Five" [1971]), we included her novel *Meridian* (1976), which explores the heavy personal costs and the emotional ramifications of a young woman's intense political commitment to the civil rights struggle. The South African writer Sindiwe Magona proved to be a significant addition to our South African section because, like Gordimer, she provides keen insights into realities surrounding race and a crisp sense of both situation and character. Besides Magona's stories ("Nosisa" [1991a], "Two Little Girls and a City" [1991b], and "I'm Not Talking about That, Now" [1996]), we focused on her novel *Mother to Mother* (1998), which gives an account of the 1993 killing of the young Fulbright scholar Amy Biehl from the perspective of the mother of one of the township boys who took part in her stabbing.

To illustrate the comparative analysis and types of discussions our classes engaged in, I offer a close examination of four stories that worked especially well in our classes. This group of stories, which includes one story by each of our four major writers, invites comparisons first of the two American stories and then of the two South African stories. The American and the South African texts are compared side by side, thereby layering international comparisons onto the insights already gained from the juxtaposition of works from a single national context.

The two stories from the United States, Walker's "Nineteen Fifty-Five" and Welty's "Powerhouse," make a compelling pairing for cross-racial analysis because they both are devoted to the same subject, the inequalities in the music industry that allowed white singers to cover music written by black composers and make enormous amounts of money, while the black performers performed in relative obscurity and with little compensation. Additionally, both stories depict real-life figures who achieved great fame through performance, though their names have been changed in these fictionalized recountings of their lives. "Nineteen Fifty-Five" is narrated by a black female performer named Gracie Mae Still (meant to be "Big Mama" Thornton) as she reflects upon her interactions with the young white man named Traynor who covers her most famous song. From the descriptions she provides of him (about five feet nine with "real dark white skin," a "red pouting mouth," and "black and curly" hair [Walker 1971:4]), it is clear that Walker is referencing Elvis Presley, who did indeed sing a version of "Big Mama" Thornton's "Hound Dog" song. In Welty's "Powerhouse," a white narrator attending a white dance in the small town of Alligator, Mississippi describes the musical feats and theatrical antics of a performer she refers to as Powerhouse. This character is meant to represent the jazz pianist, organist, composer, and comedic entertainer Fats Waller, whose performance so inspired Welty that she wrote this story in one sitting after coming home from one of his concerts.

Walker couches her complaint about the music industry in the unflattering way Gracie Mae describes Traynor's manager, whose cold, pink eyes lead her to conclude that "nobody I'd care to know is behind them" (1971:5). Half of the $1,000 this man offers Gracie Mae for the song is intended to compensate her for her creativity; the other half buys her permission for him to buy up all the remaining copies from the shelves of the "race record" shops. By removing her original version from circulation, he ensures that the song's success will be credited to Traynor. This is exactly what happens, for Traynor's fame is in large part due to this song, which he is asked to sing at every concert. The fact that Elvis's version of "Hound Dog" made its way to the 19th spot on *Rolling Stone*'s list of the "500 Greatest Songs of All Times" suggests that Walker was not exaggerating the importance of this piece to his career.

Another, more significant criticism of the society's racial bias comes through the relationship that Gracie Mae forms with Traynor during the 22-year period she recounts in the story. Traynor is depicted as an empty man who continually returns to her to inquire about the meaning of her song. "Where out of your life did it come from?" (Walker 1971:11) is his constant refrain. Traynor is incapable of understanding the real human suffering expressed in "Hound Dog," and yet his insatiable fans demand his version of her song. As Traynor tells Gracie Mae: "They want what you got but they don't want you. They want what I got only it ain't mine. That's what makes 'em so hungry for me when I sing. They getting the flavor of something but they ain't getting the thing itself. They like a pack of hound dogs trying to gobble up a scent" (Walker 1971:17). As a result, Traynor's own life is falsified by the racial biases of his listeners, and Gracie Mae is cheated out of her rightful recognition. None of the many gifts the guilt-ridden Traynor bestows upon her can make up for her lost compensation.

In Walker's story, Gracie Mae says that her husband loves the way that her singing "made the dirt farmers cry like babies and the womens shout Honey, hush!" (1971:6). In Welty's "Powerhouse," the performer named in the title is also clearly the "thing itself" and not just the flavoring of musical genius. The story is, in large part, a tribute to Waller's amazing skills as a musician and performer, as the narrator goes to lengths to suggest that he, as the artist figure, is larger than life. "He's in a trance; he's a person of joy, a fanatic," she says. "He listens as much as he performs, a look of hideous, powerful rapture on his face" (Welty 1980c:131). Similarly, a black waitress in the second half of the story exclaims to the other black townspeople who have gathered to be in Powerhouse's presence, "The Mississippi River's here" (Welty 1980c:137).

There are two methods Welty uses to shed light upon the restrictions Waller faced as a black performer in the 1930s and 1940s. First, the narrator is not the author herself but rather a townsperson whose language Welty uses to honor Powerhouse. Nevertheless, the narrator's enthusiasm about the music is heavily inflected with racial stereotype, creating a complicated mix of praise and degradation:

Powerhouse is playing!

He's here on tour from the city—"Powerhouse and His Keyboard"—"Powerhouse and His Tasmanians"—think of the things he calls himself! There's no one in the world like him. You can't tell what he is. "Negro man"?—he looks more Asiatic, monkey, Jewish, Babylonian, Peruvian, fanatic, devil. He has pale gray eyes, heavy lids, maybe horny like a lizard's, but big glowing eyes when they're open. He has African feet of the greatest size, stomping, both together, on each side of the pedals. He's not coal black—beverage colored—looks like a preacher when his mouth is shut, but then it opens—vast and obscene. And his mouth is going every minute: like a monkey's when it looks for something. Improvising, coming on a light and childish melody—smooch—he loves it with his mouth. (Welty 1980c:131)

The stereotypes run so thick here and elsewhere in the story that they primarily serve to point out the absurdity of this perspective and cancel themselves out, leaving the essence of the narrator's admiration and awe instead. This narrator also drops out by the second section of the story, which details the trip that Powerhouse and his musicians make during intermission to the World Café in Negrotown and their return back to the white dance for a closing set.

The story's second, more poignant, means of racial critique occurs when Powerhouse introduces the improvised tale of Uranus Knockwood into his performance. When he tells his white audience that his wife committed suicide by throwing herself out the window because she missed him so badly, the narrator (as well as the reader) is uncertain whether this story is true. However, when Powerhouse continues this riff in front of his black audience at the café and among his musicians on the walk back, it becomes increasingly obvious that the story is emblematic of something larger. Suggesting that Uranus Knockwood was somehow involved with his wife's suicide, Powerhouse says of him: "That no-good pussyfooted crooning creeper, that creeper that follow around after me, coming up like weeds behind me, following around after me everything I do and messing around on the trail I leave. Bets my numbers, sings my songs, gets close to my agent like a Betsy-bug; when I going out he just coming in" (Welty 1980c:138).

Knockwood becomes a symbol of white agents who seek out black music for others to perform, and his role in taking Powerhouse's wife away from him is a metaphor for Powerhouse's loss of economic control over his own creativity. The story provides evidence of what happens when white singers cover black music; for when Powerhouse's musicians look for songs to play on the nickelodeon at the World Café, they cannot find songs performed by black bands. When Powerhouse asks whose version of "Tuxedo Junction" is on the machine, the reply comes back, "You know whose" (Welty 1980c:136). This detail clarifies the point that while bands like the Glenn Miller Band were recording songs written by black musicians and getting them played on the radio as the dominant version, Fats Waller and his crew were trudging from one small town to another to do performances, enduring the separation from their families, the injustice of inadequate compensation, and the humiliation of segregated accommodations. Powerhouse makes note of this treatment when explaining that to find the room they were provided for accommodations in Alligator, Mississippi, one has to "go way downstairs along a long cor-ri-dor to where they puts us" (Welty 1980c:134).

These works by Walker and Welty, taken together, give a rounded view of the way that musical artists were affected by the obvious inequalities of the entertainment world, emphasizing the insecurity engendered in white performers and the resignation and frustration felt by black performers. Students respond with great interest to "Nineteen Fifty-Five" and "Powerhouse" because they recognize that many of the realities depicted are still operational in the contemporary music industry. The pairing of stories from South Africa that serve as meaningful counterparts to these American stories are Magona's "Two Little Girls and a City" and Gordimer's "Happy Event." These stories also focus on inequalities, but not those related to public spaces; rather, they are concerned with the devastation that apartheid wrecked upon the domestic sphere of South African families.

"Two Little Girls and a City" is based on the heart-wrenching tale of two girls, one white and one black, who were raped and murdered on the same day in Cape Town. Magona recalls the two incidents by moving back and forth between descriptions of the two families, detailing the actions of each of the girls on that fateful day, before they go missing, and recounting the respective searches for them, the eventual discovery of their bodies, and each family's expression of grief. These descriptions quickly reveal the extreme differences in the living conditions of the two families. Nina's family (the white family) lives "high up the slopes of Table Mountain" (Magona 1991b:120) in relative affluence. The children, who are tended to by a domestic servant and are taken to the beach on a daily basis, enjoy an abundance of possessions and are encouraged to imagine a successful future for themselves. The ambitions of the black family are far less bold. Phumla has come from her village with her mother and little sister, to the single men's quarters assigned to dockworkers in Cape Town, with the intention of staying only long enough for the mother to become pregnant with the family's third child, a trip necessitated by the realities of migrant labor that separated families for all but a few weeks each year. Phumla's life in the men's quarter, where her father shares a room with eight others, is surrounded by danger, whether in the form of busy roads that run alongside their accommodations or untrustworthy strangers who prey on naïve newcomers.

The central irony of the story is that while their economic circumstances are as dissimilar as they can be, the two families end up sharing the same vulnerability to attacks upon their children. Nina and Phumla are parallel victims in death, for Nina is described as "a day-old chick in the claws of a hawk," while Phumla's cry is likened to "the bleat of a lamb during a storm" (Magona 1991b:127, 132). In similar fashion, the two sets of parents mirror each other in their shock and grief, as do the two communities that bond together to assist the traumatized families.

While the story posits that humans are essentially the same, regardless of race, it also gives a stinging reminder of South African society's tragic refusal to recognize this fact, for the public response to the two murders proves entirely oppositional. The police are quick to investigate Nina's case, and the white community finds it "very reassuring" (Magona 1991b:131) to watch them at work. The black community members, however, are so distrustful of the police that they do not inform them of Phumla's disappearance until "to not do so would land them in more trouble than they were in already" (Magona 1991b:135). The two officers who respond to the call after Phumla's body is discovered in a garbage can behave like indifferent bystanders. Equally unjust is the fact that Phumla's death is never reported in the papers, and she is only ever remembered in her own community as the girl whose "knees had to be sawed to fit her into a coffin" (Magona 1991b:141). Nina's death, in contrast, is widely covered, and the news leads to a crackdown on any black person seen walking about after a certain hour. Nina's killer is not likely to be such a person, as the story strongly suggests that each girl was killed by someone of her own race. Nina registers fear of the man on the beach who approaches her, but she never notes a racial difference. Further, a black man would not go undetected on the white beach, just as a white man would be out of place in the workers' quarters. Despite this reality, the police assume that Nina's killer was a black man, and residents of the township find themselves "foremost among suspects," leading them to experience "great sorrow" and "burning anger" at the remembrance of the two little girls (Magona 1991b:142).

"Two Little Girls and a City" unveils the racial biases of the police under apartheid as they suspect black men of the white child's death while refusing to consider white men as possible culprits in either case. Gordimer's "Happy Event" also exposes discriminatory practices, but these have to do with the hypocrisies that operate in the most personal details of individual lives instead. In this story, with its title that anticipates the welcome arrival of new life, Gordimer narrows in on double standards surrounding the question of abortion. The main character, an Afrikaner woman named Ella Plaistow, expresses moral outrage that Lena, the domestic servant she hired two months earlier, supposedly kills her own baby after she gives birth to it and then buries it in a nightgown that Ella had given to her a few days before. This story is written in the third person, but with liberal use of free indirect discourse, meaning that much of the narrator's language is flavored by Ella's own thoughts and expressions. Therefore, details about the abortion that Ella herself had undergone only a few months before are hinted at rather than openly stated. She seeks to repress the memory of the abortion while simultaneously justifying her decision to have it done, something she previously considered herself incapable of doing. Gordimer likens Ella's mental processing to "ants teeming to repair a broken anthill" or "white corpuscles rushing to a wound," both symbolic of how one adjusts one's self-image and thereby "protects oneself from oneself" (1976a:107). In presenting such a damning image of Ella, Gordimer does not seek to take a stance against abortion; rather, she criticizes Ella's harsh judgment of Lena as well as her unwillingness to recognize that their individual acts fulfilled the same goal. Further, if Lena did indeed kill the child (she contends it was born dead), it would have been due to her fears of losing her employment; Ella, however, had the abortion so that she and her husband wouldn't have to postpone a long-awaited European vacation, "when they would suddenly lift themselves clear of whatever it was that their lives had settled into, and land, free of it, lightly in another country" (Gordimer 1976a:108).

In this story, when the police arrive at Ella's doorstep to question her about the bloody nightgown, she senses a sudden fear and "a throb in some organ [she] didn't know [she] had" (Gordimer 1976a:115); by contrast, Lena's reaction to the police is marked by a surprising calmness. Gordimer explains that "for Africans there is no stigma attached to any involvement with the forces of the law; the innumerable restrictions by which their lives are hedged from the day they are born make transgressions commonplace and punishment inevitable" (1976a:117). But despite their differing responses, the story aims to create numerous points of connection between the white and black women: in their names that are near reversals of each other, in the descriptions used to liken each woman to a cat, and in the nightgown that links their pregnancies since the garment used to wrap the dead child was also worn by Ella at the "nursing home" where she went to have her abortion. The many parallels grow steadily more ironic as Ella and her society do all they can to distance themselves from the African race. The story ends with such an insistence when the doctor at the court case testifies that Lena could have returned to work only 24 hours after giving birth to the infant whose death is being investigated. He states: "Were the woman in question a European, I should, of course, say this would be most unlikely. Most unlikely. But a native woman. I should say yes—yes, it would be possible" (Gordimer 1976a:120).

These two South African stories go to great lengths to insist upon the commonalities between races and to show the harmful effects that occur when these links are intentionally denied. The double standards that appear to be accepted as truths (that only a black man could rape and murder a child and that only a black woman could abort her own child and be back at work the next day) are the inevitable consequence of assumed differences. Both stories also indicate the political nature of the intimate world in South Africa, whether involving private grief or personal decisions concerning reproduction, for the implications of apartheid legislation cannot be barred from either the nursery or the bedroom.

When the two pairings of stories are placed side by side, comparative analyses quickly rise to the surface. The difference in degree asserts itself, for the South African stories about child murder are much more violent in nature than the American stories about economic injustices. While this is due in part to the subject matter chosen, there is a sense that brutality and extreme danger teem just beneath the surface in all South African writing. More extreme, too, are the divisions between races in the South African fiction. It is jarring for American readers to hear the words "master" and "madam" used for white characters and "boy" and "girl" used for the black domestic workers, but these are accepted in the nomenclature of South Africans living under apartheid. Further, racist assumptions are not censured in these stories as they might be in American fiction. This is seen in the character Ella, who quite freely thinks of her domestics in animalistic terms. She prefers hiring servants who belong to the same tribe, for example, just as it would be better "to have two Siamese cats instead of one Siamese and one tabby" (Gordimer 1976a:109). Her thoughts about her male domestic are even more shocking: "It was difficult to think of old Thomasi as something quite like oneself, when he rose to his hind legs. (Yes, one had the feeling that this was *exactly* what happened when he got up from polishing the floor)" (Gordimer 1976a:109).

The sharp contrasts in degree contribute to a difference in tone between the two sets of stories. In the American stories, the black characters respond to their situations with humor, in the case of Powerhouse, and compassion, in the case of Gracie Mae; conversely, the South African characters are left with "burning anger" or crushing defeat. Humor and compassion are not easily found in South African writing; rather, sharp and biting ironies often prevail, as seen in the last line of "Happy Event," which reads that "[Lena's prison] sentence coincided roughly with the time Ella and [her husband] spent in Europe, but though she was out of prison by the time they returned, she did not go back to work for them again" (Gordimer 1976a:121).

At the same time that the literary works from these two countries differ widely in content and texture, the underlying parallels between them cannot be overlooked. For whether they are concerned with how much money and recognition black professionals deserve to be rewarded for their work or with how capable blacks are of murder in comparison to their white counterparts, the motivations for and the overall effects of the double standards are the same. All four stories equally assert that the assumptions of privilege that give life to inequalities and consequently to double standards are allowed to exist because of the intentional barriers that are set up between the different races. "Happy Event" speaks of the "no-man's-land" that lies between "the lives of the white people in the house and the black people in their back-yard quarters" (Gordimer 1976a:111). A "no-man's-land" of racial divide exists in all these works. The only exception to this divide is seen in the story "Nineteen Fifty-Five" where Traynor invites Gracie Mae to his house (Graceland) and asks her to share a spot with him on the Johnny Carson show; however, in both instances, he is openly laughed at or scorned for making such an effort.

This consideration of points of contrast and convergence in these four stories provides an example of the types of discussions we conducted in our institute and our classes, whether we were examining stories, novels, or the historical materials we integrated into the curriculum. The course evaluations of our students and NEH participants reinforced our beliefs about the value of such comparative exercises. The evaluations conveyed student appreciation for the knowledge they gained about the history and culture of South Africa, something they would have been unlikely to acquire unless they happened to take a course in African Studies. One student commented: "I didn't know any South African authors and I had never read a short story about South Africa. I learned about a whole new world across the globe." Another added, "It was particularly enlightening to get outside of the United States' cultural-literary mind-set and read the works of black South Africans, forcing me to push beyond my ethnocentric viewpoint." The evaluations also gave credence to our contention that comparative study enhances self-knowledge and national awareness. "The South African literature almost reexposes you to the Southern American literature," said one student; another offered, "The South African stories made American stories speak louder to me."

Additionally, students discovered that because the literature directly dealt with sensitive topics, they were able to find a safe space for honest discussions about critically charged issues in the classroom. As one institute member suggested, "The discussion in class about the literature and perceptions of race were exceptional and, in my opinion, a cut about the conversations one normally has about these topics." They further valued the way comparative study allowed them to see that the United States is not alone in its struggles with race. As one student wrote: "When there is such a commonality in history in these two countries, it causes a person to further question the reasons racial issues continue to bring forth conflicts. You want to question why the things are the way they are and how these things came to be!" This student's comments affirmed our pedagogical principle that comparative study fosters more substantial analysis of the underlying issues behind cultural practices than what might occur in a study of a single context.

While this comparison has focused on the rich interplay of ideas on women authors' roles in the resistance movements of South Africa and the United States, there is great potential for comparative study in the postapartheid era as well. One such idea comes from Russell Samolsky's *Safundi* article "On Teaching South African Literature in the Age of Terror" (2004). He writes that before 2001, students in his comparative literature courses were surprised by and unable to relate to the information about police abuse and brutality that was revealed during South Africa's Truth and Reconciliation Commission (TRC) hearings. They felt that the "torture and the utter degradation of the racial Other was conceived as something radically alien and outside the ambit of contemporary American consciousness" (Samolsky 2004:1).

But their attitude changed overnight when information about the torture and abuse of prisoners at Abu Ghraib prison was disseminated to the American public, producing "the same kind of shock and dislocation that the revelations of the TRC had earlier provided" (Samolsky 2004:1). Samolsky further writes: "The effect for me was one of the uncanny in the Freudian sense of something once familiar that has been displaced and now returns. The effect upon my students was to shift problems of torture in South African literature from the realm of the purely Other to a more nuanced and somber reading of the war on terror" (2004:2). In this example, as with the earlier comparative topic, it is clear that the study of a particular topic's application to two locations does not merely double the knowledge gained. Rather, the pedagogical emphasis on difference and similitude, on global interconnectedness, and on personal awareness also promises to result in a deep level of understanding about the topic and a critical curiosity about realities beyond the self.

Notes

This chapter was developed from an article titled "Women's Literature from South Africa and the American South," which was cowritten with Pearl McHaney and appeared in *Safundi: The Journal of South African and American Studies* in October 2004.

1. *Safundi*, http://www.safundi.com/about/default.asp.

13 Stereotypes, Myths, and Realities Regarding African Music in the African and American Academy

Jean Ngoya Kidula

Introduction

For several years, the University of Georgia's African Students Association has hosted an "African Night." The occasion, managed by students who are recent immigrants or first-generation Africans, usually features a fashion show, a dance routine, and a play. The play typically addresses students' transitions into college and American life. In 2009 and 2010, the plot involved a male who relocated to the United States to go to college, leaving his wife or girlfriend in Africa. While in school, the man met and married someone else: an African or an African American woman. In due course, he communicated sporadically with his family in Africa, usually leaving out controversial or "unsavory" details about the transitions or the struggles undergone to survive in the "land of plenty." Music either framed the scenes or was central or formed a backdrop to the action. The dance routines and the fashion shows were inserted in the narrative or performed as interludes between scenes. The dances were generally of a popular urban Congolese type with a nondescript African ethnic root. The fashion show typically consisted of "African" materials and cloth sewn in contemporary trends, along with a catwalk; the modeling was set to live or canned music that was recognizably rooted in Africa.

After the event, students in world music, Africa American music, and African music classes were asked to provide a written narrative of their impressions of the event. Non-African attendees, regardless of their ethnic or racial background, stated that they felt as if something was "lost in translation." They enjoyed the different music and the general entertainment value of the event. However, scenes that required prior knowledge of the condensed plot, the music, or the dances confused them. On the other hand, students from Africa described the presentation as a satire on their initial encounter and subsequent accommodation to life in America. These two reactions can be understood to be rooted in different experiences, expectations, perceptions, and interpretations of what "Africa" was, is, or should be.

In this chapter, I draw on my experiences as a teacher and student in the United States and in Kenya to explore how stereotypes, myths, and realities about African music have been, or are, continually reinforced, negated, or negotiated in the classroom. This discussion is motivated by the fact that despite its ubiquitous presence in the soundscape of African and American life, African music in the academy is placed on the fringes of the mainstream music canon and usually located in peripheral, related disciplines such as ethnomusicology, culture studies, folklore, or anthropology. Disciplinary nomenclatures partly contribute to the marginalization of African music or music of/in Africa.

Background

Because I grew up in Kenya in the 1970s and 1980s and received my undergraduate degree in music there, my exposure to Kenyan and African music occurred in both formal and informal learning situations. The scholarly study of the music of Africa was approached from the prevailing anthropological worldviews that located the music in the "other" category. Thus, while Kenyan music practice was intrinsic to my identity and location, most available texts presented it as an "other," effectively marginalizing its disciplinary value in music studies. I began my music-teaching career with high school students in Kenya. Due mostly to the lack of written resources, our offerings of Kenyan and other African music continued to place its performance and musicology on the academic fringes, although it was highly valued as a cultural and entertainment art.

I had spent one year in the United States right after I graduated with my first degree, learning and teaching African music, among other things. Most students were fascinated more with the exoticism of the cultural African past than with contemporary music developments that reflected contact and change. Thus, my Luo dance troupe attracted more students than the choral singing of arranged Kenyan folk repertoire. On my return to Kenya, where I taught at a local university, students found Western European music more exotic and challenging than African music. The choral standard canonic repertoire and African American arranged spirituals attracted more students than the Luo dance troupe. It was only when I incorporated transcriptions of Kenyan melodies in sight-reading and ear-training classes that students gained respect for the complexity inherent in the styling of the local music they took for granted.

My graduate studies in the United States in the 1980s and 1990s were punctuated by teaching in Kenya, before I eventually relocated to teach at a university in the United States. Among my teaching and learning assignments in both locations were African music history, theory, musicianship, and performance. While my students in Kenya understood *African music* and *music in/of Africa* as interchangeable, I found distinctions in the ways the terms were generally understood among students, colleagues, and the public in the United States. While these differences in perception may account for my students' varied reception of "African Night," I believe that part of the reason lies in the students' exposure and understanding of the historical factors influencing the musical journeys of colonized and nationalized Africans on the continent, in contrast to the path of Africans who were enslaved, relocated, and nationalized elsewhere.

Relative to my experiences in the United States, music in/of Africa and African music should be understood as different concepts. Music in/of Africa, on the one hand, can be conceived of as music styles, types, structures, and practices developed and performed in Africa by past and current populations including recent immigrants from the continent whose primary musical formation was on the continent or strongly informed by trends in "modern" Africa. African music, on the other hand, typically consists of structures, forms, and practices that are considered Afrogenic, or stereotypical representations of African music on the continent and in the African diaspora. In the former, the focus is on products emanating from the continent, many of which are initially associated with a specific African culture group (such as Isugudi, a dance music of the Luyia of western Kenya) or an African country (such as juju, a popular music genre from Nigeria). The latter case expands the geographic and historical space to the roots and transformations of music over time, not just on the continent, but wherever Afrogenic music has established new traditions. Such products include blues in the United States, reggae in Jamaica, or samba in Brazil—music whose origins are associated with people of African descent. It is this music that most influenced growth, development, and creativity in global styles in the 20th century.

Stereotypes and Generalizations

A database search of the term *African music* yields information mostly about the African diaspora, since it is these populations that are the most researched and written about by scholars and those in the music industry as being representative of the African ethos. Such a search term posits the problematic of a nominal that essentially marginalizes the developments and innovations made by musicians, scholars, and music critics on the continent or those whose primary formation was on the continent. As such, the term privileges the innovation and achievements located or emanating from the historical African diaspora. Meanwhile, an African Music course in most schools in the United States focuses on Africa, with a tendency to generalize findings rooted in prescriptive stereotypes emanating from the diaspora regarding characteristics and practices perceived as "African." However, an African Music course on the continent is always understood to be about African music on the continent.

A possible reason for the overwhelming generalization of "African music" may actually be a function of the academy relative to developments in sister disciplines. For at least 50 years, a corpus of literature—such as novels and plays by African writers, regarded as African and not African-diasporic—has existed. A similar body of arts, crafts, and dances from continental Africa is distinguished from its diasporic heritage. However, little exists in the academy resembling a canon of African music distinctly separated from that in the African diaspora; neither has there been a body of composers or writings identified in the way that such a constituency exists in literature, fine art, or drama.[1] Thus, not only African, but African American music and musicians are marginalized in the canon of works incorporated in music schools' repertoires unless there is a concerted nationalist effort to include them, as has been the case in countries such as Brazil, Cuba, Ghana, and Nigeria. In the United States, African music and African American music are taught as separate subjects, usually on the periphery of required courses. Teaching these courses as a special class, usually as an elective, intimates that these types of music are nonessential to music study. While African American music is not usually taught in the canon of academic music courses, spirituals and gospel music are frequently performed and accorded special privilege in university choruses or in music festivals.[2]

Another possible reason for the generalizations about African music may be due to the historical tendency in the West to reference "African" concepts from a racial position. While people on the continent do identify themselves as African, there are regional, national, ethnic, clan, and even social and generational distinctions that are recognized as identity markers.

Students in Kenya are profoundly aware of ethnic and generational differences in tandem with political developments that align their *musicking* (processing and producing music) in different ways from that of their elders and other ethnicities. They often excuse their lack of performance expertise of certain dances, attributing it to cultural formation and generational distance. For example, students of Logooli descent, whose idiomatic hip and shoulder movements are classic markers, may find it difficult to jump with a straight torso in the manner of the Maasai. While all of these groups are Kenyan, there is a great awareness and pride in the profound musical and dance distinctions. Further, a student of Maasai heritage may be unable to execute a proper Maasai jump because he grew up in a space far from his ethnic roots or among a generation for whom the dance no longer holds a justifiable function.

African linguistic and ethnic identifiers may not be applicable to populations such as African Americans, Afro-Cubans, or Afro-Brazilians, who historically were culturally and socially segregated by race and, in the process, amalgamated "Africanisms" from the languages, styles, and musicians of the diaspora. These newly developed characteristics became archetypal contributions to the development of folk, popular, and classical music in their respective countries. Unfortunately, these features also became the basis for generalizations about continental Africa.

In an effort to sensitize students at the beginning of any course on African or African-American music in the United States, then, I require them to list stereotypes that are constructed, informed, and maintained by prevalent historical and mediated worldviews. The catalogue usually includes generalizations such as all Africans make music; Africans have rhythm; African music is simple to learn—folk and primitive; African music involves dancing or movement—always vigorous; African music is tribal and entails face painting and jumping wildly; Africans have drums; Africans understand one another's music and languages (usually dialects); African music has been that way from time immemorial; Africans should/can perform only "African music"; and Africans had no classical or popular music until Westerners introduced it.

One reads from these statements that African music is a distinct, uniform entity. The language used to describe it suggests that it is universally popular and universally practiced. Many of these insights are drawn from European worldviews prevalent since the Enlightenment period that saturated popular thought, as well as from journalistic and scholarly reports about the continent generated at historical events and moments.

In the case of the United States, I believe that a fascination with African ways of performing was drawn from observing African American slaves. Their musicking appeared radically different from European ways. Apart from various musical instruments, the body seemed to be an instrument in that it "spoke," similar to notions held about talking drums, and it created sounds as an idiophone and moved, creating rhythm or dancing. While initial observations may have begun with slaves, the curiosity led to explorations in Africa, where similar behaviors were observed in places from which slaves originated.[3]

Studies in anthropology further crystallized approaches in studying African music as a way of life or music in the people's way of life.[4] In due course, certain definitions were adopted that located "African music in a constellation of arts" integrating sound, motion, art, drama, touch, language, and history (Stone 1998:7). The fascination with African approaches to rhythm, traditionally aligned to European thinking that rhythm is located in percussion instruments, led to generalizations about drumming and Africa.[5] Thus, stereotypical "Africanisms" are in part derived from discussions about people of African descent and their musical behavior and practices that are considered different from those believed to be of a Eurogenic source. These concepts eventually became commonplace in studies of music in Africa.

It is difficult to canonize the music of Africa in the same way that music was canonized in Europe. The history of African music took a different trajectory than what developed in imperial courts in Europe or Asia, where sacred or philosophical traditions spread through political or religious alliances and conquests. Europe experienced a period of urbanization that collated in the establishment of diverse, but related, popular forms of music. There were few court alliances in precolonial Africa. However, some instruments and musical styles were disseminated through interethnic contact and warfare.[6] The nation-states created by colonialism and foreign religions such as Christianity and Islam redirected the progression of music in Africa. These developments, and their subsequent history, differed from those encountered by enslaved or indentured Africans in the diaspora. In the latter case, music with a preponderance of African elements or music of the African diaspora had the single most significant influence on global popular music in the 20th century, including what developed on the continent sourced from diasporic forms such as rumba, but transformed in mainland African contexts.

Due to different historical trajectories, developments in popular African music cannot be accounted for with the same theories applied to sister European or American music. On the continent, ethnic African music informs the backdrop of popular music and music adopted in religious and academic institutions. A wide range of factors informs any one direction suggested by the adoption of a foreign ideology in a given African country. The result is a diverse musical amalgamation marketed under singular industrial labels, as has been the case with gospel music.

On Teaching and Learning Music of/in Africa

In this section, I discuss how I have approached and introduced the music of Africa in the academy. Given the diversity of nations and people in Africa, a wide range of music exists. These *musics'* histories inform formal and stylistic features. Bonnie Wade's assertion (2009:1) that "people make music meaningful and useful in their lives" is reiterated by Jeff Todd Titon (2008:16), who, in his music-culture model, defines "music in performance as meaningfully organized sound that proceeds by rules." The model presents music as a performance circumscribed by a community that "carries on the traditions and norms, the social processes and activities, and the ideas of performance" (Titon 2008:7). The community is "situated in history and borne by memory. . . . Musical experiences, performances, and communities change over time and space; . . . history reflects changes in the rules governing music as well as the effect of music on human relationships" (Titon 2008:7, 8).

Over time and space in tandem with other developments on the continent, I classify the contemporary music of Africa broadly as (a) indigenous, ethnic, rural, peri-urban, ethnopop; (b) popular, urban, national, Pan-African, international, global; (c) academic compositions from African sources, Eurogenic forms by African performers; and (d) religious, supranational, global. Such a demarcation already speaks of different contexts of compositions and performance. It further suggests possibilities of chronological historical developments, moving away from previous studies that presented the music of Africa in the ethnographic present, solidifying the stereotype of stagnant rather than dynamic musical processes. Beyond that, these categories imply opportunities for fusions and the creation of new genres.

Layers of musical preferences also exist relative to different affiliations such as social (ethnic, class, generation, education, exposure), political (ethnic, class, national, economic), and religious (indigenous, Christian, Islamic). For example, in Kenya most members of a given village belong to one ethnic group. The national radio and other media introduce the villagers to music of other Kenyans and to what is conceptualized as "national" music in Kiswahili, as well as to popular global music. Formal schooling may introduce other types of European music. Movement into an urban area layers on experiences that are part of the social soundscapes of the modern city. Like other people, Africans and their musicians are fascinated by new sounds, which they adopt and appropriate. The most visible and audible display is found in contemporary fusions of popular secular, profane, and religious music from different parts of the world. American students are usually fascinated to learn of the diverse musical exposures present in continental Africa.

For almost 25 years, one classic text informed the global academy regarding music in Africa: Professor J. H. Kwabena Nketia's *The Music of Africa* (1974a).[7] The text was translated into several European and Asian languages and was *the* definitive authority on African music. Scholars of African diasporic forms referenced the text to defend those features considered or perceived as idiomatically African.[8] In fact, in high schools and colleges in Africa, this work was the standard text in the study of African music. My own British teacher often told us that we were not true Africans because we did not appear to possess the stereotypical instrumental ensembles associated with Africa in the general European worldview. It was assumed that drums were of exclusive African origin. Any African ethnic group without indigenous drums or drum ensembles that either "talked" or displayed polyrhythmic complexity had been compromised by modernity. The irony of this statement was that our high school was located within an ethnic community that had recently adopted drums because of church and military activities in the region. The group's name for the drum was *ndarama*—a corruption of the English word "drum."

However, it is not that Nketia's text inscribed specific characteristics as seminal to all African cultures. To the contrary, he highlighted broad differences in instrument types, genres, and musical styles found in diverse areas and among ethnic groups even within one country. The general media and Eurogenic stereotypes about African music dominated previous and subsequent discourse to the text, using the book to justify certain assertions and, in the process, selectively underlining generalities about music in Africa. In any case, the book was also written mostly in the ethnographic present, thereby suggesting a static overarching "African" culture. Its primary audience was Europeans or Americans interested in general characteristics, as was the norm in the academy at that time.[9] I believe that the resulting general "Africanisms" were appropriated to diasporic genres. They accounted for acceptable explanations for the developments initiated by these groups whose historical progression and amalgamation into the New World was rooted in Africa, but without being assigned specific ethnic, national, or regional communities. Essentially, the "Africanisms" negated or sidelined individual and community contributions. It was not until 1998 that a widely accepted and more diversified text edited by Ruth Stone was released. Nketia's text was, by that time, perceived as a historic text in independent and nationalized Africa.

It is therefore no surprise that in many universities in the United States, African students tend not to enroll in African drum, dance, or music ensemble classes. Either the music studied is long outdated—the music of their grandparents or some imagined nostalgic or embarrassing past, similar to reactions by students from the Southern United States to old-time music—or else contemporary Africans studying in the United States are interested in learning something new, something different, similar to the desires of non-African students who study African music. Apart from nostalgia, there is little challenge or novelty. Some students also feel that African music has moved into new and more exciting directions.

Therefore, most University of Georgia students who take African music classes are usually white. In addition, courses on the music of/in Africa and African music service disciplines such as folklore, comparative literature, sociology, anthropology, history, and linguistics. Disparate disciplines invoking African music are simultaneously useful and unhelpful in codifying the historical and theoretical aspects of the music of Africa. The lack of a canon of an African musical repertoire in music departments coupled with generalizations about music in Africa and associations with other disciplines suggests that African music lacks the wherewithal to stand on its own in the U.S. academy.

The most frequently recorded and aired repertoire is popular music, which traditionally has a low status in schools of music. Folkloric performances are staples at events focusing on some aspect of Africa or for entertainment purposes. Writings on music in Africa by scholars and researchers are distributed among the disciplines mentioned above. Literature on these topics by Africans on the continent rarely finds its way into libraries throughout the United States. Yet the fact that African music pervades these other disciplines suggests and probably promotes the stereotype that music permeates African people's lives.

In my experiences in the Kenyan academy, there was little available literature or notated repertoire of African music in the 1980s. Resources were drawn from writings by European or American scholars. It was not until the 1990s that the school's curriculum was enhanced by scholarly writings by Africans other than the Nketia text and a few others such as, in the case of Kenya, that by George Senoga-Zake. Most articles or books approached the study of Kenyan music through anthropological lenses, rather than musicological, theoretical, or compositional perspectives. However, an enormous drive to promote the performance of African music in schools was endorsed by the government's ministries of culture and education through competitive festivals. The repertoire most notated was choral music, which at first focused on arrangements of folk songs similar to the approach by Fisk University's arrangements of spirituals (see note 2).

By the mid-1990s, a concerted effort was launched to encourage choral compositions in African idioms drawing inspiration from cultural groups in the country and, eventually, the continent. While playing African instruments was encouraged at music festivals and in high schools and colleges, little was done to develop gradated exercises or repertoires. This situation continues to contribute to the deficiency of African instrumental performance experiences outside of drumming, which in turn affirms the stereotype that drums are the most common African instruments. It further leads to a loss of historical repertoire in that it curtails the lineage or guild of, and respect for, instrumental specialists.

Ethnomusicology and the Study of Music of Africa

In the United States, scholarship in African music, established in the fusion of anthropology and musicology, is located in the discipline of ethnomusicology. Some schools offer a cultural-social approach, and others have performing ensembles that introduce particular African national, ethnic, choral, and instrumental music practices.[10] The cultural approach creates awareness about similarities and differences among African peoples. It also helps build a healthy respect for other music traditions in the United States, even if they are not necessarily visible in music departments. Students are further exposed to various ways that different cultures theorize about music, its forms, structures, and styles, by analyzing select pieces from the large pool of available repertoire. Diverse music from the Smithsonian Global Sounds database and others such as Naxos has accelerated the aural availability of African music for analysis. By observing the dates when the music was recorded or collected and comparing progressive bites through to contemporary trends, it is possible to trace historical layers of existing sound samples.

Ethnomusicology as a discipline in Kenya was, however, not positively embraced by the music academy. The beginnings and development of ethnomusicology as a discipline sought out differences and generalizations in a less than positive light regarding African music. The approach alienated African scholars and practitioners from the performance of their music, perhaps creating ambivalence between the lived experience and the studied reports. African scholars were trained in European music in accordance with the academy, with no models of African compositional practices. Instructors in the performance of African music in the academy were often rural musicians from different ethnic groups, without a common language for discussing the intricacies of their styles. They taught adult students from cultures different from their own, using the "unnatural" environment of the modern school.

The African academy has also been slow in developing a guild of indigenous local performers to service the tertiary education level. In my first tenure at Kenyatta University in the 1980s, we had no gradated repertoire for African music performance skills. Students selected traditions they were most familiar with. In my last position, from 2001 to 2003, we encouraged students to build a body of progressive repertoire and learn the musical language of the tradition being studied. Such a challenge saw students shifting their major instruments from European to Kenyan ones and proceeding to graduate studies on indigenous instruments. The antagonism to locating African music study in ethnomusicology is gradually diminishing as terms such as *African musicology* gain currency, moving the discipline from theories and methods rooted in anthropology and sister disciplines to theory, history, composition, and performance from a musician's, music theorist's, or musicologist's perception.

My tenure in the U.S. academy relative to African music has been as a performer and a scholar. As a student in the 1980s, I taught an African dance class. The bulk of the students interested in indigenous African dances were white female students. The males were fascinated mostly with drums. In my later experiences in the 1990s, I was expected to join and quickly excel in African drum and dance classes regardless of whether their African origin was of a different tradition from my cultural and social background, exposure, and education. I was not so shocked that I was expected to play the drum and dance, since these stereotypes were prevalent everywhere. I was, however, surprised by the assumption that I would instantly sing and move correctly to any "African" music.

In my experience in the U.S. academy, African music is very rarely an integral part of a music department—it is more likely an elective. African Music is taught as a performance ensemble or as an elective from a cultural perspective. Schools with general introduction to world music courses often offer one module dedicated to African music. Popular texts with such a module emphasize the general characteristics and provide samples that until recently focused on conservative indigenous styles frozen in time and recounted in the ethnographic present. In these classes, African music is one among many topics in a given semester. Usually, the required texts contain a negligible sample of five to six musical excerpts.[11] Such offerings compare poorly to the similar examples afforded countries such as Japan and reinforce the stereotype of Africa as one large uniform country.

Perhaps the largest transformation in relation to African music and musicology has occurred in courses that focus on genres or styles such as popular or gospel music in Africa. While the cultural dimension is expected, most students are surprised that music genres in Africa have histories; that there are ethnic, national, and Pan-African popular music forms; and that religious music with European or Asian roots has established derivatives in African countries, each with unique idiomatic characteristics. Given the ethnomusicological disciplinary bias, most students view the music of Africa through the cultural rather than compositional lens with a formal history that has developed over time. Even popular music in Africa, with almost 100 years of history since the beginning of its documentation, is scrutinized from a cultural angle or marketed as "world music," the quintessential fusionist label. Once American students identify their own cultural and subcultural practices, informed and punctuated by various rituals, they recognize not just the historicity of any culture's music, but also how music reinforces individual, historical, cultural, social, religious, political, and geophysical identities.

Students also come with certain expectations. African diasporic music such as rumba, reggae, or blues was the backbone of global popular music of the 20th century. Because these musical forms are commonplace in mainstream America, students are often blind to stereotypes that are perpetuated, disguised, transformed, and embedded in the contemporary media. The burden created by historical and mediated myths, stereotypes, and realities about the music of Africa and the musicality of people of African heritage and descent may play a role in why some students avoid taking African music classes.

Some schools have African music performing ensembles integrated into other course offerings. Usually, the ensemble is either a choir or a hand-drumming class. The students are often unprepared to learn specific patterns related to different styles or cultures and amazed at the time it takes to attain correct stroke mannerisms or move in time with the appropriate body posture. Students thereafter become appreciative of the diversities of musical styles and practices on the continent. They also begin to respect the processes that any musician undergoes to perfect his or her skills, through practice and an understanding of concepts central to the music style. I seek to move students beyond folkloric appreciation to the appropriate musicianship. I often provide notation for students for whom the written score is a primary pedagogical tool. These students, regardless of their level of music literacy, tend to respect the transcribed score.

In the Kenyan academy, I had few problems with choral music in different Kenyan and African languages. Because Kenyans grew up with diverse languages spoken at home, in the street, and at school, they were quick to grasp foreign words, whereas my students in the United States always approach the exercise with trepidation. For the latter, I transcribe the text, explain the meaning, and go over the orthography and pronunciation for several weeks. In both situations, the students drew on their indigenous musical and linguistic intonation in interpreting the texture, such as employing Southern diphthongs to a Kiswahili text or, in the Kenyan case, a Kikuyu singer of a Luyia language text used an inappropriate thin nasal texture.

The most difficult aspect of working with students used to thinking of music as separate from movement has been teaching dance or helping them to approach the whole body as an instrument that not only responds to music, but actually makes music. This is where I meet the most resistance. My Kenyan students were quick to learn new dances because of early and regular exposure to diverse African dances in school and at music festivals. They recognized body rhythm as intrinsic to the music, articulating pulse or timeline versus dance. For my U.S. students, any movement is dance. Apart from formal dance students or those involved in recreational dance, there was great resistance to any movement including choreographed instrumental techniques. It was even more intimidating to sing and dance at the same time. I believe that part of the problem lies in the scarcity of regular music models for U.S. students. In Kenya, students saw these dances on the street, on television, and elsewhere, reinforcing the visual images and facilitating connections.

My African music ensemble class is required to perform before a sizable audience. Students' reviews of the experience have gradually shown excitement, awe, and great pride. For example, we normally perform at Africa Culture Day, an event organized by the University of Georgia's faculty members who teach African languages. The audiences at this event are primarily fellow students with an understanding of diversity in Africa beyond that of their peers. While they likely understand certain cultural nuances, they also expect a higher level of musicianship than that expected in their language classes, where song is used to reinforce linguistic structures. This sympathetic audience also recognizes that the group is learning to perform in much the same way as they are learning a language. My subsequent scheduled performance ensemble always draws participants from this audience.

In 2009, we also performed at a community event attended by the public. I introduced the pieces after a short discussion on the diversity of Africa. The event occurred after the performance at the university's Culture Day. My students were more confident at the second performance. The crowd was enthusiastic, and the students were ecstatic. They felt as if they were authorities and presented themselves well. Part of their assessment was based on their ability to adequately respond to the audience's questions about the music and culture without my input. I had required that they learn the cultural information.

In 2010, we performed for a different community as our first out-of-class event. It was a fund-raising event for Uganda. The students were nervous, so I preceded each piece in the set with an explanation. The attention and reception by this mixed audience of campus and general community members was remarked upon by students in their evaluation of the event. The questions and observations by the audience allowed students to comment on different manifestations of African music. Maybe even more validating for the students was the presence at the event of "real"

Africans, from the cultures we showcased, who commented positively and proudly on our musical representation of Africa. I concluded that the students had grasped that, beyond culture and socialization, instruction and practice enable good performance, appreciation, and knowledge of African and Afrogenic music and deconstruct and negate stereotypes and myths about any genre.

On Appreciation and Dissemination

How does a teacher help students in the U.S. academy gain greater appreciation for African music or music in Africa? Students have become more cognizant of Africa as part of contemporary culture. Given the availability of media and technology, students should be encouraged to interview African music students and musicians online or in chat rooms. The dialogue invigorates class discussions. While generalizations do exist, national, ethnic, family, and individual musical preferences can be outlined through case studies. I have advocated for the presence of case studies on music in specific African countries or cultures in world music texts to be commensurate with counterpart chapters in other parts of the world.

Adequate literature is available on individual countries such as Ghana, with a focused study of the Ewe to demonstrate indigenous folk, classical, and popular music in historical and cultural contexts, with modern developments. Students can conduct group and individual research projects on African music to gain knowledge and also to dispel historical and popular myths and deconstruct stereotypes. They can then share their findings in oral and written presentations. It is possible to date performances, instruments, and people that were seminal in developing certain repertoire and instruments. Documentation on iconic figures and styles from the 20th century is now available, particularly on popular music figures. For example, Fela Kuti of Nigeria has been written about in various disciplines and has a sizable output of music that can be analyzed from historical, musicological, political, and cultural perspectives. Students can further interview Africans in the United States or even in Africa to discover their tastes, preferences, and opinions on music and musicians. While live interviews are most effective, the Internet's social networks are an amazing resource.

While I involve students in ensemble performances, I also require them to attend concerts of indigenous, folkloristic, and contemporary fusions of African music. Of the groups that have performed under the auspices of the University of Georgia's School of Music, one from Botswana deconstructed some prevalent myths. When the troupe visited the campus in 2004, I did not prepare the students in any way regarding what to expect. I wanted them to form a raw impression and then to follow up the concert with a report and discussion. The group had no instruments of any kind. The body generated intricate rhythms and dances. Anyone listening to the performance without seeing the performers assumed that the polyrhythms heard were played on drums. Students were surprised that Khoisan groups from Botswana did not possess an indigenous drumming tradition. However, dancers clapped and stomped to create complex melodic and rhythmic relationships. Since these students from Botswana spoke English (the country was previously an English colony), students were able to interview several members of the troupe. At the end of the one-and-a-half-hour concert, the crowd refused to leave. Among the audience's comments was the great wonder that one can enjoy a concert of African music that doesn't involve the use of drums. Further connections were made with tap dancing and clogging, traditions associated respectively with African American Greek fraternities and sororities and with the Irish through the popular marketing of the Riverdance performance group and movie. Connections were therefore made and appreciated in regard not only to the African diaspora, but also to non-Africans in a way that facilitated discussion of how dances based on a fundamental idea have been presented and interpreted by different culture groups over time.

Travel to Africa through study abroad and other programs can expose students to music in contemporary Africa. It is also possible to work on a music project using archival, library, and ethnographic methods before and after the study abroad experience. Other resources such as radio shows also assist in disseminating knowledge. For example, one of my American students began a radio show in fall 2009, airing popular music from different African countries. The show attracted African students, who expressed their surprise on hearing classic popular songs from their countries. They called in with requests or suggestions for other artists. Several African students even became regulars at the studio. They were interested in authentic representations and felt that their presence validated the show. The program provided a bridge between what the American student had learned and the expectations of the African students.

Students are gradually learning to identify idiomatic instruments, styles, and popular musicians associated with different peoples or nations of Africa. In this process of education, myths, stereotypes, and realities about the music of Africa are finally being dynamically assessed, shared, and bridged.

Notes

1. This situation is slowly changing with works such as William H. Nyaho (2007) and Fred Onovwerosuoke (2007). Nyaho and Onovwerosuoke have transcribed works that could possibly be included in a canon of piano exercises or in the repertoire taught in a music school. I do not make the case relative to popular or folk music because of how these genres relate to other disciplines such as folklore, anthropology, and cultural and media studies rather than music departments. I also am not suggesting that there are no African composers in the manner prescribed by the canonic music academy. Several African composers have adopted Eurogenic structures and forms. For example, Akin Euba wrote the opera *Chaka* in the 1970s, but it has had limited performances. *Chaka* is rooted in Yoruba musical, lyrical, and poetic idioms, but it is arranged for a Western orchestra, with some West African modern and indigenous instruments. This Pan-African opera dramatizes the life of a well-known southern African king, Shaka the Zulu, using ideas drawn from Senegalese poets and philosophers and President Léopold Sédar Senghor, while mingling English text with Yoruba Oriki

poetry. The composer quotes classic works like the Dies Irae (Day of Wrath) from the work of French composer Hector Berlioz, among other devices, as part of his compositional strategy garnered from the various worlds that inform his musical and cultural formation. For more analytical readings of the work, see Omojola (2000).

2. It is usual to include African American choral works; the long-standing tradition traces back to the Fisk Jubilee Singers, whose arranged spirituals became an American choral signature. The original Fisk Jubilee Singers were an African American performing group from Fisk University (one of the earliest integrated universities), formed in 1871 to fund-raise for the institution. The group's renditions of arranged spirituals became a model for other such repertoires and led to the establishment of jubilee groups at many black universities. For more on the Fisk Jubilee Singers, see Southern (1997:225–228).

3. Eileen Southern's classic text *The Music of Black Americans: A History* (1997) and her edited volume *Readings in Black American Music* (1983) include introductory chapters focused on the African heritage of music, with examples of musical and other performance behaviors drawn from Western and Central Africa that were replicated in the United States.

4. Alan P. Merriam's *The Anthropology of Music* (1964) solidified this approach to studying non-Western music.

5. For a deconstructive reading of African rhythm, see Agawu (1995).

6. See, for example, Trowell and Wachsmann (1953) regarding Uganda's instruments and Charry (2000) on Mande music.

7. Professor Nketia, of Ghana, is a musicologist, composer, and educator. He has been the foremost Africanist in music studies since the 1950s. He has written extensively on music and music education in Africa and, more specifically, in Ghana. He has had an extensive impact on developments in music education in Africa and advocates through his teaching, composition, and policy statements. For some perspective on his impact, see Akrofi (2002) and DjeDje and Carter (1989).

8. Two other texts were written during this period: Francis Bebey's *African Music: A People's Art* (1975), which while also quite widely read was not extensively adopted as a text in many schools, and Ashenafi Kebede's *Roots of Black Music: The Vocal, Instrumental, and Dance Heritage of Africa and Black America* (1982), which had limited circulation. Kebede's work addresses many issues in a noncomprehensive manner and focuses more on Ethiopia's role rather than introduce the diversity found in Africa. The next most useful text is an edited volume from the Garland Encyclopedia of World Music series (Stone 1998). It contains regional and national summaries of indigenous African music styles and practices, with a few case studies of some ethnic groups. A section labeled "Issues and Processes in African Music" (Stone 1998:101–438) presents the most studied interests by European and North American scholars.

9. During the 1960s and 1970s when civil rights movements were directly questioning the marginalization and disenfranchisement of African Americans, Nketia's text (1974a), I believe, helped reinforce the broad African musical heritage and identity that was essential to this constituency. Nketia also wrote, in this period, a number of articles that highlighted the connections between Africa and its diaspora, such as "The Musical Heritage of Africa" (1974b) and "African Roots of Music in the Americas: An African View," which was published in the *Jamaica Journal* (1979). Nketia has since reprinted essays considered seminal to scholarship on music in Africa in *Ethnomusicology and African Music: Collected Papers* (2005).

10. Ghanaian drum ensembles are the most dominant ensemble type, partly due to the influence of Nketia, who introduced Ghanaian Ewe musicians into the American academy during his tenure at the University of California, Los Angeles (UCLA), the premier ethnomusicology institution in the 1960s through the 1980s. For more information on the timeline and impact of the UCLA program, see http://www.ethnomusic.ucla.edu/celebrating50years/timeline.htm, accessed April 28, 2010.

11. An examination of the standard texts for these classes such as Titon (2008), Nettl et al. (2007), and Shelemay (2006) or case studies produced by Oxford University Press demonstrates the inequities accorded African music (see Oxford University Press's Global Music Series). For example, while whole chapters are devoted to Japan, Indonesia, Ecuador, and Poland, with even more specific genre, instrumental, or regional emphases, no African country receives the same treatment.

14 What Paltry Learning in Dumb Books!

Teaching the Power of Oral Narrative

Caleb Corkery

The ancient kingdoms of West Africa thrived from the 4th to the 16th centuries, passing power from Ghana to Mali to Songhai for over a thousand years. Though these medieval empires were distinct, they oversaw a region of people with common ancestry and shared cultural practices. One role that runs through these various empires and centuries is the community historian or storyteller, the "griot" as the French generically labeled the many regional variants. The griot's knowledge and skill provide cultural cohesion as they connect a community's history to the present through narrative. Trained to memorize and perform stories, griots pass on these stories to educate and inspire their listeners. This position as storyteller, historian, and social critic makes griots both powerful and feared. Before going to battle, for instance, a warrior might pay to hear of the past glories of his ancestors.

When European explorers and missionaries encountered West Africans in the 16th century, they described griots as social pariahs: "disreputable," "buffoons," "gross and indecent," "depraved," and "sycophants" (Hale 1998:81–113). These terms were all used to describe a thousand-year-old profession that sustained social relations and cultural knowledge.

Classroom material that uncovers the long forgotten and misrepresented can make for a strong impression on students. The oral tradition of the West African griot provides such an opportunity, a distinct representation of cultural values students from Western cultures find counterintuitive and challenging to the worldview they have inculcated. The pedagogy discussed here attempts to access elements of a traditional West African perspective through an oral history project.

Western cultural attitudes typically oppose the perspective offered by the West African griot. Educators encourage students to imagine new visions of themselves that move with the future trends of society, rather than encourage students to draw strength and ambition from their pasts. Instead of valuing spoken words that recount the past, they are taught the importance of reading printed material and learning to write similarly. In some ways, the values of this educational system directly contradict the cultural perspective taught in traditional West African societies. Pointing out such contrast gives students a reference for understanding a West African perspective; it also gives them a lens through which to critique their own cultural assumptions.

The pedagogy developed in this chapter aims to raise students' appreciation for oral culture and to challenge their privileged notions of literacy. Specifically, the oral history project focuses on teaching the following: (1) oral narrative is flexible enough to represent people's lives in accordance with the rhetorical situation; (2) drawing from the past, oral narrative is a vehicle for shaping one's identity; and (3) while narrative allows one control over how the past is remembered, spoken narrative also shapes how the past connects to the present. In this chapter, these themes are brought out in a literature course through the use of interviews. The course is titled African American Literature, but the pedagogy could be productively applied to other literature and history courses as well. After providing an overview on the West African griot, this chapter outlines the oral history project, providing samples of students' work as they proceed through the lesson.

West African Griots

The griot tradition institutionalizes a cultural perspective drawn from the past. Moreover, the narrative products inherited from that long history reflect the core of what the culture has passed down (Johnson 1986:25). As historian David Conrad points out about surviving West African epic narratives, "These texts provide avenues to understanding the rich fabric of the brilliantly creative cultures from which the traditions emerge" (2006:76). The griot's role, as Foday Musa Suso explains, is designated to preserve history in narrative form: "Griots would ride along beside kings, singing their praises. They recited the warriors' names and words of inspiration and encouragement: Tell me what you will do on the battlefield, they might sing. Do something that I can pass on to future generations so you'll never be forgotten" (quoted in Kopka and Brooks 1996:36).

The West African history perspective does not ensure that oral texts passed down are accurate records of past events. The nature of oral performance leads the texts to be altered to suit the needs of the present. In fact, the griot directs the narrative to illuminate currently relevant themes or to bring out familial lineages to establish a common ancestry. According to Jan Jansen, a scholar of Mande culture, griots use historical narratives to reconstruct the past to "give an historical dimension to and validate a contemporary social relationship" (2000:9).

Some of the social functions performed by griots in the savanna of West Africa require poetic and musical talent, but most of the duties of the griot require extensive rhetorical skill. As genealogist, the griot may need to convince a prospective bride's family of the noteworthy heritage of the proposer's family. As an advisor, rulers, patrons, and members of society may call upon the griot. According to Lavalliere, a French administrator in Upper Guinea in 1911, the griot managed the cultural affairs of the chief and was not allowed to leave his side, "especially during discussions, trials, and deliberations, in order to support his criticisms and to approve his decisions" (Hale 1998:27). As spokesperson, the griot explains and elaborates the will of his patron. The griot accentuates the power of the person he speaks for by acting as his instrument, but the wordsmith possesses power by shaping meaning through his rephrasing. As diplomat or ambassador, the griot conveys messages from the rulers in a context broad enough for foreigners to understand. As mediator, the griot may be called upon to resolve disputes within a family (Hale 1998:28–30).

Of the many roles demanding oratory skill, the most prominent are praise singers and epic storytellers, which are often combined into the same performance. Praise singing, a description of someone's deeds and qualities, is the griot's most common function (Hale 1998:115). New names are often ascribed to an individual in recognition of an accomplishment, sometimes connecting the subject to other great moments or people in history. The praises become "verbal monuments that fix both the hero [the subject] and the griot ancestors of the narrator in a specific moment on the timeline of [West African] history" (Hale 1998:117).

As the griot performs, the history told has great sway over the audience, since one derives power from the past in the West African worldview (Hale 1998:119). Nobles are known to empty their purses to griots to hear their praise songs. Praises motivate the listener, but the power they engender is also associated with a mysterious life force called *nyama*, according to the Mande. The griot imparts power of the occult by channeling the past to praise, insult, and shape an individual's behavior and reputation (Hale 1998:119–121).

The griot represents a challenge to Western cultural perspectives. The knowledge and power of the griot—profound as it may be—is local and personal, and inaccessible to outsiders. Orienting to the oral accounts of the lives that have created their surroundings, the griot taps into an aesthetic and understanding that dwarfs what cultural outsiders can appreciate.

Oral History Project

Grounding in Cultural Perspective

The first goal of this pedagogy is to expose students to the history and perspective of West African griots. Assisted by the earlier material in this chapter, students can appreciate the griot as a critique to their cultural assumptions. Specifically, the griot's role offers a sharp contrast in perspective that makes the privileged status of literacy over orality noticeable. Hearing griots promote the advantage of orality over literacy can help students recognize the need to adjust their perspective as they enter into the role of oral historian. In *Sundiata: An Epic of Old Mali*, Djibril Tamsir Niane (1970) represents griots as able to read the country's future by knowing its past. The faculty of memory and the warmth of the human voice are lost in written cultures, as he proclaims: "What paltry learning is that which is congealed in dumb books!" (Niane 1970:28). West African scholar Samba Diop describes the griot as constituting "the living chain between the contemporaries and their ancestors" (1995:36). Diop claims that written texts are "mummified, fixed" (1995:16) compared to the song or tale performed orally that continues to live and grow with variations and embellishments.

Training Oral Historians

Facing a project of conducting or interpreting an interview, students are likely to be receptive to interview training. The student goals for this unit are (1) to develop skills in bringing out a person's story by establishing rapport, asking directive questions, and asking follow-up questions and (2) to develop sensitivity to the influences on the narrator's presentation: the purpose of the interview and the perception of the interviewer's role. As a first step, students might read Linda Shopes's "Making Sense of Oral History" (2002). Shopes provides much of what students need in a single document by assisting oral historians in processing an interview with questions about the narrator's identity, possible issues the narrator might experience given the interviewer's identity, and ways to focus the conversation (2002:1).

With Shopes's guide, the students are asked to analyze an interview, using both an audio file and the written transcript. Their comments from listening to the interview reveal considerable insight into the particular dynamic of personal information conveyed orally. Students notice many missed opportunities by the interviewer to draw out the narrator's story. Many also comment on the awkwardness of asking questions of a stranger and the difficulty of shifting the interviewer's role to someone interested in another person's life.

Regarding the content of the interview and the narrator's self-presentation, several notice a narrative shape emerging based on self-perception. Processing one's life through oral narrative gives one the opportunity to ground one's life, presenting a secure identity. In other words, your story illustrates who you are. Many students comment on how the narrator tells her story in a way that makes her progression into education very natural. Students quickly spot how identity is constructed through the narrative; as one student put it: "[The narrator] has a really strong identity as an educator; from her story, it's what she was meant to do."

Much like the performing griot, the narrator gives an account that suits the needs of the moment, pulling out the necessary history to convey the desired message, while concealing history just as purposefully. For instance, one student summarized the interview as not focusing "on the negative things that may have occurred in her life, she more focuses on the positives of what she has made of herself." Another student pointed out how the "plot" directs us to see what the narrator overcame to develop her current sense of pride. The narrative presents a positive impression for a project collecting the life stories of community leaders. As one student explains, "[The narrator] likes what she is doing and is proud of it because she feels like she is making a difference in the lives of children."

The constructed narrative performance appeared conspicuous to another student, who commented on the lack of detail surrounding the narrator's account as an African American female at a predominately white university. Another student noticed the empowering effect of the constructed self-narrative: "Even though she grew up in a highly segregated setting, we can see that her present understanding of that time is generally based on a positive outlook as can be seen in the way she talks about her childhood." Many students noticed the opportunity in oral narrative for self-empowerment.

Like the "warmth" in the griot's voice as Niane describes, one of the students pointed out how much deeper the individual's perspective is conveyed through the oral narrative and questioned how much he may have missed by only learning the history through written media. By processing the interview together using Shopes's questions, students observe how oral narratives assist identity formation, rhetorical strategies, and self-empowerment. By the end of the exercise, students have keen eyes for analyzing an interview on their own.

Reflecting on the Interview Project

While participating in the interview assignment, students processed their impressions through a discussion board, allowing them to step outside of their analysis and reflect on how working with this project has affected their understanding of orality. Though many students rehashed the comments from their analyses of the interviews, some gave helpful connections to larger cultural themes. In particular, the power of oral history came out in the postings. For instance, one student challenged the griot's ability compared to her own experience with oral narrative: "I learned that oral history captures emotions of that time. I am not sure if a griot could communicate that same emotion that the original storyteller gives." Another response calls attention to the distinct advantage of oral over written history: "In keeping the audio [of the interview] intact, the oral tradition of storytelling is kept alive. I think this is an important aspect of history. Oral tradition reaches back much farther than written records, giving it an appeal that cannot be met by just reading words on a page."

A developing appreciation for the significance of our histories comes through in another student's response: "There is something to be said about looking to our past, our family, our traditions . . . to discover who we really are. [The narrator] spoke of coming from a 'proud people.' She grew up in an atmosphere of love and strength, and that carried her into adulthood, and eventually into mothering and teaching."

Lessons Learned

Several encouraging outcomes emerged through this assignment. Most notably, many students referred to the griot's role as they processed the course material, demonstrating some ability to apply the West African perspective to enrich their own. Considering the griot's use of the past to understand the present, many observed how individual accounts are shaped by connections backward in time. In addition, narrative constructions may not be adequately shaped by knowledge of the past, as one student critiqued her narrator's story as "Westernized and watered down." Many students became attuned to how an individual's actions are not without past influences.

Another positive learning outcome was recognizing the rhetorical power and advantage of oral narrative. Students observed the oral form as shaping constructive identities for the narrators we studied. Though only some noticed the power of delivering one's story in the spoken rather than written form, many students pointed out the empowered stance the narrators created for themselves in the interview moment.

Compared to previous experiences teaching this course, students came away with an increased cultural appreciation for the course material. Applying the lessons from the oral history project, one student noted that the course material represents a "blend that is 'African American'—a knowledge and power in the past, but also a drive toward the future." Overlaying the course material with a West African perspective added to their engagement with the material and to the quality of their analyses.

The uneven quality of the interviews can create frustration or disengagement for some students. Putting them into groups to experience other students' interviews helps alleviate this problem, but the amount of potential analysis for each interview is unavoidably imbalanced.

This project seems incomplete without some experience with presenting oral narrative. The analytical perspective we are asking students to develop relies on an appreciation for the individual's experience related within a rhetorical context. Without the experience of being the narrator, the student remains distantly objective; oral historians, on the other hand, value the history represented in each individual. Also, appreciation for the griot's role is hard to imagine fully without exploring and presenting one's own history.

Conclusion

The pedagogy outlined here uses the perspective of the West African griot as the basis for analyzing written and spoken primary source material. After learning about griots, students applied their understanding to readings in African American literature and to oral narratives from a prior interview project. Each student was assigned an interview to analyze, and, in groups, students developed presentations to represent themes in the narratives. Additionally, students individually produced more in-depth written analyses on the following issues: the intersecting forces of race, class, and sex; the use of memory to bring meaning to their current lives; attempts to connect to larger societal narratives and counter-narratives; evidence of leadership roles; and possibilities for identification with the narrator.

The resulting analyses and response papers revealed that a productive analytical lens had developed. Students provided many insights into the value of oral narrative. In particular, they brought out themes of constructing a positive identity by drawing from one's past, communicating effectively through recreations of personal history, and shaping the past strategically for the rhetorical situation.

The role of the griot provides a concrete illustration of a traditional West African perspective. As a repository of a group's history, the griot uses oral narratives to channel historical power into the present and to help sustain social structures. Studying the griot's perspective gives one access to a worldview representative of a vast section and history of the African continent. The griot's perspective seems antithetical to the Western ethos of facing a future one can influence with skills in writing. Students can readily perceive the challenge posed by the griot's work and can apply the different perspective to course material. Griots present a clear departure from what students are used to, helping them critique and enrich their own cultural perspectives.

The added demands of implementing an oral history project may displace other course material. However, in this project, the course material drives the lessons of the oral history pedagogy. Instead of seeing the additional project as a sacrifice, the process outlined enhanced the material covered in class. In terms of educational objectives, oral history projects also enhance the criteria a liberal arts curriculum may use to evaluate students. The critical thinking in this project demands that students not only use a different cultural perspective for analysis, but also engage in a form of expression that increases their understanding of the power of effective communication. Though oral history projects may not replicate the command wielded by griot's as they perform, they do bring out lessons that tap a rich cultural history in Africa. The interviewed narrator, like the griot, draws from history to shape meaning in the moment. And the student, like the gathered audience, glimpses the construction of a narrative that brings an individual's history to life.

15 Teaching about Africa

Violence and Conflict Management

Linda M. Johnston and Oumar Chérif Diop

MANY AFRICAN WRITERS have addressed the rule of tyranny and violence in postcolonial Africa in their work. Attempts to teach about this literature of violence in Africa can be a challenge for any academic, especially when working with undergraduate students who may or may not have had some prior exposure to African writers or the literature of Africa in particular. Working in interdisciplinary teaching teams can be one way to combine skill sets and expertise in order to provide a better and easier learning experience for the students. Students can begin to understand the context and conflicts that produce the literature, the aims of the authors in presenting the literature, and the role the literature plays in helping to understand conflicts and ways to resolve them.

To understand the role of historical violence in African studies, it is important to understand how the oppressors in Africa controlled their victims and perpetrated horrible crimes. The literature of violence that developed in the postcolonial period functions to both deconstruct the language of oppression and contribute to overcoming tyrannical rule. If the language of oppression is removed, the new resultant narrative that develops is fundamentally different from the original, both in structure and in purpose (Johnston 2000). By the time most students reach the college level, they will have been exposed to analyzing literary work. Adding the tools of conflict analysis, students can zero in on the aspects of the literature that are conflictual. This process helps the students to better understand the violence in general. Our two-pronged approach assists with this in-depth analysis by focusing on (1) the types of conflict and (2) how the literary text dramatizes this conflict. By combining these two types of analysis, students can better understand what the African author is portraying about the conflict he or she is trying to describe.

In this chapter, the focus is on the strategy and the instruments for analysis utilized for teaching a module on African studies and conflict management. The chapter discusses the theoretical models utilized, the process of analysis, and the instruments used. In developing this pedagogical approach, the focus is on literature (in both text and film) produced by Africans.

Our multidisciplinary course on Africa focuses on the struggles for liberty and considers issues dealing with the intersection of politics, culture, race, class, ethnicity, and gender. It also actively connects with issues that are intimately influenced by the sociocultural and political conditions of Africa, as well as promotes a discussion on the theory and issues that inform and affect African studies. Because of students' low exposure to African literature as a discipline, the class helps them acclimatize to the literary discourse and enhances their reading and interpretation skills.

Given most U.S. students' unfamiliarity with the context of African literature, the critical analysis of literatures of violence, or the analysis tools utilized by the conflict resolution field, along with the cultural, historical, and social factors that inform the literary text, it would be counterproductive to start any course with complex narrative structures punctuated by various allusions. More than anything, the students need to learn to conduct a careful and thorough analysis of what they are reading. Instead of burdening them immediately with the most complex works, we start the module with texts that are short and fairly easy to grapple with. The fact that students are not initially intimidated by the length and the complexity of the cases eases them into the different layers of the text, one layer at a time. As a case in point, the reading and discussion of Chinua Achebe's "Dead Men's Path" (2005) or Ngugi wa Thiong'o's "The Martyr" (1975) or "A Meeting in the Dark" (1997) reveal some major issues that have been central to the postcolonial African experience such as the racial, cultural, and political antagonisms. Students are often more comfortable navigating such texts that are not burdened by intricate narrative structures and too culture-specific elements.

These stepping-stones allow the students to grapple with historical, cultural, and social issues and to engage progressively with longer and more complex texts. Subsequently, instructors can expand on the religious and cultural issues that are at the heart of these works. Furthermore, these preliminary readings and discussions prepare the students for their exploration of more complex texts. For example, the importance of education as argued by the character Njoroje in *Weep Not, Child* (Wa Thiong'o 1967) could be an entry point into the discussion of education in *My Children! My Africa!* (Fugard 2001). Both Mr. M in *My Children! My Africa!* and Njoroje in *Weep Not, Child* believe that education is the gateway to the emancipation of blacks in Africa.

In order to guide the students' analysis of conflict, this chapter recommends a concise overview of a study of conflicts that focuses on several dimensions of conflict: definitions of conflict, conflict and communication, cooperation and competition, the phenomenon of mutual influence, interdependence and independence, compatible versus incompatible goals, and the impact of scarce resources. The students can be encouraged to construct a conflict-analysis framework based on these concepts and dimensions, using five tools (outlined below) in their analysis of the works of literature and film. Each of these tools can help the students to understand the conflict in the literary work or film in a different way. Students should be able to each use the models they deem appropriate for their conflict, work together to analyze one model at a time, or each use different models to compare results. Each approach adds to the flexibility of both the teaching and the learning.

The Five Conflict Analysis Tools

This chapter recommends the use of five conflict analysis tools for examining conflict particularly related to the African literature of violence:

1. The *SPITCEROW model*, developed by Christopher Mitchell (1981; Mitchell and Banks 1996), which examines the sources of the conflict, the parties involved, the pertinent issues, the tactics used by the parties, the changes and enlargement of the conflict, the roles of various parties, the potential outcomes, and the winner;
2. A *Worldview model*, developed by Lloyd Kwast (1992), which examines the belief systems, the values, and the behaviors of the parties;
3. A *Dimensions of Conflict model*, developed by Lee Gardenswartz and Anita Rowe (1994), which examines influences such as geography, income, status, seniority, religion, appearance, race, ethnicity, education, gender, and age;
4. A *Levels of Analysis model* that for our purposes involves the intergroup, intragroup, interpersonal, and intrapersonal dimensions; and
5. The *Types of Conflict model*, developed by Christopher Moore (2003), which involves the categories, relationships, data, interests, structures, and values.

Each of these models can be examined to determine its usefulness for the conflict that is being studied. They may be used alone or in tandem.

The combination of these five conflict analysis tools can help students achieve a very thorough and deep understanding of the conflict and violence present in African literature. Additional learning could involve the students beginning to decide which tools may be relevant for which types of texts or films, as well as which tools are most useful for the type of conflict they perceive in the literary work.

Student Learning: The Meta-analysis of Conflict

The meta-analysis of conflict requires the combination of all five models. Students need to be able to analyze, process, and assess a conflict situation, that is, to draw a map of the conflict and what is occurring. Having several models of analysis at their disposal contributes to their ability to analyze the conflict from a literary point of view and also strengthens their ability to conduct an in-depth analysis in order to better understand the conflict. The literary analysis informs the conflict analysis and vice versa.

Let us take one example of an identity- and land-based conflict that has been covered extensively by African authors: that of the far-reaching repercussions of the Great Trek on the indigenous people across South Africa. For example, if the student determines that this is a value- or structure-based conflict using the Type of Conflict model, at the intragroup Level of Analysis, which involves geographic location in the Dimensions of Conflict, which is complicated by a Worldview that attaches the character only to this particular geographic space, and that the conflict is Changed and Enlarged by any threat to that geographic space, then the student has a much more thorough understanding of the complexity of the conflict. It would also help the student to understand some of the reasons why, in this example, characters would become so wedded to and anxious about any perceived threat to their land or their identity based on that land. Given this enhanced understanding of and knowledge about the conflict, the student is much better equipped to understand why the literary characters take the actions to protect their land as they do. The analysis also assists students in understanding how and under what circumstances characters would act similarly in the future.

In the following example, students are asked to identify the central conflict in Ngugi wa Thiong'o's "The Martyr" (1975) before proceeding with a literary analysis. "The Martyr" opens with the murder of two European settlers, Mr. and Mrs. Garstone, by their own Kenyan "houseboy." Mrs. Hardy and Mrs. Smiles visit Mrs. Hill to discuss the news. The husband of Mrs. Hill, one of the first settlers to the area, has died, and her children are at school in England. While she prides herself on her decent treatment of the Africans whom she employs, Mrs. Hardy and Mrs. Smiles see the African people as "savages" who will never be civilized. Mrs. Hill boasts of the loyalty of her servant, Njoroge, who has planned this night to kill her as an act of rebellion with the aid of members of the Freedom Movement. However, thinking of her deceased husband and her children, Njoroge loses the heart to kill Mrs. Hill. He decides, instead, to run to her house and warn her before the arrival of the Freedom Boys. When she hears Njoroge knocking at her door, Mrs. Hill assumes that he has come to kill her, and she shoots him. After identifying the conflicts using the conflict analysis tools, students are then asked to use two literary models to suggest a literary interpretation of the story.

Two Additional Literary Models

The first of these models is an adaptation of the analytical moves as defined by David Rosenwasser and Jill Stephen (2009) and is used to analyze a conflict situation by identifying its various literary features. The students can analyze the conflict both from the perceived perspective of each character in the literature and by looking at the conflict as a whole, from a perspective outside of the conflict. Maintaining this balance both between the literary analysis and the conflict analysis as well as between the individual's perspective within the conflict and the outsider's perspective can be very effective.

By looking at it from the outside, students can learn to ask themselves "How would the conflict seem if I were this character?" and "What do I know about the conflict?"

Rossenwasser and Stephen (2009) argue that understanding and interpreting a work of art is an ongoing process which takes time, that to really understand any one part of a work the reader needs to understand the whole, and in order to understand the whole, the reader needs to understand all of the parts. They go on to say that as more information about the work is acquired, interpretation gradually changes to incorporate that information. Effective analysis pays close attention to details: moving from generalization to analysis and moving from larger subject to key components.

Rossenwasser and Stephen claim that in order to understand a subject, the reader or viewer must get past a generic or evaluative response, discover particulars that contribute to the character of the whole, break the whole down into parts, discover how parts contribute to understanding the whole, and consider how the parts are related to one another and how they relate to the subject as a whole. They encourage readers to look for patterns in the reading. If anomalies are found, they can be used to help revise previously held stereotypical assumptions. They suggest that the student would infer what is implied by asking the right questions, determining which details seem significant, and by seeing what the details have in common.

A shortened version of Roland Barthes's (1975) codes serves as the second literary model of critical analysis. Barthes argues in *S/Z* that every narrative is interwoven with multiple codes. Any text is marked by the multiple meanings suggested by codes, two of which are relevant for conflict analysis in African literature:

1. The semantic code, which marks out those semantic connotations that have special meaning for the work at hand,
2. The cultural codes, which tend to point to shared knowledge about the way the world works.

In the study of Wa Thiong'o's "The Martyr," after using the conflict management instruments to analyze the conflicts, a majority of students' literary interpretations converge toward the following:

- Written in the third-person limited point of view, "The Martyr" conveys the thoughts and perspectives of a limited number of characters.
- The perspective of the story switches between three points of view:
  - Mrs. Hardy and Mrs. Smiles, who represent the racist European settlers in the area,
  - Mrs. Hill, who represents the liberal, condescending white settlers, and
  - Njoroge, who represents the native people and who is torn between his humanistic feelings and his radical anticolonial views.
- Through exploring each of these people's thoughts, the author is able to show the cultural blindness that leads to racism and conflict.

- Mrs. Hill wants to be kind and humane, but she has no perspective on the native people and their lives.
- Njoroge, however, harbors feelings of hatred toward his condescending employer. He perceives her as worse than those white settlers who blatantly assume their racism.
- Njoroge is willing to resort to killing because he only sees injustice, until he perceives Mrs. Hill as a wife and mother.

In exploring racism and cultural misunderstanding, this work suggests that colonization breeds a form of racism whose root cause is economic exploitation and political oppression. Only will the characters end the cycle of hatred and racism when they can view each other as human beings. The ironic and tragic ending of the story seems to suggest that this level of humanism cannot be attained under colonial rule.

Conclusion

This chapter has shown how the two-pronged approach to the study of conflict in Africa and in African literature uses a method that helps students to methodically analyze conflict in works of fiction. The combination of (1) the conflict management tools, (2) Rosenwasser and Stephen's analytical moves, and (3) Barthes's codes can give the students an analytical framework with which to thoroughly examine the representation of conflicts in African literature. This interdisciplinary approach to African studies can assist students in their understanding of the postcolonial literature of violence in Africa, the oppressors who sought to control the lives of the people, and the resultant narrative of liberty and liberation. With the conflict management tools, students can identify all aspects of the conflict and then proceed with an analysis of the more complicated intersections of literary, political, cultural, and social issues.

16 Contextualizing the Teaching of Africa in the 21st Century

A Student-Centered Pedagogical Approach to Demystify Africa as the "Heart of Darkness"

Lucie Viakinnou-Brinson

Pᴇʀsᴏɴᴀʟ ᴇxᴘᴇʀɪᴇɴᴄᴇs ɪɴ American universities, including my first encounter with Joseph Conrad's *Heart of Darkness* (1999[1902]), led me to reexamine my role as an African in the West and subsequently as a professor of French and Francophone literatures and cultures. Despite advances in technology and the growing role of the media in attempting to present Africa in a more sophisticated light, a widespread "Afro ignorance" among American students concerning Africa remains. The situation frustrates many African students studying in America, and they are often dismayed at how little their fellow American students know about Africa. I demonstrate how the theoretical-based approach known as global simulation can be implemented and adapted for an African context to balance negative images of Africa and to foster deeper connections with its culture, literature, and people.

Encountering *Heart of Darkness*

As a Beninese studying in the United States, I was plunged into the North American educational system without much preparation. Almost every day, I encountered people who heard my accent and inquired about my origins, asking me questions such as *Where are you from? How did you get here? I heard there is war and poverty in Africa? Is it true that in Africa you have lions as pets?* In the beginning, I welcomed every opportunity to "teach" about Benin and Africa in general and answered questions enthusiastically. Gradually, however, I grew weary of the questions, mainly the ones centering on war, poverty, and animals, and began to shy away at the thought of having to constantly explain the continent I knew and, more especially, Benin, the African country where I grew up. Because many of my interlocutors already held strong views about "Africa," it was not an easy task to bring them to understand its diversity and complexity or to urge them to critically analyze the often decontextualized negative images of Africa that prevailed in the media. As a result, I slowly refrained from joining circles in which I would have to "defend" Africa. I did not revel in my new role as Africa's "defense attorney" and considered removing myself from the "courtroom" as the best action to take. Unfortunately, I adopted the same attitude in my classes as a student. The rare attempts to emerge from my cocoon and to participate in class discussions often failed because of my inability to determine the right moment to "jump" into conversations. Hence, silence, nodding, and smiling became my preferred methods of communication.

One book, however, would end my voiceless confinement: Conrad's *Heart of Darkness* (1999[1902]). The book was assigned in my English literature class, and I became uneasy with its depiction of Africans. When the discussions in class focused solely on Marlow and the other "important characters" in the novel at the expense of the "natives" and the setting (the Belgian Congo), my initial discomfort reemerged. I could no longer remain silent and felt compelled to intervene. For the first time, and very reluctantly, I garnered enough courage to "jump" into the conversation. I expressed my dissatisfaction with the book's portrayal of Africa and African characters. I questioned why a book that perpetrated stereotypical images of a group of people, a country, and a continent could be hailed among the greatest novels in the English literary canon. My comments were met with silence; both my fellow students and the instructor appeared taken aback that I had spoken and, further, that I had questioned the status of a book that for so long was (and continues to be) held in English departments as one of the finest literary works, regardless of its content. My comments about stereotyping appeared to have disturbed and disrupted a shared and widely accepted assumption, and none of the critical essays assigned by the instructor supported my analysis.

While discussing my discontent about the book with senior professors of African literature, they recommended that I read the essay "An Image of Africa: Racism in Conrad's *Heart of Darkness*," by Chinua Achebe (1989). In the piece, Achebe argues that *Heart of Darkness* "projects the image of Africa as 'the other world,' the antithesis of Europe and therefore of civilization, a place where man's vaunted intelligence and refinement are finally mocked by triumphant bestiality" (1989:4). I had finally found supporting evidence for my analysis and shared the article with the instructor. He shared it with the class and described it as eye-opening; he later admitted that the article forced him to reexamine the way he had taught the book for the past 15 years. For me, the experience was also eye-opening; it played a catalytic role in my "coming out" of the veil of silence and indignation to fully embrace my responsibility as an "African," to teach and educate about Africa. As an educator, I have been exposed to several pedagogical practices to teach various subjects.

The exposure led me to select global simulation, an approach that has seldom been used, to teach about Africa and promote a deeper understanding of the continent's various countries and people.

Global Simulation: Definition and Characteristics

The use of education simulation is not new. Educators have designed, used, and evaluated simulations for more than 40 years (Hertel and Millis 2002). Simulation has been credited with motivating students to pursue deep learning (Mills and Péron 2009). Global simulation, another form of simulation often used in foreign-language classrooms, emerged from the *Bureau pour l'enseignement de la langue de la civilisation française à l'étranger* (BELC) in the 1970s in France. The BELC was a response to dissatisfaction with traditional and structural approaches to teaching the French language and civilization abroad. As a result, it began to promote approaches that put the learners at the center and validated their creativity and personal expression. Since then, definitions of global simulation have been multiple. Beatrice Dupuy (2006) describes global simulation as the creation of a fictive yet culturally grounded world in which students develop the role of a character and collaborate with other members of their community to create and invent their own world. Glenn Levine (2004:26, 27) defines the format of global simulation courses as a set of classroom activities used to facilitate cultural literacy and the acquisition of communicative competence. Francis Debyser (1996), proposes *l'immeuble* (the building) as a creative framework to implement global simulation. In the *immeuble* model of global simulation, each student is a fictional tenant of a building, and together with other tenants (fellow classmates) he or she creates and records in writing the happenings of his or her virtual world. Although definitions and conceptualization of simulation models vary, all share the following three key characteristics as articulated by Ken Jones (1984): (1) reality of function, (2) simulated environment, and (3) structure.

Reality of Function

Reality of function suggests that learners create a new identity and embrace that identity. They must behave and act as if their function in the simulation is real. For instance, in a simulation, the student who chooses to be a lawyer must behave and communicate as a lawyer; similarly, a student who chooses to be a journalist must ask pertinent questions, report the news, and perform journalistic duties effectively. As Jones states, "They [students] must stop thinking of themselves as students and avoid standing one step away from their own activities; they must step inside the function mentally and behaviorally and do the best to carry out their duties and responsibilities in the situation they find themselves in" (1984:4).

Simulated Environment

"The environment must be simulated, otherwise it is not a simulation" (Jones 1984:5). In other words, inside a simulated environment, participants create a safe reproduction of a given world filled with "real" people and events. However, the world of the simulation should not have any repercussions on the real world. According to Jones, "There must be no contact, interaction or consequences between the participants and the world outside of the classroom" (1984:5).

Structure

In order to preserve reality of function and a simulated environment, the simulation must have a cohesive structure. Students are to be briefed and debriefed. At the briefing stage, the instructor explains the context, the format, and the length of the simulation and provides the various tasks and makes resources available to the participants. Levine (2004:9) argues that the instructor, often referred to as the controller, in a global simulation must be "a resource person" who aids participants in fulfilling their assigned functions and achieving their stated goals. Jones (1984:7) warns, however, that although structure is important for global simulation, the best part of the simulation is the question minus the answer, which is supplied not in the resources, but rather in the action of the participants. In the debriefing stage, students assess the project and their performance in the simulations.

Adapted Global Simulation in an African Context

Global simulation as a pedagogical tool has been used in several French classrooms (Dupuy 2006; Magnin 2002; Mills and Péron 2009). However, although African countries make up the largest percentage of French speakers, very few global simulation studies have been conducted in African contexts. This section presents an adaptation of a global simulation that has been conducted with advanced learners of French. This project was conducted at a southeastern state university in the United States. The project's title, "Regarder l'Afrique autrement" ("Look at Africa Differently"), was borrowed from the French television news channel TV5Monde. Class was conducted in French only, and discussion and tasks were also in French.

"Look at Africa Differently" ("Regarder l'Afrique autrement")

Unlike conventional global simulation projects conducted in foreign-language contexts that focus chiefly on language skills and culture acquisition, the primary goal of the proposed global simulation was to explore and demystify specific stereotypes about Africa, mainly Francophone Africa. However, it was expected that through writing and research, students would also strengthen their French linguistic skills and cultural acquisition. The project was conducted in an advanced French class.

STEP ONE: PRESENTING THE GOALS OF THE GLOBAL SIMULATION

Prior to briefing and presenting the goals of the simulation, the instructor conducted a pretest to evaluate students' knowledge of Africa. Depending on the goals of the global simulation, the pretest incorporates specific cultural, sociopolitical, and historical elements that the instructor expects the students to master by the end of the simulation. The goals of the present global simulation were as follows: (1) demystify the notion that Africa is a country; (2) demystify the notion that Africans are the same and that Africa is not diverse; (3) demystify the notion that problems and issues such as wars, famine, and AIDS are inherent only to Africa and do not cross continental boundaries; and (4) bring others to look at Africa differently.

Given the multiple stereotypes on Africa, providing a set of clear goals at the outset of the simulation gave students a sense of direction and led them to reflect on the various stereotypes prior to engaging in the simulation.

STEP TWO: PRESENTING THE SIMULATED ENVIRONMENT

Although simulated environments for global simulation have often been created around buildings or apartments, the following global simulation was created around a virtual conference with the following scenario at its core: Recruits each received a letter from the U.S. Peace Corps acknowledging that they were selected to serve in respective Francophone African countries. They individually decided to attend a conference on Africa to strengthen their knowledge of the continent. They fortuitously met at the conference and discovered that they had much in common.

Choosing a conference site as opposed to a building or an apartment allowed students to learn extensively about a variety of topics in selected regions and countries in Africa. It also gave the instructor greater flexibility concerning stereotypes to explore and demystify. Finally, it afforded both students and the instructor greater integration of 21st-century technology in the classroom.

STEP THREE: WEEKLY SIMULATED TASKS

In order to ensure maximization of the target language in the class, all writing assignments and oral discussions and presentations were conducted in French. Journal reflections, however, which were to be included in students' portfolios and returned at the end of the semester, were written in English.

Week One: Getting to Know One Another and Discussing Stereotypes

Simulated Environment One: Presentation of Global Simulation Participants

As they enter the lobby of the Marriott Hotel where they will stay for the duration of the conference, the recruits spontaneously strike up a conversation. Very soon, they discover the following: (1) they are from the same town; (2) they have been selected as future U.S. Peace Corps volunteers and are preparing to go to Francophone Africa; (3) they are at the conference to expand their knowledge about Africa; and, finally, (4) their parents' stereotypes about Africa make them overly concerned and reluctant to fully embrace their children's decision to serve in what they referred to as the "middle of nowhere."

Simulated Environment Two: Discussing Stereotypes

After introducing themselves, the recruits meet again at the opening session of the conference, where the main speaker, a prominent Nigerian writer, Chimamanda Ngozi Adichie, discusses her personal experience as an African student in America. In her speech, she relates stereotypes she encountered and exhorts the crowd not to become prey to a single story of a group of people. The recruits eagerly take notes and, following Adichie's speech, discuss and reflect on her presentation.

Tasks
1. Recruits retreat to their hotel room to watch a recorded tape of Adichie's speech (2009). As a group, they orally reflect in French on her speech.
2. Recruits each write a reflection in their portfolios about lessons learned from Adichie's speech.

Week Two: Exploring Stereotypes at the Conference and Inviting Parents to "Virtually" Learn about Africa

The length of this section will depend on the number of stereotypes the instructor plans to explore and on the number of virtual presentations students wish to attend. In this example, three stereotypes were explored: (1) Africa is a country, (2) Africa and Africans are the same, and (3) Africa is a land of calamities. Other presentation topics at the "virtual conference" might include the exploration of negative images of Africa in the news media, the notion that African women are subservient, or the idea that Africans have minimally contributed to intellectual global thought. Conference presentations might also explore or highlight everyday lives of Africans, politics, or environmental issues.

Simulated Environment One: Africa! A Country?

Recruits individually attend separate presentations on pre- and postmodern Africa. Presenters consist of teachers and/or invited guests to the classroom. During the various presentations, recruits learn about African kingdoms, Africa's balkanization, colonialism, postcolonialism, and modernism. Following the presentations, they meet over dinner to orally exchange newly acquired knowledge.

Simulated Environment Two: How Diverse Is Africa?

The next day, recruits attend French television news channel TV5MONDE's presentations on Africa's diversity. Recruits watch documentaries that present everyday life in various African countries. During the documentaries, they get a glimpse of their future host country. They see and experience firsthand the diversity of Francophone Africa and discuss differences and similarities between African and American cities.

Tasks
1. Recruits orally discuss with peers what they learned from the various presentations and how presentations are contributing to a better understanding of Africa.
2. Recruits write a letter to their parents and explain to them the geography of Africa before and after the Treaty of Berlin, the roles played by Africans during the treaty, and the linguistic and political consequences of the treaty. To conclude and to help their parents put Africa's balkanization in perspective, students compare the balkanization of Africa to other countries in Europe or elsewhere.
3. Recruits write a letter to their parents and share TV5MONDE's (2010) links so they too can virtually travel to Africa and explore its diversity. In the letter, they discuss their impressions of the African country where they will serve as well as their excitement about their upcoming trip.

Week Three: Responding to Parents' Concerns

Simulated Environment One: Parents Take a Virtual Tour to Respective Country with Their Children

Via telephone, parents acknowledge receipt of the letter and agree to virtually tour Africa with their children while communicating simultaneously via Skype. The recruits enthusiastically agree and take the tour again with their parents. However, after each virtual stop, parents are quick to make comments that demonstrate that they continue to hold stereotypes toward Africans and Africa. The recruits do their best to answer their parents' queries during their online conversation.

Simulated Environment Two: Are Stories of Disasters and Catastrophes in Africa Inherent Only to Africa?

As recruits gather to discuss the virtual trip with parents, they receive a text message from their parents urging them to watch CNN's news of wars, famine, and other calamities in a region of Africa they cannot remember. The parents also urge their children to renounce their trip to Africa and return home. The recruits do not respond immediately, but rather begin to design plans that would appease and help their parents see Africa in a different light.

Task
1. Recruits write a letter to their parents in which they (1) discuss and contextualize Africa's calamities, (2) provide specific examples of similar calamities elsewhere in the world, and (3) demonstrate that some calamities are not inherent only to Africa but cut across continents.

Week Four: Celebration before Departure

Simulated Environment One: Departing from the Conference and Returning Home

Prior to departing from the conference, recruits collaboratively research and select online videos, Internet links, and authentic resources that present balanced images of African countries. They collectively agree that, once they return home, they will share with their parents the garnered information and reflections on the conference. Further, they discuss the best methods of presentation including digital storytelling, photo-novella, PowerPoint presentations, postings on Facebook, and the creation of a collective website (Wiki).

Simulated Environment Two: Back Home

Back home, recruits invite their respective families to celebrate their upcoming trip to Africa amid food and music from their respective future host country. Recruits present African countries visually as well as offer reflections on their conference. Family members ask questions, and from the types of questions, comments, and discussions that follow their presentation, the students realize that they have succeeded in alleviating their parents' fears and in helping them to look at Africa differently.

Tasks
1. Recruits present PowerPoint presentations of an individual African country where they will serve as U.S. Peace Corps volunteers. Presentations are followed by parents' questions and recruits' answers.
2. Recruits reflect on the simulation in their reflective portfolio.
3. Recruits complete the posttest (same as the pretest).
4. Instructor debriefs about the simulation.

Discussion: Why Use Global Simulation to Demystify Africa as the "Heart of Darkness"?

Teaching and exposing the dangers of stereotyping to students is closely related to intercultural education. In discussing the importance of teaching cross-cultural understanding in foreign-language classrooms, H. Ned Seelye maintains that acquiring facts only is "meaningless until interpreted within a problem-solving context" (1984[1974]:3). Linda Crawford-Lange and Dale Lange espouse the same stance and argue that an "information-only" approach to teaching culture may establish stereotypes rather than diminish them (1984:157). Yet the most commonly used strategies to teach intercultural and cross-cultural understanding in the foreign-language class-room rely heavily on fact-only approaches including lectures, cross-cultural inter-views, and observation. In fact-only environments, learners tend to be passive recipients of knowledge and lack opportunities to tangibly apply what they have learned.

While global simulation also relies on fact-finding, its additive advantages are that learners are placed in simulated environments that force them to immediately apply newly acquired knowledge and solve problems. In this global simulation, learners are placed in real-life scenarios where they have to solve a specific problem: allay the stereotypical views their parents hold on Africa. Hence, they are actively and continuously engaged in the learning process. They experiment with various roles, including those of researchers, critical observers, persuaders, defenders, and educators. Taking on these new roles challenges them in many ways to become more objective and analytical as they sift through garnered facts to present balanced images of their respective country. In the reflective portfolio, one student wrote, "I had to write some convincing and persuasive papers in order to convince my parents that it was safe to travel to Benin, my virtual country." Another echoed the same sentiment and wrote, "The global simulation did challenge me in a number of ways. It made me become an expert on a country . . . and be able to argue on its behalf."

"Arguing on behalf of" was a recurring theme that emanated from students' responses during the debriefing session. For the first time, they were thrust in roles that challenged them to examine and recognize their own possible stereotypes and speak from the perspective of the "Other," the perspective of the stereotyped. Although the reversal of roles might have been challenging at first, students appeared to be transformed by the experience, as demonstrated by responses in their reflective portfolios. One student stated, "In researching and sharing the research of other class members, I have been able to overcome many stereotypes I myself had formed about Africa, and the knowledge I gained will help me educate people who have those same stereotypes."

In addition to fostering a collaborative, intellectually stimulating, and sharing environment, the global simulation afforded students opportunities to explore stories that were not readily available in mainstream media. One student wrote: "When researching the country, there are endless possibilities of what you will find. I would not have known about their political standpoint, their long-lasting friendship with the United States. I would not have known about their efforts to stop the spread of the AIDS epidemic or about their daily efforts to raise and educate their children. I learned a lot." The use of technology during the simulation also allowed students to argue visually their "case" and contextualize Africa's problems. Through vivid PowerPoint presentations, students juxtaposed striking images of wars and violence in Africa and elsewhere to demonstrate to their parents that Africa's socioeconomic and political challenges do indeed cut across continents.

As early as the 1930s, John Dewey (1933) advocated learning that was active and student-centered and afforded shared inquiry. The present global simulation as demonstrated by students' work and reflection afforded situational contexts in which all three goals were attained. Embedded in experiential learning, the global simulation afforded students unique possibilities to learn, explore, and share inquiry; further, on the basis of students' reflections, it seems to have equipped them with tools to educate others about Africa and influenced their own ways of viewing Africa from a different perspective.

Conclusion

Lack of exposure, ignorance, fear, and stories about the "Other" are main reasons why stereotypes persist. As Adichie (2009) eloquently stated, the problem with stereotypes is not that they are untrue, but that they are incomplete. She argued that when the diverse stories of a group of people, and African people in particular, are reduced to a single story that is told repeatedly, stereotypes easily begin to form and become ingrained in our minds. Constant, repeated, single negative stories about Africa in Western media and in canonized literature such as *Heart of Darkness* have failed to reveal the many untold positive stories of Africans. They have failed to contextualize the catastrophes that plague Africa and to stress that the same catastrophes are also present on other continents. Single stories, as argued by Adichie, have emphasized how negatively different Africa is.

As we move in the new millennium, global simulation, a student-centered pedagogical global approach conducted in a Francophone African context, will provide an ideal framework for learners of French to begin to explore for themselves the many untold positive, balanced stories about Africa. For example, the French TV channel Portail de l'Afrique (Gate to Africa) provides a mine of authentic resources where students can draw from a mosaic of images on Francophone African countries.

The incorporation of today's technology in the global simulation makes it possible for students to work individually and collaboratively to explore, reflect on gained knowledge, and take action. According to Diana Oblinger and James Oblinger (2010), today's "Net generation" (people born in the early 1980s to the late 1990s) prefer teamwork and experiential activities; for them, doing is more important than knowing and knowing alone is unproductive. Studies have shown that by doing, learners know and retain information better. A global simulation environment that focuses on "doing" and leading students to discover other images of Africa will afford them opportunities to uncover how positively similar Africa is to the rest of the world.

PART III

APPLICATION OF APPROACHES
Experiencing African Particulars

Part III of *Teaching Africa* concludes the journey by deplaning the reader at the final destination, learning experiences that actively engage him or her to participate in his or her own education. In this final section, a leap is made from theory into practice. In six chapters, authors portray their involvements in fashioning social activism (Chapter 17), model African Union teams (Chapter 18), study abroad programs (Chapter 19), anthropological methodology field-schools (Chapter 20), global health and social medicine courses in situ (Chapter 21), and host-country Ph.D. programs (Chapter 22).

The third and ultimate domain of Bloom's Taxonomy is "doing/hands"; the chapters in Part III expand the classroom to include real-world settings. Pedagogical research continues to show that *practice by doing* increases the average retention rate for students, while retention rates for *teaching others / immediate use of learning* are even higher. Therefore, if students are able to directly and personally engage with Africa in some real way, they will begin to serve as their own *guides for the 21st-century classroom.*

Some of the chapters in referencing health clinics in Uganda (Chapter 21), historic coastal towns in Zanzibar (Chapter 20), and a host-country Ph.D. program in Ethiopia (Chapter 22) offer opportunities for students who wish to travel to Africa; other chapters in discussing historical treatments (Chapter 19), U.S.-based opportunities for engagement (Chapter 17), and involvement in university-wide clubs, associations, and programs (Chapter 18) are dedicated to the study and understanding of Africa and its diaspora through alternatives to direct travel. As these chapters attest, collaboration with Africans continues to be the primary theme and conceptual framework for this volume. It is the intent of this work that the reader is left standing at the threshold of a new collaborative and pedagogical initiative, one that will not only emphasize *why* Africa is so important in a globalizing world, but will also critically raise their awareness of and need for understanding and *experiencing African particulars* as they relate to the broader political economy of a world system.

17 Shaping U.S.-Based Activism toward Africa

The Role of a Mix of Critical Pedagogies

Amy C. Finnegan

An INFLUX OF American students traveling to study or volunteer in Africa and other regions of the global South (Grusky 2000; Panosian and Coates 2006; Parker and Dautoff 2007; Roberts 2006), the success of several Hollywood films set in Africa (e.g., *Blood Diamond* [Zwick 2006], *The Constant Gardner* [Meirelles 2005], *Hotel Rwanda* [George 2005], and *The Last King of Scotland* [Macdonald 2006]), and celebrity philanthropy performed for Africa-related causes by Bono, Angelina Jolie, and Oprah Winfrey (Bono 2007; Z. Magubane 2007, 2008), all have contributed to a notable increase in young Americans' interest in addressing social problems in Africa in the past decade. Yet, uncritically performed, activism to address "problems in Africa" can entrench essentialized identities, serve as an escape from examining and addressing social problems closer to home or those issues that may directly implicate Americans, and lead to a narrow understanding of social change that does not take into account the efforts of African activists.

Based on critical reflections from teaching at universities in both the United States and Uganda, alongside ethnographic fieldwork conducted with U.S. activists involved in the Invisible Children campaign, this chapter seeks to illuminate the relationship between pedagogy about Africa in the university classroom and students' decisions to participate in social action aimed at addressing social problems experienced on the African continent.[1] It argues that a mix of critical pedagogical approaches is essential to mobilizing young Americans to prudently engage problems experienced in Africa. Specifically, it advocates for a curriculum that includes a focus on African narratives, a critical structural analysis, a social movement analysis, a framework for conceptualizing intervention in Africa, and dialogue on Western perceptions of Africa. Since there is danger of heightened essentialization and paternalism when outsiders focus on social problems in Africa, these varied pedagogical approaches not only require both teachers and students to be deeply reflexive, but they also convey the gravity of social problems such as famine and collective violence, analyze global and regional responses, and inspire thoughtful activism as students recognize their own (and their country's) role in the global context.

The backdrop that currently informs much of the U.S.-based activism toward Africa includes the tendency for young Americans interested in working in Africa to resist risky confrontation through the ongoing efforts of groups such as Invisible Children and the Save Darfur Coalition, the impact of the Rwandan genocide on the contemporary U.S. consciousness, and the historical American politico-cultural orientation toward Africa. It is in response to this backdrop and in an effort to understand it that the mix of critical pedagogical approaches presented in this chapter was developed.

Contemporary Activist Efforts for Africa: Averting Confrontation

Since its inception in 2004, the Save Darfur Coalition—an alliance comprising over 180 national and regional nonprofit groups that are organized primarily on the basis of race, politics, and religion—has relentlessly called for "military involvement in Darfur and pressure on the United Nations" to address the violent conflict occurring in this region in western Sudan (Eichler-Levine and Hicks 2007:713). The tactics of the Save Darfur Coalition have included public rallies and die-ins, various speaking tours, letters to politicians, school fund-raising for humanitarian relief and further advocacy efforts, and a divestment campaign.[2] Similarly, Invisible Children—a U.S.-based education and advocacy organization that began work in northern Uganda and is striving to "end the longest running war in Africa"—has mobilized hundreds of thousands of young people since its inception in 2003.[3] Primarily through the production and circulation of various creative forms of media (e.g., films, podcasts, websites, and social media such as Twitter and Facebook) about the Lord's Resistance Army (LRA) insurgency and its impact on children, Invisible Children has compelled thousands of young Americans to fund-raise millions of dollars and volunteer months of their lives.

Within both the Save Darfur Coalition and Invisible Children, activists demonstrate "their Americanness by assuming the identities of powerful saviors" (Eichler-Levine and Hicks 2007:712). Furthermore, focusing on exotic "othered" locations—such as Sudan, Uganda, South Sudan, the Democratic Republic of the Congo, and the Central African Republic—allows the activists to face less controversy and less personal implication. This circumstance is due in part to the general public's minimal understanding of the history of East and Central Africa, but also to a reiterated narrative about Africa that simplifies categories into good and evil (Mamdani 2007).

While many young Americans are motivated by the Save Darfur Coalition and Invisible Children to take action on critical social concerns in Africa, most appear unwilling to be too contentious, perhaps in fear of derailing attractive personal future opportunities. The activists of Invisible Children are predominately young, white, upper-middle-class students, many of whom attend private colleges and high schools (Finnegan 2013). Most are on an upwardly mobile trajectory and therefore have much to lose by being too confrontational with those in power. Nina Eliasoph (1998) suggests that an avoidance of controversy may be due in part to an American culture that normalizes the avoidance of public political conversation by valuing politeness and suggesting that doing "doable" projects where one person can make a difference is actually better for the common good.

Since few people in the United States know about the complexity of the history and current situation in the East Africa region, it is rather straightforward for young, privileged U.S. students to take a clear, moral stance. After all, who can disagree with ending the use of child soldiers by some insurrection in the jungle of Eastern and Central Africa? Or stopping a genocide? Indeed, striving to address an ongoing political issue in northern Uganda or Darfur, Sudan, is for American young people much less controversial and requires less personal vulnerability than addressing a political issue more directly linked to them—such as the ongoing U.S.-led war in Afghanistan or even addressing a domestic political issue such as the ongoing housing foreclosure crisis or immigration. This remoteness of the issue of concern for Invisible Children and Save Darfur Coalition activists—violence in Sudan and the LRA-affected communities of Eastern and Central Africa—is aligned with a historical narrative of "otherness" (Said 2003[1978]) in which Westerners perceive those from the East as largely distinct and inferior from themselves.

A second critical component that frames many American young people's orientation to global problems is the history of genocide in Rwanda in conjunction with the international community's failure to comprehensively respond, resulting in nearly one million needless African deaths. The thinking is that Western countries' historic failure to respond to Africa's gravest problems has resulted in tragedy; yet, this generation of youth, rife with energy and a new form of global awareness, can behave better. Mahmood Mamdani explicates how the Save Darfur movement claims to have learned from what transpired with Rwanda, namely, that "the lesson is to rescue before it is too late, to act before seeking to understand" (2009:3). Interestingly, the role of the Western outsider in Rwanda, Darfur, and LRA-affected communities becomes apparent at the precise moment of crisis, a humanitarian rescuer. There is no discussion or implication of Western responsibility for structural or historical factors that have shaped these contemporary problems in Africa. In 1994 Rwanda, the international community is faulted for acting as a passive bystander amid an ongoing genocide, not for anything that it did or failed to do that produced the conditions in which the genocide could occur.

This notion that nearly one million Africans died because of the indifference of the international community weighs heavily on many young Americans' consciousness. Mamdani summarizes, "Rwanda is the guilt that America must expiate, and to do so, it must be ready to intervene, for good and against evil, globally" (2009:67). Uncritically performed, this activism, also informed by the American politico-cultural orientation toward Africa that is outlined in this volume's introduction and by a general reluctance to risk confrontation such as noted through the efforts of Invisible Children and the Save Darfur Coalition, will fail to lead to progressive social change. Thus, I have developed a mix of critical pedagogies for teaching Africa in the 21st-century classroom, which can, perhaps, inspire more thoughtful activism toward Africa. It is to this experiential narrative, that I now turn.

Education for Change: A Mixed Critical Pedagogical Approach

This chapter's teaching philosophy is to educate about Africa in such a way as to inspire students to actively work for progressive social change. As liberation theologians and many others who work for social justice agree, there is "something terribly wrong" today in the world (Farmer 2005:153; Gutiérrez 1973). Inequality, the dominance of market approaches, and war all drive the suffering experienced through poverty and disease in northern Uganda and Darfur, among other locales in Africa and beyond. As an educator, my aspiration is to use the classroom and this curriculum on Africa as a springboard for analysis and action. As John Paul Lederach outlines: "Education is never neutral. It always involves a project ultimately aimed at either keeping things as they are or changing them" (1995:26).

My aim is to inspire meaningful activism for students and teachers. I've found that it is critical to take into account the aforementioned social forces shaping activism toward Africa: the ongoing efforts of Invisible Children and the Save Darfur Coalition that present opportunities for young Americans to engage Africa with minimal controversy or risk of implication, the impact of the Rwandan genocide on the contemporary U.S. consciousness, and the historical and contemporary American politico-cultural orientation toward Africa that emphasizes Africa and Africans as "other," inferior to the West, and peripheral to U.S. interests. These dimensions are strong social influences that press upon contemporary young peoples' orientation toward Africa. As an educator committed to encouraging meaningful civic engagement, I have designed my pedagogy with an understanding of the role that these social dynamics play in young peoples' lives before, during, and after their participation in my classroom.

Specifically, I have identified several critical aspects to teaching about Africa in a way that attempts to foster more collaborative U.S. activism with African activists. This varied pedagogical approach comprises the inclusion of African narratives in course readings, a critical structural analysis of problems associated with and experienced in some communities in Africa such as poverty and war, an analysis of social movements, a solid analytical framework for understanding different forms of intervention to address social problems in Africa, and a discussion of common American-held perceptions of Africa and Africans. In what follows, I describe each of these while offering some examples that may be of use to other educators.

African Narratives

Compared to other regions of the world, the amount of scholarship and narratives from Africa written by Africans and available in the United States is minimal; many U.S. university syllabi lack African voices discussing African issues. What too often results is the dominance of people from the global North speaking about African social issues, rather than Africans themselves speaking about African issues. In the sociology course African World Perspectives, a deliberate effort was made to include at least one African narrative for each unit of the course. In the choice of African narratives, I learned to ensure a diversity of standpoints, to send the message that there is multiplicity, contradiction, and complexity within the African populace. Over the years, narratives from South Africa, Uganda, Rwanda, and Nigeria were utilized. Efforts were also made to include shorter selections by African scholars and practitioners that are less personal and more analytical. Some of these thematic areas and their corresponding references are war in Uganda (Akallo and McDonnell 2007); post-conflict transition and justice in South Africa (Gobodo-Madikizela 2003); the female experience of HIV/AIDS in Uganda (Kiguli and Barungi 2007); social movements in South Africa (Mandela 1994); genocide in Rwanda (Rusesabagina 2006); social movements and the impact of transnational corporations in Nigeria (Wiwa 2001); peace building and justice in Uganda (Afako 2002; Oywa 2002); colonialism in Africa (Boahen 1989); globalization in Uganda (Ekobu, n.d.; Mao 2003); and Western intervention in Africa (Iweala 2007).

Critical Structural Analysis

It is also essential to provide a critical structural analysis for understanding disease, war, and poverty among other social problems experienced in some parts of Africa. Specifically in my courses, I refer to globalization, particularly as it pertains to economic trade; European colonialism and its legacy; global militarism; and contemporary Western donor influence in Africa. These factors are each important dimensions that play a role in perpetuating the social issues of disease, war, and poverty that are pervasive in northern Uganda and some other parts of Africa today. I incorporate these units into my pedagogy through lectures on the history of globalization, statistics on global arms sales and U.S. military involvement overseas, a case study discussion of the surge in donor and nongovernmental organization (NGO) involvement in Uganda since the mid-1980s, and powerful films on colonialism such as Basil Davidson et al.'s *This Magnificent African Cake* (1984). The reasoning for including these units is that: "There is an enormous difference between seeing people as the victims of innate shortcomings and seeing them as the victims of structural violence" (Farmer 2005:153).

Understanding how structural violence functions and is reproduced is critical to shifting students' orientation toward Africa.

While teaching these topics requires a heavy emphasis on dynamics, events, and actors that originate outside the African continent, each of these themes has also played an instrumental role in determining the realities of social problems experienced by Africans on the African continent. A comprehensive curriculum on Africa must cover these topics as well as the responses and resistance to them. While complex and challenging to teach in a succinct way, their inclusion in curriculum can contribute to encouraging students to have an analytical framework that looks for underlying causes to social issues, often even linking back to the United States. This practice serves as a powerful antidote to the U.S.-based activism on behalf of Africa, which rarely brings in U.S. causation and seemingly allows young Americans to escape rigorous analysis of the policies and practices of the powerful country from which they originate.

While infuriating, surprising, and often disturbing for many U.S. students, the structural analysis that sometimes implicates the United States can also be deeply motivating toward taking action to address specific social issues. An awareness of structural causation of social problems experienced in various countries in Africa can be a stimulus to act as students personalize and internalize that people of affluence from the global North, many like them, can be implicated in the suffering of people in Africa. They see themselves and their country-mates on the analytical map of social problems in Africa and often feel more compelled to strive for constructive change. Some young Americans with whom I have worked have even used the language of guilt, suggesting that a sense of responsibility has partly thwarted passionate action.

Social Movement Analysis

Alongside a critical structural analysis, emphasis on the role of social movements is also integral to instruction about Africa. Social movements are the work of collectives of ordinary people who challenge policies, institutions, and persons responsible for the perpetuation of social problems and collective suffering (Della Porta and Diani 2006; McAdam and Snow 1997). For many students, the structural determinants of social concerns in Africa, such as economic trade, are simply overwhelming to understand and tackle. Thus, highlighting the efforts of social movement activism—whether it is indigenously based or of a more transnational dynamic—is critical to students' understanding of how ordinary people make a difference in addressing social problems in northern Uganda and in other disenfranchised communities. One example of social movement activism that I have used alongside my lessons on globalization and debt in Africa is the efforts of Jubilee 2000, an international coalition that arose with the goal of canceling "Third World debt" by the year 2000. Highlighting the broad-based coalition that makes up the movement, which was built on the Catholic Church's Jubilee celebration of the year 2000, is important, as is presenting its tactics of working through faith communities, enacting demonstrations, and generating public political pressure. It is also integral to emphasize the coalition's tangible results in producing partial debt relief for many poor countries by the year 2000 as well as generating further activism that has led to full debt relief for some African countries in more recent years.[4] Including such a concrete example of the work of Jubilee 2000 offers a clear indication to students of how social movement activism can be immensely useful in undoing some of the structural factors causing suffering in northern Uganda and in other communities in Africa.

In my lessons on African social movements, I also present on the role of media in social movements (Ryan 1991), in particular the concept of framing. Frames are mechanisms used to succinctly convey a movement's messages; they highlight an implicit worldview of the movement, which helps to hold together the justifications for activists' claims (Snow et al. 1986). Within social movements, frames are used for multiple purposes, including recruiting new members, mobilizing followers, and acquiring resources (Benford and Snow 2000). By teaching students the fundamentals of how information is presented through media and how activists work to put forward their own frames in the media, students critically analyze the logic of claims made in the media by both activists and their adversaries. A discussion on this theme facilitates a deeper understanding of activism as well as a more critical interpretation of media sources. I initiate it by presenting a framing analysis of the efforts of the Treatment Action Campaign (TAC), a grassroots social movement working for access to HIV/AIDS prevention and treatment services in South Africa (Friedman and Mottiar 2004; De Waal 2006). An example of how TAC frames its work versus how its adversary, the South African Government (SAG), frames its claims is presented in a dialogue format between TAC and SAG:

ISSUE

TAC   AIDS is decimating our population, and people have a right to access lifesaving medications.

SAG   Never again should Western entities (governments or corporations) be the driving force in our country, profiteering off of our problems.

WHO IS RESPONSIBLE?

TAC   Originally, it was the drug companies that were responsible for not availing lifesaving medications. Now it is the SAG that is reluctant to roll out an effective national HIV treatment program.

SAG   Western-based pharmaceutical companies that are profiteering.

WHAT IS THE SOLUTION?

TAC   Low-cost generic antiretroviral (ARV) drugs (which are available in South Africa now) should be disseminated through the public health infrastructure. The SAG ought to promote the use of these lifesaving medications by providing the resources through a national treatment program and not advancing confusing AIDS denialism rhetoric. Furthermore, poor South Africans ought to have other social and economic rights addressed.

SAG We'll handle the AIDS problem in our country our way (not by being bullied by international companies and governments). We need poverty eradication before we can take on HIV/AIDS exclusively. HIV/AIDS treatment can be handled through traditional mechanisms such as herbs, etc.

PHRASES, EXAMPLES, AND SLOGANS THAT CONVEY THE FRAME

TAC

- *Catchphrases/slogans:* "universal access," "equal treatment," "we stand up for our lives"
- *Appeal to principles and a historical example:* As in the antiapartheid struggle, our civil disobedience actions reinforce rights enshrined in the South African constitution. We are nonviolent and have the moral high ground. Acting boldly and collectively, South Africans are change agents in society.
- *Supporting argument:* AIDS denialism sends confusing messages to South Africans, leading to 1,000 HIV/AIDS deaths every day. While anticolonialism is important, there is an urgency to tackling HIV/AIDS now and pragmatically preventing new infections and treating those who currently have the disease.
- *Supporting argument:* AIDS is situated within a more comprehensive call for social and economic rights.
- *Visual image:* HIV+ t-shirts, hand fist of resistance, masses in public protest on the streets

SAG

- *Catchphrases/slogans:* "African solutions for African problems"; ARVs are "toxic," "damaging," and "poisonous"; "Stop AIDS genocide by the drug cartel"
- *Appeal to principles:* Freedom of speech in South Africa should allow AIDS denialism to have a voice in the public AIDS discourse.
- *Historical example of mistrust:* The medical field in South Africa, with its antecedents in the West, was used to exploit black South Africans during apartheid.
- *Supporting argument:* We must combat racial stereotypes of African sexuality.
- *Possible conspiracy theory:* AIDS is part of a race war and was created to wipe out Africans. Does HIV even cause AIDS?
- *Visual Image:* African herbs

After presenting this dialogue, I read some excerpts from the media that exemplify each frame. I invite students to look for similarities and differences in the frames, while at the same time, I move them toward a group discussion on why it is important for activists to understand their opponent's frames.

As a sociologist particularly interested in social movements, I also have developed case study modules of contemporary social movements in Africa. In particular,

I include the aforementioned TAC from South Africa and the Movement for the Survival of the Ogoni People (MOSOP) in Nigeria in my curriculum. TAC has targeted both pharmaceutical companies that profiteer from the sales of HIV/AIDS medications and the SAG, which has been reluctant to acknowledge and address the gravity of HIV/AIDS within the country. The movement has had several noteworthy successes including introducing HIV/AIDS to the public agenda; pressuring drug companies to drop their case against the SAG regarding the right to produce lower-cost generic drugs within the country; ensuring that the SAG rolled out a national HIV treatment program; and cultural change that has reduced the stigma connected to HIV/AIDS.

MOSOP, as a second example, is an environmental and self-determination movement of indigenous peoples in Nigeria that was founded in 1990 as a vehicle to "mobilize the Ogoni people and empower them to protest the devastation of their environment by Shell, and their denigration and dehumanization by Nigeria's military dictators" (Saro-Wiwa 2002:121). Under the leadership of Ken Saro-Wiwa, MOSOP began its initiative by creating the Ogoni bill of rights, which laid out a demand for economic, social, and environmental justice. The bill was a strategy to challenge the human rights violations at the national, regional, and international levels by exposing violations of the Nigerian constitution, the African Charter on Human and Peoples' Rights, and the Universal Declaration of Human Rights. Utilizing nonviolent action strategies, dedicated efforts to build transnational coalitions, and the human rights framework of the Ogoni bill of rights, MOSOP was able to challenge the powerful agenda of a military regime and its multinational corporate ally, Shell, resulting in the temporary removal of Shell employees from Ogoniland. Years later, MOSOP efforts led to Shell's $15.5 million settlement to families of Ogoni activists who were killed by the military regime in 1995. Yet, perhaps most notable of all of MOSOP's achievements are (1) inspiring the marginalized Ogoni people to surmount the "psychological barrier of fear" and form a collective voice of resistance (Cooper 1999:195) and (2) creating international solidarity around human rights violations carried out by powerful actors against African indigenous people, resulting in the launch of the One Naira Ogoni Survival Fund and the World Ogoni Week in 1994.

The inclusion of TAC and MOSOP social movement activism in my curriculum, with their relative successes and failures, is an important springboard for discussion on the agency of Africans and African activism. For U.S. students, it is an imperative reminder that some of the most monumental changes to address social issues in Africa have come from the collective struggle of Africans themselves. This feature goes to great lengths to undermine the essentialized notions of the African "Other" so pervasive in the American politico-cultural orientation. It also fights American paternalistic tendencies to want "to save" or "to rescue."

Conceptualizing Frameworks for Intervention in Africa

Another central component of pedagogy on Africa is an analytical framework of paradigms of intervention. Utilizing Paul Farmer's (2005) analysis of charity, development, and social justice interventions, linked closely with the roots of liberation theology (Gutiérrez 1973; Pixley and Boff 1989), I encourage students to examine the underlying logic behind various interventions in Africa. By providing Farmer's straightforward framework as a guide, students are able to identify the advantages and disadvantages of various approaches. For example, while development can be measured relatively straightforwardly through socioeconomic factors, development also conceptualizes progress in a linear fashion, in which African countries are "backward" and must "catch up" to the United States and other industrialized countries. As an illustration of these concepts, students examine three different ongoing forms of intervention in northern Uganda, which exemplify the divergent paradigms: a humanitarian food project, representing "charity"; a large United States Agency for International Development (USAID) project, exemplifying "development"; and a local human rights organization, resembling "social justice." The students reflect on the advantages and disadvantages of each approach to addressing social problems in Uganda, highlighting at the same time that rarely does one intervention exclusively embody one of the three paradigms presented in Farmer's typology. In the African World Perspectives course, the final assignment asks the students to pick any intervention in Africa to analyze and, among other queries, apply Farmer's framework to determine what kind of logic grounds a particular intervention. Students research international NGOs, local initiatives, and social change campaigns to learn how they function and with what philosophy. With a perhaps not-so-subtle emphasis on the importance of social justice interventions, students become more discriminatory in their understanding of interventions in Africa, keen to identify those that address structural determinants of social issues, of which collective activist struggles are often included.

Perceiving Africa

Finally, in a U.S.-based curriculum on African issues, it is also essential to include a unit on Western perceptions of Africa. When I was in Uganda in 2007, I worked for several months alongside four Ugandan undergraduate students on a participatory research project about perceptions of activism and social movements. Toward the end of our time together, after trust had been established, an exercise was conducted in which the students reflected on "five ways you think the West perceives Africa," "five ways the West *should* perceive Africa," and "how Africans perceive the West." Examples of how they thought the West perceived Africa included "poor," "backward," "rich with minerals," "inferior to whites," and a "potential market." Their responses to how they thought the West should perceive Africa included "Africans as people who love peace"; "a developing continent that is yearning for help from people who have no ulterior motives"; "as a continent which is not entangled with diseases, but the prevalence of such diseases is due to poor health facilities"; "can develop with global partnership"; and "Africans have conflicts [in which] sometimes the key players are from the West."

The result from the exercise was a fruitful discussion on how and why groups hold various perceptions of others and how and why perceptions can be turned into reality. The exercise was carried out with the underlying conviction that perceptions of Americans and Africans need to be reshaped in order for everyone to see one another as equal partners, which is vital to building meaningful dialogue and more effective transnational activism. The exercise on perceptions led into a discussion on the discourse of "saving Africa," which circulates in U.S. popular culture. Contrary to what I expected, Ugandan students were not nearly as upset about the "save Africa" narrative as I was. Many held a strong conviction about the critical importance of international support and seemed to believe that a certain degree of pragmatism was necessary for marketing purposes.

Upon return to Boston, I engaged U.S. students with the same exercise on perceptions. In the ensuing discussion, I presented the responses of their Ugandan peers to the identical queries. It led to a very fertile dialogue on what was surprising in terms of perceptions Africans held about the West and vice versa, what was expected, and what social factors may have given birth to the perceptions. Many of the students were surprised to learn of their Ugandan counterparts' responses, and some were saddened by the notion that Africans thought that they were viewed relatively negatively by the West. The U.S. students were mostly curious to learn more about the Ugandan students. While the exercise in the United States was carried out, photographs of the four students from Uganda were projected on a screen. Indeed, the notion of perceptions of one another became much less abstract when U.S. students listened to some of the responses and saw the images from their peers on the other side of the world.

In a more recent iteration of the discussion of perceptions of Africa in the U.S. classroom, I showed five different photographs I took in Uganda and asked students to identify (1) which image is most common in terms of how Africa is represented in the West, and why, and (2) why we are used to seeing some of these images more than others. The particular images represented various aspects of life in Africa, some that are familiar to most Americans and others that are not. They included a distraught child on the back of its mother, a group of men working together to lift a cement slab, a cluster of playful young children surrounding a younger me in a field, a glowing mother and father and their child shortly after the birth of their daughter, and a medical team posing in the radiology department at a hospital. For many of the students, some of these images were quite surprising; for much of American society, clear notions of good and evil—innocent women and children victims versus corrupt and violent male authorities and warlords—had been their predominant illustrations of African society.

In the unit on perceptions of Africa, I also bring in the work of Eric Gottesman, a U.S. collaborative artist who for many years has worked with children affected by HIV/AIDS in Addis Abba, Ethiopia. The presentation begins by showing a cover from a 2003

New York Times Magazine (Bearak 2003) that is full of black-and-white photographs of emaciated Africans and the bold words "Why Famine Persists." Using Gottesman's words as he shared them with me, I explain that "even images intended for social change can create stereotypes that separate the viewer from the subject and thus allow for future tolerance of inequality," and then I ask the students, "What do image makers do to change this context?" Gottesman's work and that of his collaborators through Sudden Flowers Productions, a group of youth based in Ethiopia, offers a unique interrogation of images coming from Africa and of who creates them (Bleiker and Kay 2007). Gottesman and the youth he works with collaboratively create photographic images and film productions to tell the story of the experience of children affected by HIV/AIDS in sub-Saharan Africa.[5] In their work, African children are not simply objects affected by a terrible disease, but rather subjects with agency who are engaged in narrating their own stories and initiating dialogue around a stigmatized topic in their communities.

Outcomes: Inspiring Activism for Social Change

The greatest indicator of the success of the pedagogies I use to teach about Africa is when students ask to see me outside of class to brainstorm how they might personally take action. As I stated earlier, many students in the United States want to go to Africa—to study, to intern, or to volunteer over the summer. To facilitate this travel, I have prepared a document with blurbs about organizations working in Uganda (where I have extensive networks), with which they might find placement. As demand for these sorts of opportunities has increased, I have become more discriminatory about sharing my personal contacts. To my surprise, though, I often find that Ugandans are quite willing to receive Americans on short-term placement in their organizations, even though they are likely to put much more effort into hosting them than they will receive in return through the labor of the intern. This inclination is likely due to the fundamental conviction of many Ugandans that international cooperation, and the potentially constructive role that outsiders can play, ameliorates social problems experienced in Africa, often through transfer of resources. All the same, it is important to instill a notion of reciprocity in my students, and I encourage them to think about what small contribution they can make to the African communities that may host them. Furthermore, as I am trying to promote activism and engagement with structural causation of problems experienced in Africa, I also suggest to my U.S. students that they become plugged into Africa-focused activist organizations based in the United States. As I am involved with some pertaining to Uganda, I have invited them to join me for various events or ongoing campaigns.

There is much space for improvement in the mix of pedagogical approaches I use in my teaching about Africa to shape more thoughtful activism. I currently do not provide comprehensive sessions on activist skills building, for example. *Activism* is quite a broad term with many divergent connotations, particularly across cultures. If unaccompanied by specific tools—such as writing press releases or organizing a campaign—students' inspiration to take action in Africa may easily default into efforts that are not really about changing the status quo, such as working for large, mainstream development NGO projects. While they are often well equipped to host international students, I have found that such large mainstream organizations are also frequently less about sustainable social change in communities than about maintaining jobs for their employees. To that end, for the U.S. students, I direct them to a list of activist organizations focusing on issues in Africa, with which they might become involved, even when these are based in the United States.

Toward Efforts for Thoughtful Activism

As outlined earlier, contemporary U.S.-based activism toward Africa is currently shaped by many factors, including the ongoing efforts of Invisible Children and the Save Darfur Coalition, which present opportunities for young Americans to engage Africa with minimal controversy or risk of implication; the impact of the Rwandan genocide on the contemporary U.S. consciousness; and the broader historical American politico-cultural orientation toward Africa that emphasizes Africa and Africans as "other," inferior to the West, and peripheral to U.S. interests. The implications of these factors are momentous. First, and perhaps most importantly, a focus on "the Other" with no structural analysis allows young, privileged Americans to overlook their own power and complicity in an oppressive system. Paying no attention to how the United States, as a global hegemony, contributes to suffering in Africa can pave the way for more imperialistic endeavors that primarily serve outsider interests as opposed to local interests, just as has historically occurred in Africa through slavery, colonialism, missionaries, and social science ventures (McClintock 1995). Second, efforts that uncritically implore U.S. intervention into crises in Africa undermine local activists' efforts that have sought to address the problems in their communities for years. In such a case, not only is indigenous knowledge not respected, but unthoughtful outsider endeavors may actually contribute to destruction of efforts by those more well versed with the dynamics of the situation.

Many university students who are drawn to U.S.-based activism toward Africa are at a critical stage in their lives where they are formulating their own independent beliefs about both Africa and activism. In line with the findings of M. Kent Jennings (2002), Paul Rogat Loeb notes: "Students' choices of retreat and engagement matter beyond their immediate political impact. Many use their college years to settle on fundamental ways of understanding their role in the world, and to embark on paths that will set the directions of their lives" (1994:367). A classroom in which a true learning community is built offers a unique opportunity for students and teachers alike to address some of the dangerous aforementioned concerns and reflect honestly on sensitive, but important topics such as power, misconceptions and perceptions of other people, structural determinants of social problems, and activist strategies for addressing such problems. The mixed pedagogical approach that I presented ties together African narratives, a critical structural analysis, social movement analysis, conceptualizing frameworks for intervention in Africa, and dialogue on perceptions of Africa. In my experience, the pedagogy has yielded two important outcomes. First, it attempts to deliberately respond to the ongoing aforementioned social forces that are currently shaping U.S. engagement toward Africa. Second, the pedagogy aims to mobilize young Americans to thoughtfully engage problems that are experienced in Africa through utilizing activist strategies.

As many students are provoked to take social action on the social problems they learn about in Africa, my goal is that they do so thoughtfully and without reiterating narrowly construed stereotypes of African people or the African continent. I strive for a balance between inspiring, even empowering young people to take action on the problems they observe and learn about and emphasizing reflexivity, self-criticism, and rigorous analysis of one's (and one's country's) relative power. The dangers are that if the balance is not achieved, the result can be either well-intentioned action that is not based on collaboration and trust, and therefore unsustainable, or paralysis because the exercise of reflexivity and self-critique is too disempowering. My hope is to foster thoughtful activism with a mind-set of collaboration and to encourage students to question whether it is justice in Africa they are working for or rather global justice, which both includes and implicates Americans.

Notes

I am especially grateful to my students in both the United States and Uganda, who have taught me a great deal and have been instrumental in the development of my pedagogy on Africa. In particular, I am grateful to my students from African World Perspectives at Boston College. In Uganda, I have special appreciation for students at Gulu University, Institute of Peace and Strategic Studies, who participated in the working group seminar on conflict studies, as well as students from Ethnic Identity and Conflict Transformation; Human Rights, Development, and Social Justice; Conflict, Power, and Change; Civil Society and Peace Building; and also the medical students (Ugandan and international) who have participated in the social medicine course, Beyond the Biologic Basis of Disease. Finally, I acknowledge and appreciate the contribution of my co-instructors Zine Magubane, Shelley White, Michael Westerhaus, and Julian Jane Atim.

1. Invisible Children is a U.S.-based education and advocacy organization that works in eastern and central Africa. For more information, please see http://invisiblechildren.com. While I present pedagogical approaches and experiences from teaching in both the United States and Africa, the overall focus of this chapter is on critical pedagogies that lead to effective U.S.-based activism toward Africa.

2. For more information on the Save Darfur Coalition, please see http://www.savedarfur.org.

3. The Lord's Resistance Army (LRA) war began in northern Uganda in the late 1980s; since 2006, however, northern Uganda has not experienced active LRA violence as the group has shifted its activities to southern Sudan, the Central African Republic, and the Democratic Republic of the Congo. Invisible Children's activist efforts now extend beyond northern Uganda to the region of Central Africa. "End the longest running war in Africa" was a frequently used phrase at Invisible Children events, in its e-mails, and on its website throughout 2009-2010. Since then, Invisible Children has changed its phrasing, and this phrase is no longer apparent on the website. This phrase is still reflected at the StayClassy website, http://www.stayclassy.org/case-studies/invisible-children, accessed October 17, 2012.

4. For more information on Jubilee 2000 and the ongoing activism to address debt relief, please see http://www.jubileeusa.org.

5. For more information on Eric Gottesman's work, please see http://www.ericgottesman.net.

18 The Model AU as a Pedagogical Method of Teaching American Students about Africa

Babacar M'Baye

THE MODEL AFRICAN Union (hereafter referred to as the Model AU) is an annual convention in which students from many American colleges and universities meet for three days in Washington, D.C., to discuss and vote on resolutions that address major challenges in Africa. Students learn the role, structure, and performance of the African Union (AU) while searching for solutions to Africa's key economic, social, and political obstacles. As Professor Michael C. Nwanze and Professor Jack Parson, the founders of the Model AU, explain, "Through simulation, augmented by briefings at African Embassies in Washington, D.C., participants gain a better and clearer understanding of the multi-various determinants, capabilities and constraints that shape the domestic and foreign policies of African countries as well as the patterns of cooperation and conflict that characterize intra-African diplomacy."[1] After visiting African embassies in Washington, D.C., students return to a hotel in the metropolitan city, where they bring and discuss their numerous resolutions in various simulated committees of the AU (the Committee on Economic Matters, the Committee on Social Matters, the Committee on Union Government, and the Peace and Security Committee). Through these meetings, students gain a better understanding of Pan-African agency as it is applied in the AU's effort to create and foster unity and development among African people. The conference enables students to learn and practice diplomacy by representing their chosen nations in distinctive ways. In this vein, Parson argues that "the model [AU] puts Africa and African issues at the center of debate and discussion. For those interested in teaching about Africa, it offers a unique opportunity to immerse students in such discussions"

(1994:294). Likewise, Professor John Bing of Heidelberg College says: "The [AU] simulation models what the 'real world' is like. Some of the resolutions passed in the past have given real-world diplomats ideas that have become policy" (quoted in Gosche 2011).

Reflecting on experiences from teaching a course titled Pan-Africanism and the Model AU, I show in this chapter how the convention effectively teaches students about contemporary issues in Africa while introducing them to the agency in Pan-Africanism. As Imanuel Geiss defines it, "Pan-Africanism" is an ideology of "political cooperation" among Africans who attempt to eradicate "the present poverty of Africa, the lack of modern communications, the predominance of production at the subsistence economic level, and the orientation of most new states towards the former 'mother country'" (1969:200).

Preparing Students for the Model AU

Students are introduced to readings that emphasize the agency of African people, such as Geiss's "Pan-Africanism" (1969) and J. Ayo Langley's "Pan-Africanism in Paris, 1924–36" (1969), which explore the solidarity among blacks on the two sides of the Atlantic Ocean, a unity that inspired Africans to create the AU in 1963 (formerly called the Organization of African Unity [OAU], the organization's name changed to AU on May 26, 2001) (AU 2011). Discussing the resistance of Quobna Ottobah Cugoano and Edward Wilmot Blyden against slavery and the struggles of Henry Sylvester Williams, W. E. B. Du Bois, George Padmore, and Nnamdi Azikiwe against colonialism, Geiss's essay gives students a history of black solidarity against oppression that predates the AU. Langley's essay examines similar agency in the solidarity of Francophone Africans such as Blaise Diagne and Kojo Touvalou Houénou alongside other Pan-Africanists such as Du Bois and Marcus Garvey during the 1920s. Once students understand this solidarity, they read Claude Welch's essay "The Organization of African Unity and the Promotion of Human Rights" (1991). This article introduces students to the various charters, commissions, and committees of the AU while helping them understand that "protection of human rights in the [African] continent depends ultimately on the active, effective role of African governments, assisted by outside pressures and far greater activity by human rights NGOs [nongovernmental organizations]" (Welch 1991:555).

Once students are familiar with the history of the AU, they tackle the institution's agenda, which contains a list of the topics that committees discuss at each convention. To prepare for the agenda topics, which change each year, students are assigned (1) three position papers and (2) four resolutions. The position papers explain the position of a particular country about an issue on the agenda of either the Executive Council or the AU's committees. This assignment allows students to gather and organize specific information on their country's opinions about the AU's agenda. In order to compile this information, students read chapters of *Lonely Planet: West Africa* (Gordon et al. 2002) that contain accessible statistics, maps, and basic facts on the people, geography, government, politics, economy, education, arts, and cultures of each West African country. These chapters are supplemented with sections from David M. Haugen's *Africa: Opposing*

Viewpoints (2008), which discusses the following central questions: What are the most serious problems facing Africa? What economic policies will benefit Africa? And, what is the state of democracy and human rights in Africa? These chapters provide students with arguments that they can develop to support or refute a position about their selected country. Also, the readings help students write the resolutions that they must bring to the convention for debate, passage, or, in the worst case, dismissal, at either a committee or Executive Council meeting.

Moreover, students read the first and second chapters of Guy Martin's *Africa in World Politics: A Pan-African Perspective* (2002) in which he shows that the ideology of "EurAfrica," theoretically "based on the twin concepts of 'complementarity' and 'interdependence'" between Europe and Africa, is "a convenient justification for colonialism" since it "views the complete integration of the two continents—or the absorption of Africa by Europe—as the ideal solution" (2). By identifying EurAfrica as neocolonialism, Martin helps students understand the unequal relationships between Africa and Europe and their manifestations in policies of Western financial institutions such as the International Monetary Fund (IMF) and the World Bank.

To complement the above readings with visual aids, students view a number of documentaries and films such as Ali A. Mazrui's *Tools of Exploitation* (1986) and Raoul Peck's *Lumumba: A True Story* (2000), both of which show the continual European scramble for wealth throughout the African continent with serious socioeconomic consequences. Throughout the duration of the class, students are made to understand the direct and indirect links between historical circumstances (e.g., slavery and imperialism) and contemporary issues plaguing many African countries (e.g., racism, neocolonialism, and gender oppression).

Since a major goal of the course is to help the student delegation prepare its resolutions, students are also provided with links to relevant websites that cover major issues in Africa.[2] Once the content is decided, students then spend the remainder of their time discussing strategies for writing resolutions, including ways of composing "basis statements" and "action statements." According to the *Ninth Annual National Model African Union Delegation and Officers' Handbook*, basis statements identify "the nature of the issue" to which the resolution would like to draw attention and explain "the reasons" for the AU's "attention to the matter" (2011:10). A basis statement begins with words such as "Noticing," "Recognizing," "Given," or "Knowing," while an action statement begins with words such as "Condemns," "Urges," "Demands," or "Recommends" (2011:10). Once students complete their basis statements and action statements, they create their resolutions and submit them for instructor review. Prior to this submission of drafts, students attempt to improve the documents by reviewing successful resolutions written by former peers of the Model AU.[3]

Writing resolutions allows students to do background library research that helps them make informed statements about both particular African countries and Pan-Africanism. Furthermore, writing resolutions helps students learn how meaning derives not just from regurgitating received information gained from the classroom, but from analyzing and applying such information in social, experiential, and diplomatic contexts in which students test them. This teaching philosophy challenges the popular belief that "strong education is run from inside—not from outside the institution," a concept that K. Patricia Cross also opposes in her essay "Classroom Research: Implementing the Scholarship of Teaching" (1996:403). The Model AU summit contradicts this pedagogical philosophy by showing how good education also arises from both personal and private spaces. In order to understand the AU and its Pan-African spirit of solidarity, students combine knowledge received from both the classroom and the outside world. Discussing this integrative nature of the Model AU, Parson writes: "Participation in the model [AU] is the payoff for the teaching process that has taken place at home universities. [The *Faculty Advisors' Handbook* for the Model AU describes it as an 'extension of the classroom.'] The preparatory period, before the model takes place, is excellent for developing student interest and interdisciplinary skills" (1994:295). Since it is a complement to, rather than a replacement of, the classroom learning, the Model AU cannot be substituted with the classroom learning because it is an experience that cannot be fully replicated outside of the "real-life" context. Therefore, as Parson argues, one can describe the Model AU as a "second experiential learning" (1994:294).

The Model AU Summit

The national Model AU convention begins with a briefing session in which every participant receives a name tag and a copy of the conference program and identifies the room where his or her committee will meet the next day. During this session, the faculty members submit their students' resolutions to the conference organizers, who distribute them to each participant the following day. At the start of the convention, every student is well dressed and joins a committee on which he or she will serve as a chair, vice chair, rapporteur, delegate, or other important functionary. For two and a half days, these delegates discuss the strengths and weaknesses of various student-written resolutions that were brought before their committee; they are charged with selecting the best ones to submit to the Assembly of Heads of State and Government, and a similar and decisive process takes place in the presence of all delegates at the end of the summit.

A major figure of the Model AU is the chair, whose role is to instruct delegates on the voting procedures, which appear in the *Delegation and Officers' Handbook*, and remind them that when they wish to speak to always raise their placards bearing the name of their country. At the beginning of each committee meeting, the chair reads the names of the nations represented in the committee and asks the delegates to sit according to the alphabetical order of their state. The chair then asks, "Is there more than one delegate for a specific nation?" If there is more than one delegate for a country, the chair asks the alternate representatives to sit outside of the formal delegation. The chair also reminds participants that during the meeting they should use the *Robert's Rules of Order* (Robert et al. 2004), a guide for facilitating discussions and group decision making. Then the chair lets students examine each resolution and allows five points of inquiry about each.

When recognized, the delegates who have consolidated or sponsored a resolution are given time to speak about it. The chair tells delegates, "Before speaking, please raise your placard to be recognized by Mr. Chair or Madame Chair." When a delegate speaks without having been recognized, the chair says, "Out of order!" In addition to calling the delegates to "stay in order," the chair lets them address any of the "basis clauses" and "action clauses" on the resolution. Each point that these delegates raise is called "a point of inquiry," which is a question on a matter of procedure and not on the resolution itself. According to the *Ninth Annual National Model African Union Delegation and Officers' Handbook*: "A Point of Inquiry may be used to question a speaker after he/she has finished his/her remarks: a questioner will address the Point to the Chair, who will then ask the speaker if he/she 'wishes to yield.' . . . The Chair will ensure that Points of Inquiry are only used to raise questions of clarifications or for additional information" (2011:25). Yielding is an important part of the discussion of resolutions. If, after speaking, a delegate realizes that he or she did not have a lot to say, he or she can state, "I yield my time to the delegate of . . . ," and at that point the delegate from this other nation can speak for a duration that the chair determines.

Furthermore, the chair makes a number of motions during committee meetings. As is apparent in the *Robert's Rules of Order*, a "motion" is a statement in which a meeting participant, after obtaining the floor, says, "I move that . . . " and then clearly describes the proposal he or she wants to make (Robert et al. 2004:20). A regular motion that a chair makes is to propose that members of a committee vote on specific items of a resolution. Once this motion is carried, the chair says: "The motion to vote is made. How many are in favor of this motion? Are there any abstentions?" Oftentimes, the motion is carried with a clear majority, and, in other cases, a delegate may ask representatives to explain their country's position on a particular issue.

When a delegate makes a motion to have a caucus, which is a short pause that allows a committee or a delegation to discuss a resolution without the interference of the chair, the delegate needs to say whether the caucus is to be moderated or unmoderated and how long it should last. According to the *Ninth Annual National Model African Union Delegation and Officers' Handbook*, "caucusing" usually gives delegations the opportunity "to gain sponsorship for draft resolutions" (2011:22). In the moderated caucus, students cannot talk among themselves without being allowed to do so by the chair. In the unmoderated caucus, students can talk among themselves whether the chair allows them to move away from their seats or not. Such a caucus allows students to practice the thorough democratic process in which consensus is reached at the real AU. Diedre L. Badejo—in her book *The African Union (Global Organizations)*—explains this process as a series of "intense meetings" in which "representatives prepare the groundwork for the negotiators and decision-makers" (2008:42). According to Badejo, institutions of the AU such as the Permanent Representatives' Committee and the Executive Council "work together to ensure that perspectives and issues are communicated at each level of authority and that the Assembly of Heads of States and Government receive the most-well-prepared documents possible so that it can make the best decisions" (2008:42). This assiduous collaboration between the AU's major branches shows Africans' capacity to exercise agency and democracy in their political deliberative process.

While much of the Model AU summit takes place in committee meetings, another substantial part of the event occurs in African embassies throughout Washington, D.C., where students spend two to three hours during the first day of the convention being briefed by embassy diplomats about their nation's official positions on the summit's agenda. For instance, on February 28, 2008, students talked with the ambassador of Senegal, Dr. Amadou Lamine Ba, and members of his staff about their country's official position on the wars between northern and southern Sudan as well as those between different factions of the Democratic Republic of the Congo. The ambassador also discussed many social and economic problems in Senegal, the business opportunities in the country, and the increasing visibility of Senegalese immigrants in the United States.

This experience gave students direct contact with knowledgeable Senegalese diplomats, who shared with them pertinent insights on the social, political, economic, and cultural history of Senegal. Such a visit to an African embassy in Washington, D.C. is consistent with the AU's increasing facilitation of exchange between African immigrants and their country's diplomatic representations in the United States. Embassies can play a major role in the lives of the people of the diaspora by "enabling" them to "have consular services" and "make economic contributions to their countries" (Ratha et al. 2011:174). By facilitating relationships between African immigrants and their embassies in the United States, the AU promotes African agency for these sojourners in both their homelands and the diaspora.

Students used the information that they received from the Embassy of Senegal in order to maximize their participation in the AU convention and write excellent research projects for the course. A week after they returned from Washington, D.C., students submitted a reflection and analysis paper that demonstrated their understanding of the history, culture, and sociopolitical situation of their country and a greater appreciation of diplomacy and international affairs. In their reflections about their participations in the Model AU, students often mentioned how the summit helped them improve their research skills while empowering them to speak confidently in front of their peers. These comments show that the Model AU gives students practical research, experiential, and analytical skills that they can transfer into their internships and future careers. Such skills need to be taught and practiced inside and outside the classroom through interactive assignments such as position papers, resolutions, committee meetings, embassy visits, reflection essays, and research projects. By taking students to the Model AU summit, educators give young scholars the chance to grow as active learners and apply the theoretical lessons they imbibe in the classrooms to active meetings with peers and major officials in Washington, D.C.

The Model AU is an irreplaceable experience that allows students to learn and discuss Africa's contemporary issues in real-life and diplomatic settings. Working on various resolutions that are discussed in many simulated committees of the AU, students demonstrate a sense of professionalism that the classroom can complement. The Model AU also enables students to develop important skills and potentials, such as the ability to present and defend their views in front of peers from other universities and colleges. Through this convention, students learn to maintain professional decorum and language in order to impress their peers and influence them to support their resolution. By the end of the summit, students understand the collaborative process of the AU and the agency that such a Pan-African organization can provide.

Notes

I thank Professor Michael C. Nwanze, Professor Jack Parson, and their wonderful colleagues from the Model AU Conference for having introduced my students and me to this amazing experience.

1. National Model African Union Conference, http://www.modelafricanunion.org, accessed April 22, 2010.

2. Students are given links to these websites: (1) IRIN, http://www.irinnews.org (managed by the United Nation Office for the Coordination of Humanitarian Affairs and offering daily humanitarian news and analysis in Africa); (2) AllAfrica, http://allafrica.com (daily news from different parts of the African continent); (3) the African Union, http://www.africa-union.org; (4) the United Nations, www.un.org; (5) the New Partnership for Africa's Development, http://www.nepad.org; and (6) Seneweb, http://www.seneweb.com (the main portal to news in French from Senegal).

3. A segment from a recent student resolution brought to a recent Model AU reads as follows:

Concerned with the plight of innocent men, women and children who are living in Somalia whose lives have been detrimentally affected by ongoing fighting between the Union of Islamic Courts and the national government;

Fully aware of Somali children's suffering as a result of recruitment and abduction into opposition forces, their increased vulnerability to becoming orphaned and neglected, and the hindrances to their educational development that are imposed upon them beyond their free will;

Considering that several of the countries, including Somalia, that have been black-listed by the UN [United Nations] for such activities, are indeed African nations;

Urges the Model African Union to act on its authority to formulate and adopt legislation that is aimed at safeguarding children, with a central focus on Somali nationals, as Somalia is the most recent African nation to experience a renewed explosion of political upheaval;

Insists that the legislation includes explicit provisions for family reunification and the social reintegration of reclaimed child soldiers.

This is an impressive resolution because it shows strong position statements and action statements while revealing the kind of injustices that influence the AU to sanction oppression against civilians in war-torn nations. The resolution reflects the severity of the divisions between the Union of Islamic Courts (Midowga Maxkamadaha Islaamiga) and the national government of Somali over issues of religion and political representation in Somali in 2008.

19 The Kalamazoo / Fourah Bay College Partnership

A Context for Understanding Study Abroad with Africa

Daniel J. Paracka, Jr.

ACCORDING TO STATISTICS compiled by the Institute of International Education, U.S. students studying abroad in Africa represented just 4.5 percent of the global total (Open Doors 2010). Why do so few students choose to study in Africa? Rather than generalize about study abroad to Africa, this chapter examines the particular context and experience of Kalamazoo College's study abroad program with Fourah Bay College (FBC) in Sierra Leone, one of the first and longest-running programs of its kind. The focus of this chapter is to understand the broader socioeconomic, cultural, and political forces that framed the relationship and influenced student learning.

The Kalamazoo and FBC connection started at a time when study abroad first began to gain prominence as a valuable part of the college experience in the United States. Kalamazoo College, founded in 1833, sent its first group of students abroad to Europe in 1958 and to Sierra Leone in 1962. This was a period marked by the beginning of both the Cold War and the African independence movement. It was a period of high hopes in Africa. Many young African universities were just starting to take shape. Others, such as FBC, had a long history, one marked by a struggle for survival, immense pressures to outperform European counterparts, and a desire to differentiate itself from the traditional Western academy.[1]

Origins of the Kalamazoo / Fourah Bay College Connection

In 1962, John Peterson, one of the newly trained American "Africanists," helped Kalamazoo College in Michigan initiate a study abroad program with FBC in Freetown, Sierra

Leone. FBC, founded in 1827, is the oldest non-Islamic institution of higher learning in Africa and was a prestigious choice. Kalamazoo students were directly enrolled at FBC and lived in residence halls on campus with African roommates. They usually stayed at FBC for one academic year. The Kalamazoo program was for undergraduates; it was not set up with the goal of training specialists or experts, although many of its graduates went on to pursue graduate work in African studies. The study abroad program itself did not directly receive any government funding. The two universities would sustain this partnership for over 30 years, a remarkable accomplishment given the many challenges that FBC faced throughout this period.

Peterson was one of a few U.S. scholars to make long-term commitments to the study of Sierra Leone. As a graduate student at Northwestern University, Peterson received a Ford Foundation Foreign Area Training Fellowship in 1958 to conduct research in Freetown on the Muslim Krio of Sierra Leone. He developed an in-depth understanding and appreciation for Sierra Leonean cultures and was able to communicate and pass on this knowledge and passion to others. Indeed, it was this type of "in-depth, local-based knowledge grounded in extensive fieldwork, language facility and interdisciplinary training" that became the hallmark of area studies (Lloyd 2000:103).

The Early Years of Study Abroad Experience at FBC

Between 1962 and 1994, Kalamazoo College sent 308 students to Sierra Leone, most to FBC for their junior year abroad. At one point, Kalamazoo conducted study abroad programs to seven different African countries in the same year (Greene 1994:244). In many ways, Kalamazoo College pioneered study abroad to Africa from the United States. Peterson first joined the two-person history department at Kalamazoo College in 1961, where he was encouraged to develop courses in African history and a study abroad program to FBC. Along with Peterson, Bill Pruitt, Joe Fugate, and James Buschman all worked to develop Kalamazoo's study abroad programs in Africa. More than most African universities at that time, FBC was an international university attracting numerous students from across the continent and especially from the English-speaking regions.

The Kalamazoo study abroad students learned about Africa, but they also learned about the United States and themselves. As an early Kalamazoo College document about study abroad students noted: "[The question of] racial problems in America was clearly high in the thoughts of ordinary African students. Segregation is the omnipresent ink blot. We arrived here right after the Mississippi incident and ever since this has constantly come up. . . . Americans have to know more about their own country to answer or explain effectively the many questions they were asked" (International Programs Collection 1967). Student participants of the Kalamazoo Africa study programs gained new and different perspectives on race relations. "For the white Americans, it is often the first experience that he or she will have as a very visible minority. The Black American experiences what it means to be in the majority and comes to a better understanding of his own history and heritage" (Fugate 1987:14). African American students participated in the Kalamazoo program every year of its existence, although the majority of students in the program were of European descent.[2] The African context provided an invaluable encounter with difference for students visiting from the United States. As such, study abroad to Africa supports "fruitful dialogue about race, racism, and the racial legacy in America" (Tolliver 2000:115).

Courses related to Africa were practically nonexistent at both FBC and Kalamazoo when the study abroad program began. For example, Kalamazoo students enrolled in the following classes at FBC in 1962: "Greek and Roman Culture, Greek New Testament, Ethics, Metaphysics, English, Geography, Economics, Botany, and African History" (International Programs Collection 1962). In contrast, by 1987, Kalamazoo students enrolled in "African Literature, West African History, History of Sierra Leone, Politics of Development, Sociology of Development, Krio, African Political Systems, Problems of Nation-Building, Pidgin and Creole Languages, Ethnography, and West African Indigenous Religions" (International Programs Collection 1987). The change in course offerings reflected the growth and changes to the field of African Studies, although these latter courses often enrolled more foreign students than Sierra Leonean students. While many alumni of the Kalamazoo Africa programs went on to specialize in African Studies, only a few Sierra Leoneans pursued graduate work in the field. Few Africans conducted research of local cultures, instead pursuing more professional and technical degrees abroad so that these skills could be put into the service of the country upon return. This discrepancy underscores the pressure that African students felt to develop and modernize their newly independent nations.

Throughout the 1970s and 1980s, as the political process in Sierra Leone was corrupted through the increasingly predatory and self-interested regime of Sierra Leone's prime minister and president Siaka Stevens (1967–1985), student protests at FBC grew ever more frequent and desperate. As FBC suffered budget cuts due to the ever-worsening economic situation, more and more faculty resigned and left the country. The number of Kalamazoo participants in the study abroad program also declined as economic conditions worsened and political unrest became more common. As Sandra Greene noted, "Food, water, and electricity shortages, and limited healthcare and transportation caused by the local economic difficulties, made the experience of studying in Africa additionally challenging" (1994:249). Kalamazoo College students witnessed the protests firsthand and were increasingly advised to distance themselves from such protests; on occasion they had to remove themselves from the campus for their safety. Participants in the study abroad program during this period had to be carefully screened and prepared for the political milieu. Eventually, all participants were required to take part in a 10-week predeparture course. In addition, Kalamazoo administrators made annual site visits, sometimes visiting on multiple occasions in a single year. The program cultivated valuable relationships with numerous local contacts ranging from top university administrators to drivers and a wide variety of community members. Kalamazoo shared information and lessons learned with other colleges and universities in the United States that were interested in developing similar study abroad experiences to Africa.

On Saturday, January 29, 1977, the 150th anniversary of FBC, students openly criticized President Stevens during his commencement address, accusing him of diverting government funds for personal use. Students held up placards that read "Bring Back Our Money from the Swiss Banks," "Shaki Must Resign," "We Want Jobs Not Just Degrees," and "President Should Decrease His Cabinet by 40%" (Daramy 1993:189). About 50 students were involved in the demonstrations at the commencement. When students began marching and singing, they drowned out President Stevens's speech, making it impossible to hear, and he was unable to finish. He left, his car being chased amid jeers of "Tifi, Tifi, Jan Conico," a chant usually used in the schoolyard when a child is caught stealing.[3]

Stevens, who had come to power in 1967 opposing one-party rule, had created just that in Sierra Leone by 1977 (Roberts 1982:332). The student protest was followed by swift government retaliation, and several students were killed including a Nigerian student and a student from Zimbabwe (then Rhodesia). The Kalamazoo students, after a terror-filled evening, were eventually taken unharmed to the U.S. ambassador's home. Government thugs had been instructed not to harm foreign students, although as noted above, these instructions had not protected all foreign students. Kalamazoo administrators received updates on the situation from the U.S. State Department, but communication was difficult and limited. A letter dated February 9, 1977, to the Kalamazoo students at FBC from Kalamazoo administrators emphasized to students: "Your safety is the first consideration. Do not stay if it is not safe" (FBC Program Report 1977). These students ended up staying at FBC through the end of the semester as originally scheduled and completed all of their course work.

From 1977 onward, campus closures and strikes became annual occurrences. However, the corruption and intimidation of the Stevens regime did not seem to register with educational or political leaders outside of Sierra Leone. Instead, President Stevens actually received honors from abroad. Students did demonstrate at Lincoln University in Pennsylvania on October 29, 1979, when Lincoln University conferred on Siaka Stevens an honorary doctor of law degree. Estimates of the number of protesters ranged from 100 to 400. Stevens was booed and called a murderer as he spoke. Pictures of people who had been executed in Sierra Leone were circulated. Stevens canceled later appearances on the campus (West Africa Magazine 1979a:2135; 1979b:2069). When Stevens returned to Sierra Leone from the United States, FBC students refused to attend a special welcome reception (West Africa Magazine 1979c:2259). President Stevens received a letter from U.S. president Jimmy Carter congratulating him on his award. In November 1980, Stevens also accepted a knighthood from the Queen of England (Sesay 1981:32). These awards were no doubt bestowed on Stevens because he was such a devoted ally of the West, when many other African countries were aligned with the Soviet Union during the Cold War.

In November 1980, protests on the FBC campus resulted in the cancellation of classes and led to violence. A nationwide strike that also closed the college followed in September 1981. On October 26, 1983, Vice-Chancellor Arthur Porter, Principal Eldred Jones, and Warden Jenkin Smith were all doused with powdered milk and marched downhill in the middle of the day to the statehouse, where the students used them as hostages to arrange a tête-à-tête with Siaka Stevens (FBC Program Report 1983). Four students and the three administrators met with the Sierra Leone president. The campus was shut down for two weeks following the protest. On Thursday, January 12, 1984, students again protested. Tear gas was used on the marchers, and there was some looting and one reported death. Between September 1980 and January 1984, no fewer than 22 professors, lecturers, and technicians left FBC (Kutubu Commission of Inquiry 1984). While Kalamazoo students were there primarily to learn about African culture, they were confronted with serious local and international political issues. It is a testament to the close collaboration and relationship between educators at Kalamazoo College and FBC that the program was able to maintain continuity through this extremely difficult period. It is doubtful that today very many U.S. universities would offer study abroad with an African partner university under such conditions. Instead, many universities now elect to organize their own "island" programs in part to avoid the possibility of African university closures.

On January 26, 1992, the University of Sierra Leone faculty and students were tear-gassed during a peaceful march to commemorate the student protests of 1977. Cyril P. Foray, FBC principal from 1985 to 1993, led the march. Visiting Kalamazoo College students and their faculty advisors had planned to observe the march from a distance but were caught up in the ensuing melee. President Joseph Saidu Momoh accused FBC students of using American students as shields (FBC Program Report 1992). Obviously, the Kalamazoo students did not experience a sanitized or romanticized Africa; they faced a difficult reality.

Because of the continuing and escalating violence, in November 1994, Kalamazoo College indefinitely suspended its study abroad program with FBC and the University of Sierra Leone. Six of the seven students participating in the Kalamazoo program transferred to the Kalamazoo program in Kenya, while the remaining student returned home. The program is yet to be resumed.

Lessons Learned

What are the lessons learned through this partnership? Today, study abroad to Africa is slowly expanding, although most U.S. study abroad programs are of a much shorter duration, usually just a few weeks rather than the yearlong program that Kalamazoo and FBC operated. How can students from the United States be effectively and appropriately engaged in the study of Africa in Africa today? And how can they gain an appreciation for the diversity and complexity of African society in just a few weeks? Most faculty and students in the United States still know very little about Africa and tend to perceive Africa in the negative terms promoted by static media representations of past events. Global issues of race and gender, power and privilege, social justice, and sustainable development remain critically important subjects in need of greater attention, mutual accountability, and shared understanding. While programs of short duration may allow for greater participation, it is unclear whether such programs provide adequate context for significant understanding of complex issues to develop. One of the ways to foster greater engagement is through internships and service-learning projects where visiting students, as participant observers, can learn from local leaders about how they are tackling for themselves their own local issues and concerns. This approach encourages a philosophical switch from learning about Africa to learning from and with Africans.

Undoubtedly, the context has changed. There is now much more information, knowledge, and experience available to draw upon for preparing students to study abroad in Africa. The literature gained through the numerous partnerships and collaboration between Africa, the United States, and other regions of the world is extensive. The scholarship about African history, culture, and society has matured, as has African leadership. The rebel war in Sierra Leone ended in 2002, and since the war, democratic elections have successfully occurred and many positive steps have been taken to increase the functionality of the government. Today, an Internet search for study abroad to Sierra Leone identifies five U.S. universities currently offering programs. All of these programs are relatively short, however, of between two and six weeks.

The question of reciprocity and mutual benefits is critical to any U.S. university that wants to effectively collaborate on study abroad with African partners. Over the years, a number of Sierra Leonean students attended Kalamazoo College, several with the help of scholarship funds from Kalamazoo, but it appears that the number is very small. There were also several FBC faculty members who came to teach at Kalamazoo. Writing in 1994, Greene noted: "This exchange is [predominantly] one-way . . . this problem is particularly acute in Africa programs like that at Kalamazoo College" (1994:251–252). Historically, universities in the United States have often had an unequal advantage in funding for such programs and activities compared to their African partners. In recent years, improved funding models have emerged that enable a more reciprocal exchange process. However, for many critical observers, international education in the United States is still primarily an export industry aimed at generating revenues. And while one-to-one tuition exchange programs may benefit individual African students, such arrangements may also represent a burden to African universities (Coffman and Brennan 2003:141).

Reciprocity is a key component for successful international partnerships. The long life of the FBC-Kalamazoo partnership is a good indication that the partnership was viewed as mutually beneficial. Reciprocity is a broad construct that not only includes financial considerations but also focuses on the educational goal of obtaining a true exchange of ideas and values, including those that may be in conflict. The greatest value of study abroad with African partners is the potential to develop mutual understanding around common interests and problems in order to foster greater collaboration.

Defining common interests is imperative, and educators must do their best to make explicit and transparent the sometimes hidden or unconscious sociocultural, political, and economic dynamics and reasoning at work in order to create a more open, honest, and ethical space for communication, interaction, and learning to occur. Learning how to interpret and negotiate among different value systems becomes the critical context for developing intercultural partnerships and therefore a basis for mutual problem solving of today's complex interdependent global issues. Study abroad programs with African partners must have clear, mutually defined learning goals. U.S. students traveling to Africa must come prepared to learn about Africa from their African hosts; they must be engaged with local communities at all levels and segments of society; and they should definitely not be there on some type of cultural rescue mission.

Thirty-six of the 308 participants in the Kalamazoo study abroad program to Sierra Leone obtained advanced degrees in African studies or related studies, 16 at the master's level and 20 at the doctoral level, an impressive statistic for a small liberal arts undergraduate college (Greene 1994:247). Students studied a broad range of topics. A 1991 Kalamazoo alumni magazine highlighted a few of the wide-ranging cultural studies of students who had studied at FBC in the 1980s, covering topics such as cloth design, Krio theater, historic cultural representation, and photography. Alumni such as Chris Corcoran, for example, went on to receive a Fulbright award for her work. She completed her doctorate degree in linguistics from the University of Chicago and documented the existence of over 70 theater troupes, 120 playwrights, and 355 plays active in Sierra Leone in the 1980s (Kalamazoo College Quarterly Review 1991). Kalamazoo students learned a great deal about themselves and about Sierra Leone. Student interest in learning about Sierra Leone and Africa helped to drive curricular change at both colleges.

While it is beyond the scope of this chapter to fully evaluate the policies and effectiveness of international educational exchanges in Africa or the degree to which government funding was manipulated by political ideologies, it does seem reasonable to suggest that the soft diplomacy of personal relationships forged through study abroad programs such as that between Kalamazoo College and FBC were efficacious in promoting intercultural learning. One Kalamazoo administrator reported, "I remember being told by a Sierra Leone educator that the presence of our students at his university was probably worth the equivalent of one million dollars in AID funds" (Stavig 1974:11). It is unclear just how much national governments will be willing to spend on international education exchange in the future. Rather than depend upon government funding, it is most likely that colleges and universities in the United States and Africa will have to work together to find ways to create programs that are self-supporting and mutually beneficial, if they are to be sustainable. One of the ways to do this financially may be to exchange groups of American students involved in short-term course experiences for several African students on longer-term degree programs. No matter what form partnerships take, the real value of the learning exchange experience for both the individual participants and the broader institutions and communities must be evaluated, and not just the dollar amounts. There is not likely to be one formula that can be applied to the great diversity of African and U.S. colleges and universities. Certainly, these study abroad programs must be grounded within academic programs and not add-on courses disconnected from students' major fields of study.

International education alone cannot and should not be the primary means for addressing local political issues, but it has the potential to bring to light injustices and lend support to more informed policy decisions. It can especially help to illuminate the connections between local and global issues. A globally relevant education should help bring together multicultural communities to equitably and cooperatively solve common problems, ensure human dignity, protect the diversity of life on the planet, and conserve precious resources. While the dysfunctional politics of the Cold War era undermined the overall effectiveness of international education exchange, it did not defeat the laudable and serious goals of those involved in and committed to intercultural learning and engagement. Developing effective international partnerships requires serious commitments that are part of a broader institutional vision and that go beyond study abroad to engage all stakeholders and inform curricular change. Study abroad to Africa should be grounded in the interdisciplinary theories and research of African studies. Programs should involve partnerships that connect diverse public and private segments of society including the arts, small businesses, multinational corporations, schools, health-care providers, religious groups, and environmental, nongovernmental, and not-for-profit organizations. It is also critically important if such relationships are to flourish that educators give particular focus to preparing and supporting students throughout their intercultural learning experiences. In this way, such programs are most likely to be mutually beneficial and sustainable.

Study abroad programs with African partners should be conceived as part of a larger effort by U.S. colleges and universities to effectively build relationships, conduct joint research, deliver classroom instruction, and collaborate on joint projects. International partnership relationships need to extend beyond the limited impact of one or two researchers working together. Such programs need to be strategically integrated within degree programs and across disciplines, including African Studies. African studies is critically important today to anyone genuinely interested in collaborating effectively across cultures to solve local and global issues.

Universities and governments cannot operate effectively under antagonistic circumstances, nor can universities remove themselves from the larger social contexts. The Cold War is over, and most African universities have abandoned partisan politics for more practical problem solving. Universities in the United States and in Africa are now much more able than before to forge mutually beneficial relationships focused on educational exchange rather than political ideology, although serious value differences remain. Where the middle ground between communism, socialism, and capitalism is located is, of course, open for debate, but it is widely agreed upon that providing access to quality education is a critically important goal for the future stability and sustainability of our increasingly global society no matter the political ideology. Cold War politics were not conducive to promoting healthy civil societies in Africa, but despite this context, the FBC–Kalamazoo College collaboration managed to find ways to infuse important curricular changes and impact student lives in very meaningful ways. Certainly, the time is right (if not long overdue) for institutions of higher learning within Africa and the United States to further elevate their level of commitment, coordination, and collaboration to each other.

Notes

1. For more about the history of the FBC, see Daniel J. Paracka, Jr., *The Athens of West Africa: A History of International Education at Fourah Bay College, Freetown, Sierra Leone* (2003).

2. For an in-depth analysis of one African American student's experiences of the Kalamazoo study abroad program at FBC, see Oni Faida Lampley's play *The Dark Kalamazoo* (1997; debuted in 1999).

3. FBC Program Report (1977) and personal interview with Joe Opala (Savannah, GA, November 19, 2000).

20 Teaching Culture, Health, and Political Economy in the Field

Ground-Level Perspectives on Africa in the 21st Century

James Ellison

Introduction

Early in the 21st century, Africa is more intimately connected to transnationally circulating forces of political economy than at any time in the past. Africa has been tied to such forces throughout history, of course, as both a contributor and a recipient of cultural movements, commodities, and technologies, and some Africanists rightly warn that the enticing models of "globalization" can mask such long-standing ties (Cooper 2001). The close of the 20th century saw increases in the speed and ubiquity of communications technologies, electronic transfers of capital, and movements of people both within the continent and to and from overseas destinations. Political and economic liberalization following the Cold War increased the flow of international capital into African countries, often to purchase newly privatized resources and take advantage of relaxed import and export restrictions, and it dramatically expanded the presence of international nongovernmental organizations (NGOs).

Scholars face challenges in conceptualizing and researching Africa's new economic, political, and social realities. Teachers face a familiar dilemma of how to teach students about everyday life in Africa under these new conditions. Teaching about Africa in the United States once meant deconstructing stereotypes about a place most students had never visited and would likely never go, stereotypes that circulated in popular media and even in college classrooms. Africa scholars sought creative ways to represent Africa accurately and in its fullness, using African films, literature, art, and music to convey understandings of African experiences (Bastian and Parpart 1999).

However, like other aspects of culture, stereotypes are not static. Along with neoliberal changes in Africa's politics and economics, Africa scholars now face new challenges when teaching about daily life in Africa in part because students today have more access to Africa than did students in the past. There are also new possibilities for teaching about Africa—including through field-based courses.

This chapter examines the conditions that make a field-based course in Africa possible and desirable in the 21st century. A field-based course offers an incomparable way to teach students about everyday life in Africa in a form that many Africanists are already prepared to teach. Many Africanists develop or expand detailed, on-the-ground knowledge of African countries when they conduct research for advanced degrees. In the past, such experiences provided useful anecdotes and slides for classes. Taking students to Africa was rarely an option; it was unaffordable for students and faculty, most U.S. schools lacked the infrastructure to support such a project, and the logistical difficulties in potential host countries were enormous. Changes in political and economic conditions and infrastructures, however, have made field-based courses more feasible. Such courses can create opportunities for faculty and meet the challenges presented by students who already have some firsthand experiences with Africa.

A centerpiece of this chapter is a discussion of the field-based course I designed and direct in Tanzania, drawing on knowledge and relationships established over many years of research. In this six-week course, students learn about public health, livelihoods, and culture in changing political and economic contexts while they are immersed in the social and cultural diversity of eastern Africa. In Dar es Salaam, students experience urban life and learn about current political, economic, and public health concerns in the country. In Zanzibar, they learn about Islam and western Indian Ocean cosmopolitanism during intensive Swahili language instruction. Through a more sustained immersion in rural southwest Tanzania, they learn about village life and people's changing livelihoods and health. The course is an ethnographic "field school," teaching students qualitative research methods that they use to learn about people's day-to-day lives and experiences.[1] Unlike study abroad programs centered on classroom learning at host universities and short-term travel programs, field schools involve students in actual fieldwork and provide related readings, lectures, and discussions. Students spend the bulk of their time traversing village paths and interacting with people at their homes and farms. The field school is a life-changing and career-shaping event for students; it offers an incomparable way for them to learn about new and changing conditions in Tanzania, and it helps them envision careers working with Africans as central, knowledgeable actors.

Neoliberalism, Public Health, and New Stereotypes

In the past two decades, Africa's economic, political, and cultural landscapes have changed with increased flows of people and commodities. Liberalization reconfigured socioeconomic hierarchies and created new obstacles to things like health care. Entrepreneurs with capital or government connections often benefited from privatization, while the gap between the wealthy and the poor has grown.[2] Health care in Tanzania, once a right provided by the government, much like primary education, became fee based and partly privatized.

Students—even those with firsthand experiences with Africa and Africans—often find it difficult to comprehend connections between political economy and health. In a popular class I teach on health in Africa, students arrive ready to learn about contemporary health problems—particularly HIV/AIDS; they have studied it in other classes and seen documentaries on AIDS in Africa. They respond well to readings that outline historical links between economic changes and malaria (Packard 2007) and associations between poverty and AIDS (Nolen 2007). They are more inclined to view Africans as helpless in the face of health catastrophes or even as deserving blame for their health conditions—because of bad decisions about treatment or poor "cultural" or "hygiene" habits—than to understand people as complex and knowledgeable agents living in political-economic contexts that challenge their abilities to be healthy (Maharaj and Roberts 2006; Susser 2009; Whyte et al. 2006). In other words, students who "self-select" into a course on African health and healing are often prepared to see Africans as sufferers—even as self-afflicted victims—in need of external expertise. Students who have firsthand experience with Africa or Africans even summon their experiences to support such assumptions.[3] Like the experts in biomedical fields that some of these students aspire to join, they are initially unprepared to understand local narratives and knowledge of health and illness (Thomas 2008).

Working against pernicious stereotypes about Africa, such as those concerning health, is a long-standing goal in teaching about Africa in the United States (e.g., Gilbert and Reynolds 2012:xxi–xxiv), but such stereotypes have developed a particular 21st-century form in political and economic realms and in popular culture. Africa is seen as marginal and a target for "extractive neoliberalism" (Ferguson 2006:210), its ill-used and underexploited resources in need of taking in an era of "free" markets. Popular films dealing with Africa have largely abandoned the blatantly racist themes of the past and today address social issues like the human costs of the international diamond trade and the impact of the international pharmaceutical industry and nonconsensual drug testing on Africans. Yet even these films present Africa and Africans as a backdrop to the experiences and agency of white Europeans and Americans. Students today tend to be concerned about the global economy, and many oppose the exploitation of Africa, but they view the continent and its maladies through this 21st-century lens.

Today, paradoxically, students in U.S. college and university classes often refer to their personal experiences with Africa when using stereotypes about Africa, such as those concerning health. Like many Africanists, I try to identify and counteract flawed stereotypes about Africa. Students begin my overview class on Africa by completing a map quiz and listing 10 things they know about Africa. In the past, their misshapen maps contained one or two key features—Egyptian pyramids, for example. Their lists provided unsurprising associations—for example, witch doctors, safaris, and tribes. Over the years, these results have changed. Students now map places they have visited or studied and list African leaders and recent historical events. Many eschew older stereotypes and racism that once passed as acceptable. Each year, I have a few more students who have traveled to Africa—for family vacations, study abroad, or with secondary school or religious programs. Many more have family members who have lived, worked, or traveled in Africa. Some have Internet "friends" in Africa, and most have African friends on campus—or in churches, mosques, or their home communities. An increasing number are children of Africans who came to the United States since the 1980s or are African students who came specifically for secondary or higher education. Rather than experience creating unproblematic understandings of Africa, however, these students often cite their experiences when using current stereotypes about Africa, giving apparent authority to their perspectives.

These new demographic patterns and experiences among our students suggest that our pedagogical models must also change. Our task may be more difficult than it was when we taught about "real" places and people in order to change what students knew wrongly through film or popular representations. Our teaching often involved two interrelated efforts. The first was to make Africa seem less exotic while making common stereotypes explicit. We exposed flaws in "common knowledge" about Africa by using more accurate information about Africa and Africans' lives, drawing on media from Africa wherever possible. A second effort was to introduce students to the cultural, social, economic, and political conditions of life in Africa as different from what they are used to or would assume. Through films, art, literature, guest speakers, and Internet exercises, we sought to bring Africa and Africans to life for students—somewhat on African terms. These efforts remain crucial to our teaching, but stereotypes supported by the self-affirmation of experience require us to rethink how to accomplish them.

A field-based course offers important new ways to confront current stereotypes by teaching about everyday life in Africa. It also addresses students' growing interests in doing practical work in Africa. Critics may rightly point out that student participation in such a program can be limited by space and costs. Financial aid may be available to help students cover program costs, and some types of external funding exist for faculty running such programs, which can reduce student expenses. In this time of market influence in higher education, a field-based course is also appealing to administrators seeking to boast of "experience-based learning" and global opportunities in their institutions.[4] Field-based courses are an important way to teach about Africa as well as to create profound new opportunities for students to engage with people in Africa. They have the potential to contribute to the lives of people we work with in

Africa—colleagues and those living in fieldwork sites, as discussed below—and such courses have personal and professional rewards for the scholars who design and direct them.

Deciding to Create a Fieldwork-Based Course in Africa

Among the principal arguments for creating a field-based course in Africa is that many Africanists already have the expertise needed to design and direct one. That experience is gained through training and research; in the past, we viewed that experience as an asset for ongoing research, but neglected to consider it as an opportunity for creating important and unique field-based pedagogy. To be clear, in referring to such experience, I mean having knowledge of host-country research institutions—universities, research clearance offices, organizations, and so on—and people in them; having knowledge of the physical and social infrastructures in the countries where we work; and having created (and reworked) research and travel itineraries. These are incomparable experiences for setting up a successful field-based course for undergraduates. A field-based course can also contribute to our own ongoing professional development in ways that regular course work cannot, as we collaborate with colleagues in Africa and consider new ways to involve undergraduate students in our research.

There are other strong arguments for creating such a course. We have long sought ways to present "African voices" in our classes, and a field-based course places our students solidly in African contexts. It creates the opportunity for students to learn directly from African people in their daily lives and from intellectuals in African universities, NGOs, government offices, and clinics, and through it, students can learn alongside African peers. A field-based course comprises an incomparable set of experiences through which our students learn by doing. Students gain a new sense of seriousness about Africa and their overall studies from participating in such a program (Gmelch and Gmelch 1999; Houlihan 2007; Iris 2004). It can clarify for them possible career options that place Africa and Africans at the center of their thinking. Alumni of our program in Tanzania have found the experience a catalyst and gone on to study environmental law, public health, and anthropology at the graduate level and to work in these and other related fields after graduation.

In 2003, I developed the fieldwork-based course in Tanzania with my colleague Karen Weinstein, a biological anthropologist at Dickinson College. Our reasons for establishing the program involved our own research, our pedagogy and students' experiences, and our colleagues and friends in Tanzania. We have devoted much of our lives to learning about Africa, learning to live, work, and conduct research there; our intention has always been to continue our fieldwork throughout our careers. We sought to provide students with firsthand experiences of Tanzania in field research situations, to create opportunities for them to meet, collaborate with, and befriend people there through fieldwork rather than through commercial transactions of tourism or the patron-client dynamics that can exist when wealthy students study in poor countries. Ideally, our students would learn about the complexities of Tanzanians' everyday lives directly from Tanzanians, undermining stereotypes about Africa they had absorbed in the United States. The practical research skills students learn are useful to them in a range of fields after graduation. The program also helps them develop a realistic vision of careers working with people in Africa, something alumni of our program have said would have been difficult otherwise. "We did not merely learn about an academic subject," wrote one student following her experience in 2005, "but were personally changed in various ways, from our worldview and outlook on life, to our academic aspirations" (Kirner 2005:5). Several alumni are working to return to Tanzania or go elsewhere in Africa to work on projects directed in part by African researchers.

As scholars in the United States who by global standards are relatively well funded, we consider it important for our work to bring some benefit to the people in our field sites and our Tanzanian colleagues. To those ends, we direct our program through local contacts and businesses. We organize our students to contribute to the University of Dar es Salaam library, and we have involved them in small development projects in our host community. The current effort, in which students have taken initiative, involves a piped water project for a sub-village of our fieldwork, because, as our fieldwork demonstrated, local women and children currently draw virtually all water for drinking and washing from a local stream. We also place Tanzanian experts at the heart of our program, to teach our students and receive recognition for their expertise—as well as the compensation due for their contributions. We emphasize to our students that Tanzanians are the experts of their own lives. In terms of the broad structural inequalities between the United States and East Africa, these are small benefits, but they are important and are directly related to the field-based course. In the future, we hope to expand our efforts to include student exchanges and greater co-involvement of Tanzanian faculty and students in the program as a whole.

The Field School in Tanzania

Students in our program remain off the beaten track, spending time with Tanzanians in their communities to understand their everyday social and cultural lives and their articulations with national and transnational forces. Our six-week field school has two main academic purposes: to teach students qualitative field research methods and to teach them about the interconnections among culture, nutrition, health, and changing global political and economic conditions in eastern Africa. Readings and lectures explain fieldwork methods—such as recording field notes, conducting interviews, and logging fieldwork with a global positioning system (GPS)—and students carry out exercises in each region we visit. In the last month of the program, students apply these methods to independent research projects that they choose in connection with the theme of the course and their research interests. We stress the imperative of ethical practice, through readings—including the field school Institutional Review Board (IRB) documents—and discussions, and students learn the importance of openness and informed consent.[5] To successfully engage in field research, students must listen to and learn from the people they interact with; their enjoyment of this unique intercultural experience is also part of the learning process.

Formal lessons about eastern Africa involve lectures by and discussions with the field school directors and Tanzanian scholars, professionals, and activists. Readings provide historical and ethnographic overviews and address society, culture, and changes in economics and health at specific sites we visit. Readings, lectures, and visits link student experiences to practical life and scholarship, making a student's knowledge of Tanzania both intensely personal and academically sound. Students also receive an intensive introduction to Swahili language in Zanzibar, early in the program, and in rural southwest Tanzania each student works with a local multilingual peer on a fieldwork project. Nearly all students maintain contact with their Tanzanian peers after the program, and as a result of the field school some have changed their career plans to concentrate on Africa, having carried out meaningful research showing links between Tanzania's liberalization and rural people's changing livelihoods and health conditions (Weinstein and Ellison 2010). Students receive two course credits when they complete the program.[6]

Long before reaching East Africa, while students are applying for summer programs, we hold public information sessions to promote our course, and we try to involve program alumni to discuss their experiences and answer questions. We want prospective students to know that our program is not a common study-tour. After accepting student applicants, we hold three on-campus orientation sessions. In the initial session, we outline the program and basic travel necessities—obtaining visas and vaccinations and plans for packing. In the subsequent sessions, we discuss the program's academic core, specific packing and travel arrangements and our itinerary, and cultural immersion. At each session, we try to prepare students for situations they might confront if they are inexperienced travelers or have not ventured off the beaten track in a place like Tanzania. We discuss the ethical issues in our project, and we repeatedly urge students to view themselves as fortunate guests and to approach the experience with humility and readiness to learn from people in Tanzania. We try to expose and discard common views of North American superiority to Africa and desires to save Africans from "self-evident" troubles. Finally, we distribute a handbook that details our travel and what to expect in Tanzania, along with information for emergencies, including contact information for the college and the directors. We encourage students to share the handbook with their families.

Our field school has been successful in large measure due to our long-term relationships with people in Tanzania. We designed the program to run on a budget of roughly $20,000 in 2008. The budget includes costs for host-country transportation, lodging, and meals and fees for guest speakers, student translators, trips, and entertainment. Costs depend on the number of students participating and variables like the changing price of food and particularly fuel, which can wreak havoc on the budget.

Each student pays approximately $5,000 for the program, which covers tuition and fees and all of the things just discussed and overhead for our college (which contributes financial assistance for students going abroad). Students pay for their own travel within the United States, airfare to Tanzania (which we arrange for group discounts), vaccinations, passports and visas, and personal materials. Fieldwork equipment is either already owned by our college or purchased with other monies. Faculty experience in a host country can bring knowledge about inexpensive options for lodging, eating, and travel that can make such a program feasible. We operate our program with two directors, although to do so may not always be possible. Having a single director concentrates responsibility on one person; it also makes it hard to create contingency plans while shielding students from schedule disruptions.

The first field school included an initial stop in Tanzania's "safari circuit" as a way to immediately confront students' stereotypes about Africa while also teaching them about political ecology, tourism, economic liberalization, and economic diversification. We subsequently eliminated the safari circuit because it claimed a disproportionately large share of the program's budget, due to the high costs of lodging, meals, park fees, and transportation associated with tourism. Students see wildlife and tourism at other sites, and past participants supported eliminating the safari, which became relatively insignificant to them compared to other experiences on the program. Among the readings we assigned for the safari circuit was an article by anthropologist Mwenda Ntarangwi (2000), who for years has taken U.S. students to rural Kenya. Ntarangwi writes that students scoff at tourists who are interested in African wildlife and commodities, but he argues that students themselves engage in similar behaviors and therefore their motives resemble tourism. Our students balk at Ntarangwi's claim, insisting that their interests differ fundamentally from those of tourists, although we sense in their response that Ntarangwi's argument hits close to home. His contention seems to have a lasting influence on students, and it remains a point for serious reflection throughout the program—and even beyond. We continue to assign the article because of this impact.

Our current design is to arrive in Dar es Salaam, Tanzania's most populous urban center, where people from the University of Dar es Salaam (UDSM) Links Office, the office that oversees ties with foreign universities and colleges, meet us. Major universities in Africa tend to have such an office, and it is important to work with them: they have expertise and experience with similar programs; they control important resources; and working with them is appropriate. Chances are they can make cost-saving and itinerary-enhancing suggestions. UDSM's office has been helpful in planning and logistics. Most of our travel in the city involves local transportation, either riding on *daladala* (minibuses) on regular routes or negotiating with drivers for private trips. Links Office staff provide some help as favors, and we are expected to give honoraria and gratuities to drivers, staff, and a student assistant, as well as to pay for any use of university vehicles. In designing a field-based program, be sure to include gratuities in your budget.

Like many major universities, the UDSM has residence facilities that can house visiting students. We arrange for our students to stay in a university dormitory, the preferred option of the university and a cost-effective option for us. Our students find the dormitory basic, but it is also a good introduction to the life of a student in Tanzania. The potential for petty theft exists, as students are clearly short-term visitors; we recommend consulting with university housing staff about their security recommendations. The directors stay with friends nearby or at a university-provided house, if one is available. We give our students a locally purchased cell phone to contact us for planning and in case of an emergency; we discourage students from buying cell phones because we want them to focus on their interactions in Tanzania and not on contact with their friends and family back home.

Students meet with senior and junior scholars in anthropology, sociology, and other fields in the social sciences at the UDSM who discuss their work, its place in the university and in Tanzania today, and current social and political situations in Dar es Salaam and the country. We take our students to Muhimbili University of Health and Allied Sciences in Dar es Salaam, the central teaching and research hospital in the country. There our students meet with a professor who works in public health and has experience in medical anthropology; having taught in the United States, he easily finds the right level to address our students about culture, nutrition, health, and national health priorities, which he situates in national and international political and economic contexts. These and other lectures and visits set the stage for subsequent lessons, and our students refer to them throughout the rest of the program. They also incorporate information from them in their final projects.

From Dar es Salaam, we travel to Zanzibar by ferry, lodging on the edge of "Stone Town" at a guesthouse that is decorated with 19th- and 20th-century artifacts and photographs of Zanzibar and western Indian Ocean cosmopolitan lifestyles. Each morning after tea on the rooftop, our students walk through town to the State University of Zanzibar and the Institute of Swahili and Foreign Languages for their intensive course in Swahili language. Their course includes morning classroom sessions and individual tutorials in the afternoons, through which students learn practical use of the language and how to navigate cultural encounters as they walk in town and visit their instructors' friends and family. We have no illusions that our students gain real use of Swahili; the purpose of the language training is to get them familiar with basic sounds in Swahili and to learn some basic greetings.

Through lectures and reading assignments, students learn about Zanzibar's place in the history of Swahili language and culture and in Indian Ocean trade (Gilbert 2004; Prestholdt 2008) and how the coast is linked with the mainland. Through fieldwork exercises, students observe and make notes about people's gendered practices, religious identities, and cultural backgrounds to elicit the historical and cultural complexity of the island, while also leading students to dismantle assumptions about gender and ethnicity. They learn that the coast is home to "Arabs" (Omanis, Hadhramauts,

Yemenis), "Asians" (Hindu, Goan), and "Africans" ("Nyasa," "Yao," Makonde, Swahili, Somali) from across the western Indian Ocean and that, contrary to stereotypes, it is not necessarily obvious how one can distinguish among these people. During our stay, students freely tour "Stone Town," sample Zanzibar's excellent restaurants, and attend performances by internationally renowned Taarab bands. At the end of our stay, there is a feast for the students and the language faculty and staff who work with them.

Dar es Salaam and Zanzibar give students two very different experiences, and from there we head to the Rift Valley of southwestern Tanzania for the most intensive part of our program. We embark for the city of Mbeya on the Tanzania Zambia Railway Authority (TAZARA) line, Africa's "Freedom Railway" built in the 1970s with assistance from China, connecting Zambia and southern Africa with Dar es Salaam's Indian Ocean seaport (Monson 2009). Common delays in the overnight trip teach students about train travel in East Africa and can bring the good fortune of a daytime pass through the Selous Game Reserve, letting students see spectacular wildlife from their compartments. Captive inside the train, they also find numerous opportunities to meet and talk with other travelers from Tanzania, Zambia, and elsewhere. In Mbeya, a longtime friend and business owner in a district administrative town meets us at the train station and takes us to his guesthouse for a meal. We lodge in a village south of the district capital at a hostel attached to a theological college, home to a late-19th-century Moravian church and a mid-20th-century Moravian school. The hostel affords rural fieldwork opportunities and the ability to connect students with multilingual translators, some of whom attend the local school. Costs of lodging and meals are low when compared with options that are more formal; we continue to consider arranging homestay opportunities for students, although language is a main obstacle.

Local government officials grant permission for our students to do fieldwork projects in the villages around the hostel, all within a single ward. We arrange visits with doctors and hospital staff at the government's district hospital and a comparatively well-funded rural Catholic hospital farther to the north. At these hospitals students learn about health problems in the district, how these facilities address those problems, and the constraints they face locally, nationally, and with regard to international funding. These are outstanding opportunities, as our hosts at the hospitals invite students to ask questions and to return if they wish for follow-up information. In the community, students also meet with local health practitioners and people involved in farming cooperatives and economic ventures, although a student's individual project determines the people he or she will spend the most time with. If other scholars in relevant fields are doing fieldwork in the area, we ask them to talk with our students about their work.

For fieldwork, we pair each student with a local peer who has facility with English, Swahili, and Nyakyusa languages. Peers include local secondary school students, new teachers at the school who are in their early twenties, and local people who recently finished secondary school and are planning to attend university or begin work as teachers. Students work with these peers to engage with the local community, using the academic lessons and methods we teach them. In 2008 and 2011, we designed and had students complete a demographic and health survey of every household in one village, and they plotted research sites using GPS technology. The survey generated data to compare with national surveys in 2004 and 2010, and it helps us quantify economic and health issues we understood through qualitative data and to see new patterns in people's experiences (Weinstein and Ellison 2010). The survey was an important way for students and peers to begin conversations with villagers at their homes, helping students to develop and begin their own independent projects. During the program, we hold workshops for students to discuss their fieldwork and receive feedback, and we work with each student to shape and refine his or her project. Students have some latitude in selecting fieldwork topics, but their projects—ranging from a study of pregnancy and midwifery to examinations of changes in farming after socialism—align with our own research interests.

The data and information students generate have enabled us to document, among other things, that in nearly all households in our village site, women and children carry water for drinking and cooking uphill from streams exposed to contaminants including livestock. The directors, the students, and an elected community board are now addressing this water situation. In the field, we gauged the students' interest in tackling this problem and met with district engineers and the community board. The clearest solution is to install centrally located water spigots in the village, drawing from a spring uphill. Our students began fund-raising in the 2008–2009 academic year with assistance from our college. The project met some opposition among stakeholders controlling water sources, and, in 2011, we helped with additional surveys and negotiations. A successful piped water project will mean improved health and reduced workload for women and children in the village. It is a strong lesson for the students in the practical value of fieldwork and learning from local communities about their lives and needs, as well as an extraordinary example of student-engaged learning.

On weekends, the students travel to a beachfront lodge on the shores of Lake Nyasa, a site with buildings dating to the 1890s settlements of German missionaries. Students relax in thatched-roof bungalows and spend time swimming, hiking, and visiting a local periodic market, giving them the chance to collect their thoughts before returning to their fieldwork. Because the area is in the same broad cultural region as their fieldwork and is near another hospital, some students pursue informal conversations with local people related to their fieldwork interests.

At the end of our stay in the southwest, we hold a large feast to thank members of the community, local government and ceremonial authorities, staff at the hostel, and the students' local peers. At the feast, we voice our thanks to the people who have helped us, and our hosts take the opportunity to offer speeches thanking us and inviting future collaborations. The students select a representative to give a speech of thanks, which they prepare in Swahili with the help of a peer. More than these particular exchanges, our students see again that fieldwork in a place like rural Tanzania is not just an academic exercise, but also a personal commitment. Back in Dar es Salaam, again lodging at the UDSM, we meet with Tanzanian colleagues and friends to discuss the field season and lay out future collaborations. The students present the preliminary results of their fieldwork, and they have time before departing to shop and sightsee, either on their own or with the assistance of a student staff member of the university's Links Office. They write and submit final papers after returning to the United States.

The best-laid plans are subject to changing prices, in particular related to the global price of oil.[7] We have incurred these costs most clearly in the price of fuel, but they also emerge in the price of food and lodging. Others developing such a program should anticipate possible price fluctuations and have some emergency money that can be sent from the home university or college (e.g., through Western Union). One should also budget for gifts and tipping; wages can be low, and a tip is much appreciated and often expected—for people who help carry luggage or run errands and also for people who are paid regular wages, such as hotel employees, university office workers, and drivers. At the UDSM, for example, visiting programs may be asked to provide "bus fare" for student assistants and university drivers when they work beyond regular hours on evenings and weekends. Similarly, fieldwork depends on rapport and goodwill. Although we do not pay people to participate in our students' fieldwork, we acknowledge the demands of the survey and our students on people's time by having the students give a small gift to each participating household, such as a kilogram bag of sugar. We want our students to express their thanks and hope that people in the community will view the students (and us) as grateful guests.

Students generally adapt well to conditions in Tanzania and excel with the experience. Health is always a concern when leading students on a program abroad, and we try to prepare students for their health needs prior to our departure. We direct them to health facilities that deal with international travel for vaccinations, immunizations, and prescriptions for antimalarials. Others designing field-based programs should work with their home institutions to understand or design appropriate procedures for disciplinary or medical problems and to be sure that students are aware such procedures exist.

Concluding Thoughts: A Field-Based Course Is Possible

The very issues we seek to understand—the effects of political and economic liberalization at global, national, and local scales—make possible our field-based course in Tanzania. Economic and political changes have opened many countries in Africa to increased flows of international visitors. This has meant an expansion of infrastructures related to tourism and international students and a relative ease of obtaining visas, airline tickets, and accommodations in a host country. Unlike two decades ago, much planning for a group trip to Africa today can take place from abroad using the

Internet and new cell phone connectivity. Today, it is common for African universities to have offices that specifically deal with international programs. As I discussed above, those offices can help enormously with setting up field-based courses involving foreign institutions and students. At the same time, colleges and universities in the United States have new commitments to and infrastructures for supporting "experience-based learning" programs, in which international study has become extremely important. Institutions of higher education find such programs highly marketable, and most are seeking new ways to maintain their commitment to them in the current economic crisis.

Changes in the realm of finance associated with global neoliberalism create new ways for students to fund their involvement in field-based courses in Africa. This is more of an observation of new economic practices than an endorsement of these changes; students and their families live in this new economy, as do the home institutions, and they are often willing to use it for a variety of purposes. Many students today travel to Africa for other reasons; some have relative ease gaining family support for an academic program. Other ways to help pay for participation also exist. Some colleges and universities pool overhead funds from abroad programs to support students needing financial assistance, thereby encouraging the creation of new abroad offerings. Small grants are sometimes available to students from within a student's home university or college or from outside associations and foundations. If a field-based program is tied to faculty research, external funding options also exist in the United States, such as the National Science Foundation, where the Research Experience for Undergraduates (REU) program helps support student research.[8]

A field-based course is an incomparable way to teach about Africa in the 21st century. Alumni of our program consistently tell us that the field school is a unique and rewarding experience. Students learn about Africa from Africans through their intensive, on-the-ground experiences and as they travel a long path from the Indian Ocean coast to the Rift Valley in southwest Tanzania. They conduct directed fieldwork projects side by side with local peers, and they connect that work and their experiences with scholarship about local culture and Tanzania's history and current predicaments. We are proud of what alumni have done with the experience, and other students are excited about the possibility of participating in the future. Our hosts always warmly welcome our students and invite us to return. Through the program, students can envision new career possibilities that involve Africa and through which they might establish their own connections with people in Africa.

Notes

I wish to thank the many people in Tanzania—far too many to name—who have graciously contributed to the success of the ethnographic field school at different times and locations; Dickinson College, for supporting the program; and the students who have participated over the years. My colleague Karen Weinstein has been a perfect partner in the process throughout, and I am grateful for our ongoing collaboration.

1. Field schools are common in archaeology, a subdiscipline of anthropology, and increasingly so in social and cultural anthropology (Iris 2004). Analogous fieldwork experiences are also becoming available through organizations such as the School for Field Studies (Houlihan 2007).

2. As cited in Mensah (2008:2), the United Nations Development Programme's (UNDP) Human Development Report for 2006 notes that in recent years, "sub-Saharan Africa is the only region that has witnessed an increase in both the incidence of poverty and in the absolute numbers of poor." See also the UNDP's current information (http://hdr.undp.org/en).

3. As an analogy, sociologists expect not that students will understand class relations based on mere experiences in the United States, but rather that students adopt folk explanations that sociologists work to counteract.

4. The expansion of study abroad opportunities including to sites in Africa is examined in Hoffa and DePaul (2010) and at the Institute of International Education (http://www.iie.org/en/research-and-publications/open-doors).

5. The codirectors submit the field school as a whole for IRB review and present possible student projects as parts of that whole. This model works because students use a common set of methods; their work is part of a course; we set parameters on topics; and we set standards of confidentiality. We employ a uniform consent process that gives people several options for participation. Such practices may vary with the structure of a program.

6. At Dickinson, a typical semester-long course earns one course credit, which is equivalent to a three- or four-credit course at other universities and colleges.

7. We have not encountered disruptions due to political troubles, such as those after Kenya's 2007 elections, and so I cannot recommend ways to manage a program in such a context. We have had to amend our plans for various other reasons, such as the loss of electricity in Zanzibar throughout our stay in 2008. Maintaining good communication with your friends and colleagues in your host country will always help.

8. See the National Science Foundation's website, at http://www.nsf.gov.

21 Beyond the Biologic Basis of Disease

Collaborative Study of the Social and Economic Causation of Disease in Africa

Amy C. Finnegan, Julian Jane Atim,

and Michael J. Westerhaus

Introduction

On a dry, hot Friday afternoon in January 2010 in northern Uganda, medical students from Uganda, Holland, and the United States gathered in a large circle and reflected on Paul Farmer's book *Pathologies of Power: Health, Human Rights, and the New War on the Poor* (2005). Excitedly, the students shared inspirations, critiques, and real-life experiences in response to the issues raised by the book. One Ugandan student, captivated by the concept of structural violence, expressed how he had seen corruption, gender inequality, and poor governance ruin the lives of sick patients, but he had not previously known what to call it. A student from the United States with experience working in Central America expressed concern about the sustainability of the sorts of resource-intensive health solutions for the poor that Farmer advocates for in the book. Another student beamed with the hopeful message of the book. And one other commented that she now sees that solutions for the global health challenges facing our world today rest on forming networks and building "togetherness."

The engaged conversation that afternoon symbolizes the interactive and collaborative classroom dynamics that characterized Beyond the Biologic Basis of Disease: The Social and Economic Causation of Illness, a social medicine course taught in Gulu, Uganda, from January 18 to February 12, 2010. The course brought together 21 medical students from around the world—12 from different regions of Uganda, 8 from the United States, and 1 from Holland.[1] Through patient case discussions, bedside clinical teaching, didactic lectures, group discussions and interactive activities, and field visits, the course merged the teaching of clinical and social medicine to provide a unique immersion into global health in the Ugandan context.

The course originated in response to swelling global health interest over the past decade among aspiring medical students. The factors propelling this increase include enhanced media networks that regularly confront us with troubling stories about poverty and disease (Boltanski 1999), the implementation of community-based models of care with demonstrated efficacy for reducing health inequities (Farmer 2005), and reinvigorated calls for social justice and primary care to form the basis of new initiatives (Lancet 2008:863). For these reasons, dramatically increased numbers of medical students are venturing abroad and facing the ethical, emotional, social, and clinical challenges of health-care delivery in resource-limited settings (Hurt 2007; Panosian and Coates 2006; Roberts 2006).

Given cautionary historical precedents in which biomedicine drove the adverse objectification of Africans (Vaughn 1991), the practice and study of global health in Africa warrants meticulous attention to questions about its origins, logic, values, and intentions. In what ways can global health education steer away from sole reliance on objective, positivist biomedicine as the dominant paradigm for understanding disease in Africa? How can curricula be created that juxtapose medical, social, political, economic, cultural, and historical understandings of illness in Africa? Can global health immersion experiences maximize collaborative learning and partnership by welcoming African and foreign students into the same classroom? And, in such settings, how can instructors mindfully attend to the economic and power inequalities in the classroom to ultimately build unity and cohesion?

The experience and pedagogy of Beyond the Biologic Basis of Disease offers an opportunity to engage these critical questions. This chapter argues that the design and pedagogy of this course offered a creative and rich opportunity for teaching global health in Africa in the 21st century built upon reflexivity, partnerships, and empowerment. Through personal confrontation with privilege and power both in the classroom and in the world, careful scrutiny of global and local relations, and concurrent teaching of clinical and social medicine, the course replaced customary, stereotyped teachings of Africa with personalized, self-critical, and contextual understandings of global health in Uganda.

In this chapter, an overview of the course pedagogy, objectives, and content is first provided. Second, experiential narratives from the perspectives of previous participant instructors and students are shared in order to demonstrate how the unique curriculum fostered collaboration and partnership. This discussion is followed by a presentation of the course's limitations and opportunities for growth. The chapter concludes with a discussion on how novel approaches to teaching global health can inspire social change.

Toward a New Paradigm of Teaching Global Health in Africa

In *Pedagogy of the Oppressed*, Paulo Freire (1970) contrasted two educational models—the "banking" model and the "problem-posing" model. In the "banking" model, students are passive "receptacles" into which teachers "deposit" information, thereby denying students of creative power and active engagement with the world. In contrast, the "problem-posing" method encourages collaboration and partnership between teachers and students in order to pursue "a constant unveiling of reality" (Freire 1970:81). As a liberating model of education, the latter model initiates a process in which "students, as they are increasingly posed with problems relating to themselves in the world and with the world, will feel increasingly challenged and obliged to respond to that challenge" (Freire 1970:81).

While originally developed as a critique of educational relationships between oppressors and the oppressed, Freire's concepts hold great salience for the pedagogical stances of teaching global health in Africa in the 21st century. Global health educational initiatives rooted in the banking model—of which there are many—collude with societal processes of African objectification and blind students to the potential of sustained collaborative action for bringing about systemic change in the provision of health care for the poor. Further, banking model pedagogies in global health entrench assumptions about the need for paternalistic outsider intervention. In contrast, problem-based initiatives combining reflection and action (praxis) offer empowerment in the learning process and partnership between teachers and students that holds promise for meaningful response to the recognition that "something is terribly wrong" in the world (Farmer 2005:142).

Previous witness of extensive reliance on the banking model in global health education spurred the birth of the social medicine course described here. Personal experience with global health rotation electives offered by U.S. medical schools typically revealed a lack of structure and curriculum beyond exposure to the clinical presentation and management of tropical disease, inadequate integration with local medical students, and minimal engagement with the local social, political, and economic context both prior to and during the rotation. Observation of, and participation in Ugandan medical education demonstrated a formalized system of teaching reliant on didactic lectures, rote memorization, and the regurgitation of material for exams to fill students with biological understandings of disease. In both cases, clinical teaching was divorced from formal social medicine teaching, which occurred either thousands of miles or years away from the clinical teaching.

Thus, through a collaborative effort involving Ugandan and U.S. physicians and social scientists, this course was developed as a "problem-posing" model of global health education aiming to achieve the following objectives: (1) provide a structured global health immersion experience for medical students with dedicated supervision and teaching in clinical medicine and social medicine; (2) study issues related to global health in a resource-poor setting with an emphasis on local and global context; (3)

foster critical analysis of global health interventions in resource-poor settings; (4) facilitate the development of a clinical approach to disease and illness using a biosocial model through structured supervision and teaching; (5) build an understanding and skill set associated with physician advocacy; and (6) promote international solidarity and partnership in generating solutions to global health challenges facing societies throughout the world.

With these objectives as guiding principles for the curriculum, all elements of the course aimed toward continual *conscientization*, or "consciousness-raising" (Freire 1970:101). Prior to the course, students were required to read *Pathologies of Power* in order to build familiarity with narratives depicting how inequality and structural violence impinge upon patients' lives to cause disease. As illustrated in the chapter's introduction, Farmer's work and student reactions to it provided a meaningful starting point for our course-long critical analysis of global health in Africa.

Following this introductory discussion, the curriculum then merged clinical tropical medicine with social medicine topics through a combination of interactive lectures, discussions, films, community field visits, ward rounds, and clinical case discussions. A typical day started with a case discussion emblematic of the disease topic for the day followed by bedside teaching with a preselected patient. Special emphasis was placed on gathering a social history from patients and determining the advantages and limitations of the physical exam in an area with minimal diagnostic medical technology. Clinical topics covered during the course included malaria, tuberculosis, tetanus, malnutrition, HIV/AIDS, mental health, schistosomiasis, acute respiratory infections, measles, and rheumatic heart disease.

Afternoons were dedicated to explicit engagement with social medicine topics. These topics were covered through small and large group discussions, panels with invited guests, films, and lectures from individuals actively involved in work related to the day's topics. Efforts were continually made to link the clinical conditions discussed in the morning with the afternoon's social medicine topics to clearly delineate the ways in which social factors translate into biological disease. The content of the curriculum was broadly divided into five topics with specific subtopics as delineated below.

SECTION 1—DETERMINANTS OF HEALTH BEYOND BIOLOGY: SOCIAL
AND ECONOMIC CAUSATION OF DISEASE:

- Colonialism in Africa (Boahen 1989)
- The historical and political context of northern Uganda (Finnström 2008)
- Globalization and health (Ferguson 2006; Kaiser 1996)
- International trade and access to medicines (Westerhaus and Castro 2009)
- The impact of war on health (Garfield and Neugut 2000)
- African traditions in medicine
- Linkages between structural violence and disease (Farmer 2005; Galtung 1969)

SECTION 2—GLOBAL HEALTH INTERVENTIONS: PARADIGMS OF CHARITY, HUMANITARIANISM, AND STRUCTURAL CHANGE:

- Practicing medicine as a foreigner (Hurt 2007; Roberts 2006)
- Models of global health intervention (Farmer 1995)
- Witnessing and responding to suffering
- The World Health Organization in northern Uganda
- Governmental public health work

SECTION 3—SOCIAL JUSTICE IN HEALTH INTERVENTIONS: MODELS OF COMMUNITY-BASED HEALTH CARE:

- Philosophy and history of social justice
- Models of community-based health care (Behforouz et al. 2004; Morgan 1993)
- Partners in Health: mission and model of care (Partners in Health 2006)
- Liberation medicine (Smith and Hilsbos 1999)

SECTION 4—HEALTH AND HUMAN RIGHTS AND THE HEALTH-CARE WORKER AS ADVOCATE:

- Human rights: what are they?
- Health as a tool for peace
- Training health-care workers as advocates (AGHA Uganda 2006)
- The Treatment Action Campaign (De Waal 2006; Power 2003)

SECTION 5—TOOLS FOR EFFECTIVE APPLICATION OF GLOBAL HEALTH EXPERIENCE: WRITING, PHOTOGRAPHY, RESEARCH, AND POLITICAL ENGAGEMENT:

- Narrative medicine (Charon 2006)
- Writing as advocacy
- Media and health in Africa (Bleiker and Kay 2007)
- Participatory action research (Cornwall and Jewkes 1995)

In addition, student participants led teaching sessions on personal experiences with the creation of sustainable humanitarian relief efforts, building community-based nutrition programs in resource-poor settings, and health activism.

Classroom-based teaching was enhanced through field visits to sites illustrating different models of health intervention. Field visits were made to (1) the AIDS Service Organisation (TASO), Gulu Branch—a Ugandan organization started in the late 1980s to provide support, care, and treatment to individuals and families affected by HIV/AIDS (http://www.tasouganda.org); (2) the Northern Uganda Malaria, AIDS, and Tuberculosis initiative (NUMAT)—a five-year project funded by the United States Agency for International Development (USAID) to expand access to HIV, tuberculosis, and malaria prevention and treatment services through strengthening local government and community initiatives (http://numat.jsi.com); (3) the Amuru Health Center—a community health center affiliated with St. Mary's Hospital Lacor that provides outpatient primary care, basic inpatient management of common diseases, and community outreach activities (http://www.lacorhospital.org); and (4) the Gulu Municipality Prison—the regional prison for Gulu town and district, with approximately 700 male and female inmates. These visits allowed students to contrast and compare the philosophies, funding mechanisms, concrete activities, and impacts of different types of health interventions.

Evening film showings provided another venue for students to engage the course content. Those shown included *Uganda Rising* (McCormack and Miller 2006); *State of Denial* (Epstein 2003); *War Dance* (Fine and Nix 2007); *A Closer Walk* (Bilheimer 2003); *The Mask Videos* (Negatu et al. 2008); *Invisible Children* (Bailey et al. 2006); *This Magnificent African Cake* (Davidson et al. 1984); *The Constant Gardener* (Meirelles 2005); and films illustrating the work of Partners in Health. Finally, a course reader incorporating articles and book chapters exploring the topics covered was provided to all students to stimulate and complement discussions during the course.

Together the course content and methodologies aimed to provide students with a dynamic, challenging, and interactive environment in which to face the local and global context of illness production beyond biological causation. In addition to providing familiarity with a core set of clinical tropical medicine and social medicine topics necessary to understand global health issues in Uganda in the 21st century, the course design chiseled away at stereotypes of Africans as passive recipients of outsider intervention. Simultaneously, students were urged to make the uncomfortable realization that "the poor are a by-product of the system in which we live and for which we are responsible" (Gutiérrez 1983). We encouraged such *conscientization* not only through close, personal encounters with patients suffering under the dual weight of illness and oppression, but also through activities designed to explore the linkages between personal power and privilege and the global systems of structural violence.

Instructor Reflections: Emphasizing Collaborative Learning and Teaching

Exploring the linkages between power on a personal level and the global systems of structural violence and hierarchy requires the creation of an equitable classroom conducive to collaboration. Far too often global health educational programs revolve around North American and European teachers and students teaching about and studying problems in resource-poor settings from which they do not originate. Thus, the course organizers strove to build a learning community that comprised both instructors and students from Africa, the United States, and Europe. The team of instructors emerged from a network of already established friendships, and together they identified deficiencies in global health education and began to devise the course. After two years of conversation, networking, and consultation with mentors, the instructors completed the curriculum design and initiated publicity for the course.

Recruitment of Ugandan students began through personal connections that linked the instructors to an existing student association dedicated to health equity, founded several years earlier by one of the instructors. Leaders from this group played a pivotal role in identifying the 12 Ugandan student participants as well as handling numerous organizational logistics and liaising with Gulu University's Faculty of Medicine. Recruitment of international students took place through medical student e-mail networks (such as the Global Health Education Consortium and the American Medical Student Organization) as well as through outreach to particular medical schools with departments dedicated to providing global health opportunities such as the University of Minnesota, the University of Washington, the University of Massachusetts, and Case Western University.

In the end, the fusion of students from the United States and Holland with those from Uganda became an absolutely integral aspect of the course, enhancing learning by bringing in a plurality of perspectives to the subjects tackled. It promoted respect and sensitivity as students and instructors engaged the complex course material. An example to illustrate this point occurred on the second day of the course during a session on the history of northern Uganda. An American instructor and a Ugandan student from the north co-led the session. The student opened the session with a very colorful presentation full of photographs and maps, emphasizing both the cultural richness of the region and the recent tragedies of political violence. After he concluded, the American instructor began with a historical narrative of Uganda since precolonial times. As she guided the class through her slides outlining different eras—from precolonialism to colonialism to postcolonial independence—she stopped and invited the Ugandan students, who originated from nearly every region in the country, to add to or amend the outline in order to incorporate their unique perspectives of how they were taught their country's history.

While facilitating such an interactive session that allowed for the emergence of multiple truths around Ugandan history was challenging, what resulted was a collaborative co-creation of knowledge and learning in which all present received a deeply textured understanding of the history of Uganda and the war in the north. During the discussion, a medical student from southwestern Uganda explained that the British aligned closely with the Bantu peoples in the south because of perceived tendencies toward conflict among the northerners. As he concluded his view, likely taught by teachers from the southern and central regions of the country, a fifth-year medical student from northern Uganda, shot her hand up to interject: "It's not that we were more warrior-like, rather it was just that we resisted the colonialists much more than the southerners." Their comments resonated with the publicized division between northerners and southerners within Uganda, a factor regarded as partly responsible for the recent war in northern Uganda. And as Sverker Finnström suggests, "The causes and consequences of the war in northern Uganda, the reasons for it, and the facts about it— they all differ, depending on whom you are listening to" (2008:8). Given that history depends on who is telling it, students and instructors in the course were able to engage with a more nuanced and comprehensive understanding of the history of northern Uganda because of the collaborative emphasis of the course.

In addition to creating a comfortable space for divergent viewpoints, promoting collaboration required explicit recognition of the numerous power inequities among participants. First, the international students held passports that allowed them to travel freely in and out of Uganda without burdensome visa processes, while the 12 students carrying Ugandan passports would be extremely restricted in trying to travel to their counterparts' countries of origin. Indeed, restrictions on Ugandan travel limit the possibility of having a future course immersed in the global North. Second, the international medical students all attend medical schools well endowed with resources—books in the library, medical supplies in the wards, instructors who are compensated fairly enough to motivate them to regularly teach, and readily available computers with Internet access to journals that summarize the latest medical research. Such resources are sorely lacking for Ugandan students. Third, there was significant variance of the students' economic means. The international students, on the one hand, had each paid a course fee of several hundred dollars to attend on top of airfare and accommodations. The Ugandan students, on the other hand, as per design and with respect to their meager economic resources, paid nothing for the course. The international students could afford a weekend trip to a nearby national park, while many of the local students struggled to pay their regular university fees. Fourth, there were gender inequities, as can be expected in most mixed-sex groups. Female medical students both from Uganda and from the United States embark on their careers keenly aware that they must balance demanding medical careers with the societal expectation that they also raise children and maintain the home. Fifth, and finally, for the international students, a "career in global health" means a trajectory of working in resource-poor settings, which leads to recognized novelty and adventure, a high-paying salary, and advancement within Western institutions. For the Ugandan students, a "career in global health" is often the only option for practicing clinical medicine and one that will likely be accompanied with low enumeration and a dearth of needed medical supplies to satisfactorily complete the tasks, particularly if they choose to work in the public sector.

Recognition of the personal inequities among the students challenged the instructors to proactively work to build equity in the classroom. The instructors embraced this challenge even though aware that it would only result in partial equity, since the aforementioned inequalities were very real and would not easily disappear, despite the most genuine efforts. The overarching aspiration was to create enough equity in the classroom for students to see each other as peers. As global health work requires solidarity and strong mutually respectful relationships, the instructors strove to create an atmosphere in which students could envision future partnerships with each other where the international student was seen not just as "the donor" or "the technical expert" and the Ugandan student as "the local staff" or the "implementer." For real collaboration to unfold there had to be a reciprocal dialogue between locals and internationals based on mutual respect.

To accomplish this aim, efforts were made to be cognizant of the very real material inequalities, regardless of how small, among our students. For example, given the poor quality of libraries in Gulu coupled with the difficulty and expense of purchasing new books and having them sent by post to northern Uganda, the instructors put significant energy into financially and logistically ensuring that each Ugandan student received his or her own new copy of *Pathologies of Power*. Such efforts were made because the instructors recognized that Ugandan students were accustomed to reading photocopied versions of material or outdated editions of books, often with the sense that they didn't deserve or couldn't access the most current, up-to-date material. While perhaps trivial in appearance, the creation of an equitable classroom requires attentiveness to the most microscopic levels of inequality.

Similarly, even though students were accommodated at different locations, the Ugandan and international students shared lunch together every day to promote socializing and relationship building. Indeed, small groups often ventured to town together after finishing lunch, and several students regularly swam together in a nearby pool. One of the U.S. students led swimming lessons, which were particularly exciting for some of the Ugandan students who had not had the opportunity to take formal swimming instruction. One Ugandan student even commented that those swimming lessons stimulated some important self-reflection, reminding her of her formative childhood years spent in Canada. While an unstructured part of the course, these opportunities in fact proved critical for our attempts at building a collaborative community.

Three structured activities were also utilized to build equity, trust, and collaboration among the students—a privilege walk, a facilitated conversation on sexual orientation, and partner activities. The privilege walk pushed students to explore their own personal levels of privilege and power (McIntosh 1989). The exercise began with students lining up along one wall of the classroom, with all the desks and tables pushed to the perimeters. The facilitator then read aloud statements to which students were supposed to reflect on personally and respond accordingly: "If one or both of your parents completed a university degree, take one step forward. If you were raised in an area where there was crime or violence, take one step backward," and so forth. At the end of the exercise, students were dispersed throughout the room; those with the most privilege had advanced to the opposite side of the room from where the walk began, and those with the least amounts of power and privilege were nearby or even touching the wall of origin. The walk was done in silence and was a grave reminder, for some students, of the challenges they had faced in their lives. It was also an interesting opportunity to depict visually the diverse backgrounds from which the students came, even among the group of Ugandan students and those from the United States and Europe. For example, several of the international students were from working-class backgrounds in which they experienced much less privilege and access to resources when back at home. Likewise, among the Ugandan students, often along subregional lines, students had varying exposure to violence and economic security. In the emotional and deeply personal discussion following the exercise, all students shared personal vignettes about what it meant for them to reflect personally on power and privilege and why it was critical to their future trajectories in global health. Many came to the conclusion, as hoped for by the instructors, that personal reflection on where one comes from is an important step forward in working for social justice in resource-poor settings; similarly, attention must be paid to these dynamics when forming partnerships with colleagues across the divide of the global North and the global South.

A facilitated dialogue on sexual orientation was also incorporated because of the recent introduction of a bill to the Ugandan parliament that authorized the death penalty for individuals engaged in homosexuality and that criminalized condoning homosexuality. Many of the Ugandan students were accustomed to church sermons and local media condemning homosexuality. Students from the United States and Europe, in comparison, were accustomed to openness to sexual minorities since many had friends and family members who were openly gay, lesbian, or bisexual. Thus, tension had developed around this issue, which the instructors felt needed to be addressed both as an opportunity for learning and as a mechanism to deepen understanding of one another. The instructors started the dialogue by inviting students to question only one another—on things they were curious about or did not understand related to homosexuality, to the laws governing it, or to various populations' perceptions. What followed was a deeply rich dialogue about culture, about moral values, about stories of abuse and exploitation, about faith, and about stigma—which was likely only possible because of the trust that had been built in earlier weeks among the group. While an unplanned session, it turned out to be a significant opportunity for genuine dialogue and further collaborative learning. Students from all perspectives on the issue came away with a deeper and more nuanced understanding of sexual orientation in both Uganda and the United States.

Lastly, partner activities were utilized to create equity and more humanizing understandings of one another. Prior to the course, at the suggestion of the Ugandan students, each international student was paired with one Ugandan student. Through e-mail, each pair communicated and started getting to know each other. At the start of the course, this partnering ensured that every student knew at least one other student on a slightly less than surface level. These preestablished pairings served as easy groupings for several activities throughout the course, from ward visits to discussion groups. We also prepared discussion questions about personal experiences and affiliations and encouraged the pairs to find time to discuss them over lunch or during free time. In our evaluations, several students commented on these pairs as a meaningful platform for building friendships.

As demonstrated by the instructor's experiences with the class, remaining cognizant of power inequalities among students is a crucial step that encourages sensitivity to these dynamics in the classroom. In this course, it led the instructors to think through details like getting new books for the Ugandan students and ensuring that all could enjoy lunch together as well as structured activities like the privilege walk, the dialogue on homosexuality, and the partner activity. Attentiveness to such details built a collaborative learning community—including students and instructors from both the West and Africa—which was critical to the course's success.

Student Reflection and Evaluation: Social Medicine
Built on Partnership and Togetherness

An examination of student reflections indicates that the course provided a transformative and rich learning experience. On the final day of the course, the students anonymously jotted down something that they learned during the course. Among the things listed were the following: (1) "Working with the community requires a lifelong commitment and also involving the community at every single step of the program"; (2) "I have been inspired to call upon my elected officials in the United States to make changes for health and human rights both in the United States and abroad"; (3) "I learned about all the politics behind poverty—the things that cause poverty and the factors that allow poverty to continue"; and (4) "I've learned that although battling the factors that contribute to poverty and health care inequities are difficult, it is doable." These and other comments revealed that the course gave students the tools to identify and confront obstacles to the provision of high-quality health care to all. As the previous sections highlighted, these lessons were learned not as individuals but as a collaborative international class tightly linked through respectful relationships as friends and colleagues.

As friends, many of the students formed deep bonds through sharing personal life experiences and social outings. Despite the anticipated challenges of the earlier mentioned power inequalities within the group, an amazing synergy of friendship developed between the Ugandan and international students. As instructors, it was astonishing and inspiring to witness the students' efforts to undo their power inequities and see each other as equals. Following the first week of the course, the international students organized and financed a goat roast that was thoroughly enjoyed by all on a Sunday afternoon. Two weeks later, the Ugandan students returned the favor and organized a large dinner party. Numerous social outings to Ugandan students' homes, to graduation parties, to church, to the market, and to pubs and nightclubs occurred throughout the course. Near the end, students exchanged gifts with one another as a sign of gratitude for friendship and the time spent together.

Such shared social experiences built trust and respect, making it easier to acknowledge the differences in the classroom. For example, during the debriefing following the privilege walk described above, the majority of the students stated that they had realized the barriers that most of them had to overcome to reach their current status. Many of the students also stated that they were ready to use their respective pasts, whether of privilege or scarcity and oppression, as platforms to advocate for and work toward best practices in global health.

This foundation of friendship also helped build collaborative relationships as colleagues committed to addressing health inequities. Fruitful class discussions led to student-directed efforts to build networks and develop projects to reverse health disparities witnessed in the course. In the final days, they developed working groups to take on pressing issues such as antiretroviral drug stockouts in Uganda, inadequate medical supply provision to health centers, and food supplementation for malnutrition in rural areas. Further, the class initiated an e-mail listserv to promote communication related to the course projects and other news of interest related to social medicine. After the course concluded, a group of student participants and one instructor attended an international conference in Kisumu, Kenya, on health activism organized by the People's Health Movement. Another small group of students and one of the instructors jointly wrote an article on lessons learned from the course for the *Gulu University Medical Journal*. Two of the international medical students returned to Gulu to complete further clinical rotations and continue work on projects initiated during the course.

The course offered the opportunity for cultural exchange and the formation of long-lasting relationships as colleagues and friends, key ingredients in teaching global health in Africa in a way that prioritizes reflexivity, partnerships, and empowerment. This aspect of the course led one student to reflect, "I have gained a much deeper appreciation of what it means to work through international collaborations and the vast difference that a deeper understanding in local history, culture, etc. can make in how you approach an issue." Another student asserted at the end of the course, "To establish change in Africa, one will have to transparently INVOLVE the community itself. In fact, the community knows better." Students clearly emerged from the course with a deep valuation of partnerships—among each other, with communities, and across international borders—in working to transform the social, economic, and political conditions that limit access to high-quality health care in Africa.

The course also offered an intensive, hands-on immersion opportunity for learning about the practice of clinical tropical medicine in a way that incorporates social understandings of disease. One student stated: "[The course offered] a greater understanding / a more practical understanding of what it means to practice social medicine. I feel that this is an understanding that I could not have obtained from any textbook." Overall, the majority of the course participants reported an improvement in the level of knowledge and experience with global health and social medicine. In particular, 83 percent of local students moved from minimal to moderate or advanced levels, while 63 percent of the international students reported that they had improved their levels of knowledge. At the end of the course, most of the students also stated that they had gained exposure and familiarity with social justice models for health care.

The students ranked the field visits to health facilities and organizations implementing health interventions very highly among the course activities. Specifically, most students enjoyed the field visit to the Amuru Health Center because it allowed them to interact one-on-one with patients and experience the realities of practicing medicine in resource-poor settings. During that field visit, students paired up with their partners and together either saw patients in the health center followed by case discussions with one of the course instructors or participated in a community outreach to a school. Near the end of the day at the Amuru Health Center, the class gathered to reflect. In general, the comments shared suggested that the Ugandan students were not surprised by the experience and were even excited. One Ugandan student shared: "This was not boring at all. It is really exciting to get out into the community and see patients and the social issues we have been discussing." For the international students, the experience was more troubling. A U.S. student reflected: "I feel upset by the fact that people here aren't more upset by the poor care they receive here. People deserve so much more and they aren't even aware of it." One of the course instructors from the United States reflected in response: "It is really hard to not know what to do. At the school, we met a sick child with a treatable condition. Poverty, poor schooling, and a lack of proper nutrition at home were all partly responsible. It is easy to identify the big problems contributing to the situation, but what do you then do for the one sick child in front of you?" Following the reflection, the day ended with a soccer game with the clinic staff. These sorts of experiences encountered during the field visits gave students the opportunity to face the really difficult questions and realities confronting patients and medical providers in a resource-poor setting.

A final outcome worthy of noting was the successful integration of ongoing evaluation throughout the four-week course in order to create a teacher-student partnership in shaping the course. The instructors built in continual course evaluation through informal talks with students, debriefings after activities, meetings with class representatives, and written assessments. For example, at the end of the first week, students were asked to provide a written response to two questions: "What has worked well and not worked well during the first week of the course?" and "What are your hopes and expectations for what is to come in the course?" Answers to these questions helped the instructors recognize the need for more guided discussions, increased small group activities, and more explicit linking of the clinical and social medicine aspects of the course. Such evaluative processes allowed for dynamic, in-process modification of the course structure and content, a technique previously demonstrated to improve learning in medical education (Braden 2008). Regular evaluation also moved the course closer to a cocreative process between teacher and student, in which "the Students—no longer docile listeners—are now critical co-investigators in dialogue with the teacher" (Freire 1970:68).

Course Limitations and Areas for Growth

The class had a number of limitations and areas for future improvement. Occasionally, inadequate time was set aside for discussion. For example, films about the history of northern Uganda were particularly troubling and emotive for some Ugandan students because they triggered personal memories of trauma and family death. On one occasion, the film *Uganda Rising* (McCormack and Miller 2006) finished and no discussion was facilitated afterward due to the late hour, leaving many students uncomfortable and unsure how to process the disturbing footage. More structured discussions and sensitivity to potentially upsetting experiences will be needed in the future. In addition, many students felt that improved facilitation by the course instructors would enhance the course experience. During the course, certain discussions wandered far from their primary topic. Some visiting lecturers delivered overly long, dull presentations and failed to invite audience participation. In such situations, the course instructors could have intervened and served as stronger facilitators.

Another potential limitation of the course is inadvertent creation of unsupported frustration among students, particularly those from Uganda, after they finish the course and reenter their regular rotations. Following the completion of the course, most Ugandan students entered regular rotations in community health, surgery, or obstetrics and gynecology. While empowered by the social medicine course and able to critically analyze disease from social, political, and economic perspectives, they struggled to make concrete changes in clinical situations faced by their patients. One student, completing a rotation in obstetrics and gynecology, described the horror of watching a patient deliver on the floor at a public hospital and being able to identify structural reasons for this situation, but not knowing how to respond tangibly in the moment. Another student reported similar feelings of powerlessness when sent to a health center lacking adequate staff, medicines, and medical supplies and therefore woefully unprepared to handle sick patients. Without careful attentiveness to and preparation for these types of transitions after the course, student participants may become hopeless and demoralized, feelings previously described by medical professionals working in resource-poor settings (Raviola et al. 2002).

These limitations will be addressed in coming years as we continue to improve upon the course. In addition, ideas for improvement and expansion include increasing the enrollment space available, publicizing the course throughout Africa and the world, and the creation of a second component of the course that takes place in the United States (if travel visa restrictions can be overcome) and focuses upon an up close examination of the United States' health-care system, the United States government and its role in global health and development, and global institutions such as the International Monetary Fund (IMF) and the World Bank. Other ideas include incorporating student community research and advocacy projects into the course curriculum and making the social medicine course contiguous with an enhanced community health rotation in Uganda.

Conclusion: Forging Social Change through Up Close and Personal Global Health

This chapter has demonstrated that the social medicine course Beyond the Biologic Basis of Disease offers an alternative to teachings of tropical medicine and health in Africa that frequently lack structure, undervalue social understandings of disease, and promote—often unknowingly—continued objectification of Africans as victims desperate for outsider intervention. Drawing on the disciplines of medical anthropology, sociology, political science, public health, and clinical medicine, the course curriculum advances an understanding of disease as the result of converging social, cultural, political, economic, and biological factors. Rooted in the local context of northern Uganda, the course methods and content allow for contextual understandings of illness that are "historically deep" and "geographically broad" to emerge (Farmer 2005:158).

Beyond the Biologic Basis of Disease also makes engagement with global health deeply personal. By attending to power and privilege differentials in the classroom, students are asked to confront their own power and privilege in the world as participatory in the structural violence that silences the poor and precludes their liberation from disease and poverty. In essence, they face the uncomfortable queries of Jesuit priest James Guadalupe Carney: "Do we North Americans eat well because the poor in the third world do not eat at all? Are we North Americans powerful, because we keep the poor in the third world weak? Are we North Americans free, because we help keep the poor in the third world oppressed?" (1987:xi). A willingness to face such difficult questions, however, is also what potentiates change in the world. Thus, drawing on the strength of respectful, trusting relationships as colleagues and friends, participants in the social medicine course are uniquely positioned to catalyze social change through partnership and collaboration.

The social medicine course held in northern Uganda in January 2010 revealed great determination, a willingness to collaborate, and creativity among a group of tremendously gifted and inspirational students who are ready to embrace the global health challenges facing Uganda and the rest of Africa in the 21st century. Illustrative of this spirit, one student expressed at the end of the class: "The course has empowered me with various ways of handling or solving problems in a diplomatic way. . . . I feel my eyes are open, my muscles are contracted, and the hand and body is ready to start acting against problems." The world eagerly awaits the fruits of these students' determination.

Notes

We would like to acknowledge St. Mary's Hospital Lacor, Gulu University Faculty of Medicine, Students for Equity in Health Care, and the student participants in the 2010 social medicine course for their roles in successfully helping to build an innovative, engaged curriculum.

1. Throughout the essay, for clear identification, "international" medical students refers to students from the United States and Europe who came to Uganda to study and "local" medical students refers to students from Uganda who are enrolled at Gulu University.

22 Educating the Educators

Ethiopia's IT Ph.D. Program

Solomon Negash and Julian M. Bass

Higher education was willfully neglected in Africa during the late 20th century (Bloom et al. 2006). In the 1980s, African government officials with limited budgets argued that social returns on primary and secondary education were substantially higher than the returns on tertiary education (Colclough 1980; Psacharopoulos 1980). The "Washington Consensus" is a phrase that describes a set of policies "aligned with the commercial and financial interests of advanced industrial countries" (Stiglitz 2002:20). Institutions pursuing Washington Consensus policies, such as the International Monetary Fund (IMF) and the World Bank, actively discouraged higher education investment in low-income countries. University funding was reduced, causing deterioration in staff working conditions, the built environment, and research capacity. Learning support environments for students were adversely affected. After the turn of the century, there was growing recognition that, in an information-based world, societies need the capacity to generate, transmit, and consume new knowledge. Technically trained professionals need to be equipped to analyze local and national problems, policies, and opportunities as well as train future generations in these emerging economies. Serious and productive universities are required to engage with and develop intellectual communities to pursue these functions (Szanton and Manyika 2001:1–3). As Malcolm Gillis stated in 1999:

> Today, more than ever before in human history, the wealth—or poverty—of nations depends on the quality of higher education. Those with a larger repertoire of skills and a greater capacity for learning can look forward to lifetimes of unprecedented economic fulfillment. But in the coming decades the poorly educated face little

better than the dreary prospects of lives of quiet desperation. (quoted in Task Force on Higher Education and Society 2000)

Paul Collier (2007) echoes these thoughts in his study of the "bottom billion." Increasing availability and enrollment in higher education must therefore be part of the strategy for low-income countries to achieve economic growth and become better connected to the global economy.

Africa has a very low (less than 5 percent compared to 50 percent in the United States) enrollment in higher education (Bloom et al. 2006). It has been estimated that in 1999, 174 education institutions were designated as universities in Africa (AAU 1999). There were 26 countries having only one or two universities, while South Africa, Nigeria, and Sudan had several.

Information and communication technologies (ICTs) have permeated the business and academic consciousness of low-income countries. Many have established ministerial and directorate positions in information technology (IT) and launched certificate programs, but advanced academic degree programs, especially Ph.D. programs, have lagged behind. From among the 225 member universities of the Association of African Universities (AAU) in 2010, we found 1,364 degree programs in 23 countries. We followed the uniform resource locator (URL) provided for each AAU member university and searched its website for Ph.D. programs (AAU 2010). There were 25 Ph.D. programs in ICT-related fields from 11 countries. It is important to note that the AAU membership list is not exhaustive. For example, in Ethiopia, the focus of this chapter, only 4 universities out of the more than 50 established in the country are members of the AAU; hence the numbers may have been underrepresented.

IT offers many countries the opportunity to quickly create a First World industry, as demonstrated by India's success with outsourcing. This model has spread to other countries, including the Philippines, Russia, Vietnam, Brazil, and Uruguay. That Ethiopia's instructional language for secondary and tertiary education is English, coupled with its large population, 85 million people, makes IT a potential growth industry. First, however, Ethiopia must create a cadre of professors who can educate those who will become the critical resource for such an industry.

We argue that the IT Ph.D. program in Ethiopia has merit for consideration in other subject areas and locations. Although in its early stages, one program can already demonstrate some published research outputs. Student numbers in the program as a whole are steadily being increased to build a self-supporting local research infrastructure. The program has attracted contributions from a significant number of foreign faculty members.

Before discussing the specifics of the Ph.D. program, the chapter presents a brief overview of the educational context in Ethiopia. We introduce the overall education system and the achievements in terms of increasing student numbers and overall quality.

An Overview of Ethiopia's Education System

Management of education institutions in Ethiopia is partially decentralized, with the Ministry of Education overseeing the government-run universities and regional educational bureaus. Regional educational bureaus in turn oversee several educational units including primary schools, high schools, higher education preparatory schools, and colleges of teacher education. These regional education bureaus have responsibility for both financing and supervising schools and the college of teacher education sector.

School student progression in Ethiopia is based on a system of national examinations at grades 8, 10, and 12. Children are entitled to free education up to grade 10, after which placement is based on achievement. Thus, students achieving sufficiently high grades to qualify for the academic track attend a two-year college preparatory program (grades 11 and 12) followed by tertiary education. Students who qualify for the technical track attend a two-year diploma program and join the job market.

In an effort to drive up the quality of education since 2006, Ethiopia has imposed a requirement for all primary school teachers to qualify with a two-year college of teacher education diploma. Those teaching in high schools and at university levels require at least a bachelor's degree from a university.

Ethiopia has a history of higher education, in the form of education for Orthodox Christian clergy that dates back to 1711. Formal public universities were not established, however, until 1947, at Alemaya University, with a focus on agriculture, and in 1950, at Addis Ababa University. These two universities remained the only higher education institutions until 1991. Between 1991 and 2005, Ethiopia's public universities increased from 2 to 9, and in 2007 from 9 to 22, with a further 10 new institutions added in 2010–2011. The first private higher education institution, Unity College, was established in 1998. Today, there are more than 50 public and private universities in the country and many more certificate- and diploma-granting institutions.

There has been government support for expanding the public education system in Ethiopia. Considerable resources have been devoted to increasing primary school access, which has had a ripple effect in other parts of the system. Secondary (high) school expansion demands increased numbers of first-degree qualified teachers. University expansion followed this trend, when the number of higher education institutions in the country more than doubled (admittedly starting from a relatively low base) in 2007. The total number of students enrolled increased from 54,285 in 2002–2003 to 263,001 in 2007–2008 (Government of Ethiopia 2008, 2009). The government has received some credit for the ambition and achievements of the expansion program (Saint 2004). However, the ability to increase student numbers while also maintaining and enhancing quality has been questioned. It has been argued that the expansion process has adversely affected staff workloads in the university sector and that the quality of teaching has declined (Tessema 2009).

Ph.D. Program Design

Reduced teaching and research capacity during the 1980s and 1990s in the indigenous higher education sector led to increased overseas education, particularly at universities in high-income countries. The overall migration of Africans with advanced degrees is estimated at 20,000 annually (ICAD 2006). The International Organization for Migration (IOM) estimated that Ethiopia lost 74.6 percent of its human capital from various institutions between 1980 and 1991 (IRIN 2004). Another estimate shows that 60,000 Ethiopian professionals including physicians, professors, and engineers left the country between 1985 and 1990 (Odumasi-Ashanti 2003). An estimate from 2003 showed a 15-year average reporting that 50 percent of Ethiopians who went abroad for advanced studies did not return. Many of these professionals go to the United States and the United Kingdom. The 2000 U.S. census showed that Africans with bachelor's and advanced degrees led all other U.S. immigrant groups (U.S. Census Bureau 2000). Establishing local Ph.D. programs is one way to address the nonreturn of skilled professionals from abroad.

Ph.D. Program Rationale and Motivation

The IT Ph.D. program design will fail Ethiopia if it does not curb the migration of talent. To mitigate this threat, the IT Ph.D. program is designed as a local program. The international faculty travel to Ethiopia in lieu of sending students abroad. The structure of the program is based on the not unreasonable assumption that students who are educated in Ethiopia are much more likely to remain living and working in Ethiopia. The Ph.D. program initiative was conceived by a consortium of academic departments that offer master's degrees in the computing field, including three at Addis Ababa University—computer science, information science, and electrical and computer engineering—and the departments of IT and telecom engineering in the Graduate School of Telecommunications and Information Technology.

The primary objective of the Ph.D. program is to develop Ph.D. graduate students who have the capacity to identify and solve problems related to IT policy, design, development, and implementation in Ethiopia. Students learn to apply technical and scientific methods and innovative thinking. The program prepares candidates for successful academic and professional careers in Ethiopia. It also tries to foster the development of Ethiopia as an IT outsourcing center through the courses it offers, the skills developed, and the research undertaken. Though it would be a loss to Ethiopia if successful completion of the Ph.D. program serves only as an entry point to a career in a high-income country, we should, nevertheless, educate and acculturate Ph.D. students to present their work at appropriate international conferences and publish in journals.

The demand for terminally qualified faculty in Ethiopia is high. Over 200 Ph.D. holders were needed to meet the 2008–2009 academic year demand for teaching at public universities. This projection is only for public academic institutions and does not include private institutions, industry, and other research and development needs. The 2007–2008 Addis Ababa University 10-year strategic plan calls for 5,000 Ph.D. graduates from 85 disciplines and thus provides evidence of institutional support for the proposed Ph.D. in IT.

Curriculum Design

The IT Ph.D. program currently has 70 students. Students are spread across six tracks at different levels including coursework, proposal writing, and dissertation work. The program has six complementary specialty tracks (Addis Ababa University IT Ph.D. Consortium 2007). The tracks, listed in alphabetical order, are information retrieval (5 students); information systems (IS) (17 students); Internet protocol (IP) networking and mobile Internet (13 students); language technology (15 students); software engineering (15 students); and wireless communication systems (5 students).

The proposed Ph.D. program complements the Ethiopian government's emphasis on ICT as a key development agent. The government has established a ministerial position for ICT. Ethiopia's vision to overcome underdevelopment by using ICT as a strategic agent was articulated in a 2005 speech by the late prime minister Meles Zenawi: "We believe we are too poor not to save everything we can and invest as much as possible in ICT. We recognize that while ICT may be a luxury for the rich, for us the poor countries, it is a vital and essential tool for fighting poverty, for beating poverty that kills and ensuring our survival" (ICT Regulation Toolkit, n.d.).

The Ph.D. program is designed as a hybrid between the European research-only and single-supervisor model and the U.S. model of coursework, comprehensive exams, team of supervisors, and dissertation. It is intended to span four years, with course work in the first year and dissertation research in subsequent years. Doctoral candidates are expected to have completed a master's degree in a related field before admission to the Ph.D. program. Incoming doctoral students will join a cohort in their track, with a minimum of five students per cohort.

At least one foreign professor for each course travels to Ethiopia for one to three weeks during the face-to-face mode of the course. Both a local and a foreign advisor jointly chair the dissertation. The dissertation process requires intense collaboration between the student and dissertation advisors. Doctoral candidates write and orally defend their dissertation. Students are expected to defend their dissertation proposal in their second year, following coursework completion.

The Ph.D. program is a suitable candidate for applying a scarce resource principle to its design. The scarce resource in this case is the foreign faculty member willing to travel to Ethiopia on multiple occasions. Thus, the program is designed around the scarcity of foreign faculty willing to commit to multiple trips to Ethiopia. This design aspect means that the transfer of doctoral teaching and supervision needs to occur as rapidly as feasible, and we believe that the goal should be to transfer all teaching to local faculty within three to five cohorts and all dissertation supervision within 10 years. Local faculty will take over the teaching of a course after it has been taught two or three times jointly with a foreign faculty member. For this transition to occur, an appropriate foreign faculty member must be at Addis Ababa University during the face-to-face mode of the course for the first two or three offerings. Local faculty will take over dissertation supervision after they have co-supervised two dissertations.

The taught components vary among tracks. For example, core (compulsory) courses in the software engineering track include Research Methodology and Ethics, Advanced Seminar in Software Engineering I, Human Computer Interaction, Software Design and Management, Advanced Seminar in Software Engineering II, and Software Architecture and Construction. Similarly, the core courses in the IS track include Systems Thinking on Sustainability, Advanced Topics in Information Systems, Research Methods in Information Systems, Advanced Seminar in Information Systems I, Advanced Seminar in Information Systems II, and IT Management, Leadership, and Implementation.

Candidates must achieve a 3.0 grade point average in the taught component, before being eligible to move into the individual research element of the program. Following the taught component, candidates prepare a research proposal. The proposal guidelines dictate the following sections: introduction, literature survey, research questions, research objectives, scope, and ethical considerations. The individual research phase commences once the proposal has been approved. During the research phase, local and international faculty members provide supervision.

Ph.D. Program Implementation

The program uses a professor-focused model. The focus in this approach is to recruit renowned researchers who are well recognized in the discipline. Participation by lead researchers has given the program instant international recognition. Recruiting faculty to teach and supervise dissertations has become relatively manageable. Over three dozen professors have indicated their willingness to teach. In 2009 alone, 20 international faculty taught in the program. So how, specifically, was the program implemented?

Innovation in the IS Track

The six tracks in the program apply different techniques; as an example, we note four innovative approaches used in the IS track: joint coordination, a communities of practice framework, an eminent researcher, and scarce resource management. When the IS program was initially conceived, there was no one holding an IS Ph.D. among the local core team members. It was thus agreed that two roles should be created, one each for a local and an international coordinator. The international coordinator was tasked in leading the development of the draft curriculum; the communities of practice theory was used to develop this curriculum.

The communities of practice theory lays out a framework for professionals with a common interest to come together and share ideas. The international coordinator linked IS professors from eight universities (six from the United States, one from Australia, and one from Ethiopia) to draft the curriculum. E-mail and videoconferencing were used as tools to facilitate the discussion. The draft curriculum was completed after an interactive videoconference discussion between participating professors and follow-up e-mail communication. A joint discussion between the local and international team via videoconferencing was conducted to finalize the curriculum. Groups of faculty were assigned to develop the syllabus for each course.

Eminent researchers were invited to launch the IS Ph.D. program. Several eminent researchers took part in a conference in Addis Ababa, in which 15 international faculty members (8 from the United States, 5 from Europe, 1 from South Africa, and 1 from Australia) attended. This conference provided the opportunity to introduce the final curriculum, recruit students, and demonstrate the support from eminent researchers. The researchers also led in teaching the coursework. Involvement of the eminent researchers gave the program instant recognition by the IS field internationally, including a published recognition by the Association for Information Systems in March 2010. This acceptance has made recruiting faculty easier; in a period of two years, the IS program was able to garner three dozen professors from around the world who have volunteered, if called upon, to teach or supervise dissertations. Such broad recognition would have been difficult without the participation of the eminent researchers.

A scarce resource management approach was used for scheduling classes. With teaching faculty coming from overseas, coordinating international faculty time to teach in Ethiopia was challenging. The international faculty members were recognized as the scarce resource; hence international faculty availability became the primary factor for class scheduling. The teaching faculty provided their availability, and classes were scheduled accordingly.

Built Environment

The Ph.D. program enjoys a suite of offices in a modern building on the College of Business and Economics campus (the formal reference in Ethiopia is Faculty of Business and Economics; the word Faculty is used in lieu of College). Each student has shared desk space and access to a personal computer; many use their own laptops. There is a large seminar room, which accommodates up to 30 people and is used for taught courses and research seminars. In addition, there are newly partitioned spaces for equipment storage, network support, and shared office areas for students, track coordinators, and administrative support staff.

Electricity

In the early years of the program, a reliable electricity supply was a challenge. The Ph.D. program suite shares electricity with others in the building. For most of the year, the electricity supply is reliable. However, for about three months of the year, electricity was being rationed with a rolling program of power outages. This problem is due to reliance on hydroelectric power and water shortages prior to seasonal rains. Currently, electricity rationing is minimized since supply to the national grid has increased. Ethiopia has tripled its electricity generation capacity and is in the process of exporting electricity to neighboring countries. This progress promises to overcome the electricity supply challenges.

Internet Connectivity

The program staff members have established a wireless network and small intranet. This dedicated Ph.D. program connection has a rated bandwidth of two megabits per second. Staff, visiting faculty, and several of the candidates who have access to a laptop with wireless connectivity use this Internet connection.

The offices also have access to the Addis Ababa University intranet. The university intranet gives access to online resources, notably the Institute of Electrical and Electronics Engineers (IEEE) digital library and conferences and journals from the Association for Information Systems, as well as several other electronic journals. The university intranet also blocks access to certain sites, such as SourceForge, YouTube, and Facebook, for bandwidth management purposes.

Remote Teaching and Advising

Internet-based technologies are used to facilitate communication among the students, local faculty advisors, and foreign advisors. However, network-intensive, synchronized technologies (e.g., videoconferencing) are often unreliable due to lack of bandwidth. We find that e-mail is widely used because of its low bandwidth needs, as well as the time zone difference between Ethiopia and some of the locations of the foreign supervisors, and thus is the expected media preference for many remote supervisors. In addition, foreign advisors use calling cards or Skype to make low-cost international calls to their students and the local advisors.

Research Results and Program Outputs

Success of the program implementation is corroborated by student research output. Students from the IS Ph.D. track have presented at international conferences and published in international journals. Overall the IS track students have produced six journal papers, three book chapters, and twenty conference proceedings. These intellectual contributions are in international venues in addition to several publications locally. The publications are varied in topic as shown in the list below:

Acceptance of WoredaNet E-Government Services in Ethiopia: Applying the UTAUT Model

Assessing the Employees' Information Security Awareness Status in Ethiopian Financial Institutions

Promises and Perils of the Virtuous Knowledge Exchange Cycle in Ethiopian Higher
    Education Institutions

The Role of IT Infrastructure in IS Success Model: Applying the IS Success Model in
    Low-Income Countries Context

Salary and Incentive Structure in the Ethiopian Higher Education

The Success of Student Information Management System: The Case of Higher
    Education Institution in Ethiopia

The Tradition of Validating Knowledge Production in Higher Education

The Use of Information Architecture towards Effective Road Safety Data
    Management

Using Data Mining Technique to Predict Student Dropout at St. Mary's University
    College: Its Implication to Quality of Education

Using Data Mining to Combat Infrastructure Inefficiencies: The Case of Predicting
    Non-Payment for Ethiopian Telecom

In addition to the research papers published by the IS track students, students on the software engineering track of the Ph.D. program have published two papers and have several projects in progress:

Service-Oriented Organizational Interoperability Architectural Framework

Business Service Modeling Using SOA: A Core Component of Business Architecture

Requirements Engineering Using a Goal-Oriented Requirements Pattern Approach

Enterprise Resource Planning Systems in an Ethiopian Context and Service-
    Oriented Architectures

Students have started annual workshops where they present and review one another's papers and have started a local chapter of the Association for Information Systems. Students have also given research seminar presentations, for example, in defense of their research proposals.

Lessons Learned

The Ph.D. candidates are selected from among the brightest computing and IS information systems technologists in the country. They are almost all experienced university faculty, have obtained master's degrees, and have been teaching undergraduate computing courses for some years. Several of the candidates have commercial business interests in IT-related fields, having undertaken system development and deployment or consulting engagements. Prior to traveling to Ethiopia, professors held a common preconception about the students, expressed by one as follows: "The best I expected was the same level of student caliber as my students from the United States."

After their teaching experience, the common response from the professors was that "students are more experienced and more highly motivated than those at home [United States]. Their cognitive skills are as good as those of any reputable institution [in the United States]." Further evidence for the high levels of student motivation was provided by a professor who said, "We had eight-hour-per-day classes with overnight assignments for a whole week; the students wanted it all." Another visiting professor said:

> I learned more from the students; the students bring the local context. Students tell me what applies to their local context and what does not. The interaction was productive. The students came with work experience. When I discuss a topic with them, they tell me that it does not apply in their country context. Students often help me put the subject in the local context. I teach the same subject in Ethiopia as the one I teach in the United States. The only thing I needed to change was its application, making it fit the local context.

A sustainable program needs to recruit a steady flow of high-caliber, motivated, and dependable students. The long-term success of the program depends on the success of its students. The program model depends on successful students who will become future teachers and dissertation chairs. Visiting faculty provide much of the current teaching and dissertation support. To achieve long-term sustainability, some of the teaching and dissertation supervision has to be transferred to local faculty. The current plan is to accomplish the transition in five to seven years.

Visiting international faculty tended to find that the experience opened their eyes to current realities and helped them overcome some incorrect preconceptions about the country and sub-Saharan Africa in general. Visiting professors were unanimous in their view that visiting in person was the best way to understand Ethiopia, its people and culture. While many may have read about Ethiopia, they do not see the full story until they make a personal visit. One professor said: "After listening to the news and reading about Ethiopia, I was worried, a female professor, traveling alone; friends had warned me, and I too was worried for my safety. I had the best experience—safe, secure, place and the people were very friendly. No one bothered you when walking alone, day or evening." After one visiting professor shared his experience in Ethiopia with his class in the United States, one of his graduate students ended up doing his term paper on Ethiopian coffee. Teaching in the program is truly international. For example, at the local conference where the IS Ph.D. program was formed, participants from a dozen universities across five continents took part. Of these, only two had Ethiopian origins. Visiting faculty report benefits through expansion of their teaching portfolio. The courses offered by visitors at Addis Ababa University rarely map precisely to current teaching needs at home institutions. As a result, visiting faculty are provided with new opportunities to develop areas of expertise related to their core interests. These new skills acquired while teaching in Addis Ababa then contribute to research supervision and teaching back home. For the diaspora of Ethiopian origin (only one member of the diaspora has participated so far), the program presents a welcome opportunity for funded visits to see family and friends. International faculty members report that students have the cognitive skills required to undertake excellent research. The recruitment selection process means that the Ph.D. candidates are top-scoring graduates at master's levels, often with some years of teaching experience in the higher education sector. The prevailing education system in Ethiopia tends to favor broad and shallow learning that typically results from a culture of lectures and terminal examinations (Bass and Heeks 2011). This leads to a lack of emphasis on practical teaching sessions that reinforce subject-specific skills in the syllabus. This is, in turn, exacerbated by a lack of resources for investment in laboratory infrastructure. As a result, Ph.D. candidates may not have had the opportunity to gain firsthand experience of advanced subject-specific skills in their area of expertise. The taught component of the Ph.D. program provides an opportunity for candidates to undertake laboratory and project work that can counteract this disadvantage during earlier phases of education.

Current Program Challenges

The Ph.D. program is successfully using an innovative model to accelerate the process of creating an IT research community. The program has succeeded in attracting some eminent faculty members to contribute toward the teaching and supervision of candidates. However, the program is not without challenges. In general terms, the transition to an indigenous self-supporting and sustainable program over the next three to five years remains a major task. It is too early to tell whether this transition will be successful. Currently, there are two major challenges that would benefit from greater attention, namely, (1) research supervision and (2) a sufficient critical mass of active researchers.

Research Supervision

A challenge for the program is translating the goodwill of visiting faculty from teaching classes to supervising students. This difficulty will include institutional challenges; for example, some international institutions see risks in their staff providing supervision to candidates at another institution. Further, there are the logistical issues of supervising geographically remote candidates. The limited telecommunication facilities present challenges to technology-based, face-to-face supervision, and the costs of telephone communication are high. Being restricted to written communication with supervisors will become unattractive as Ph.D. projects advance in their development.

Critical Mass

Another challenge for the Ph.D. program will be establishing a vibrant research culture. The Ph.D. program is designed to provide research training. This aim will be difficult to achieve in an environment where no actual research is being undertaken.

Research is best conducted where there is sufficient critical mass of active researchers. Faculty members and research staff will need to demonstrate research outputs in order to contribute credibly to the supervision of candidates.

Summary and Concluding Remarks

There is government support for expanding the education system in Ethiopia. School-sector expansion has led to a dramatic increase in demand for new academic staff members in universities. Computing departments at the public universities have been unable to provide sufficient numbers of Ph.D.-qualified faculty. The IT Ph.D. program managers report anecdotally that 90 percent of the candidates sent abroad in the past have not returned to Ethiopia, many having established successful careers in academia elsewhere. These pressures of dramatically increased demand, insufficient indigenous research-active staff capacity, and difficulties with retaining staff acquiring higher degrees abroad have led to the development of a novel, Addis Ababa–based, solution.

The IT Ph.D. program in Addis Ababa is using an innovative approach to building a sustainable research community. The curriculum includes a one-year taught component followed by a three-to-four-year research project. The approach uses international faculty to bring teaching and supervision resources. The program is attracting sufficient numbers of international faculty members. The IS track has successfully recruited visiting faculty to supervise the dissertations of all its first cohorts; however, the same is not true for the other IT Ph.D. tracks, for which visiting faculty teaching courses has not translated into visiting faculty supervising research candidates. It is also necessary to establish a broader research culture within which research training should be taking place.

The program has benefits for visiting faculty, including (1) expanding their teaching-research portfolio of expertise and (2) increasing their cultural awareness of sub-Saharan Africa. The model used in staffing the Ph.D. program has been successful. Some professors have shown interest in replicating this model in other regions and countries. The program will face considerable challenges to transform into a local, self-sustainable program. It is challenged currently by difficulties with remote research supervision and an insufficient number of research-active local faculty members attempting to support and supervise Ph.D. candidates. Despite these challenges, the program is breaking new ground in establishing a novel model for developing research capacity.

Conclusion

Knowledge Circulation and Diasporic Interfacing

Toyin Falola

THERE ARE SEVERAL ways to strengthen the connections between Africa and the world, and vice versa, and then use these connections to generate relevance, progress, development, and peace.

First, we as scholars have to keep extending the frontier of knowledge, use our resources to transform scholarship in and about Africa, and ensure that our studies also inform mainstream scholarship. We must be fully inserted into all the mainstream knowledge systems and must struggle to be at the center. While we should continue to support area studies, we have to understand their limitations in academies that use the universalism of ideas as a key source of power. Africa is part of "universal knowledge" and not so-called local knowledge with less value. This advancement of the "universality" of African / African diaspora knowledge (about them, and by them) must be presented in such a way that the academic world, irrespective of location, will see both value and need in the knowledge being generated.

To individuals, the acquisition of quality education remains the main source of mobility, especially to the segment of the population lacking access to inheritance and start-up capital to establish businesses on their own. This education has to be based on various components: the acquisition of knowledge in various disciplines (inter- and multidisciplinary); the acquisition of skill sets connected with occupations in both the formal and informal sectors of the economy; and the cultivation of emotional intelligence to process data and information in a careful, objective, and rational manner.

As scholars, our research and the way we teach must reflect the concerns not just of our specific disciplines, but of the universities where we work, the locations where we live, our community and the people who constitute our communities, and our colleagues. We have the special role to link the Americas with Africa, the academy with the public, and knowledge with occupations. On our campuses, we have to represent the very best in the understanding of Africa and the people of African descent, as well as the value of diversity and culture. Off campuses, we need to let entrepreneurs, politicians, and policy makers benefit from our knowledge. As cultural brokers, we must bring the knowledge of Africa to the Americas and that of the Americas to Africa. Insularity must give way to internationalization. As we promote study abroad programs for those in the United States to go to Africa, those from Africa must come to the United States as well. And there must be domestic "study abroad" programs as well in which students understand different and diverse communities within and beyond their regions.

The suggestions on education combine merit and non-merit factors of success. Quality education will ensure the understanding of the very process of development, even the ability to question the ideology of meritocracy and confront it with alternatives. Abilities and talents have to be discovered, then cultivated, and then put to use. As all first-generation migrants do genuinely understand and practice, there is no shortcut to success and no substitute for hard work. The large numbers of immigrants since the 1980s still belong to a first generation. As they succeed, many will leave inheritance to their children as a "non-merit" factor to not only consolidate, but also expand, the wealth and knowledge base of their successors. We are already noticing the trend in the placement of Africans in all the major colleges and institutions across the country. Focused and interested in degrees tied to occupations, the second generation are proving that they may acquire greater influence than the first.

Second, the African, Africanist, and African diasporic knowledge must be converted into value added for institutions and people to grow. The growth can be by way of humane values, the cultivation of cosmopolitan minds, the ability to understand the complexity of society, the management of resources and people, and the promotion of global peace. Sure, many will expect far more tangible things by way of technical advancement, poverty elimination, and massive development within Africa and between Africa and the rest of the world. It is not selfish for some to demand that the knowledge we generate must transform Africa and black people. If they are transformed, the entire world is transformed; also millions of people will be less poor, migrations will reduce, interstate relations will improve, and market and democratic spaces will expand.

Third, we have to theorize more on the nature and uses of power, with the main goal of seeking the means for more and more Africans to be part of the institutions and structures of governance. Without power, it is difficult to control resources and create appropriate mechanisms of allocation. Power is difficult to acquire without social capital. Immigrants and the marginalized find it very difficult to acquire social capital, that is, an extended network of highly connected people. Social capital is an integral part of how the institutions of society work in relation to the acquisition of power and wealth.

Fourth, we have to increase the rates of business ownership and then generate more sales, hire more people, and create more profits. For success to occur, we must understand the importance of financial and human capital and seek the means to create start-up capital that can make businesses more competitive. The possibility of creating higher start-up capital lies in only one strategy: the ability to pool and combine resources. Just as we have been successful in forming religious and ethnic associations, we have to move beyond both to create business associations. Through the acquisition of greater managerial skills and capital, there is now a large pool of African petty bourgeoisie who can now move to the next stage in the Marxian categorization: entrepreneurial capitalists who work in their own businesses and are also able to hire the labor of others. In other words, the entrepreneur-capitalists are able to use the proletariat (those who sell their labor) to create more capital.

Fifth, and finally, be it in education, politics, or business, alliances have to be forged: the creation of what Martin Luther King Jr. once described as the "network of mutuality" (1965). This network will be in stages, within cities, between cities, and between hosts and homelands. For example, the USA-Africa Dialogue discussion group is an initiative that has created a Pan-Africanist framework with a global reach. Today, the USA-Africa Dialogue discussion group has become the most successful in using the Internet to link black people in different continents and to document, interpret, and disseminate the experiences of the "new African diaspora." These alliances need to revive some of the agenda of older Pan-Africanist networks that sought the elimination of exploitation and domination of black people. The members of the new diaspora must support those of the older diaspora to attain empowerment and full citizenship. Networking has to be conceived in terms of the creation of support mechanisms within the United States and of development mechanisms between the United States and Africa.

Through resources such as *Teaching Africa: A Guide for the 21st-Century Classroom*, the infrastructures of capacity building, knowledge circulation, and diasporic interfacing are being created and consolidated. This work shows how the study of Africa can interface with that of Europe and the Americas, giving us ideas on how we can begin to rethink how we teach and organize the disciplines and how some area study programs can think outside of their boxes. It also advocates for links between the community and the academy, through activist engagements to put the ivory tower in the service of the community. This book shows how creative people are so valuable in the conceptual values that they bring to the table and in their portrayal of marginalized subjectivities. In tandem, these essays reveal ideas on culture, race, people, and aspirations in ways that help us talk about various subjects and issues that are crucial to the pedagogy of the black and the American experience. Intellectual power is the very first condition for both economic and political power. As we generate sound scholarship, we are now laying a solid foundation of intellectual power to transform lives and societies.

Note

This piece was first presented as the final section of the keynote address at the Ninth Annual Africana Studies Conference, "Crossroads 1: The New African Diasporas in the United States," University of North Carolina at Charlotte, April 13, 2011.

References

AAU (Association of African Universities). 1999. Guide to Higher Education in Africa. Accra, Ghana: AAU.

AAU (Association of African Universities). 2010. Membership. Electronic document, http://www.aau.org/membership/fullmembers.php, accessed December 4.

ABC Australia. 1999. Africa: The AIDS Highway. 21 min. Surrey: Journeyman Pictures.

Abrahamsen, Rita. 2000. Disciplining Democracy: Development Discourse and Good Governance in Africa. London: Zed Books.

Abrahamsen, Rita. 2003. African Studies and the Postcolonial Challenge. African Affairs 102(407):189–210.

Achebe, Chinua. 1989. An Image of Africa: Racism in Conrad's *Heart of Darkness. In* Hopes and Impediments: Selected Essays. Pp. 1–20. New York: Doubleday.

Achebe, Chinua. 2005. A Dead Man's Path. *In* Literature: An Introduction to Fiction, Poetry, and Drama. Ninth Edition. X. J. Kennedy and D. Gioia, eds. New York: Longman.

Adams, Jonathan, and Randy Foote. 2010. Sudden Climate Change through Human History. Electronic document, http://dieoff.org/page127.htm.

Adams, Jonathan, Mark Maslin, and Ellen Thomas. 1999. Sudden climate transitions during the Quaternary. Progress in Physical Geography 23(1):1–36.

Adams, Maurianne, Lee Anne Bell, and Pat Griffin, eds. 2007. Teaching for Diversity and Social Justice. Second Edition. New York: Taylor and Francis Group.

Addis Ababa University IT Ph.D. Consortium. 2007. Curriculum for Ph.D. Program in IT. Addis Ababa, Ethiopia: Addis Ababa University.

Adichie, Chimamanda Ngozi. 2006. Half of a Yellow Sun. New York: Anchor.

Adichie, Chimamanda Ngozi. 2009. The Danger of a Single Story. Electronic document, http://www.ted.com/talks/chimamanda_adichie_the_danger_of_a_single_story.html.

Afako, Barney. 2002. Reconciliation and Justice: "Mato Oput" and the Amnesty Act. *In* Protracted Conflict, Elusive Peace: Initiatives to End the Violence in Northern Uganda. Okello Lucima, ed. Pp. 64-67. Accord: An International Review of Peace Initiatives 11.

African Journal of Teacher Education. 2010. Global Teacher Education Initiatives, Sustainable Development and Poverty Alleviation Strategiesi n Africa. African Journal of Education 1(1).

African News Service. 1990. Africa: Savage Beasts and Beastly Savages. Electronic document, http://allafrica.com/stories/200101080390.html, accessed October 22, 2009.

African Studies Center. 2009. Africa: Urban Inequality in Global Perspective. Electronic document, http://www.africa.upenn.edu/afrfocus/afrfocus102409.html, accessed April 6, 2010.

Agawu, Kofi. 1995. The Invention of African Rhythm. Journal of the American Musicological Society 48(3):380–395.

AGHA Uganda (Action Group for Health, Human Rights, and HIV/AIDS, Uganda). 2006. A Promise Unmet: A Survey Report on Access to Essential Medicines in Uganda. Electronic document, http://physiciansforhumanrights.org/library/report-2007-10-01.html, accessed April 29, 2010.

Ahluwalia, Pal. 2001. Politics and Post-colonial Theory: African Inflections. New York: Routledge.

Akallo, Grace, and Faith J. H. McDonnell. 2007. Girl Solider: A Story of Hope for Northern Uganda's Children. Grand Rapids, MI: Chosen.

Akrofi, Eric Ayisi. 2002. Sharing Knowledge and Experience: A Profile of Kwabena Nketia, Scholar and Music Educator. Accra, Ghana: Afram Publications.

Alden, Patricia, David T. Lloyd, and Ahmed I. Samatar, eds. 1994. African Studies and the Undergraduate Curriculum. Boulder, CO: Lynne Rienner Publishers.

Alpers, Edward A. 1995. Reflections on the Studying and Teaching about Africa in America. Issue: A Journal of Opinion 23(1):9–10.

Alpers, Edward A., and Allen F. Roberts. 2002. What Is African Studies? Some Reflections. African Issues 30(2):11–18.

Ambler, Charles. 2011. "A School in the Interior" African Studies: Engagement and Interdisciplinarity. African Studies Review 54(1):1–17.

Ansell, Nicola. 2002. Using Films in Teaching about Africa. Journal of Geography in Higher Education 26(3):355–368.

ap Gareth, Owain Llŷr. 2009. Welshing on Postcolonialism: Complicity and Resistance in the Construction of Welsh Identities. Ph.D. dissertation, Aberystwyth University.

Appiah, Kwame Anthony. 1991. Is the Post- in Postmodernism the Post- in Postcolonialism? Critical Inquiry 17(2):336–357.

Appiah, Kwame Anthony, and Henry Louis Gates Jr., eds. 1999. Africana: The Encyclopedia of the African and African American Experience. New York: Basic Civitas Books.

Aryeetey-Attoh, Samuel, ed. 2010. Geography of Sub-Saharan Africa. Third Edition. Upper Saddle River, NJ: Prentice Hall.

Ashcroft, Bill, Gareth Griffiths, and Helen Tiffin. 2002. The Empire Writes Back: Theory and Practice in Post-colonial Literatures. New York: Routledge.

Attenborough, Richard, dir. 1987. Cry Freedom. 157 min. Hollywood, CA: Universal Pictures.

Attwell, David. 2005. Rewriting Modernity: Studies in Black South African Literary History. Athens: Ohio University Press.

AU (African Union). 2011. Inventory of International Nonproliferation Organizations and Regimes. Electronic document, http://cns.miis.edu/inventory/pdfs/au.pdf, accessed September 25, 2011.

Badejo, Diedre L. 2008. The African Union (Global Organizations). New York: Chelsea House Publications.

Bailey, Bobby, Laren Poole, and Jason Russell, dirs. 2006. Invisible Children—the Rough Cut. 55 min. San Diego, CA: Invisible Children.

Bakupa-Kanyinda, Balufu, dir. 2003. Afro@Digital: An African Look at Digital Technology. 52 min. San Francisco: California Newsreel.

Ballentine, Karen, and Jake Sherman, eds. 2003. The Political Economy of Armed Conflicts: Beyond Greed and Grievance. Boulder, CO: Lynne Rienner Publishers.

Banks, James A. 2006. Cultural Diversity and Education: Foundations, Curriculum, and Teaching. Fifth Edition. Boston: Pearson Education.

Banks, James A. 2008. An Introduction to Multicultural Education. Fourth Edition. Boston: Pearson Education.

Barber, Karin, ed. 1997. Readings in African Popular Culture. Oxford: James Currey.

Barber, Karin, ed. 2006. Africa's Hidden Histories: Everyday Literacy and Making the Self. Bloomington: Indiana University Press.

Barthes, Roland. 1975. S/Z. Richard Miller, transl. New York: Hill and Wang.

Bass, Julian M., and Richard Heeks. 2011. Changing Computing Curricula in African Universities: Evaluating Progress and Challenges via Design-Reality Gap Analysis. Electronic Journal of Information Systems in Developing Countries 48(5):1–39.

Bastian, Misty L., and Jane L. Parpart, eds. 1999. Great Ideas for Teaching about Africa. Boulder, CO: Lynne Rienner Publishers.

Bates, Robert H., V. Y. Mudimbe, and Jean F. O'Barr, eds. 1993. Africa and the Disciplines: The Contributions of Research in Africa to the Social Sciences and Humanities. Chicago: University of Chicago Press.

Bayart, Jean-François. 1993. The State in Africa: The Politics of the Belly. London: Longman.

Bayart, Jean-François. 2008. Global Subjects: A Political Critique of Globalization. Andrew Brown, transl. Cambridge: Polity.

Bayart, Jean-François. 2009. The State in Africa: The Politics of the Belly. Second Edition. Mary Harper, Christopher Harrison, and Elizabeth Harrison, transl. Cambridge: Polity.

Bearak, Barry. 2003 Why Famine Persists. New York Times Magazine, July 13.

Bebey, Francis. 1975. African Music: A People's Art. London: Harrap.

Behdad, Ali. 2005. On Globalization, Again! In Postcolonial Studies and Beyond. Suvir Kaul and Ania Lumba, eds. Durham, NC: Duke University Press.

Behforouz, Heidi, Paul Farmer, and Joia Mukherjee. 2004. From Directly Observed Therapy to Accompagnateurs: Enhancing AIDS Treatment Outcomes in Haiti and Boston. Clinical Infectious Disease 38(S5):S429–S436.

Benford, Robert D., and David A. Snow. 2000. Framing Processes and Social Movements: An Overview and Assessment. American Review of Sociology 26:611–639.

Berry, Sara. 1992. Hegemony on a Shoestring: Indirect Rule and Access to Agricultural Land. Journal of the International African Institute 62(3):327–355.

Besteman, Catherine. 2008. "Beware of Those Bearing Gifts": An Anthropologist's View of AFRICOM. Anthropology Today 24(5):20–21.

Biggs, John. 2003. Teaching for Quality Learning at University: What the Student Does. Buckingham, UK: Society for Research into Higher Education and Open University Press.

Biko, Steve. 1979. I Write What I Like: A Selection of His Writings. A. Stubbs, ed. Portsmouth, NH: Heinemann.

Bilheimer, Robert, dir. 2003. A Closer Walk. 82 min. Bloomfield, NY: Worldwide Documentaries.

Bleiker, Roland, and Amy Kay. 2007. Representing HIV/AIDS in Africa: Pluralist Photography and Local Empowerment. International Studies Quarterly 51(4):139–163.

Bloom, Benjamin S., Max D. Engelhart, Edward J. Furst, Walker H. Hill, and David R. Krathwohl. 1956. Taxonomy of Educational Objectives: The Classification of Educational Goals. Handbook 1: Cognitive Domain. New York: Longmans, Green.

Bloom, David, David Canning, and Kevin Chan. 2006. Higher Education and Economic Development in Africa. Washington, DC: World Bank. Electronic document, http://siteresources.worldbank.org/INTAFRREGTOPTEIA/Resource /Higher Education Econ Dev.pdf.

Boahen, A. Adu. 1989. African Perspectives on Colonialism. Baltimore, MD: Johns Hopkins University Press.

Bohata, Kirsti. 2004. Postcolonialism Revisited: Writing Wales in English. Cardiff: University of Wales Press.

Boltanski, Luc. 1999. Distant Suffering: Morality, Media, and Politics. New York: Cambridge University Press.

Bono, ed. 2007. Special Issue: Africa. Vanity Fair, July.

Bowman, Larry W., ed. 2002. Identifying New Directions for African Studies. African Issues 30(2).

Bowman, Larry W., and Diana T. Cohen. 2002. Identifying New Directions for African Studies: The National Survey of African Studies. African Issues 30(2):2–10.

Braden, Beau R. 2008. In-Process Modification Yields Improved Teaching Outcomes for International Emergency Medicine. International Journal of Emergency Medicine 1:279–286.

Bradford, Helen. 2001. Through Gendered Eyes: Nongqawuse and the Great Xhosa Cattle-Killing. South African and Contemporary History Seminar, University of the Western Cape.

Bradshaw, M. J. 1990. New Regional Geography, Foreign-Area Studies, and Perestroika. Area 22(4):315–322.

Bradshaw, Steve, Augustine Adongo, Thomas Ocran, Tony Mensah, James D. Wolfensohn, Paul R. Krugman, and Pascal Lamy, dirs. 2002. The Trade Trap. Life 3. Oley, PA: Bullfrog Films.

Bramble, Dennis M., and Daniel E. Lieberman. 2004. Endurance Running and the Evolution of Homo. Nature 432:345–352.

Brookfield, Stephen. 2005. Learning Democratic Reason: The Adult Education Project of Jürgen Habermas. Teachers College Record 107(6):1127–1168.

Brotton, Jerry. 1998. "This Tunis, Sir, Was Carthage": Contesting Colonialism in The Tempest. In Post-colonial Shakespeares. Ania Loomba and Martin Orkin, eds. Pp. 23–42. New York: Routledge.

Bundy, Colin. 2007. New Nation, New History? Constructing the Past in Post-apartheid South Africa. In History Making and Present Day Politics: The Meaning of Collective Memory in South Africa. Hans Erik Stolten, ed. Pp. 74–76. Uppsala: Nordic Africa Institute.

Burger, William. 2003. Perfect Planet, Clever Species: How Unique Are We? Amherst, NY: Prometheus Books.

Callahan, Bryan. 1997. Veni, VD, Vici? Reassessing the Ila Syphilis Epidemic. Journal of Southern African Studies 23(3):421–440.

Carney, James Guadalupe. 1987. To Be a Revolutionary. San Francisco, CA: Harper and Row.

Chang, Ha-Joon. 2002. Kicking Away the Ladder: Development Strategy in Historical Perspective. London: Anthem Press.

Chapman, Graham P. 2007.-graphy: The Remains of a British Discipline. Journal of Geography in Higher Education 31(3):353–379.

Charon, Rita. 2006. Narrative Medicine: Honoring the Stories of Illness. New York: Oxford University Press.

Charry, Eric. 2000. Mande Music: Traditional and Modern Music of the Maninka and Mandinka of Western Africa. Chicago: Chicago University Press.

Chinweizu, Onwuchekwa Jemie, and Ihechukwu Madubuike. 1983. Toward the Decolonization of African Literature. Washington, DC: Howard University Press.

Christie, Hazel, Lyn Tett, Vivienne E. Cree, Jenny Hounsell, and Velda McCune. 2008. "A Real Rollercoaster of Confidence and Emotions": Learning to Be a University Student. Studies in Higher Education 33(5):567–581.

Coe, Michael T., and Jonathan A. Foley. 2001. Human and Natural Impacts on the Water Resources of the Lake Chad Basin. Journal of Geophysical Research 106(D4):3349–3356.

Coffman, Jennifer E. 2009. Teaching Globalization and Cultural Context through Music. Anthropology News 50(8):40.

Coffman, Jennifer E., and Kevin Brennan. 2003. African Studies Abroad: Meaning and Impact of America's Burgeoning Export Industry. Frontiers: The Interdisciplinary Journal of Study Abroad 9(Fall):139–147.

Cohen, Lizabeth. 1990. Making a New Deal: Industrial Workers in Chicago, 1919–1939. Edinburgh: Cambridge University Press.

Colclough, Christopher. 1980. Primary Schooling and Economic Development: Review of the Evidence. World Bank Staff Working Paper, No. 399. Washington, DC: World Bank.

Cole, Roy. 2008. The Regionalization of Africa in Undergraduate Geography of Africa Textbooks, 1953 to 2004. Journal of Geography 107:61–74.

Cole, Roy, and H. J. de Blij. 2007. Survey of Subsaharan Africa: A Regional Geography. New York: Oxford University Press.

Collier, Paul. 2007. The Bottom Billion: Why the Poorest Countries Are Failing and What Can Be Done about It. New York: Oxford University Press.

Conrad, David. 2006. Oral Traditions and Perceptions of History from the Manding Peoples of West Africa. *In* Themes in West Africa's History. E. K. Akyeampong, ed. Pp. 73–96. Athens: Ohio University Press.

Conrad, Joseph. 1999[1902]. Heart of Darkness. New York: Penguin Group.

Cooper, Frederick. 2001. What Is the Concept of Globalization Good For? African Affairs 100(399):189–213.

Cooper, Joshua. 1999. The Ogoni Struggle for Human Rights and a Civil Society in Nigeria. *In* Nonviolent Social Movements: A Geographical Perspective. Stephen Zunes, Lester R. Kurtz, and Sarah Beth Asher, eds. Pp. 189–202. Malden, MA: Blackwell Publishing.

Cornell, Carohn, and Leslie Witz. 1994a. The Debate Continues: Critical Perspectives on the Development of the History 1 Curriculum at the University of the Western Cape. *In* AD Dialogues, 2. M. Walker, ed. Pp. 97–102. Bellville: University of the Western Cape.

Cornell, Carohn, and Leslie Witz. 1994b. "It Is My Right to Participate in the Subject": Contesting Histories in the First Year Lecture Room. Social Dynamics 20:49–74.

Cornwall, Andrea, and Rachel Jewkes. 1995. What Is Participatory Research? Social Science and Medicine 41(12):1667–1676.

Coundouriotis, Eleni. 2009. Why History Matters in the African Novel. *In* Teaching the African Novel. Gaurav Desai, ed. Pp. 53–69. New York: Modern Language Association of America.

Crawford-Lange, Linda, and Dale Lange. 1984. Doing the Unthinkable in the Second-Language Classroom: A Process for the Integration of Language and Culture. *In* Teaching for Proficiency: The Organizing Principle. American Council on the Teaching of Foreign Languages (ACTFL), Foreign Language Education Series, Volume 15. Theodore V. Higgs, ed. Pp. 139–177. Lincolnwood, IL: National Textbook Company.

Cross, K. Patricia. 1996. Classroom Research: Implementing the Scholarship of Teaching. American Journal of Pharmaceutical Education 60(Winter):402–407.

Curtin, Philip, Steven Feierman, Leonard Thompson, and Jan Vansina. 1995[1978]. African History: From Earliest Times to Independence. New York: Longman.

Daramy, Sheikh Batu. 1993. Constitutional Developments in the Post-colonial State of Sierra Leone 1961–1984. Lewiston, NY: Edwin Mellen Press.

Davidson, Basil, Christopher Ralling, and Andrew Harries, dirs. 1984. This Magnificent African Cake. *In* Africa: The Story of a Continent, Program 6. 57 min. Chicago: Home Vision Select.

Davies, R. R. 1974. Colonial Wales. Past and Present 65:3–23.

Davis, Thomas J., and Azubike Kalu-Nwiwu. 2001. Education, Ethnicity and National Integration in the History of Nigeria: Continuing Problems of Africa's Colonial Legacy. Journal of Negro History 86(1):1–11.

De Waal, Alex. 2006. AIDS and Power: Why There Is No Political Crisis—Yet. New York: Zed Books.

Death, Carl. 2010. Governing Sustainable Development: Partnerships, Protests, and Power at the World Summit. New York: Routledge.

Debyser, Francis. 1996. L'immeuble [The Building]. Paris: Hachette FLE.

Della Porta, Donatella, and Mario Diani. 2006. Social Movements: An Introduction. Second Edition. Malden, MA: Blackwell Publishing.

Delpit, Lisa D. 1988. The Silenced Dialogue: Power and Pedagogy in Educating Other People's Children. Harvard Educational Review 58(3):280–299.

Delpit, Lisa. D. 1995. Other People's Children: Cultural Conflict in the Classroom. New York: New Press.

Dewey, John. 1933. How We Think: A Restatement of the Relation of Reflective Thinking to the Educative Process. Boston: D.C. Heath and Company.

Diamond, Jared. 1997. Guns, Germs, and Steel: The Fates of Human Societies. New York: W. W. Norton.

Diop, Samba. 1995. The Oral History and Literature of the Wolof People of Waalo, Northern Senegal. Lewiston, NY: Edwin Mellen Press.

Dittmer, Jason. 2006. Teaching the Social Construction of Regions in Regional Geography Courses; or, Why Do Vampires Come from Eastern Europe? Journal of Geography in Higher Education 30(1):49–61.

DjeDje, Jacqueline Cogdell, and William G. Carter, eds. 1989. African Musicology: Current Trends; A Festschrift Presented to J. H. Kwabena Nketia. African Studies Center and African Arts Magazine, University of California, Los Angeles.

Douglass, Frederick. 1995[1845]. Narrative of the Life of Frederick Douglass. New York: Dover.

Duffield, Mark. 2007. Development, Security and Unending War: Governing the World of Peoples. Cambridge: Polity.

Dunn, Kevin C. 2009. Contested State Spaces: African National Parks and the State. European Journal of International Relations 15(3):423–446.

Dupasquier, Chantal, and Patrick N. Osakwe. 2005. Foreign Direct Investment in Africa: Performance, Challenges, and Responsibilities. African Trade Policy Centre (ATPC), Work in Progress No. 21. United Nations Economic Commission for Africa, Addis Ababa, Ethiopia.

Dupuy, Beatrice. 2006. "L'immeuble": French Language and Culture Teaching and Learning through Projects in a Global Simulation. In Project-Based Learning in Second Language Education: Past, Present, and Future. Volume 5. JoAnn Hammadou-Sullivan, ed. Pp. 195–214. Greenwich, CT: Information Age Publishing.

Edusei, Krobo, Jr. 2009. Executive chairman's statements during a seminar on the business climate in Africa. The 14th CNN African Journalist of the Year Awards, July 21. Accra, Ghana.

Ehret, Christopher. 2002. The Civilizations of Africa: A History to 1800. Charlottesville: University of Virginia Press.

Eichler-Levine, Jodi, and Rosemary R. Hicks. 2007. "As Americans against Genocide": The Crisis in Darfur and Interreligious Political Activism. American Quarterly 59(3):711–735.

Ekobu, Caroline. N.d. The Poverty Trap: A Ugandan Perspective on Globalization. Electronic document, http://www.africafiles.org/printableversion.asp?id=19110, accessed October 18, 2008.

Eliasoph, Nina. 1998. Avoiding Politics: How Americans Produce Apathy in Everyday Life. New York: Cambridge University Press.

Eliot-Hurst, Michael E. 1985. Geography Has Neither Existence Nor Future. *In* The Future of Geography. R. J. Johnston, ed. Pp. 59–91. London: Methuen.

Ellipsis Arts. 1994. Africa: Never Stand Still. Roslyn, NY: Ellipsis Arts.

Ellis, Stephen. 2009. West Africa's International Drug Trade. African Affairs 108(431):171–196.

Epstein, Elaine, dir. 2003. State of Denial. 86 min. New York: Lovett Productions.

Evans-Pritchard, E. E. 1976[1937]. Witchcraft, Oracles, and Magic among the Azande. Abridged Edition. New York: Oxford University Press.

Fanon, Frantz. 1963. The Wretched of the Earth. Constance Farrington, transl. New York: Grove Press.

Fanon, Frantz. 1986[1952]. Black Skin, White Masks. Charles Lam Markmann, transl. London: Pluto.

Farmer, B. H. 1973. Geography, Area Studies, and the Study of Area. Transactions Institute of British Geographers 60:1–15.

Farmer, Paul. 1995. Medicine and Social Justice. America 173(2):13–17.

Farmer, Paul. 2005. Pathologies of Power: Health, Human Rights, and the New War on the Poor. Berkeley: University of California Press.

FBC (Fourah Bay College) Program Report. 1977–1992. International Program Files, Kalamazoo College Archives, Kalamazoo, MI.

Ferguson, James. 2006. Global Shadows: Africa in the Neoliberal World Order. Durham, NC: Duke University Press.

Ferguson, Niall. 2003. Empire: How Britain Made the Modern World. London: Allen Lane.

Fine, Sean, and Andrea Nix, dirs. 2007. War Dance. 105 min. Washington, DC: Fine Films Productions.

Finnegan, Amy C. 2013. The White Girl's Burden. Contexts: Understanding People in their Social Worlds 12(1).

Finnström, Sverker. 2008. Living with Bad Surroundings: War, History, and Everyday Moments in Northern Uganda. Durham, NC: Duke University Press.

Florida, Richard. 2005. The World Is Spiky. Atlantic Monthly, October. Electronic document, http://www.theatlantic.com/images/issues/200510/world-is-spiky.pdf.

Foley, Jonathan A., Michael T. Coe, Marten Scheffer, and Guiling Wang. 2003. Regime Shifts in the Sahara and Sahel: Interactions between Ecological and Climatic Systems in Northern Africa. Ecosystems 6:524–539.

Fox, Robin. 1975. Encounter with Anthropology. Harmondsworth, UK: Penguin.

Francis, Mark, and Nick Francis, dirs. 2006. Black Gold. 77 min. San Francisco: California Newsreel.

Fratkin, Elliot. 1991. Surviving Drought and Development: Ariaal Pastoralists of Northern Kenya. Boulder, CO: Westview Press.

Fratkin, Elliot. 1998. Ariaal Pastoralists of Kenya: Studying Pastoralism, Drought, and Development in Africa's Arid Lands. Boston: Pearson Education.

Fredrickson, George. 1981. White Supremacy: A Comparative Study in American and South African History. New York: Oxford University Press.

Fredrickson, George. 1995. Black Liberation: A Comparative History of Black Ideologies in the United States and South Africa. New York: Oxford University Press.

Freedman, Sarah W., Harvey M. Weinstein, and Timothy Longman. 2006. Education for Reconciliation: Creating a History Curriculum after Genocide. Final Narrative and Financial Report. Human Rights Center, University of California, Berkeley. Electronic document, http://www.law.berkeley.edu/HRCweb/pdfs/RCIntroduction.pdf.

Freire, Paulo. 1970. Pedagogy of the Oppressed. Myra Bergman Ramos, transl. New York: Continuum Publishing Company.

French, Howard W., and Lydia Polgreen. 2007. Chinese Flocking in Numbers to a New Frontier: Africa. New York Times, August 17.

Friedman, Steven, and Shauna Mottiar. 2004. A Moral to the Tale: The Treatment Action Campaign and the Politics of HIV/AIDS. A case study for the University of KwaZulu-Natal (UKZN) project titled: Globalisation, Marginalisation, and New Social Movements in Post-apartheid South Africa. Centre for Policy Studies, the Centre for Civil Society, and the School of Development Studies, UKZN, South Africa.

Friedman, Thomas L. 2005. The World Is Flat: A Brief History of the Twenty-First Century. New York: Farrar, Straus and Giroux.

Fuchs, Eckhardt, and Benedikt Stuchtey. 2002. Across Cultural Borders: Historiography in Global Perspective. Lanham, MD: Rowman and Littlefield.

Fugard, Athol. 2001. My Children! My Africa! New York: Theatre Communications Group.

Fugate, Joe. 1987. Hallmarks of Successful Programs in the Developing World: Academic Programs in Universities in Sub-Saharan Africa for Undergraduates. Council on International Educational Exchange (CIEE) Occasional Papers, No. 22. CIEE, New York.

Gabriel, Peter. 1980. Peter Gabriel. New York: Mercury Records.

Gaines, Kevin K. 2006. Black Expatriates and the Civil Rights Era: American Africans in Ghana. Chapel Hill: University of North Carolina Press.

Galtung, Johan. 1969. Violence, Peace, and Peace Research. Journal of Peace Research 6(3):167–191.

Gardenswartz, Lee, and Anita Rowe. 1994. Diverse Teams at Work: Capitalizing on the Power of Diversity. Chicago: Irwin Professional Publishing.

Garfield, Richard, and Alfred Neugut. 2000. The Human Consequences of War. In War and Public Health. Barry Levy and Victor Sidel, eds. Pp. 27–38. Washington, DC: American Journal of Public Health.

Geertz, Clifford. 1977. The Interpretation of Cultures. New York: Basic Books.

Geiss, Imanuel. 1969. Pan-Africanism. Journal of Contemporary History 4(1):187–200.

George, Terry, dir. 2005. Hotel Rwanda. 121 min. Hollywood, CA: MGM.

Gewald, Jan-Bart. 2003. Colonization, Genocide, and Resurgence: The Herero of Namibia, 1890–1923. In Genocide in German South-West Africa: The Colonial War of 1904–1908 and Its Aftermath. Jürgen Zimmerer and Joachim Zeller, eds. E. J. Neather, transl. Pp. 123–142. Monmouth, Wales: Merlin Press.

Gilbert, Anne. 1988. The New Regional Geography in English- and French-Speaking Countries. Progress in Human Geography 12(2):208–228.

Gilbert, Erik. 2004. Dhows and the Colonial Economy of Zanzibar. Athens: Ohio University Press.

Gilbert, Erik, and Jonathan T. Reynolds. 2008. Africa in World History: From Prehistory to the Present. Second Edition. Upper Saddle River, NJ: Pearson.

Gilbert, Erik, and Jonathan T. Reynolds. 2012. Trading Tastes: Commodity and Culture Exchange to 1750. Third Edition. Upper Saddle River, NJ: Pearson.

Giliomee, Hermann, and Bernard Mbenga. 2007. New History of South Africa. Cape Town: Tafelberg.

Gilroy, Paul. 1993. The Black Atlantic: Modernity and Double Consciousness. Cambridge, MA: Harvard University Press.

Gluckmann, Max. 1935. Zulu Women in Hoecultural Ritual. Bantu Studies 9:255–271.

Gmelch, George, and Sharon Bohn Gmelch. 1999. An Ethnographic Field School: What Students Do and Learn. Anthropology and Education Quarterly 30(2):220–227.

Gobodo-Madikizela, Pumla. 2003. A Human Being Died That Night: A South African Woman Confronts the Legacy of Apartheid. Boston: Houghton Mifflin.

Golmohamad, Muna. 2009. Education for World Citizenship: Beyond National Allegiance. Educational Philosophy and Theory 41(4):466–486.

Gonzales, Rhonda M. 2009. Societies, Religion, and History: Central-East Tanzanians and the World They Created, c. 200 BCE to 1800 CE. New York: Columbia University Press.

Gordimer, Nadine. 1976a. Happy Event. In Selected Stories. Pp. 107–121. New York: Viking Penguin.

Gordimer, Nadine. 1976b. Introduction. In Selected Stories. Pp. 9–15. New York: Viking Penguin.

Gordimer, Nadine. 1976c. Is There Nowhere Else Where We Can Meet? In Selected Stories. Pp. 17–20. New York: Viking Penguin.

Gordimer, Nadine. 1986a. A Chip of Glass Ruby. In Six Feet of the Country. Pp. 264–274. New York: Viking Penguin.

Gordimer, Nadine. 1986b. City Lovers. In Six Feet of the Country. Pp. 48–60. New York: Viking Penguin.

Gordimer, Nadine. 1986c. Country Lovers. In Six Feet of the Country. Pp. 61–70. New York: Viking Penguin.

Gordimer, Nadine. 1986d. Six Feet of the Country. In Six Feet of the Country. Pp. 7–20. New York: Viking Penguin.

Gordimer, Nadine. 1991. Once Upon a Time. In Jump and Other Stories. Pp. 23–30. New York: Penguin.

Gordon, David F., and Howard Wolpe. 1998. The Other Africa: An End to Afro-Pessimism. World Policy Journal 15(1):49–59.

Gordon, Frances Linzee, Anthony Ham, Amy Karafin, Kim Wildman, and Isabelle Young. 2002. Lonely Planet: West Africa. Melbourne: Lonely Planet.

Gosche, Jill. 2011. Off to the Capital: Heidelberg Students Participate in Model Government. Electronic document, http://www.advertiser-tribune.com/page/content.detail/id/521636/Off-to-the-Capital.html?nav=5062, accessed January 27.

Government of Ethiopia. 2008. Education Statistics Annual Abstract, 2006–2007. Addis Ababa, Ethiopia: Ministry of Education.

Government of Ethiopia. 2009. Education Statistics Annual Abstract, 2007–2008. Addis Ababa, Ethiopia: Ministry of Education.

Grass, Günter. 1963. *Hundejahre* [Dog Years]. Ralph Manheim, transl. New York: Harcourt, Brace and World.

Greene, Sandra. 1994. Nowhere to Hide: Perspectives on an African Foreign-Study Program. In African Studies and the Undergraduate Curriculum. Patricia Alden, David T. Lloyd, and Ahmed I. Samatar, eds. Pp. 243–254. Boulder, CO: Lynne Rienner Publishers.

Grundlingh, Albert. 1990. Politics, Principles, and Problems of a Profession: Afrikaner Historians and Their Discipline, c.1920–c.1965. Perspectives in Education 12:1–19.

Grusky, Sara. 2000. International Service Learning: A Critical Guide from an Impassioned Advocate. American Behavioral Scientist 43(5):858–867.

Guelke, Leonard. 1977. Regional Geography. Professional Geographer 29:1–7.

Gutiérrez, Gustavo. 1973. A Theology of Liberation: History, Politics, and Salvation. Maryknoll, NY: Orbis Books.

Gutiérrez, Gustavo. 1983. The Power of the Poor in History. Maryknoll, NY: Orbis Books.

Guyer, Jane I. 1996. African Studies in the United States: A Perspective. With the help of Akbar M. Virmani and Amanda Kemp. Atlanta: African Studies Association Press.

Hale, Thomas. 1998. Griots and Griottes: Masters of Words and Music. Bloomington: Indiana University Press.

Hamilton, Ruth Simms. ed. 2007. Routes of Passage: Rethinking the African Diaspora. East Lansing: Michigan State University Press.

Harrison, Graham. 2001. Post-conditionality Politics and Administrative Reform: Reflections on the Cases of Uganda and Tanzania. Development and Change 32(4):657–679.

Hart, Donna, and Robert W. Sussman. 2005. Man the Hunted: Primates, Predators, and Human Evolution. Boulder, CO: Westview Press.

Hart, John Fraser. 1982. The Highest Form of the Geographer's Art. Annals of the Association of American Geographers 72:1–29.

Hartshorne, Richard. 1939. The Nature of Geography. Lancaster, PA: Association of American Geographers.

Hastings, Adrian. 1996. The Church in Africa, 1450–1950. New York: Oxford University Press.

Hattam, Robert, and Michalinos Zembylas. 2010. What's Anger Got to Do with It? Towards a Post-indignation Pedagogy for Communities in Conflict. Social Identities 16(1):23–40.

Haugen, David M., ed. 2008. Africa: Opposing Viewpoints. San Diego: Greenhaven Press.

Hawkes, Terence. 1998. Bryn Glas. In Post-colonial Shakespeares. Ania Loomba and Martin Orkin, eds. Pp. 117–140. New York: Routledge.

Hertel, John P., and Barbara J. Millis. 2002. Using Simulations to Promote Learning in Higher Education. Sterling, VA: Stylus Publishing.

Hilliard, Asa G., III 1991. Why We Must Pluralize the Curriculum. Educational Leadership 49(4):12–14.

Hilsum, Lindsey. 2005. Re-enter the Dragon: China's New Mission in Africa. Review of African Political Economy 32(104–105):419–425.

Hine, Darlene C., William C. Hine, and Stanley Harrold. 2002. The African American Odyssey. Upper Saddle River, NJ: Prentice Hall.

Hitchcock, Peter. 1997. Postcolonial Africa: Problems of Theory. Women's Studies Quarterly 25(3/4):233–244.

Hoffa, William W., and Stephen C. DePaul, eds. 2010. A History of U.S. Study Abroad: 1965–Present. Carlisle, PA: Forum on Education Abroad and Frontiers: The Interdisciplinary Journal of Study Abroad.

Holmen, Hans. 1995. What's New and What's Regional in the "New Regional Geography"? Geografiska Annaler 77(1):47–63.

hooks, bell. 1994. Teaching to Transgress: Education as the Practice of Freedom. New York: Routledge.

Houlihan, Paul. 2007. Introduction: Supporting Undergraduates in Conducting Field-Based Research: A Perspective from On-Site Faculty and Staff. Frontiers: The Interdisciplinary Journal of Study Abroad 14:ix–xv.

Howe, Stephen. 2000. Ireland and Empire: Colonial Legacies in Irish History and Culture. Oxford: Oxford University Press.

Howe, Stephen. 2009. Minding the Gap: New Directions in the Study of Ireland and Empire. Journal of Imperial and Commonwealth History 37(1):135–149.

Hunter-Gault, Charlayne. 2007. New News out of Africa: Uncovering Africa's Renaissance. New York: Oxford University Press.

Hurt, Avery. 2007. Altruism or Tourism: Hidden Ethics of Overseas Electives. New Physician 56(9):4.

ICAD (Interagency Coalition on AIDS and Development). 2006. The Emigration of Healthcare Professionals to High-Income Countries. Ottawa: ICAD. Electronic document, http://www.icad-cisd.com/pdf/Emigration_fact_sheet_EN.pdf.

ICT Regulation Toolkit. N.d. ICTs and the Transformational Opportunity and Risks. Electronic document, http://www.ictregulationtoolkit.org /en/Section.3100.html, accessed December 2, 2010.

Iliffe, John. 2006. The African AIDS Epidemic: A History. Athens: Ohio University Press.

International Programs Collection. 1962–1987. International Program Files, Kalamazoo College Archives, Kalamazoo, MI.

IRIN (Integrated Regional Information Networks). 2004. Ethiopia: IOM [International Organization for Migration] and Government Wooing Skills and Funds from Diaspora. Nairobi, April 5. Electronic document, http://www.irinnews.org/report.aspx?reportid=49412.

Iris, Madelyn. 2004. What Is a Cultural Anthropology Field School and What Is It Good For? National Association for the Practice of Anthropology Bulletin 22:8–13.

Iweala, Uzodinma. 2007. Stop Trying to "Save" Africa. Washington Post, July 15.

Jablonski, Nina G. 2004. The Evolution of Human Skin and Skin Color. Annual Review of Anthropology 33:585–623.

James, Emily, dir. 2002. The Luckiest Nut in the World. 20 min. London: Fulcrum TV.

Jansen, Jan. 2000. The Griot's Craft: An Essay on Oral Tradition and Diplomacy. Münster: Lit Verlag.

Jennings, M. Kent. 2002. Generation Units and the Student Protest Movement in the United States: An Intra- and Intergenerational Analysis. Political Psychology 23(2):303–324.

Johnson, David. 1998. From the Colonial to the Post-colonial: Shakespeare and Education in Africa. *In* Post-colonial Shakespeares. Ania Loomba and Martin Orkin, eds. Pp. 218–234. New York: Routledge.

Johnson, Douglas L., Viola Haarmann, Merrill L. Johnson, and David L. Clawson. 2010. World Regional Geography: A Development Approach. Tenth Edition. New York: Prentice Hall.

Johnson, John Williams. 1986. Epic of Son-Jara: A West African Tradition. Bloomington: Indiana University Press.

Johnston, Linda M. 2000. The Tobacco Dispute: A Study in the Use of Discourse and Narrative Theory in the Understanding of Health-Related Conflicts. Ph.D. dissertation, George Mason University.

Johnston, Rennie. 1999. Adult Learning for Citizenship: Towards a Reconstruction of the Social Purpose Tradition. International Journal of Lifelong Education 18(3):175–190.

Jones, Ken. 1984. Designing Your Own Simulations. London: Methuen.

Jones, Terry, dir. 1979. Life of Brian. 94 min. London: Handmade Films.

Joyce, Christopher. 2010. Did Climate Change Drive Human Evolution? NPR Morning Edition, March 22. Electronic document, http://www.npr.org/templates/story/story.php?storyId=124906102.

Joyce, James. 2005[1916]. A Portrait of the Artist as a Young Man. London: Collector's Library.

Kabba, Alie, Lisa Simeone, and Shana Wills. 2009. Retooling Systems: Enhancing the Integration of African Refugees in Illinois. United African Organization Policy Brief 1(2). Electronic document, http://uniteafricans.org, accessed April 1, 2010.

Kaiser, Paul. 1996. Structural Adjustment and the Fragile Nation: The Demise of Social Unity in Tanzania. Journal of Modern African Studies 34(2):227–237.

Kalamazoo College Quarterly Review. 1991. A Magazine for Alumni, Parents, and Friends. Winter 53(1).

Kandji, Serigne Tacko, Louis Verchot, and Jens Mackensen. 2006. Climate Change and Variability in the Sahel Region: Impacts and Adaptation Strategies in the Agricultural Sector. Nairobi, Kenya: United Nations Environment Programme and World Agroforestry Centre.

Kaplan, Mark, Richard Wicksteed, and Olley Maruma, dirs. 1988. Biko: Breaking the Silence. 52 min. New York: Filmakers Library; San Francisco: California Newsreel.

Kebede, Ashenafi. 1982. Roots of Black Music: The Vocal, Instrumental, and Dance Heritage of Africa and Black America. Englewood Cliffs, NJ: Prentice-Hall.

Keenan, Jeremy. 2008. US Militarization in Africa: What Anthropologists Should Know about AFRICOM. Anthropology Today 24(5):16–20.

Keim, Curtis. 2009. Mistaking Africa: Curiosities and Inventions of the American Mind. Second Edition. Boulder, CO: Westview Press.

Kennedy, Liam. 1992. Modern Ireland: Post-colonial Society or Post-colonial Pretensions? Irish Review 13:107–121.

Kiberd, Declan. 1996. Inventing Ireland: The Literature of the Modern Nation. London: Vintage.

Kiguli, Susan N., and Violet Barungi. 2007. I Dare to Say. Kampala, Uganda: Femrite Publications Limited.

Kimble, G. H. T. 1951. The Inadequacy of the Regional Concept. In London Essays in Geography. Laurence D. Stamp and Sidney W. Wooldridge, eds. Pp. 151–174. Cambridge, MA: Harvard University Press.

King, Joyce, Etta R. Hollins, and Warren C. Hayman, eds. 1997. Preparing Teachers for Cultural Diversity. New York: Teachers College Press.

King, Martin Luther, Jr. 1965. Remaining Awake through a Great Revolution. Commencement Address for Oberlin College, June, Oberlin College Archives. Electronic document, http://www.oberlin.edu/external/EOG/BlackHistoryMonth/MLK/CommAddress.html.

Kirner, Karen. 2005. Engaging the World: Summer Field School in Tanzania. Dickinson College Community Studies Center Newsletter, Fall/Winter:4–6.

Klare, Michael, and Daniel Volman. 2006. America, China, and the Scramble for Africa's Oil. Review of African Political Economy 33(108):297–309.

Klein, Naomi. 2007. The Shock Doctrine: The Rise of Disaster Capitalism. New York: Metropolitan Books.

Knight, Chris. 1991. Blood Relations: Menstruation and the Origins of Culture. New Haven, CT: Yale University Press.

Knight, Chris. 2008. Early Human Kinship was Matrilineal. In Early Human Kinship: From Sex to Reproduction. Nicholas Allen, Hilary Callan, Robin Dunbar, and Wendy James, eds. Pp. 61–82. Malden, MA: Blackwell Publishing.

Kolchin, Peter. 2003. American Slavery, 1619–1877. New York: Hill and Wang.

Kopka, Matthew, and Iris Brooks, eds. 1996. Jali Kunda: Griots of West Africa and Beyond. Roslyn, NY: Ellipsis Arts Press.

Korang, Kwaku Larbi. 2004. Writing Ghana, Imagining Africa: Nation and African Modernity. Rochester, NY: University of Rochester Press.

Korang, Kwaku Larbi. 2010. Francophone/Anglophone Dialogue: A Roundtable on the Aesthetics and Politics of Foundational Texts in an Era of Diaspora and Transnationalism. African Studies Association 53rd Annual Meeting, San Francisco, CA, November 20.

Krabacher, Thomas, Ezekiel Kalipeni, and Azzadine Layachi. 2009. Global Studies: Africa. Twelfth Edition. Boston: McGraw-Hill Higher Education.

Krishna, Sankaran. 2009. Globalization and Postcolonialism: Hegemony and Resistance in the Twenty-First Century. Lanham, MD: Rowman and Littlefield.

Kroll, Catherine. 2010. Dogs and Dissidents at the Border: Narrative Outbreak in Patrice Nganang's *Temps de chien. In* Negotiating Afropolitanism: Essays on Borders and Spaces in Contemporary African Literature and Folklore. Jennifer Wawrzinek and J. K. S. Makokha, eds. Pp. 89–111. New York: Rodopi.

Kuper, Rudolph, and Stefan Kropelin. 2006. Climate-Controlled Holocene Occupation in the Sahara: Motor of Africa's Evolution. Science 313(5788):803–807.

Kutubu Commission of Inquiry. 1984. Freetown: Government of Sierra Leone.

Kwast, Lloyd E. 1992. Understanding Culture. *In* Perspectives on the World Christian Movement: A Reader. Second Edition. Ralph D. Winter and Steven C. Hawthorne, eds. Pasadena, CA: William Carey Library.

Ladson-Billings, Gloria. 1994. The Dreamkeepers: Successful Teachers of African American Children. San Francisco, CA: Jossey-Bass.

Ladson-Billings, Gloria. 1995a. But That's Just Good Teaching! The Case for Culturally Relevant Pedagogy. Theory into Practice 31(3):160–166.

Ladson-Billings, Gloria. 1995b. Toward a Theory of Culturally Relevant Pedagogy. American Educational Research Journal 32(3):465–491.

Lalu, Premesh, and Carohn Cornell. 1996. Staging Historical Argument: History 1 at the University of the Western Cape. South African Historical Journal 34:196–210.

Lancet. 2008. A Renaissance in Primary Health Care (Editorial). Lancet 372(9642):863.

Langer, Judith. 1995. Envisioning Literature: Literary Understanding and Literature Instruction. New York: Teachers College Press.

Langley, J. Ayo. 1969. Pan-Africanism in Paris, 1924–36. Journal of Modern African Studies 7(1):69–94.

Lederach, John Paul. 1995. Preparing for Peace: Conflict Transformation across Cultures. Syracuse, NY: Syracuse University Press.

Lee, James. 2010. Naturalizations in the United States: 2009. *In* The Annual Report of the Department of Homeland Security, Office of Immigration Statistics. Electronic document, http://www.dhs.gov/xlibrary/assets/statistics/publications/natz_fr_2009.pdf, accessed April 1, 2012.

Levine, Glenn. 2004. Global Simulation: A Student-Centered Task-Based Format for Intermediate Foreign Language Courses. Foreign Language Annals 37:26–36.

Lipsitz, George. 1994. Rainbow at Midnight: Labor and Culture in the 1940's. Urbana: University of Illinois Press.

Lischer, Richard. 1997. The Preacher King: Martin Luther King Jr. and the Word That Moved America. New York: Oxford University Press.

Lloyd, David T. 2000. African Studies and Study Abroad. Frontiers: The Interdisciplinary Journal of Study Abroad 6(Winter):99–116.

Loeb, Paul Rogat. 1994. Generation at the Crossroads: Apathy and Action on the American Campus. New Brunswick, NJ: Rutgers University Press.

Logie, Dorothy, Michael Rowson, and Robert Snyder. 2007. Should Developed Countries Provide Debt Relief to the Poorest, Indebted African Nations? *In* Taking Sides: Clashing Views on African Issues. Volume 2. William G. Moseley, ed. Pp. 120–133. Boston: McGraw-Hill.

Lonsdale, John. 2005. African Studies, Europe, and Africa. Afrika Spectrum 40(3):377–402.

Loomba, Ania. 1998. Colonialism/Postcolonialism. New York: Routledge.

Loomba, Ania, and Martin Orkin. 1998. Introduction: Shakespeare and the Post-colonial Question. *In* Post-colonial Shakespeares. Ania Loomba and Martin Orkin, eds. Pp. 1–22. New York: Routledge.

Lowry, Stephen. 1995. A Review of the History Curriculum Process. *In* Proceedings of the Workshop on School History Textbook Writing: From Principles to Practice. Janet Reid and Rob Siebörger, eds. Cape Town: University of Cape Town.

Luhrmann, Tanya M. 1989. Persuasions of the Witch's Craft: Ritual Magic in Contemporary England. Cambridge, MA: Harvard University Press.

Macdonald, Kevin, dir. 2006. The Last King of Scotland. 123 min. Los Angeles: Fox Searchlight Pictures.

MacLeod, Gordon, and Martin Jones. 2001. Renewing the Geography of Regions. Environment and Planning D: Society and Space 19:669–695.

Madge, Clare, Parvati Raghuram, and Patricia Noxolo. 2009. Engaged Pedagogy and Responsibility: A Postcolonial Analysis of International Students. Geoforum 40:34–45.

Magnin, Michèle C. 2002. An Interdisciplinary Approach to Teaching Foreign Languages with Global and Functional Simulations. Simulation and Gaming 33:395–399.

Magona, Sindiwe. 1991a. Nosisa. *In* Living, Loving, and Lying Awake at Night. Pp. 72–86. New York: Interlink Books.

Magona, Sindiwe. 1991b. Two Little Girls and a City. *In* Living, Loving, and Lying Awake at Night. Pp. 117–142. New York: Interlink Books.

Magona, Sindiwe. 1996. I'm Not Talking about That, Now. *In* Push-Push! and Other Stories. Pp. 65–85. Johannesburg: David Philip.

Magona, Sindiwe. 1998. Mother to Mother. Boston: Beacon Press.

Magubane, Bernhard M. 2007. Whose Memory—Whose History? The Illusion of Liberal and Radical Historical Debates. *In* History Making and Present Day Politics: The Meaning of Collective Memory in South Africa. Hans Erik Stolten, ed. Pp. 251–279. Uppsala: Nordic Africa Institute.

Magubane, Zine. 2007. Oprah in South Africa: The Politics of Coevalness and the Creation of a Black Public Sphere. Safundi: The Journal of South African and American Studies 8:373–393.

Magubane, Zine. 2008. The (Product) Red Man's Burden: Charity, Celebrity, and the Contradiction of Coevalness. Journal of Pan African Studies 2(6):102.1–102.25.

Maharaj, Pranitha, and Benjamin Roberts. 2006. Tripping Up: AIDS, Pharmaceuticals, and Intellectual Property in South Africa. *In* Trading Women's Health and Rights? Trade Liberalization and Reproductive Health in Developing Economies. Caren Grown, Elissa Braunstein, and Anju Malhotra, eds. Pp. 212–234. London: Zed Books.

Mama, Amina. 2007. Is It Ethical to Study Africa? Preliminary Thoughts on Scholarship and Freedom. African Studies Review 50(1):1–26.

Mamdani, Mahmood. 2007. The Politics of Naming: Genocide, Civil War, Insurgency. London Review of Books 29(5):5–8.

Mamdani, Mahmood. 2009. Saviors and Survivors: Darfur, Politics, and the War on Terror. New York: Pantheon Books.

Mandela, Nelson. 1994. Long Walk to Freedom: The Autobiography of Nelson Mandela. Boston: Little, Brown.

Mao, Norbert. 2003. Unevenly Yoked: Has Globalization Dealt Africa a Bad Hand? Yale Global Online, http://yaleglobal.yale.edu/content/unevenly-yoked.

Marquardt, Gary. 2007. Open Spaces and Closed Minds: A Socio-environmental History of Rinderpest in South Africa and Namibia, 1896–1897. Ph.D. dissertation, Department of History, University of Wisconsin.

Marston, Sallie A., Paul L. Knox, and Diana M. Liverman. 2008. World Regions in Global Context: Peoples, Places, and Environments. Third Edition. Upper Saddle River, NJ: Prentice Hall.

Martin, Guy. 2002. Africa in World Politics: A Pan-African Perspective. Trenton, NJ: Africa World Press.

Martin, James. 1995. Who Cares About Africa? America 172(17):16–20.

Masquelier, Adeline. 1999. The Medium Is the Message: Teaching Africa through Music. *In* Great Ideas for Teaching about Africa. Misty L. Bastian and Jane L. Parpart, eds. Boulder, CO: Lynne Rienner Publishers.

Mazrui, Ali A., dir. 1986. Tools of Exploitation. *In* The Africans: A Triple Heritage. 60 min. Burlington, VT: Annenberg/CPB Project.

Mbembe, Achille. 1992. Provisional Notes on the Postcolony. Africa: Journal of the International African Institute 62(1):3–37.

Mbembe, Achille. 2001. On the Postcolony. Berkeley: University of California Press.

Mbembe, Achille. 2002a. African Modes of Self-Writing. Public Culture 14(1):239–273.

Mbembe, Achille. 2002b. At the Edge of the World: Boundaries, Territoriality, and Sovereignty in Africa. *In* Beyond State Crisis? Postcolonial Africa and Post-Soviet Eurasia in Comparative Perspective. Mark R. Beissinger and Crawford Young, eds. Pp. 53–80. Washington, DC: Woodrow Wilson Center Press.

Mbembe, Achille. 2007. Sacré bleu! Mbeki and Sarkozy? Electronic document, http://mg.co.za/article/2007-08-27-sacr-bleu-mbeki-and-sarkozy, accessed August 27, 2010.

McAdam, Doug, and David A. Snow. 1997. Social Movements: Readings on Their Emergence, Mobilization, and Dynamics. New York: Oxford University Press.

McCann, James C. 1999. Climate and Causation in African History. International Journal of African Historical Studies 32(2–3):261–279.

McCann, James C. 2002. Title VI and African Studies: Prospects in a Polycentric Academic Landscape. African Issues 30(2):30–36.

McClintock, Anne. 1995. Imperial Leather: Race, Gender, and Sexuality in the Colonial Contest. New York: Routledge.

McCormack, Pete, and Jesse James Miller, dirs. 2006. Uganda Rising. 90 min. New York: Mindset Media.

McGregor, JoAnn, and Terence Ranger. 2000. Displacement and Disease: Epidemics and Ideas about Malaria in Matabeleland, Zimbabwe, 1945–1996. Past and Present 167(1):203–237.

McHaney, Pearl, and Renée Schatteman. 2004. Women's Literature from South Africa and the American South. Safundi: The Journal of South African and American Studies 5(4):1–16.

McIntosh, Peggy. 1989. White Privilege: Unpacking the Invisible Knapsack. Peace and Freedom July/August:10–12.

Mda, Zakes. 1995. Ways of Dying. Cape Town: Oxford University Press Southern Africa.

Meirelles, Fernando, dir. 2005. The Constant Gardener. 129 min. Universal City, CA: Focus Features.

Memmi, Albert. 1990[1957]. The Colonizer and the Colonized. Howard Greenfeld, transl. London: Earthscan.

Mensah, Joseph. 2008. Introduction: Neoliberalism and Globalization in Africa. *In* Neoliberalism and Globalization in Africa: Contestations from the Embattled Continent. Joseph Mensah, ed. Pp. 1–14. New York: Palgrave Macmillan.

Merriam, Alan P. 1964. The Anthropology of Music. Evanston, IL: Northwestern University Press.

Merryfield, Merry M. 2005. The Press and Global Education. *In* Social Studies and the Press: Keeping the Beast at Bay? Margaret Smith Crocco, ed. Pp. 93–108. Greenwich, CT: Information Age Publishing.

Mezirow, Jack. 1996. Contemporary Paradigms of Learning. Adult Education Quarterly 46(3):158–173.

Mills, Nicole A., and Mélanie Péron. 2009. Global Simulation and Writing Self-Beliefs of Intermediate College French Students. International Journal of Applied Linguistics 156:239–273.

Milne, Seumas. 2005. Britain: Imperial Nostalgia. Le Monde diplomatique, May. Electronic document, http://mondediplo.com/2005/05/02empire.

Mintz, Sidney W., and Richard Price. 1992. The Birth of African-American Culture: An Anthropological Perspective. Boston: Beacon Press.

Mitchell, Christopher. 1981. The Structure of International Conflict. New York: St. Martin's Press.

Mitchell, Christopher, and Michael Banks. 1996. Handbook of Conflict Resolution: The Analytical Problem-Solving Approach. London: Pinter.

Mitroff, Ian I., and Abraham Silvers. 2008. Sociopathic Capitalism: Tricked to Solve the Wrong Problem. Fellowship 74(Summer/Fall):28.

Molele, Charles. 2009. Why Africa Is Burning? Sunday Times (South Africa), August 22.

Monson, Jamie. 2009. Africa's Freedom Railway: How a Chinese Development Project Changed Lives and Livelihoods in Tanzania. Bloomington: Indiana University Press.

Moody, Anne. 2004[1968]. Coming of Age in Mississippi. New York: Delta Paperbacks.

Moore, Christopher W. 2003. The Mediation Process: Practical Strategies for Resolving Conflict. San Francisco, CA: Jossey-Bass.

Moore, Sally Falk. 1993. Changing Perspectives on a Changing Africa: The Work of Anthropology. *In* Africa and the Disciplines: The Contributions of Research in Africa to the Social Sciences and Humanities. Robert H. Bates, V. Y. Mudimbe, and Jean F. O'Barr, eds. Pp. 3–57. Chicago: University of Chicago Press.

Moore, Sally Falk. 1994. Anthropology and Africa: Changing Perspectives on a Changing Scene. Charlottesville: University Press of Virginia.

Morgan, Lynn. 1993. Community Participation in Health: The Politics of Primary Care in Costa Rica. Cambridge: Cambridge University Press.

Morris, Jerome E. 2003. What Does Africa Have to Do with Being African American? A Microethnographic Analysis of a Middle School Inquiry Unit on Africa. Anthropology and Education Quarterly 34(3):255–276.

Moseley, William G. 2005. Regional Geographies of the U.S. Southeast and Sub-Saharan Africa. Southeastern Geographer 45(1):44–53.

Moss, Todd. 2007. African Development: Making Sense of the Issues and Actors. Boulder, CO: Lynne Rienner Publishers.

Muhammad, Mustapha. 2010. Chad: Lake Communities Left High and Dry. Electronic document, http://allafrica.com/stories/201001090020.html.

Muller, Peter O. 1995. The Contribution of Textbooks to Undergraduate Geography Instruction in the USA. Journal of Geography in Higher Education 19(3):341–343.

Murphy, Alexander B. 2006. Enhancing Geography's Role in Public Debate. Annals of the Association of American Geographers 96(1):1–13.

Murphy, Alexander B. 2007. Geography's Place in Higher Education in the United States. Journal of Geography in Higher Education 31(1):121–141.

Murphy, Alexander B., and John O'Loughlin. 2009. New Horizons for Regional Geography. Eurasian Geography and Economics 50(3):241–251.

Murray, Senan. 2007. Lake Chad Fishermen Pack Up Their Nets. BBC News, January 15. Electronic document, http://news.bbc.co.uk/2/hi/africa/6261447.stm.

Muurholm, Halfdan, and Casper Erichsen, dirs. 2006. 100 Years of Silence: The Germans in Namibia. 40 min. New York: Filmakers Library.

Myers, Garth A. 2001. Introductory Human Geography Textbook Representations of Africa. Professional Geographer 53(4):522–532.

Myers, Norman. 2001. Environmental Refugees: A Growing Phenomenon of the 21st Century. Proceedings of the Royal Society of London 357:609–613.

National Model African Union. 2010. Electronic document, http://www.modelafricanunion.org/index.htm, accessed April 22.

NCATE (National Council for Accreditation of Teacher Education). 2008. Professional Standards for the Accreditation of Teacher Preparation Institutions. Washington, DC: NCATE. Electronic document, http://www.ncate.org/LinkClick.aspx?fileticket=nX43fwKc4Ak%3D&tabid=669, accessed April 1, 2010.

Negatu, Dhaniel, Biniyam Mesfin, and Eric Gottesman, dirs. 2008. The Mask Videos. 25 min. Addis Ababa, Ethiopia: Sudden Flower Productions.

Nettl, Bruno, Thomas Turino, Isabel K. F. Wong, Charles Capwell, Philip Bohlman, and Timothy Rommen. 2007. Excursions in World Music. Fifth Edition. Upper Saddle River, NJ: Prentice Hall.

Newbury, Colin Walter. 1971. British Policy towards West Africa. Oxford: Clarendon Press.

Newell, Stephanie. 2000. Ghanaian Popular Fiction: "Thrilling Discoveries in Conjugal Life" and Other Tales. Oxford: James Currey.

Newstead, Clare. 2009. Pedagogy, Post-coloniality and Care-Full Encounters in the Classroom. Geoforum 40:80–90.

Nganang, Patrice. 2005. Le Principe dissident [The Principle of Dissidence]. Yaoundé, Cameroon: Éditions L'Interlignes.

Nganang, Patrice. 2006. Dog Days: An Animal Chronicle. Amy B. Reid, transl. Charlottesville: University of Virginia Press.

Ngcobo, Lauretta. 1990. And They Didn't Die. Scottsville, South Africa: First Feminist Press.

Niane, Djibril Tamsir. 1970. Sundiata: An Epic of Old Mali. G. D. Picket, transl. London: Longman Press.

Ninth Annual National Model African Union Delegation and Officers' Handbook. 2011. Howard University, Washington, DC, February 24–27.

Nketia, J. H. Kwabena. 1974a. The Music of Africa. London: W. W. Norton.

Nketia, J. H. Kwabena. 1974b. The Musical Heritage of Africa. Daedalus 103(2):151–161.

Nketia, J. H. Kwabena. 1979. African Roots of Music in the Americas: An African View. Jamaica Journal 43:12–17.

Nketia, J. H. Kwabena. 2005. Ethnomusicology and African Music: Collected Papers. Accra, Ghana: Afram Publications.

Nkrumah, Kwame. 1957. Ghana: The Autobiography of Kwame Nkrumah. New York: Thomas Nelson.

Nkrumah, Kwame. 1965. Neo-colonialism: The Last Stage of Imperialism. New York: International Publishers.

Nolen, Stephanie. 2007. 28: Stories of AIDS in Africa. New York: Walker.

Ntarangwi, Mwenda. 2000. Education, Tourism, or Just a Visit to the Wild. African Issues 28(1–2):54–60.

Ntarangwi, Mwenda, David Mills, and Mustafa Babiker, eds. 2006. African Anthropologies: History, Critique, and Practice. Dakar, Senegal: CODESRIA.

Nuttall, Sarah, and Carli Coetzee, eds. 1998. Negotiating the Past: The Making of Memory in South Africa. New York: Oxford University Press.

Nyaho, William H., ed. 2007. Piano Music of Africa and the African Diaspora. New York: Oxford University Press.

Oblinger, Diana, and James Oblinger. 2010. Educating the Net Generation. Electronic document, http://www.educause.edu/research-and-publications/books/educating-net-generation.

O'Brien, Richard. 1992. Global Financial Integration: The End of Geography. London: Pinter.

Odamtten, Harry Nii Koney. 2010. A History of Ideas: West Africa, the "Black Atlantic," and Pan-Africanism. Ph.D. dissertation, Michigan State University.

Odumasi-Ashanti, Don. 2003. Africa Brain Drain: 70,000 Scholars Leave Yearly. Ghanaian Chronicle (Accra), March 13.

Offenburger, Andrew, Scott Rosenberg, and Christopher Saunders, eds. 2003. A South African and American Comparative Reader: The Best of Safundi and Other Selected Articles. Washington, DC: Safundi Publications.

Ogundimu, Folu. 1994. Images of Africa on U.S. Television: Do You Have Problems with That? Issue: A Journal of Opinion 22(1):7–11.

Ohmae, Kenichi. 1990. The Borderless World: Power and Strategy in the Interlinked Economy. New York: HarperBusiness.

Okpewho, Isidore. 1992. African Oral Literature: Backgrounds, Character, and Continuity. Bloomington: Indiana University Press.

Olaniyan, Tejumola. 2009. Political Critique and Resistance in African Fiction. In Teaching the African Novel. Gaurav Desai, ed. Pp. 70–86. New York: Modern Language Association of America.

Oliphant, Andries Walter. 1992. The Struggle of the Two Souths. In Broken Strings: The Politics of Poetry in South Africa. Stephen M. Finn and Rosemary Gray, eds. Cape Town: Maskew Miller Longman.

Omojola, Bode. 2000. Composition and Transmission of Modern Musical Forms in Africa: A Study of Chaka, Akin Euba's Opera. African Notes 24(1–2):61–68.

Onovwerosuoke, Fred. 2007. Twenty Studies of African Rhythms. Volume 1. St. Louis, MO: African Music Publishers.

Open Doors. 2010. Institute of International Education. Electronic document, http://www.iie. org/en/Research-and-Publications/Open-Doors.

Orlich, Donald C., Robert J. Harder, Richard C. Callahan, Michael S. Trevisian, and Abbie H. Brown. 2004. Teaching Strategies: A Guide to Effective Instruction. Seventh Edition. Boston: Houghton Mifflin.

Oywa, Rosalba. 2002. Women's Contribution to Peacebuilding in Northern Uganda. In Protracted Conflict, Elusive Peace: Initiatives to End the Violence in Northern Uganda. Okello Lucima, ed. Accord: An International Review of Peace Initiatives 11:60–61.

Paasi, Anssi. 2002. Place and Region: Regional Worlds and Words. Progress in Human Geography 26(6):802–811.

Packard, Randall. 2007. The Making of a Tropical Disease: A Short History of Malaria. Baltimore, MD: Johns Hopkins University Press.

Pai, Young, Susan A. Adler, and Linda K. Shadiow. 2006. Cultural Foundations of Education. Fourth Edition. Upper Saddle River, NJ: Pearson.

Panosian, Claire, and Thomas J. Coates. 2006. The New Medical "Missionaries"—Grooming the Next Generation of Global Health Workers. New England Journal of Medicine 354(17):1771–1773.

Paracka, Daniel J., Jr. 2003. The Athens of West Africa: A History of International Education at Fourah Bay College, Freetown, Sierra Leone. New York: Routledge.

Parker, Barbara, and Diane Altman Dautoff. 2007. Service-Learning and Study Abroad: Synergistic Learning Opportunities. Michigan Journal of Community Service Learning 13(2):40–52.

Parson, Jack. 1994. Underdevelopment and Self-Reliance in Building African Studies: Some Pedagogical, Policy, and Practical Issues at the College of Charleston. In African Studies and the Undergraduate Curriculum. Patricia Alden, David T. Lloyd, and Ahmed I. Samatar, eds. Pp. 281–297. Boulder, CO: Lynne Rienner Publishers.

Partners in Health. 2006. PIH Guide to Community-Based Treatment of HIV in Resource-Poor Settings. Boston: Partners in Health.

Paton, Alan. 1948. Cry, the Beloved Country. New York: Charles Scribner's Sons.

Pearce, Fred. 2007. With Speed and Violence: Why Scientists Fear Tipping Points in Climate Change. Boston: Beacon Press.

Peck, Raoul, dir. 2000. Lumumba: A True Story. 115 min. Toronto: Universal.

Pepetela. 2002. The Return of the Water Spirit. Luís R. Mitras, transl. Portsmouth, NH: Heinemann.

Peters, Rebecca Todd. 2008. Economic Justice Requires More than the Kindness of Strangers in Global Neighbors: Christian Faith and Moral Obligations in Today's Economy. Grand Rapids, MI: William B. Eerdmans Publishing.

Pham, J. Peter. 2007. Strategic Interests: Getting AFRICOM Right. World Defense Review. Electronic document, http://worlddefensereview.com/pham021507.shtml.

Philips, John Edward, ed. 2006. Writing African History. Rochester, NY: University of Rochester Press.

Pixley, George V., and Clodovis Boff. 1989. The Bible, the Church, and the Poor. Maryknoll, NY: Orbis Books.

Pohlandt-McCormick, Helena. 2000. 'I Saw a Nightmare . . .': Violence and the Construction of Memory (Soweto, 1976). History and Theory 39(4):23–44.

Postman, Neil, and Charles Weingartner. 1969. Teaching as a Subversive Activity. New York: Delacorte Press.

Potts, Richard. 1996. Humanity's Descent: The Consequences of Ecological Instability. New York: William Morrow and Company.

Power, Samantha. 2003. The AIDS Rebel. New Yorker, May 19.

Prestholdt, Jeremy. 2008. Domesticating the World: African Consumerism and the Genealogies of Globalization. Berkeley: University of California Press.

Psacharopoulos, George. 1980. Higher Education in Developing Countries: A Cost-Benefit Analysis. World Bank Staff Working Paper, No. 440. Washington, DC: World Bank.

Pudup, Mary Beth. 1988. Arguments within Regional Geography. Progress in Human Geography 12(3):369–390.

Rahman, Ahmad A. 2007. The Regime Change of Kwame Nkrumah: Epic Heroism in Africa and the Diaspora. New York: Palgrave Macmillan.

Rassool, Ciraj. 2000. The Rise of Heritage and the Reconstitution of History in South Africa. Kronos: Journal of Cape History 26:1–21.

Ratha, Dilip, Sanket Mohapatra, Caglar Ozden, Sonia Plaza, William Shaw, and Abede Shimeles. 2011. Leveraging Migration for Africa: Remittances, Skills, and Investments. Washington, DC: World Bank.

Raviola, Giuseppe, M'Imunya Machoki, Esther Mwaikambo, and Mary Jo Good. 2002. HIV, Disease Plague, Demoralization and "Burnout": Resident Experience of the Medical Profession in Nairobi, Kenya. Culture, Medicine, and Psychiatry 26(1):55–86.

Reich, Robert. 2007. Supercapitalism: The Transformation of Business, Democracy, and Everyday Life. New York: Alfred A. Knopf.

Reinert, Erik. 2007. How Rich Countries Got Rich . . . and Why Poor Countries Stay Poor. New York: Public Affairs.

Rincon, Paul. 2006. Predators "Drove Human Evolution." BBC News, February 19. Electronic document, http://news.bbc.co.uk/2/hi/science/nature/4729050.stm.

Rist, Gilbert. 2002. The History of Development: From Western Origins to Global Faith. Patrick Camiller, transl. London: Zed Books.

Robert, Henry M., III, William J. Evans, Daniel H. Honemann, and Thomas J. Balch. 2004. Robert's Rules of Order Newly Revised. Cambridge, MA: Da Capo Press.

Roberts, George. 1982. The Anguish of Third World Independence: The Sierra Leone Experience. Lanham, MD: University Press of America.

Roberts, Maya. 2006. Duffle Bag Medicine. Journal of the American Medical Association 295(13):1491–1492.

Robinson, Pearl T. 2004. Area Studies in Search of Africa. In The Politics of Knowledge: Area Studies and the Disciplines. David L. Szanton, ed. Pp. 119–183. Berkeley: University of California Press.

Robinson, Ronald, and John Gallagher. 1961. Africa and the Victorians: The Official Mind of Imperialism. London: Macmillan.

Robson, Elsbeth. 2002. "An Unbelievable Academic and Personal Experience": Issues around Teaching Undergraduate Field Courses in Africa. Journal of Geography in Higher Education 26(3):327–344.

Rodney, Walter. 1972. How Europe Underdeveloped Africa. Washington, DC: Howard University Press.

Roodt, Darrell, Anant Singh, Helena Spring, Kenneth Kambule, Leleti Khumalo, and Harriet Lenabe, dirs. 2006. Yesterday. 96 min. New York: Home Box Office.

Rosenwasser, David, and Jill Stephen. 2009. Writing Analytically. Boston: Thomson Wadsworth.

Rounder Select. 1992. Nairobi Beat: Kenyan Pop Music Today. Cambridge, MA: Rounder Select.

Rusesabagina, Paul. 2006. An Ordinary Man: An Autobiography. New York: Viking.

Ryan, Charlotte. 1991. Prime Time Activism: Media Strategies for Grassroots Organizing. Boston: South End Press.

Said, Edward. 1994. Culture and Imperialism. London: Vintage.

Said, Edward. 2003[1978]. Orientalism. London: Penguin.

Saidi, Christine. 2010. Women's Authority and Society in Early East-Central Africa. Rochester, NY: University of Rochester Press.

Saint, William. 2004. Higher Education in Ethiopia: The Vision and Its Challenges. Journal of Higher Education in Africa 2(3):83–113.

Samolsky, Russell. 2004. On Teaching South African Literature in the Age of Terror. Safundi: The Journal of South African and American Studies 5(4):1–2.

Sarnecki, Judith Holland. 2000. Mastering the Masters: Aimé Césaire's Creolization of Shakespeare's The Tempest. French Review 74(2):276–286.

Saro-Wiwa, Ken. 2002. To Mandy Garner. In Gathering Seaweed: African Prison Writing. Jack Mapanje, ed. Pp 121-123. Portsmouth, NH: Heinemann Publishers.

Saunders, Christopher. 1988. The Making of the South African Past: Major Historians on Race and Class. Cape Town: David Philip.

Sautman, Barry, and Yan Hairong. 2007. Friends and Interests: China's Distinctive Links with Africa. African Studies Review 50(3):75–114.

Schaefer, Fred K. 1953. Exceptionalism in Geography: A Methodological Examination. Annals of the Association of American Geographers 18:226–249.

Scheper-Hughes, Nancy. 2001. Saints, Scholars, and Schizophrenics: Mental Illness in Rural Ireland, Twentieth Anniversary Edition, Updated and Expanded. Berkeley: University of California Press.

Schmidt, Nancy. 1980. Criteria for Evaluating Precollegiate Teaching Materials on Africa. Issue: A Journal of Opinion 10(3–4):58–61.

Schuster, Mathieu, Philippe Duringer, Jean-Francois Ghienne, Claude Roquinb, Pierre Sepulchrec, Abderamane Moussab, Anne-Elisabeth Lebatarda, Hassan Taisso Mackayed, Andossa Likiusd, Patrick Vignauda, and Michel Brunete. 2009. Chad Basin: Paleoenvironments of the Sahara since the Late Miocene. Comptes Rendus Geosciences 341(8–9):603–611.

Seddon, David. 2006. China: Africa's New Business Partner. Review of African Political Economy 33(110):747–749.

Seelye, H. Ned. 1984[1974]. Teaching Culture: Strategies for Intercultural Communication. Lincolnwood, IL: National Textbook Company.

Servant, Jean-Christophe. 2005. China's Trade Safari in Africa. Le Monde diplomatique, English Edition, May 11.

Sesay, Amadu. 1981. Sierra Leone's Foreign Policy since Independence. Africana Research Bulletin 11(1–2):3–49.

Shakespeare, William. 1968[1611]. The Tempest. London: New Penguin Shakespeare.

Shanafelt, Robert, ed. 2012. Building Bridges in Anthropology: Understanding, Acting, Teaching, and Theorizing. Knoxville, TN: Newfound Press.

Shelemay, Kay Kaufmann. 2006. Soundscapes: Exploring Music in a Changing World. Second Edition. New York: W. W. Norton.

Shillington, Kevin. 1995. History of Africa. Second Edition. New York: Macmillan.

Shinn, Eugene A., Garret W. Smith, Joseph M. Prospero, Peter Betzer, Marshall L. Hayes, Virginia Garrison, and Richard T. Barber. 2000. African Dust and the Demise of Caribbean Coral Reefs. Geophysical Research Letters 27(19):3029–3032.

Shopes, Linda. 2002. Making Sense of Oral History. History Matters: The U.S. Survey Course on the Web. Electronic document, http://historymatters.gmu.edu/mse/oral.

Shuffield, Robin, dir. 2006. Thomas Sankara: The Upright Man. 52 min. Lille, France: Zorn Production International.

Silvester, Jeremy, and Jan-Bart Gewald. 2003. Words Cannot Be Found: German Colonial Rule in Namibia; An Annotated Reprint of the 1918 Blue Book. Sources for African History, Volume 1. Leiden: Brill.

Simpson, David E., dir. 2008. Milking the Rhino. 85 min. Oley, PA: Bullfrog Films.

Singer, Merrill. 2008. Drugs and Development: The Global Impact on Sustainable Growth and Human Rights. Long Grove, IL: Waveland Press.

Smith, Lanny, and Ken Hilsbos. 1999. Liberation Medicine: Health and Justice. Electronic document, http://www.dghonline.org/content/liberation-medicine-health-justice, accessed December 12, 2010.

Smythe, Kathleen R. 2009. The Dangers of Teaching about Globalization. Globalization (8)1. Electronic document, http://globalization.icaap.org/content/v8.1/Smythe.pdf, accessed October 23, 2011.

Snow, David A., E. Burke Rochford, Steven K. Worden, and Robert D. Benford. 1986. Frame Alignment Processes, Micromobilization, and Movement Participation. American Sociological Review 51(4):464–481.

South Africa Department of Education. 2000. A South African Curriculum for the Twenty First Century: Report of the Review Committee on Curriculum 2005. Pretoria: South Africa Department of Education.

Southern, Eileen, ed. 1983. Readings in Black American Music. Second Edition. New York: W. W. Norton.

Southern, Eileen. 1997. The Music of Black Americans: A History. Third Edition. New York: W. W. Norton.

Spivak, Gayatri Chakravorty. 1988. Can the Subaltern Speak? In Marxism and the Interpretation of Culture. Cary Nelson and Lawrence Grossberg, eds. Pp. 271–313. Urbana: University of Illinois Press.

Stavig, Richard. 1974. A Funny Thing Happened on My Way to Class. Kalamazoo College Quarterly 36(1)9–12.

Steinberg, Philip E., Andy Walter, and Kathleen Sherman-Morris. 2002. Using the Internet to Integrate Thematic and Regional Approaches in Geographic Education. Professional Geographer 54(3):332–348.

Steinmetz, George. 2007. The Devil's Handwriting: Precoloniality and the German Colonial State in Qingdao, Samoa, and Southwest Africa. Chicago: University of Chicago Press.

Stern, David I. 1992. Do Regions Exist? Implications of Synergetics for Regional Geography. Environment and Planning A 24:1431–1448.

Stewart, Robert. 2005. Introduction to Physical Oceanography. Electronic document, http://oceanworld.tamu.edu/resources/ocng_textbook/contents.html.

Stiglitz, Joseph E. 2002. Globalization and Its Discontents. London: Penguin.

Stock, Robert. 2004. Africa South of the Sahara: A Geographical Interpretation. Second Edition. New York: Guilford Press.

Stolten, Hans Erik, ed. 2007. History Making and Present Day Politics: The Meaning of Collective Memory in South Africa. Uppsala: Nordic Africa Institute.

Stone, Ruth, ed. 1998. The Garland Encyclopedia of World Music. Volume 1: Africa. New York: Garland Publishing.

Stringer, Christopher, and Robin McKie. 1996. African Exodus: The Origins of Modern Humanity. New York: Henry Holt and Company.

Susser, Ida. 2009. AIDS, Sex, and Culture: Global Politics and Survival in Southern Africa. Malden, MA: Wiley-Blackwell.

Swift, Jeremy. 1977. Sahelian Pastoralists: Underdevelopment, Desertification, and Famine. Annual Review of Anthropology 6:457–478.

Szanton, David L., and Sarah Manyika. 2001. PhD Programs in African Universities: Current Status and Future Prospects. A Report to the Rockefeller Foundation. University of California, Berkeley. Unpublished paper.

Táíwò, Olúfémi. 2009. How Colonialism Preempted Modernity in Africa. Bloomington: Indiana University Press.

Task Force on Higher Education and Society. 2000. Higher Education in Developing Countries: Peril and Promise. Washington, DC: World Bank. Electronic document, http://www.tfhe.net/report/Introduction.htm.

Tattersall, Ian. 2000. Once We Were Not Alone. Scientific American 282(1):56–62.

Taylor, Ian, dir. 1993. Back to Africa. 56 min. New York: Pelicula Films in association with Thirteen/WNET.

Taylor, Ian. 1998. China's Foreign Policy towards Africa in the 1990s. Journal of Modern African Studies 36(3):443–460.

Téno, Jean-Marie, dir. 1992. Afrique, je te plumerai [Africa, I Will Fleece You]. 88 min. San Francisco: California Newsreel.

Téno, Jean-Marie, and Bärbel Mauch, dirs. 2004. Le Malentendu colonial [A Colonial Misunderstanding]. 73 min. San Francisco: California Newsreel.

Terreblanche, Sampie. 2002. A History of Inequality in South Africa, 1652–2002. Pietermaritzburg: University of KwaZulu-Natal Press.

Tervonen, Taina. 2001. L'écrivain à l'école de la rue: Entretien avec Patrice Nganang [The Writer at the Street School: Interview with Patrice Nganang]. Africultures 37(April):104–105.

Tessema, K. A. 2009. The Unfolding Trends and Consequences of Expanding Higher Education in Ethiopia: Massive Universities, Massive Challenges. Higher Education Quarterly 63(1):29–45.

Thomas, David P. 2009. Revisiting Pedagogy of the Oppressed: Paulo Freire and Contemporary African Studies. Review of African Political Economy 36(120):253–269.

Thomas, Felicity. 2008. Indigenous Narratives of HIV/AIDS: Morality and Blame in a Time of Change. Medical Anthropology 27(3):227–256.

Thornton, John K. 1998. Africa and Africans in the Making of the Atlantic World, 1400–1800. Cambridge: Cambridge University Press.

Thornton, John K. 2000. Teaching Africa in an Atlantic Perspective. Radical History Review 77:123–134.

Titon, Jeff Todd, ed. 2008. Worlds of Music: An Introduction to the Music of the World's Peoples. Fifth Edition. Belmont, CA: Schirmer.

Tolliver, Denise. 2000. Study Abroad in Africa: Learning about Race, Racism, and the Racial Legacy of America. African Issues 28(1–2):112–116.

Tremonte, Colleen M., and Linda Racioppi. 2007. At the Interstices: Postcolonial Literary Studies Meets International Relations. Pedagogy 8(1):43–73.

Trouillot, Michel-Rolph. 2005. Between the Cracks. Electronic document, http://sites.jhu.edu/igs/Crosscurrents/Trouillot.pdf, accessed October 8, 2012.

Trowell, Kathleen Margaret, and Philip Klaus Wachsmann. 1953. Tribal Crafts of Uganda. New York: Oxford University Press.

Tull, Denis M. 2006. China's Engagement in Africa: Scope, Significance, and Consequences. Journal of Modern African Studies 44(3):459–479.

TV5MONDE. 2010. Afrique: Les indépendances 1960–2010. Electronic document, http://www.tv5.org/TV5Site/independancesafricaines.

United Nations. 2008. World Population Prospects: The 2008 Revision Database. Electronic document, http://esa.un.org/unpp, accessed December 22, 2010.

UNODC (United Nations Office on Drugs and Crime). 2007. Cocaine Trafficking in West Africa: The Threat to Stability and Development. Electronic document, http://www.unodc.org/documents/data-and-analysis/west_africa_cocaine_report_2007-12_en.pdf, accessed April 17, 2009.

Unwin, Tim, and Rob Potter. 1992. Undergraduate and Postgraduate Teaching on the Geography of the Third World. Area 24(1):56–62.

U.S. Census Bureau. 2000. African Immigration to the United States, 2000. Electronic document, http://www.census.gov/main/www/cen2000.html.

Van Amerom, Marloes, and Bram Büscher. 2005. Peace Parks in Southern Africa: Bringers of an African Renaissance? Journal of Modern African Studies 43(2):159–182.

Van Hensbroek, Pieter Boele. 1999. Political Discourses in African Thought: 1860 to the Present. Westport, CT: Palgrave.

Vaughn, Megan. 1991. Curing Their Ills: Colonial Power and African Illness. Stanford, CA: Stanford University Press.

Vengroff, Richard. 2002. Retirement, Replacement, and the Future of African Studies. African Issues 30(2):57–62.

Wa Thiong'o, Ngugi. 1967. Weep Not, Child. Portsmouth, NH: Heinemann.

Wa Thiong'o, Ngugi. 1975. The Martyr. *In* Secret Lives, and other stories. Pp. 181–185. Portsmouth, NH: Heinemann.

Wa Thiong'o, Ngugi. 1997. A Meeting in the Dark. *In* Under African Skies: Modern African Stories. Charles R. Larson, ed. Pp. 70–83. New York: Farrar, Straus and Giroux.

Wa Thiong'o, Ngugi. 2005. Europhone or African Memory: The Challenge of the Pan-Africanist Intellectual in the Age of Globalization. *In* African Intellectuals: Rethinking Politics, Language, Gender, and Development. Thandika Mkandawire, ed. Pp. 155–164. London: Zed Books.

Waberi, Abdourahman A. 2009. In the United States of Africa. David Ball and Nicole Ball, transl. Lincoln: University of Nebraska Press.

Wade, Bonnie. 2009. Thinking Musically: Experiencing Music, Expressing Culture. Second Edition. New York: Oxford University Press.

Wade, Charles. 2006. Editorial: A Historical Case for the Role of Regional Geography in Geographic Education. Journal of Geography in Higher Education 30(2):181–189.

Wade, Nicholas. 2010. Signs of Neanderthals Mating with Humans. New York Times, May 6. Electronic document, http://www.nytimes.com/2010/05/07/science.07neanderthal.html.

Walker, Alice. 1967a. Everyday Use. *In* In Love and Trouble. Pp. 47–59. New York: Harvest.

Walker, Alice. 1967b. Roselily. *In* In Love and Trouble. Pp. 3–9. New York: Harvest.

Walker, Alice. 1971. Nineteen Fifty-Five. *In* You Can't Keep a Good Woman Down. Pp. 3–20. New York: Harvest.

Walker, Alice. 1976. Meridian. New York: Pocket Books.

Wallace, Marion. 1998. "A Person Is Never Angry for Nothing": Women, VD, and Windhoek. *In* Namibia under South African Rule: Mobility and Containment, 1915–1946. Patricia Hayes, Jeremy Silvester, Marion Wallace, and Wolfram Hartmann, eds. Pp. 77–94. Athens: Ohio University Press.

Watkins, Mel. 1994. Talk with Toni Morrison. *In* Conversations with Toni Morrison. Danille K. Taylor-Guthrie, ed. Pp. 43–47. Jackson: University Press of Mississippi.

Wei, Yehua Dennis. 2006. Geographers and Globalization: the Future of Regional Geography. Environment and Planning A 38:1395–1400.

Weinstein, Karen, and James Ellison. 2010. Socioeconomic Change and Biological Vulnerability in Rungwe District, Tanzania: A Preliminary Qualitative and Quantitative Analysis. Thirty-Fifth Annual Meeting of the Human Biology Association, Santa Fe, NM. American Journal of Human Biology 22(2):274–275.

Welch, Claude E., Jr. 1991. The Organization of African Unity and the Promotion of Human Rights. Journal of Modern African Studies 29(4):535–555.

Welton, Michael. 1997. Repair, Defend, Invent: Civil Societarian Adult Education Faces the 21st Century. *In* Adult Learning and the Challenges of the 21st Century. Ove Korsgaard, ed. Pp.67–75. Odense: Association for World Education.

Welty, Eudora. 1957. Place in Fiction. *In* The Eye of the Story: Selected Essays and Reviews. Pp. 116–133. New York: House of Books.

Welty, Eudora. 1980a. The Demonstrators. *In* The Collected Stories. Pp. 608–622. New York: Harcourt.

Welty, Eudora. 1980b. Livvie. *In* The Collected Stories. Pp. 228–239. New York: Harcourt.

Welty, Eudora. 1980c. Powerhouse. *In* The Collected Stories. Pp. 131–141. New York: Harcourt.

Welty, Eudora. 1980d. Where Is the Voice Coming From? *In* The Collected Stories. Pp. 603–607. New York: Harcourt.

Welty, Eudora. 1980e. Why I Live at the P.O. *In* The Collected Stories. Pp. 46–56. New York: Harcourt.

Welty, Eudora. 1980f. A Worn Path. *In* The Collected Stories. Pp. 142–149. New York: Harcourt.

Wenzel, Jennifer. 2009. Bulletproof: Afterlives of Anti-colonial Prophecy in South Africa and Beyond. Chicago: University of Chicago Press.

West Africa Magazine. 1979a. Conflict over Students' Protests. November 19.

West Africa Magazine. 1979b. Honorary Doctorate of Law from Lincoln University. November 5.

West Africa Magazine. 1979c. President Stevens Welcomed Home. December 3.

Westerhaus, Michael, and Arachu Castro. 2009. Inverting the Killer Commodity Model: Withholding Medicines from the Poor. *In* Killer Commodities: Public Health, and the Corporate Production of Harm. Merrill Singer and Hans Baer, eds. Pp. 367–397. New York: AltaMira Press.

Whyte, Susan Reynolds, Michael A. Whyte, Lotte Meinert, and Betty Kyaddondo. 2006. Treating AIDS: Dilemmas of Unequal Access in Uganda. *In* Global Pharmaceuticals: Ethics, Markets, Practices. Adriana Petryna, Andrew Lakoff, and Arthur Kleinman, eds. Pp. 240–262. Durham, NC: Duke University Press.

Williams, Adebayo. 1997. The Postcolonial Flaneur and Other Fellow-Travelers: Conceits for a Narrative of Redemption. Third World Quarterly 18(5):821–841.

Williams, Chris. 2005. Problematizing Wales: An Exploration in Historiography and Postco-loniality. *In* Postcolonial Wales. Jane Aaron and Chris Williams, eds. Pp. 1–22. Cardiff: University of Wales Press.

Wilson, Angene H. 1995. Teaching about Africa: A Review of Middle/Secondary Textbooks and Supplemental Materials. Social Studies 86(6):253–259.

Witz, Leslie, and Carohn Cornell. 2000. Africa, Race and Empire in the Nineteenth Century at a South African University in 1998. Radical History Review 76:223–231.

Wiwa, Ken. 2001. In the Shadow of a Saint: A Son's Journey to Understand His Father's Legacy. South Royalton, VT: Steerforth Press.

Woods, Donald. 1981. Asking for Trouble: The Autobiography of a Banned Journalist. New York: Atheneum.

World Bank. 2010. Measuring Inequality. Electronic document, http://go.worldbank. org/3SLYUTVY00, accessed April 6.

Wyn Jones, Richard. 2005. In the Shadow of the First-Born: The Colonial Legacy in Welsh Politics. *In* Postcolonial Wales. Jane Aaron and Chris Williams, eds. Pp. 23–38. Cardiff: University of Wales Press.

Young, Robert J. C. 2001. Postcolonialism: An Historical Introduction. Oxford: Blackwell.

Zeleza, Paul Tiyambe. 1997. The Perpetual Solitudes and Crises of African Studies in the United States. Africa Today 44(2):193–210.

Zeleza, Paul Tiyambe. 2010. African Diasporas: Toward a Global History. African Studies Review 53(1):1–19.

Zukas, Alex. 1996. Different Drummers: Using Music to Teach History. Perspectives 34:6.

Zunz, Olivier. 1982. Urbanization, Industrial Development, and Immigrants in Detroit, 1880–1920: The Changing Face of Inequality. Chicago: University of Chicago Press.

Zwick, Edward, dir. 2006. Blood Diamond. 143 min. Los Angeles: Warner Bros.

Index

Abrahamsen, Rita, 87
Abu Ghraib, 139
Achebe, Chinua, 127, 164, 170–171
action statements, construction of, 197–201
active learning techniques, African politics and, 81–87
activism: African studies and use of, 15, 181–193; mixed critical pedagogy concerning, 184
Adams, Jonathan, 43–44
Addis Ababa University, 242
additive approach to diversity, 110–111
Adichie, Chimamanda Ngozi, 117, 126–127
Adjetey, Frederick, 90, 92–93
advocacy work, by health-care workers, 229–239
Africa: Chinese economic ties with, 5–7; cultural and political differences in, 6–7; geopolitical relevance of, 5–7; prehistory and history of, 12; as region, 100–103; regional map of, vii; study abroad programs in, 202–210; true size of, viii; Western misperceptions of, 190–193
Africa in World Politics: A Pan-African Perspective (Martin), 197
African AIDS Epidemic: A History, The (Life), 58–59
African Americans: African studies and, 6–7; cultural contributions of, 97n.1
"African Bingo," 107
"African Breakfast," 108
African Charter on Human and Peoples' Rights, 189
African development, African studies discussion of, 35–36
African Development: Making Sense of the Issues and Actors (Moss), 31
Africa: Never Stand Still (recordings), 24–25
Africa News, 25
African History: From Earliest Times to Independence (Curtin), 70
African Journal of Teacher Education, 3
African music: in African Studies, 14; stereotypes about, 140–154
African musicology, emergence of, 149–154
African National Congress (ANC), 62–63, 120–122
African newspapers, in African studies, 28, 32, 37n.6; globalization coverage and, 49–50; history of Africa and, 70–71

African Students Association, 140
African studies: curriculum development for teaching about, 2–4; geopolitical relevance of, 1–2; introductory exercises in, 21–26; literature survey for, 7–9; model AU as pedagogical tool for, 195–201; pretesting of knowledge and ignorance, exercises for, 22–26; regional concept in, 98–103; socially just curriculum in, 104–111; stereotypes about Africa in, 21–26, 104–111, 169–178; survey of approaches in, 9–11; Western preconceptions in, 1–2
African Studies Association, 8
African Studies in the United States: A Perspective (Guyer), 8–9
African Summer Institute for Teachers (AFSI), 104–111
African Union (Global Organizations), The, 199–200
Africa: Opposing Viewpoints (Haugen), 197
Africa Past and Present programs, 59–60
Africa South of the Sahara (Stock), 102–103
Africa: The AIDS Highway (film), 58–59
Afrikaner political supremacy: history of, 61–69; language issues and, 81
Afrique, je te plumerai (Africa, I Will Fleece You) (film), 123–125
Afro@Digital (film), 36n.3
aggression, human evolution and, 51n.4
agriculture: in African history, 41–42; climate change in Africa and, 42–48; *Ugali* Lesson and, 73–75
Ahern, Bertie, 84–85
Ahluwalia, Pal, 87
AIDS Service Organisation (TASO), 229
Aké, Claude, 82–83
Alemaya University, 242
AllAfrica.com, 49–50
American Medical Student Organization, 231
American Revolution, 92
Amin, Idi, 84
Amuru Health Center, 229–230, 237
And They Didn't Die (Ngcobo), 130
Angola: diamond mines in, 36n.1; history and politics in, 28–30
animal domestication: in African history, 41–42; climate change in Africa and, 42–48

Contributors

Julian Jane Atim is a Ugandan physician with an M.P.H. from Harvard University and the founder of Students for Equity in Health Care (SEHC). With Amy C. Finnegan and Michael Westerhaus, she developed and directs the course Beyond the Biologic Basic of Disease: The Social and Economic Causation of Illness.

Julian M. Bass was formerly the Higher Education IT Advisor at the Higher Education Strategy Center, Addis Ababa, Ethiopia, and worldwide technical Training Manager for a Silicon Valley–based enterprise customer relation management vendor. He is currently a lecturer at the School of Computing at Robert Gordon University in the United Kingdom and a director of X Lab Mentoring Ltd. He has published over 50 articles in the areas of IT for education in developing countries, software development methods, fault-tolerant computing, and hard real-time distributed systems.

Todd Cleveland is an Assistant Professor of History at Augustana College, where he teaches classes on African history, African commodities, African development, sports in Africa, and Africana studies. His past publications include examinations of African National Congress activity in Angola, the introduction of industrial education into Angola, the role of soccer in engendering Angolan nationalism, the methodological implications of conducting research in contemporary Angola, and the histories of ethnic minorities and child laborers on Angola's diamond mines.

Jennifer E. Coffman is Associate Executive Director of International Programs and Associate Professor of Integrated Science and Technology at James Madison University. She is the founder and Director of JMU's Kenya Field School and also serves as Chair of the U.S. Board of Directors for Carolina for Kibera, Inc. Coffman's research in Kenya examines the politics of land access and ownership, concepts of sustainability, resource distribution, and education.

Caleb Corkery is an Assistant Professor of English at Millersville University of Pennsylvania. He teaches courses in African American literature, writing, and the rhetoric of race. Most recently, he has developed a critical pedagogy for teaching white racial awareness, which has appeared in the journal *Teaching English in the Two-Year College*. His previous work on African literature includes "Citizen Orator in the West African Savannah" in the volume *Rhetoric in the Rest of the West* (Cambridge Scholars Publishing, 2010).

Carl Death joined the Department of International Politics at Aberystwyth University (United Kingdom) in September 2009, after having obtained a Ph.D. and M.Sc. in Economics from Aberystwyth and a B.A. from Cambridge University. In 2008–2009, he lectured in the School of Law and Government, Dublin City University. He is the author of *Governing Sustainable Development* (Routledge, 2010). He teaches the courses Power, Conflict, and Development in Africa; Protest, Power, and Resistance in Africa; and Global Environmental Politics.

Oumar Chérif Diop is an Assistant Professor of Postcolonial Literatures at Kennesaw State University. He has presented numerous papers on violence and trauma in African literatures. His forthcoming articles are on violence in Alex Laguma's works, agency in Nawal El Sadaawi's works, and trauma in Yvonne Vera's novels. Prior to his work on violence, Dr. Diop coauthored "Ousmane Sembene's *Xala*: The Novel, the Film, and Their Audiences" (Research in African Literatures, 1998). His research deals with violence and trauma in African and African diaspora literatures.

James Ellison is an Associate Professor of Anthropology at Dickinson College. A cultural anthropologist, he has conducted fieldwork in Somalia, Ethiopia, and Tanzania. He researches and teaches about the intersections of culture and political economy in Africa and health and healing in Africa. His writings have been published in venues including the journals *American Anthropologist*, *American Ethnologist*, and *Comparative Studies in Society and History*.

Toyin Falola is University Distinguished Teaching Professor and the Frances Higginbotham Nalle Centennial Professor of History at the University of Texas at Austin. He has published many books, including *Colonialism and Violence in Nigeria* (Indiana University Press, 2009).

Amy C. Finnegan is a Professor at the University of Minnesota–Rochester. She received her Ph.D. from Boston College in 2011. As a practitioner/activist, she has worked on antiwar issues and peace building, HIV/AIDS, and human rights in the United States and Uganda. Her research interests include race relations, global health, social movements, and peace and conflict. Along with Julian Jane Atim and Michael Westerhaus, she developed and directs the course Beyond the Biologic Basis of Disease: The Social and Economic Causation of Illness.

Trevor R. Getz is Professor of African History at San Francisco State University and a former Fulbright Scholar at the University of the Western Cape and the University of Stellenbosch in South Africa. He is the author or coauthor of eight books including *African Histories: New Sources and New Techniques for Studying African Pasts* (Prentice Hall, 2011), and *Abina and the Important Men: A Graphic History* (Oxford University Press, 2011). He is currently editing the Oxford University Press series African World Histories.

Linda M. Johnston is the Executive Director of the Siegel Institute for Leadership, Ethics, and Character and an Associate Professor of Conflict Management at Kennesaw State University. She received her Ph.D. at the Institute for Conflict Analysis and

Resolution at George Mason University in 2000. Dr. Johnston is the President of the International Peace Research Association Foundation, serves on the board of Hands along the Nile, and teaches at the University for Peace in Costa Rica.

Jean Ngoya Kidula is Associate Professor of Music (Ethnomusicology) at the University of Georgia in Athens, Georgia. She previously worked at Kenyatta University in Kenya. Her current research is in historical, contemporary, and popular spiritual and ritual music and musicians in Africa, with a focus on Kenya and Tanzania. The arenas for examination include ethnic, religious, academic, urban, and industrial spaces.

Catherine Kroll is an Associate Professor of English at Sonoma State University. She received her Ph.D. from the University of California, Berkeley, and was awarded a Fulbright-Hays grant for study in South Africa in 2004. Dr. Kroll is a member of the Advisory Board of *Research in African Literatures* and has published essays on the writing of Boubacar Boris Diop, Alex La Guma, and Patrice Nganang, among others.

Brandon D. Lundy is Interim Associate Director of the Ph.D. Program in International Conflict Management and an Assistant Professor of Anthropology at Kennesaw State University. He received his Ph.D. from the State University of New York, Buffalo, and *Université des Sciences et Technologies de Lille*, France, in 2009. Dr. Lundy served as a U.S. Peace Corps volunteer in Cape Verde. His ethnographic research focuses on the intersections of livelihood, cultural identity, and globalization in Guinea-Bissau.

Gary Marquardt is an Associate Professor of History at Westminster College in Salt Lake City, Utah, where he teaches African, world, and environmental history. He received his Ph.D. in African History at the University of Wisconsin–Madison and has previously taught at Virginia Commonwealth University. Beyond the standard course canon, he has also developed and taught the classes History of Coffee, Apartheid in Film and Literature, Revolution in the Graphic Novel, and Imperialism and Resistance in the Late Modern Era.

Babacar M'Baye is Associate Professor of English and Pan-African Studies at Kent State University. His work has appeared in the *Journal of African Literature and Culture*, *Journal of Pan-African Studies*, and *New England Journal of History*. He is the author of *The Trickster Comes West: Pan-African Influence in Early Black Diasporan Narratives* (University Press of Mississippi, 2009).

Solomon Negash is an Associate Professor of Information Systems at Kennesaw State University. He earned his Ph.D. from Claremont Graduate University. Dr. Negash was instrumental in creating the Ethiopian National ICT Advisory Body—for which he served as its first chairman and helped establish the Information Systems Ph.D. program at Addis Ababa University—and he served as its first international coordinator. His current research is mobile technology and e-learning. Dr. Negash heads the mobile application development lab at Kennesaw State University.

Jeanine Ntihirageza received her Ph.D. in Linguistics from the University of Chicago. As Assistant Professor at Northeastern Illinois University, she teaches classes in teaching English as a second or foreign language and in African and African American studies and coordinates the English Language Program and the African Summer Institute for Teachers. Her research interests include phonology and morphology of Bantu (African) languages, contact linguistics, ethnopragmatics, and issues of African immigrants.

Harry Nii Koney Odamtten is an Assistant Professor of African and Atlantic History at Santa Clara University, California. He received a dual Ph.D. in African American and African Studies and in History from Michigan State University and has previously taught as Visiting Assistant Professor at the University of Central Arkansas. His dissertation, "A History of Ideas: West Africa, the 'Black Atlantic,' and Pan-Africanism," received the 2010 Donald Lammers Graduate Award at Michigan State University. Dr. Odamtten is also a 2008 Compton Africa Peace fellow. His research activities and publications span African and African diaspora intellectual and social history, African and African American gender and women's studies, Pan-Africanism, and hip-hop and public culture.

Daniel J. Paracka, Jr., is Director of the Education Abroad Office and Associate Professor of Education at Kennesaw State University. His Ph.D. is in International Education Policy from Georgia State University. He is the author of *The Athens of West Africa: A History of International Education at Fourah Bay College, Freetown, Sierra Leone* (Routledge, 2003) and has an established record of publications in the field of global learning. Dr. Paracka also served with the U.S. Peace Corps in Sierra Leone from 1985 to 1987.

Ryan Ronnenberg is an Assistant Professor of History at Kennesaw State University. His writings concern the intellectual history of colonial- and independent-era southern and eastern Africa. Dr. Ronnenberg is currently documenting the historical trauma of Burundian refugees settled in western Tanzania since the 1970s, and he is partnering with the Psychiatric Department of Muhimbili University to ensure the provision of mental health and social work services to this refugee community.

Renée Schatteman is an Associate Professor of English at Georgia State University. She first traveled to Africa to serve as a secondary teacher in rural Zimbabwe. After receiving her Ph.D. in Postcolonial Literature from the University of Massachusetts in 2000, she cowrote a three-volume curriculum guide to African literature titled *Voices from the Continent* (Africa World Press, 2003) and has published articles on various writers from southern Africa, including Tsitsi Dangarembga, Sindiwe Magona, and Zakes Mda.

Kathleen R. Smythe is a Professor of History at Xavier University. She received her Ph.D. in African History from the University of Wisconsin–Madison. She is the author of *Fipa Families: Reproduction and Catholic Missionaries in Nkansi, Ufipa 1880–1960* (Heinemann, 2006) and numerous articles on Fipa history. She is currently teaching and writing at the intersection of sustainability, economic development, and globalization. Her chapter in this volume is drawn from her manuscript "Why We Need African History" (under review fall 2012).

Lucie Viakinnou-Brison is an Assistant Professor of French at Kennesaw State University. She received her Ph.D. in French and Educational Studies from Emory University in Atlanta, Georgia. Her research interests include foreign-language pedagogy and Francophone literatures.

Matthew Waller has taught in an alternative school, a middle school, and a high school in a small Tanzanian village. Since the fall semester of 2008, Mr. Waller has been a member of Kennesaw State University's adjunct faculty. In December 2009, he completed an M.A. in Geography from Georgia State University. He currently teaches World Regional Geography and the Geography of Sub-Saharan Africa. His interests include aid organizations, regional geography, Africa, and the pedagogy of geography.

Michael J. Westerhaus is a primary care physician at the Center for International Health in St. Paul, Minnesota. He received an M.D. and an M.A. in Medical Anthropology from Harvard University in 2006. With Amy C. Finnegan and Julian Jane Atim, he developed and directs the course Beyond the Biologic Basis of Disease: The Social and Economic Causation of Illness, which takes place each year in Gulu, Uganda.

Durene I. Wheeler is an Associate Professor at Northeastern Illinois University. She teaches classes in educational inquiry and curriculum studies as well as African and African American studies and women's studies. Her research interests include historical intersections of race, class, and gender in education as well as the use of multicultural feminist pedagogy to foster social justice and equity in teacher-training programs.

DISCARD

CPSIA information can be obtained at www.ICGtesting.com
Printed in the USA
LVOW131456300613

340851LV00002B/3/P